THE KABBALAH SUTRAS

A YOGI'S GUIDE TO COUNTING THE OMER

Marcus J Freed

freedthinker books
www.marcusjfreed.com

Freedthinker Books
Los Angeles, CA
www.marcusjfreed.com

Printed in the United States of America.

First edition: August 2015
Second edition: April 2019

Library of Congress Control Number: 2015907682

British Library Cataloguing in Publication Data: A catalogue record for this book is available from the British Library.

Print version: 10

ISBN: 9781797663043

Copy Editor: Gillian Freed
Cover Design & Original Book Design: Joshua Rudolph
Page Layout & Typography: Ann Steer
Photography (Gym & Yoga): Timothy Reise
Portrait Photograph: Timothy Fielding
Proof Reader: Jo Zeitouni

A NOTE ON LANGUAGE IN THE BOOK AND FONTS USED

We have followed UK English spellings and punctuation styles throughout the book. The primary font is Adobe Caslon, originally designed by William Caslon (1692-1766) in London. I chose this font because of its good readability, workability and the connection to my native England. Hebrew and Hebrew transliterations are usually in italics, titles are in Trilogy Sans. The footnote font is Candara.

The Hebrew transliterations are generally written with the modern Sephardic pronunciation, e.g. Shabbat rather than Shabbes, Shabbos or Shobbos. To represent the guttural 'Chet' sound (as in Chanukah or L'Chayim), we have written a 'Ch'.

The 'chet' sound is hard to accurately pronounce by the written word alone, without vocal instruction. You will know it is being said incorrectly when somebody articulates 'chutzpah' (or hutzpah) with a soft ch that isn't coming from the back of the throat (i.e. the 'ch' in cheese is not the 'ch' in chutzpah, but taking somebody's cheese without asking would be a chutzpah). If you really want to learn this distinction, I'd recommend viewing a video of Chaim Topol's Fiddler on the Roof recording of "To Life". Practice singing along with 'L'chayim' and you'll be well on the right path.

DISCLAIMER Please consult your health care provider and obtain full medical clearance before practicing yoga or any exercise programme. Practising under the direct supervision and careful guidance of a qualified instructor will reduce risk of injuries. The information in this book is strictly for reference only and not in any manner a substitute for medical advice or the direct teaching of a qualified yoga teacher. The author, illustrators, photographers and publishers assume no responsibility for injuries or losses that may result from following any of the advice contained herein. If, however, your life significantly improves as a result of reading, we will gladly join you to celebrate! Now, practice in safety and good health!

Cover images, courtesy: Hebrew - Maaseh Tovia (Cracow 1908, p41b). Beach (Laguna, Shutterstock licensed), Marcus backbend (Photographer: Greg Bernardi, Creative Director: Joshua Rudolph).

DEDICATION

Dedicated to the forgotten Kabbalists and to the forgotten teachers who perished in the Holocaust.

Your names may have been lost but may your memory be a blessing and may your souls ascend in the Garden of Eden.

To the memory of Avraham Avinu

To the memory of the Baal Shem Tov

To the memory of Rabbi Abraham Abulafia

To the memory of Rabbi Chayim Vital

To the memory of Rabbi Elijah ben Shlomo Zalman Kremer,
the Vilna Gaon

To the memory of Rabbi Menachem Mendel Schneerson,
the Lubavitcher Rebbe

To the memory of Rabbi Moshe Cordovero

To the memory of Rabbi Nehunia ben Kahana

To the memory of Rabbi Shimon Bar Yochai

To the memory of Rabbi Shneur Zalman of Liadi,
the Altar Rebbe

To the memory of Rabbi Sholom DovBer Schneersohn,
the Rebbe Rashab

To the memory of Rabbi Yitzhak Luria, the Ari z"l

To Rabbi Yosef ben Avraham Gikatilla

and to the memory of the Tzaddikim Nistarim,
the Hidden Righteous Ones

Zichronam L'vracha: may they be remembered for a blessing ז״ל.

THANKS & ACKNOWLEDGEMENTS

This book has been an eight-year process and gone through many drafts and incarnations. What you see is the result of help, support and input from many wonderful teachers, guides, friends and students over the years.

Thank you to Metuka Daisy Lawrence for your guidance and for saving my life. Rabbi Yitzhak Gaines, thank you for being an incredible resource of Kabbalistic wisdom. Rabbi Hillel Simon, thank you for your time and teaching from before the early days of this project. Marissa Leigh Salem, thank you for years of inspired chevruta learning, bouncing ideas and for insightful questions. Thank you to all the students over the years who have helped shape the rough diamonds of these ideas.

Rabbi Yonah and Rachel Bookstein, a huge thank you for your ongoing love and support in the Brave New World of Los Angeles, and the Pico Shul community for your passion and spirit. David Solomon, thank you for your generosity of sharing your masterful Tiqqunei haZohar translation before publication - this was the manuscript which helped my understanding soar and thank you for your fast and deep answers to difficult questions. Emeritus Chief Rabbi Lord Sacks, thank you for inspiration, encouragement and support. Thank you to Rabbi Simon Jacobson for your ever-helpful Omer book and helpful suggestions.

Mum and Dad - thank you for embarking on that great project known as parenthood. No doubt it seemed like a good idea at the time and hopefully it still does. Mum - thank you for your amazing dedication with proof-reading and copy-editing. You went above and beyond the call of duty. Thank you for all the other stuff you have edited in the decades since I lernd tu spel propalee.

Thank you to Daniel Knust for your vision and creativity as we created the crowdfunding video, shlepping through the beaches of Malibu whilst trying to bring these ideas to cinematic life. Thank you to Laura Knust, Jeff Handel and David Buchwald for additional support during the shoot. Edward Clarke - for your yogic teachings which will last a lifetime and for believing in the Kosher Sutra ideas while they were still in nascent form. Elizabeth Connolly, may your memory be a blessing, thank you for the teachings you gave and the light you brought. Seth Merewitz, thank you for welcoming me at your Albion retreat in NorCal where I wrote the first draft all those years ago. Jo Zeitouni, thank you for your superstar proof-reading. Thank you to Ann Steer, for many months of hard work laying out the pages of this book. I am grateful for your patience, attention to detail, and your ongoing dedication to this project.

Thank you to the great teachers of Kabbalah whose light and blessing continues to guide the way: The Vilna Gaon, Rabbi Aryeh Kaplan, the Baal Shem Tov, Rabbi Abraham Abulafia, Rabbi Joseph Gikatilla, Rabbi Nechuniah ben Kahana, Rabbi Moshe Cordovero (thank you for the Tomer Devorah), Rebbe Rashab (thank you for Kuntres Avodah), Rabbi Moses Ben Maimon/ Rambam (thank you for your physical-spiritual inspiration in Chapter 4 of *Hilchot De'ot*), Rabbi Shlomo Yitchaki/Rashi (thank you for the spiritual guide lamps you left us along the way), Rabbi Shneur Zalman of Liadi (thank you for the Tanya), Rabbi Yitzchak Ginsburg, Rabbi Yitzhak Luria (thank you for unleashing tremendous light), Rabbi Chayim Vital (thank you for bearing and illuminating the light of the Ari).

FUNDERS

This book was made possible through a combination of grants and crowdfunding support. A huge thank you to Lynne Schusterman and ROI for generous micro grants that helped with various stages of the book's development, along with grant-matching for the crowdfunding campaign.

A special thank you to the following people for believing in the project and pre-purchasing books, which helped bring it into being. Welcome to *The Kabbalah Sutras* "family": Tammy Abramowitz, Kathryn Barash, Robert Bray, Alexis & Jonathan Colman, Adam Coppel, Adam Edelman, Miriam Edelman, Barbara Williams Ellertson, Joseph & Jaime Esshaghian, Estelle Eugene, Jennifer Fatalevich, Gill & Barry Freed, Ze'ev Funt, Aaron Ganz, David & Maure Gardner, Carla Gavzey, Hood & Morganstein families, Daniel Housman, Elizabeth Hurvich, Katherine Golitzen, Letty Gonzalez, Babak Kanani, Eliot & Susie Kaye, William Kingston, Simon Kisner, Lori Klein, Melissa Kurtz, Rosemary Lafollette, Elliot Laniado, Eddy Levin, Lisa Levine, Nina & Sal Litvak, Terri McNicholl, Sybil Malinowski Melody, Courtney Mellblom, Seth & Tali Merewitz, Mary F Meyerson, Jon Mitchell, Dan Myers, Barnaby & Hannah Nemko, Steve Newman, Danny Newman, Christopher Nicholson & Sara Coppola, Sophie Osnah, Emily Pflaster, Keren Ram, Barak Raviv, Sandra Razieli, Davira Reichman, Richard Rose, Jessica Rosenthal, Laura Rotter, Janna Roth, Justin Rubin, Luca Rubin, Rya, Josh Sacks, Rebecca Leary Safon, Howard Saul, Lee Fowler Schwimmer, Susan Seely, Robin Smith, Rabbi Samuel Samtosha Steinberg, Aaron Sztarkman, Sam Talbot, Alison Turner, Carol Venuti, Rahel Wasserfall, Dove Weissman-Shtein, Deborah Wilfond, Ben Yossef, Kaley Zeitouni, Holly Zook, and Sharon Zulauf.

CONTENTS

Gym Exercises xiii

Yoga Postures xiv

Preface xv

Introduction 1

    Tree of Life: The Sefirot 2

    Sefirot & The Body 3

    49 Steps to Enlightenment 4

The Kabbalah Sutras 19

Bibliography 467

Index 471

Book Club Guidelines 477

Other Publications 478

THE KABBALAH SUTRAS

WEEK 1 - *CHESED* **19**

Introduction: Endless Love 20

Day 1: Lovingkindness in Lovingkindness :
All You Need is Love 29

Day 2: Discipline in Lovingkindness -
The Art of a Healthy "No" 37

Day 3: Balance in Lovingkindness: Love Me Tender 45

Day 4: Endurance in Lovingkindness: Water & Ice 53

Day 5: Humility In Lovingkindness: Behave Like A Guest:
Humble Love 61

Day 6: Bonding in Lovingkindness: Strenghtening
Relationships 69

Day 7: Mastery in Lovingkindness: The Royal Path
of Love 76

WEEK 2 - *GEVURAH* **79**

Introduction: Strength Training 80

Day 8: Lovingkindness in Discipline:
When Love Means Saying "No" 90

Day 9: Discipline in Discipline: Goal Scoring 97

Day 10: Compassion in Discipline: Soft Focus 105

Day 11: Endurance in Discipline: Marathon Man 114

Day 12: Humility in Discipline: The Humble Leader 122

Day 13: Bonding in Discipline: Stay Grounded 130

Day 14: Nobility in Discipline: Mastering Your Power 137

WEEK 3 - *TIFERET* **145**

    Introduction: Compassion: The Path of Jacob 146

    Day 15:   Lovingkindness in Compassion: Loving Balance 153

    Day 16:   Discipline in Compassion: All in the Balance 162

    Day 17:   Compassion in Compassion:
                Healer, Heal Thy World 170

    Day 18:   Endurance in Balance: The Fight for Justice 179

    Day 19:   Humility in Balance: A Fine Balance 186

    Day 20:   Bonding in Compassion: The Edge of Glory 195

    Day 21:   Nobility in Compassion: Raise Your Game............203

WEEK 4 - *NETZACH* *211*

    Introduction: The Birth of Ambition..212

    Day 22:   Lovingkindness in Endurance: 7-Year Itch.............222

    Day 23:   Discipline in Endurance: Getting Things Done 232

    Day 24:   Compassion in Endurance: Loving The Journey..239

    Day 25:   Endurance in Endurance: Don't Stop Believing...248

    Day 26:   Humility in Endurance: Pride & Fall 256

    Day 27:   Bonding in Endurance: The Pleasure Seekers......264

    Day 28:   Nobility in Endurance: Masters of Endurance 271

WEEK 5 - *HOD*... **279**

    Introduction: Sweet Surrender 280

    Day 29:   Lovingkindness in Humility: Blame & Complain ..287

    Day 30:   Discipline in Gratitude: Conditioned Thanks: 294

    Day 31:   Balanced Humility: Bend like the Reed 301

Day 32: Endurance in Humility: Good Yogi, Bad Yogi.........308

Day 33: Humility in Humility: Random Acts of Humility....315

Day 34: Bonding in Humility: Humble Splendour................323

Day 35: Nobility in Humility: Humble Rulers 332

WEEK 6 - *YESOD* **339**

Introduction: Welcome to the Pleasure Zone 340

Day 36: Lovingkindness in Bonding: The Power of Love ..348

Day 37: Discipline in Bonding: Catching Fire 356

Day 38: Compassion in Bonding: Bonds That Heal 365

Day 39: Endurance in Bonding: Friendship is Golden 372

Day 40: Humility in Bonding: This Town Ain't Big Enough 379

Day 41: Bonding in Bonding: Harness Your Life Force 387

Day 42: Nobility in Bonding: Relationship Mastery 395

WEEK 7 - *MALCHUT* **403**

Introduction: The Path of Royalty...............................404

Day 43: Lovingkindness in Nobility: Being Your Best.........412

Day 44: Discipline in Nobility: Strong Hands &
               Outstretched Arms 420

Day 45: Compassion in Nobility: The Noble Balance 428

Day 46: Endurance in Nobility: The Battle for Yourself: 437

Day 47: Humility in Nobility: Greatness through
               Gratitude 445

Day 48: Bonding in Nobility: A Little Less Than Divine 452

Day 49: Nobility in Nobility: Kiss the Bride 459

GYM EXERCISES

Day 1: Bicep Curl 33

Day 2: Front Raise 41

Day 3: Side Lateral Raise 48

Day 4: Lunge 55

Day 5: Squat 63

Day 6: Seated Overhead
        Press 69

Day 7: Knee Push-Up 76

Day 8: Push Up..........................95

Day 9: Alternate Shoulder
        Tap................................103

Day 10: Saxon Side Bend 112

Day 11: Dumbbell Lunge 120

Day 12: Dead Lift 128

Day 13: One Arm Dumbbell
        Extension 135

Day 14: 40 Punches 143

Day 15: Ab Wheel 160

Day 16: Speed Rotations 168

Day 17: Superman Stretch 177

Day 18: Jackknife Crunch 184

Day 19: Flutter Kick 193

Day 20: Sit-Ups 201

Day 21: Plank............................210

Day 22: Alt Arm &
        Leg Raises 230

Day 23: Raised Leg
        Push-Ups....................237

Day 24: Leg Raises 246

Day 25: Dumbell Split Squat..254

Day 26: Dumbbell Squat.........262

Day 27: Goblet Squat..............269

Day 28: Bridges 277

Day 29: Plank Jump-Ins 292

Day 30: Plank Leg Raises 299

Day 31: Body Fold 306

Day 32: Dumbbell
        Front Squat 313

Day 33: Bottom To Heels 321

Day 34: Half Jacks 330

Day 35: Standing Toe Raise ..337

Day 36: Star Jumps/
        Jumping Jacks 354

Day 37: Jump Knee Tucks 363

Day 38: Archer Lunge 370

Day 39: Fly Step.......................377

Day 40: Step Up 385

Day 41: Shoulder Quad
        Set 393

Day 42: Side Plank 401

Day 43: Clapping Push-Ups...418

Day 44: Seated Dumbbell
        Extension....................426

Day 45: Sitting Twist...............435

Day 46: Donkey Kick...............443

Day 47: Raised Leg Crunch 450

Day 48: Mountain Climber 457

Day 49: Mountain 464

YOGA POSTURES

Day 1: Cow Pose 34

Day 2: Warrior One 42

Day 3: Triangle 49

Day 4: Extended Side-Angle 56

Day 5: Standing Leg Raise 64

Day 6: Headstand 70

Day 7: Easy 77

Day 8: Chair 96

Day 9: Warrior 2 104

Day 10: Pyramid 113

Day 11: Downward Dog 121

Day 12: Dancer 129

Day 13: Tree 136

Day 14: Easy 144

Day 15: Cat-Cow 161

Day 16: Quarter-Dog 169

Day 17: Sphinx......................... 178

Day 18: Reverse Side-Angle ...184

Day 19: Camel 194

Day 20: Backbend 202

Day 21: Easy 210

Day 22: Triangle 231

Day 23: Extended
Side-Angle 238

Day 24: Warrior 1 247

Day 25: Warrior 2 255

Day 26: Boat 263

Day 27: Hero 270

Day 28: Extended Mountain &
Mountain 278

Day 29: Staff 293

Day 30: Seated Forward
Bend 300

Day 31: Inclined Plane 307

Day 32: Half-Moon 314

Day 33: Extended Child Pose 322

Day 34: Bound Angle or
Cobbler 331

Day 35: Bridge 338

Day 36: Horse Stance 355

Day 37: Boat 364

Day 38: Child's Pose 371

Day 39: Forward Straddle
Bend 378

Day 40: Tree 386

Day 41: The Great Seal 394

Day 42: Camel 402

Day 43: Cat-Cow 419

Day 44: Standing Forward
Bend 427

Day 45: Bridge 436

Day 46: Bow 444

Day 47: Shoulderstand 451

Day 48: Headstand 458

Day 49: Savasana 465

THE KABBALAH SUTRAS

PREFACE

Life can change in a moment. On the 3rd of November 2017 I was
hit by a car whilst walking to a Shabbat dinner in Los Angeles,
suffered a brain haemorrhage, was told I had two hours to live, unless I
underwent emergency brain surgery, and found myself in a void staring
at two bright lights. I saw a golden window to the left which I knew
represented coming back to this lifetime, this incarnation as Marcus,
and a bright window of white light to the right which meant I would
immediately transition to the next realm of existence. I intuitively knew
that if I "died" my parents would experience trauma for perhaps three
months or three years, but they would get through it. I saw there was no
death and absolutely nothing to fear because what we call death is just a
transition from one plane of existence to the next. I had been prepared
for the moment of death through my Kabbalistic training and knew I
must focus on elevating my thoughts and trusting God. All I could do
was surrender and hand myself over, as we sing in the final line of *Adon
Olam* - "*b'yado afkid ruchi*" - "into my hand I entrust your spirit".

What followed was an incredible journey. Four days later I had a second
brain haemorrhage and a second brain surgery. Big questions arose
regarding my level of recovery in terms of capacity and mobility and we
did not know how the medical bills would be paid since my insurance
was insufficient, but my friend Audrey Jacobs began a crowdfunding
campaign titled "Marcus needs a miracle". Miracles occurred and angels
appeared in my life. 1800 people supported the crowdfunding, which
was extraordinary for many reasons, not least because 18 is the gematria
(Hebrew numerology) for *Chai* (life) and the number 1800 represents
100 times life. Visitors and messages of well-wishing came in from

around the world. It felt like I had died, attended my own memorial service, heard what people would have said, and come back to life.

The Kabbalists teach that everything is a blessing, and Rabbi Shneur Zalman of Liadi explains that the more we search for a blessing, the more it will be revealed. This applies to difficult situations we may consider as "bad", although in the context of the infinite Creator of the universe, everything is good, even if we do not see it. We ask for revealed blessings, and we can reveal the hidden blessings if we look hard enough.

I have made it my mission to find the blessing in this experience, especially during challenging times. As one of my teachers used to say, "your principles don't count until you are put under pressure". It is easy to believe in God whilst standing in a synagogue on Yom Kippur or feel calm and serene whilst on a meditation retreat, but the real test is whether we can do it during uncomfortable times.

This new edition of *The Kabbalah Sutras* was the first project I took on during the recovery period, back when my brain injury had healed but I was still largely incapacitated due to recovering from brain trauma. Yoga was instrumental to my recovery. Some doctors had said I may experience headaches for months or years following the surgeries, but my friend Ida Unger, an experienced Iyengar Yoga teacher, visited regularly with specific yoga sequences designed for brain surgery recovery. The headaches were minimised and almost eradicated within three months, as was the need for continuous pain medication.

The first edition of *The Kabbalah Sutras* came out a few years ago in a larger version, but I wanted something more compact that could be offered at a lower price and reach a greater audience. This trilogy of books - *The Kosher Sutras, The Kabbalah Sutras and The Festive Sutras* - is a passion project that is intended to provide gateways for people to experience God through their body. The project grew out of my yoga teachings, although *The Kabbalah Sutras* allows way to connect to the Divine experience through business, relationships, career, and more general physical exercise.

Why yoga? The short version is that a few years after I became religiously observant, I found myself getting restless in synagogue, wanted to move around during prayer, and wondered if I could pray whilst moving around. To be fair, many people get bored in synagogue and want to move around, but at the time my restlessness peaked, my interest in yoga was simultaneously piqued. I was studying yoga as part of a postgraduate acting course at Webber Douglas in London. My teacher Edward Clarke inspired me with his beautiful asana practice and deep knowledge of the subtle energetic of yoga. After drama school, whilst completing my first yoga teacher training, Edward supported my journey as I asked the question of "how can I experience God through my body, in the context of Torah and Jewish prayer?". I simultaneously reached out to many of my Rabbis, including my teacher Rabbi Dr Dovid Ebner, whom I had learned from every day back when I lived and studied at Yeshivat Hamivtar in Efrat, Israel.

The Kabbalah Sutras was not a book I intended to write. One day in 2006 it occurred to me that there must be a physical system through which we can experience the sefirot in our body. The *Tikkunei Zohar*, a key book of Kabbalah, connects the sefirot with the body. I assumed there must be some kind of work that explores this in detail, but after several years of fruitless searching it became clear that the only way I could read the book I was looking for was to sit down and write it. Or to be more accurate, to sit down, listen and allow the book to be written through me. Here it is. I hope you enjoy it and that it uplifts your spiritual journey.

With love and blessings

Marcus Freed

Los Angeles, California, April 2019/Nissan 5779

"You shall count for yourselves – from the day after the Shabbat, from the day when you bring the Omer of the waving – seven Shabbats, they shall be complete. Until the day after the seventh shabbat you shall count, fifty days"

LEVITICUS 23:15-16

INTRODUCTION

"The end is in the beginning,
the beginning is in the end"

SEFER YETZIRAH 1:7

TREE OF LIFE: THE SEFIROT

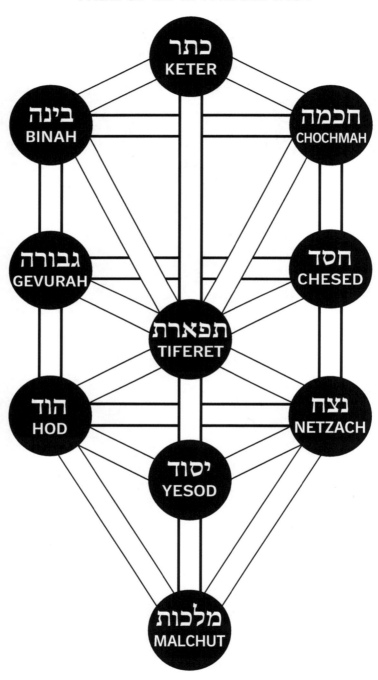

SEFIROT & THE BODY

מלכות
Malchut-Kingship

חסד
Chesed-Love

תפארת
Tiferet-Balance

גבורה
Gevurah-Strength

יסוד
Yesod-Bonding

נצח
Netzach-Endurance

הוד
Hod-Humility

We learn about the physical placement of the *Sefirot* directly from the Tikkunei Zohar 17b: "*Elijah began and said: Master of the Worlds! … You are He that has produced ten constructs (tiquninn) – and we call them 'the ten sephirot' – with which to direct hidden worlds that are not revealed, and worlds that are revealed… And they are called in this order: chesed is the right arm, gevurah is the left arm, tipheret is the body, netzach and hod are the two thighs; and yesod is the completion (siyuma) of the body – the sign of the holy covenant. Malkhut is the "mouth" – we call it the Oral Torah*"*

---

* Tiqqunei haZohar 11b, Qustha 1740: An English Translation. For a fuller explanation of how *Malchut*-Mastery is also connected with the hands and feet for the purposes of this book, please see the Introduction to *Malchut*-Mastery, page 404.

49 STEPS TO ENLIGHTENMENT

"There are more things in heaven and earth, Horatio,
than are dreamt of in your philosophy" — Hamlet [1]

The Kabbalah Sutras took eight years to write. I was troubled by one simple question: How are we to experience the Kabbalah within our bodies? There are beautiful Kabbalistic teachings which can enhance our lives, strengthen our connection with God, calm internal chaos, banish feelings of loneliness, and, even, bring an experience of heaven down to earth. The language of the Kabbalah refers to this as "unifying God"[2], which is something we will get into in very practical ways.

INTENTIONS OF THIS BOOK

These are the intentions for *The Kabbalah Sutras:*

1. To give you access to a simple yet self-empowering Kabbalistic system.

2. To give you these teachings to spread love and light.

3. To give you ways to improve your life through spiritual practices and specific exercises.

4. To give you ideas that can be applied to your work life to enjoy greater financial success and creative flow.

5. To give you techniques to move you closer to your soul's mission.

---

[1] Hamlet, 1:v.
[2] In the language of the Kabbalah, the "Unification of God" is usually referred to as "Uniting the Yud-Hey and the "Vav-Hey" of God. It refers to the four-letter name of God - known for centuries in English as "Yahweh". This topic alone could and has filled many books. We will revisit this throughout the book; it refers to the masculine and feminine aspects of both G-d and ourselves.
To pick one example of where we are "Uniting" G-d, we could look at Rabbi Yitzhak Luria's ("The Ari z"l") meditations on entering the *mikveh*, the ritual bath. At one stage in his meditative prescription he takes the four-letter name and has people meditate on it seven times (see *Meditation & Kabbalah*, p216).
On the most basic level, a practitioner might think of "where are my head & heart not aligned?", "where am I not integrating the masculine/direct and feminine/intuitive aspects of my personality". Our bodies are a microcosmic representation of God.

STEPPING OUT OF THE CAVE

The Kabbalah, the Jewish mystical tradition, teaches of 10 Divine energies that emanate different attributes of God, and seven of these are located in the body. The great second-century mystic Rabbi Shimon Bar Yochai spent 13 years hiding in a cave with his son, buried up to his neck in sand to preserve his clothes, whilst meditating on these mysteries[3]. He later wrote that a person "must act at the right time, that is, by knowing which *sefirah* [Divine energy-sphere] dominates at a particular time, he can bind himself to it and carry out the adjustment associated with the ruling attribute"[4]. This is far from tabloid astrology; the Kabbalists were focused on nothing less than channelling the power of God and teaching us how to do the same.

PRACTICE vs THEORY

Esoteric Bookshelves are replete with Kabbalistic theories and manuals. There are theories for everything ranging from the *Sefirot* (which this book is concerned with) to unifying the Higher worlds, to the theories of reincarnation and how Biblical and Rabbinic figures shared parts of their soul which revisited the earth in different incarnations[5]. *The Kabbalah Sutras* is a practical guide to experiencing the teachings in your body as an experiential pathway to connecting with God.

THE CALL: PHYSICAL MEDITATION, YOGA, TAI CHI & OTHER ENERGY WORK

Some Jewish practitioners head towards Eastern traditions to find what is "missing" in their own practice, although the mystical Jewish tradition has many references to physical meditation and energetic applications of the theories. To my knowledge, nobody has ever created a system for translating this world of Kabbalistic theory into practice.

---

3   Babylonian Talmud, Shabbat 33b.
4   Rabbi Shimon Bar Yochai's commentary on Bereisheet in The Zohar, quoted in Tomer Devorah p135.
5   See "The Gates of Reincarnation", Shaar HaGilgulim by Rabbi Yitzhak Luria (1534-1575). The book is amazing, but not for beginners.

WHY "SUTRAS"?

A 'sutra' is an aphorism, a noun from Indian literature describing a short phrase that contains a condensed teaching. Famous collections include the Yoga Sutras and the Karma Sutra. Their literary form is very close to that of the Mishna, eg Rabbi Hillel's statement *"If I am not for myself, who is for me? And if I am only for myself, what am I? And if not now, when?"*[6] . For the purposes of this book I have reimagined each Sefirah-combination as a mini-sutra, so *Gevurah Sheb'Chesed*, Discipline in Lovingkindness, is a sutra within itself. In essence *The Kabbalah Sutras* is a commentary on these Kabbalistic 'sutras'.

AUTHENTICITY

I have tried to stay completely authentic to the teachings of the sages. We are taught that Moses received the spiritual tradition on Mount Sinai[7], and our aim is to continue that tradition and stay true to it where knowingly possible. The Hebrew word for "received" is *kibel*, the root of *Kabbalah*. Writing this, I stand with an open heart and open ears listening for the words of Divine Truth. This book is based upon the teachings of the great Kabbalists, including Rabbi Abraham Abulafia, Rabbi Moshe Cordovero (the "Ramak"), Rabbi Yitzhak Luria (the "Ari z'l"), Rabbi Shneur Zalman of Liadi (the "Alter Rebbe"), Rabbi Shimon Bar Yochai (the "Rashbi") and more recent teachers including Rabbi Aryeh Kaplan z"l, The Lubavitcher Rebbe, Rabbi Menachem Mendel Schneerson z"l, and Rabbi Yitzhak Ginsberg.

KABBALISTIC CONFUSION

There is some confusion between what it means to be a Kabbalist. The snake-oil salesmen will tell you "sign up for this easy 12-part course and you will become a Kabbalist". At best this is nonsense and at worst it is deceitful and dangerous. To deeply connect with the path of Kabbalah involves integrating the other aspects of Jewish observance, including

---

6   Pirkei Avot, Ethics of the Fathers 1:14.
7   Pirkei Avot, Ethics of the Fathers, Chapter 1, Verse 1.

the fundamental pillars of *Shabbat* (Sabbath observance), *Kashrut* (dietary laws), *Taharat Mishpocha* (Family Purity & Sexual ethics), *Tefillah* (prayer) and more.

For someone to claim they are a Kabbalist without practicing the other pillars is akin to building the 20th floor of a building without first laying the foundation and building the other 19 storeys. There are repeated warnings against people who attempt to explore mystical teachings without first getting their foundations, and who suffer as a result. The story of the four rabbis entering the Orchard or "Pardes" is recounted in the Talmud:

> *"The Rabbis taught: Four entered the Pardes. They were Ben Azzai, Ben Zoma, Acher and Rabbi Akiva. Rabbi Akiva said to them, "When you come to the place of pure marble stones, do not say, 'Water! Water!' for it is said, 'He who speaks untruths shall not stand before My eyes' (Psalms 101:7)". Ben Azzai gazed and died. Regarding him the verse states, 'Precious in the eyes of G-d is the death of His pious ones' (Psalms 116:15). Ben Zoma gazed and was harmed. Regarding him the verse states, 'Did you find honey? Eat only as much as you need, lest you be overfilled and vomit it'* [8]. *Acher cut down the plantings. Rabbi Akiva entered in peace and left in peace"* [9].

This is taken as a metaphorical description of the results of mystical exploration and the price that can be paid by someone who is not sufficiently prepared. To be more explicit, if somebody starts playing with esoteric teachings and does not have a sufficient grounding, there can be a tremendous price to pay. When the story says *"Ben Zoma gazed and was harmed"*, this is a very practical warning for today. I have personally seen first-hand the dangers of ungrounded mystical meditations. This is not a game with which to toy lightly.

Rather, we are focusing on Kabbalistic Principles here. These can be applied by anyone, regardless of levels of observance, faith or belief. The core seven principles of *The Kabbalah Sutras* are based on the *Sefirot* or Divine Spheres, the emotional aspects of God which are present within

---

[8]   Proverbs 25:16.
[9]   Babylonian Talmud Hagigah 14b and Jerusalem Talmud Hagigah 2:1.

our body. The seven principles are: *Chesed*-Love, *Gevurah*-Strength, *Tiferet*-Balance, *Netzach*-Endurance, *Hod*-Gratitude, *Yesod*-Connection & *Malchut*-Mastery.

SHIFTING TRANSLATIONS & THE DIVINE FEMININE CURVES

I will be using various translations of these throughout the book. Hebrew is a deeply rich and allusive [elusive?] language, and to keep to one translation would be limiting. These *Sefirot* - the Divine Spheres - are feminine in their essence, their teachings coming to us by way of what is best described as the Divine Feminine Curves. Imagine a couple who are about to leave the house and the woman says to her man, "Sweetheart, do you like my red dress?". He replies "it's lovely". She says "Hang on, I'm just going to try on another one, the black one..how does this look?". The man replies "You look great in it". She asks, "What about the first one? Didn't that look good? What are you saying?". The man tries to answer but his answers are flaccid. He is stuck in a paradox, unwittingly wandering into a real-life Zen koan, the ultimate unanswerable question.[10]

The same is true with the Divine Feminine, the *Shechina*. The female part of God changes and moves in circles rather than straight lines. So I may translate *Chesed* as 'love', 'lovingkindness', 'giving', while *Gevurah* may be 'strength', 'discipline', 'fortitude', or something else. Sometimes Hod will be 'Humility' but it may also appear as 'Gratitude' or even 'Surrender'. This is not through lack of a thorough academic methodology but rather my higher goal of staying true to the essence of the *sefirot* (in my humble understanding) and true to the *higher* goal of the book, namely, to help you optimise your life and fulfil your Divine mission in the world. To let God shine through you. This does not demand over-thinking. If masculine thinking worked in every situation

---

[10] My friend Jeffrey Van Dyk did provide the "escape route" to this question. When a woman asks "which dress do you prefer?", the trap is to try and answer the question with a statement. Rather, answer it with a question: "which dress do you feel best in? How does it make you feel?". In answering the question-behind-the-question, you give the right answer. This is why men have failed for centuries: they only tried to answer the question.

then we would always know how to answer the question about the red dress.

Rational and logical thinking is 'masculine' in this context, while intuitive and emotionally-driven thinking is 'feminine'. One is not better than the other. Jewish styles of learning have been largely focused on the former, hence the need for practices like *The Kabbalah Sutras.*

BECOMING LIKE GOD

The aim of our work is to become like God. As we will shortly reflect upon, the essence of the Kabbalistic teachings is to reveal Godliness within. The more we activate the Divine spheres, the *sefirot*, within our body, the more we become attuned to our Godly nature. The Kabbalists taught that as we activate the lower spheres, we are also activating the Divine spheres.[11] In short, the best way to reach Heaven is through Earth.

An early Kabbalist, Rabbi Moshe Cordovero (the "Ramak", 1522–1570) wrote a beautiful work called the *Tomer Devorah* (The Palm Tree of Deborah). He taught:

> *"It is proper for man to emulate his Creator, for then he will attain the secret of Supernal Form in both image (tzelem) and likeness (demut)"*[12].

This may seem a daunting or initially unattractive task, after all, why would you want to emulate the Divine? If the answers are not initially obvious then consider the alternate route: living an entirely earth-bound life with earth-bound pleasures and earth-bound travails. Rather, we have the choice of infusing our meaning, elevating our actions, seeing everything we do in a bigger context.

---

[11]   This concept is discussed in the Tanya, the writings of the Ari z"l & elsewhere.
[12]   Tomer Devorah, (Chp 1, p3).

TO UNIFY GOD, FIRST UNIFY YOURSELF

After becoming religious at the age of 19, I studied at Orthodox *yeshivot* (Rabbinical seminaries) and wherever possible I am trying to stay faithful to the tradition. My professional life has taken me in several diverse directions as a professional actor, writer, dramatist, business coach, and teacher of yoga, and several passions have waxed and waned over the decades including surfing, salsa & breakdancing, meditation, intuitive energy work and more. We talk of becoming one with God and many seekers are looking to reach higher spiritual levels, but first we must unify the different parts of ourselves. To see that we are complex beings, often with apparent internal contradictions, but this too is also a form of oneness. Understanding the Divine begins by first understanding ourselves.

PICKING UP FROM BOOK ONE: THE KOSHER SUTRAS

The Kabbalah Sutras is intended as a deepening of my first book *The Kosher Sutras*. Whereas the focus was almost exclusively on interpreting Biblical wisdom through yoga and meditation, and integrating ancient wisdom into our modern world, this book is designed to be even more holistic and practical.

BEYOND ASANA

I realised that yoga isn't enough and my work developed beyond that practice alone, for various reasons. Yoga asana is like a hammer in the hand of a builder, a set of brushes in the hands of a painter, a spoken vocabulary in the mind of a writer. A fantastic and important tool, but a map for the journey rather than the destination. The point of yoga is not more *asanas* (physical postures); the goal of yoga is oneness with the Divine. Too many practitioners get trapped in the means as an end in itself, but that is like confusing your car for the destination you are trying to reach. The focus of the yoga conversations tend to develop along the lines of "I need to be more flexible" or "I am so flexible - look at my backbend" - whilst there are tremendous life-changing benefits to the practice and I wholeheartedly support it, my own body had begun asking for a more integrated practice. So, I began more seriously exploring insight and spiritual meditations, aerobic and weights at the gym, tai-chi and other energy work. With the current rate of change, I expect this practice to continue developing.

Thus, *The Kabbalah Sutras* will incorporate various different body-centred practices, whilst staying true to my yogic roots.

Our destination is oneness. Trying to feel whole again. This occurs everywhere within our earthly realm, whether it is feeling 'at one' with nature when you stand before the Grand Canyon, feeling 'at one' with your lover at the point of physical union, feeling 'at one' with satisfaction when you have eaten a sumptuous meal, feeling 'at one' with your work when you are in flow and in the zone, or feeling 'at one' with good friends on a good night out. The Kabbalists teach that what happens below is also happening above, and with the correct intention, awareness and vessel, all of these experiences of being 'at one' can mirror and contribute towards the unity of God.[13]

THE *SEFIROT*

The Kabbalists teach that there are ten categories of universal love, known as the *sefirot* (Divine spheres). Three are intellectual, residing in the head, and the remaining seven are emotional attributes that are associated with the body. They can also be seen as channels through which we connect with God, and each has a specific quality. Like markers on a metaphysical radio, we tune into different frequencies to hear the distinct variety of message that each offers. But that is where

---

[13] This is not, God forbid, to suggest that God is not unified. I am deliberately not going into Kabbalistic theory here. The sages go to great lengths to explain *Seder Hishtalshelus* which is the Order of Creation - i.e. how and why does a completely unified being create a lower world of disunity (e.g. the one we are living in!). This includes concepts such as the *Arba Olamot* (four worlds), *Tzimtzum* (contraction of Divine energy), *Ohr Ein Sof* (Endless Light) and more. Two 'starter manuals' would be the Tanya and "Meditation & Kabbalah" (see Bibliography).

the metaphor ends, because the Kabbalah teaches that although each sefirah is a different aspect of God, they all exist simultaneously and are inter-related. Our 49 day quest follows the path of the 'lower' seven *sefirot*, or Divine energies, that are specifically related to the body, a concept we'll explore later on.

Here are the categories of the seven emotional *sefirot*, along with various translations of each:

1. דסח *CHESED*: Lovingkindness, benevolence, giving, existence (the power of love – how can I experience more love?)

2. גבורה *GEVURA*: Justice, discipline, restraint, awe, strength, power, bonding (The power of strength)

3. טפארת *TIFERET*: Beauty, harmony, compassion, centeredness, balance (The power of balance)

4. נצח *NETZACH*: Endurance, fortitude, ambition (The power to endure)

5. הוד HOD: Humility, splendour (The power to shine)

6. יסוד YESOD: Bonding, foundation, groundedness (The power to be grounded)

7. מלכות MALCHUT: Nobility, sovereignty, leadership, monarchy (The power to be great)

The Kabbalah Sutras is designed as a seven-week practice with a different theme for each week.

THE WEEKLY THEMES

Each day there are two themes - theme of the day and theme of the week. So Day One is *Chesed Sheb'Chesed* - Love in Love, Day Two is *Gevurah Sheb'Chesed* - Discipline in Love, Day Three is *Tiferet Sheb'Chesed* - Compassion in Love and so forth. Our intention is experiential learning rather than a purely intellectual foray. Here is an overview of the exercises:

Week 1: *Chesed*/**Love**: Loving Love, Disciplined love, Compassionate love, Enduring love, Humble love, Pleasurable/Grateful love, Grounded and Connected Love, Masterful Love.

Week 2: *Gevurah*/**Discipline/Strength**: Loving Discipline, Disciplined Discipline, Compassionate Discipline, Enduring Discipline, Grateful/Humble Discipline, Grounded and Connected/ Pleasurable Discipline, Masterful Discipline.

Week 3 *Tiferet*/**Compassion:** Loving Compassion, Strong Compassion, Compassionate Compassion, Enduring Compassion, Humble/ Grateful Compassion, Connected and Pleasurable Compassion, Masterful Compassion.

Week 4 *Netzach*/**Endurance:** Loving Endurance, Disciplined Endurance, Compassionate Endurance, Enduring Endurance, Grateful Endurance, Connected and Grounded Endurance, Masterful Endurance.

Week 5 *Hod*/**Gratitude:** Loving Gratitude, Disciplined Gratitude, Compassionate Gratitude, Enduring Gratitude, Grateful/ Humble Gratitude, Masterful Gratitude.

Week 6 *Yesod*/**Connection, Pleasure, Grounding:** Loving Connections, Disciplined Connections, Compassionate Connections/Relationships, Masterful Relationships/ Relationship Mastery.

Week 7 *Malchut*/**Mastery, Nobility:** Loving Mastery, Disciplined Mastery, Compassionate Mastery, Disciplined Mastery, Grateful and Humble Mastery.

YOGIC PRECEDENTS AND THE HOLY LION

In the search for an authentic basis for physicalising the Kabbalistic teachings, our master key is in the works of perhaps the greatest Kabbalist of the last 1000 years, Rabbi Yitzhak Luria (1543-1572, known as the Ari'zal (or Ari z"l), which translates as 'The Lion, may his memory be a blessing').

The Ari z"l describes how we can do a walking meditation whilst visualising the *Sefirot*. He notes the physical connections to each of the seven Sefirah-energies and suggests ways of bringing them into action:

> *"When you walk in the street, meditate that your two feet are the Sefirot Netzach and Hod. When you look at something with your eyes, meditate that your eyes are Chochmah-wisdom and Binah-understanding. Meditate in this manner with regard to every part of your body. Also contemplate that you are a vehicle for the Highest Holiness. This is the meaning of the verse "In all your ways know Him".[14]*

> *There is no question that if you constantly make use of these meditations, you will become like an angel of heaven. You will gain an enlightenment so that you will be able to know all that you desire. This is especially true if you do not interrupt this meditation, thinking of this constantly, and not separating your mind from it. Everything depends on your intensity of concentration and attachment on high. Do not remove this from before your eyes...*

> *This is a meditation through which you can elevate your Nefesh-soul from Asiyah[15] to the Universe of Yetzirah.[16]*

> *Contemplate on the mystery of Wings. Through Wings, man can fly and ascend on high. A bird cannot fly except with its wings. Paralleling the wings of a bird are the arms of man.*

> *There are five loves (Chasadim). These permeate the Six Directions of the Body [which parallel the six Sefirot, Chesed, Gevurah, Tiferet, Netzach, Hod and Yesod].*

---

[14] Proverbs 3:6.
[15] The lowest 'world' or sphere of existence in the 'four worlds' model of reality presented in Lurianic Kabbalah.
[16] The World of Formation (in the four worlds model).

*In the arms and the upper third of the torso, these Loves
are concealed. In the lower part of the body, they are
revealed.*

*It is for this reason that man flies with his arms, which
are his Wings, and not with his legs or other wings...*

*This is the Kavannah (intention) upon which you
should meditate. Every ascent is through this Name of
Forty-Two.*

*Meditate on your right arm (Chesed-love).
Contemplate...*

*Then meditate on your left arm (Gevurah-strength).
Contemplate..."*[17]

To the best of my knowledge, there has never been a system to
comprehensively experience and practice these principles in the body.

ON WRITING IN STRAIGHT LINES & WRITING IN CIRCLES

This book did not want to be written in a straight line. I tried
many times. The nature of the *sefirot* is the Divine Feminine, the
Godly curves. True to male form, I resisted it for a while, but finally
succumbed. *The Kabbalah Sutras* is about *sefirot*. They are feminine,
circular energies. There is no 'A to B'. A leads to B but it may be via
C or via A. Think of male-female miscommunication and different
perspectives. This is a Feminine-energy book in that sense.

In other words, there is a strong precedent.

---

[17] From the Ari z'l's Twenty-First Yichud, in Meditation and Kabbalah p258. I have inserted
English names of the *sefirot* as they do not appear in the original translation.

COUNTING THE OMER

A profound spiritual opportunity is presented during a 49 day period between the festivals of Passover/Pesach and Shavuot, approximately March-April to May-June. The precise timing varies according to the Hebrew calendar but the Kabbalists make it clear: this is a time for balancing the Divine energy so that we strengthen our connection during each of the 49 days, culminating in an all-night celebration of learning and meditation at *Shavuot*.

Why are there 49 ways when there are only seven attributes? Because each of these pathways is a delicate mix of each of the energetic traits. When we bond with a friend, we can do it through acts of lovingkindness, compassion, endurance, humility, nobility or a host of other nuanced emotions. So, by exploring the seven aspects of each of these seven aspects, we reach 49, this period that the Bible refers to as *Sefirat HaOmer*, or the Counting of Omer, that coincides with the time of the spring threshing season.

HOW TO USE THE BOOK

There are three ways of using this book. Each of the essays is designed to be used in conjunction with either a yoga or gym practice, and applied directly to your relationships, business/career/job and daily outlook. There are suggestions for a posture that is appropriate for each day, and questions to meditate on. Each week has seven different yoga and gym exercises, which you begin on the first day of the week (Sunday) and add to over during the subsequent days so that you have a longer practice on the seventh day of the week (Shabbat/Saturday). If you are using the book for yoga practice, each day's posture should be preceded with four rounds of sun salutes and concluded with a basic closing sequence that includes a backbend, inversion (e.g. headstand), resting posture (eg savasana/shabbat pose/corpse pose) and seated meditation.

METHOD 1: *Counting the Omer:* This is the full 49-day method that begins on the Hebrew date of the 16th Nissan (for a reliable calendar, visit http://www.chabad.org/holidays/sefirah/omer-calendar.htm).

METHOD 2: *Any day from today!:* Choose any day of the year to start your practice sequence and begin the 49-day programme at that point.

METHOD 3: *Class motivator:* A final option is to choose any of the essays to read as a motivator before going to a yoga class or doing your self-practice. Read one that appeals to the mood that you are in and get started.

METHOD 4: *Daily Practice*

The seven *sefirot* also relate to the days of the week:

> *"These seven attributes are known as the "seven days of Creation," for it was through these seven attributes that G-d created the world. Each day's creation came about through a particular attribute: during the first day Chesed was dominant, the second day Gevurah, and so on"[18]. We can interpret this so that each day our week has a different theme, and this is a personal practice that I try to keep in mind every day.[19] The idea is that on any one day you can read some of the essays and practices for the corresponding sefirah. The "day" runs in line with the Jewish calendar, which begins at sunset and runs for 24 hours.*

---

[18] Sefer Tanya, Chapter 3.

[19] There is a far more nuanced version of this that can be deduced from the writings of the Ari z"l in Meditation & Kabbalah. For example, each hour has a dominant sefirah, so you might go more deeply into the appropriate day/hour combination. Or during the Counting of the Omer between Pesach and Shavuot, you would get extra 'layering' - e.g. Tuesday (which is *Tiferet*/Compassion) might fall on *Chesed Sheb'Gevurah*, which is Lovingkindness in Discipline. However, I have not yet developed a theory of how to apply these extra nuanced layers at this point in my personal practice and understanding. The aim is to keep our practice simple and working rather than to get lost in the realm of theory, which takes us back to the story of the Pardes/Orchard that warns us of the dangers of losing our mind in Kabbalistic practice, G-d forbid.

DAYS & CORRESPONDING *SEFIROT*

> Day #1 - *Chesed*-Love - Saturday night - Sunday[20]
>
> Day #2 - *Gevurah*-Discipline - Sunday night - Monday
>
> Day #3 - *Tiferet*-Compassion - Monday night - Tuesday
>
> Day #4 - *Netzach*-Endurance - Tuesday night - Wednesday
>
> Day #5 - *Hod*-Humility & Gratitude - Wednesday night - Thursday
>
> Day #6 - *Yesod*-Connection - Thursday night - Friday
>
> Day #7 - *Malchut*-Mastery - Friday night - Saturday (Shabbat)

TIMING

These sessions can be done in as little as 10 minutes a day; spend 3-4 minutes reading the essay and 7 minutes doing the postures so that you can physicalise and embody the idea. If you are with a friend, why not read the essay together and then discuss the ideas, before doing your yoga practice.

Practice in health, safety and unleash your light!

---

[20] This system is according to the Gra, as explained in the commentary to the Sefer Yetzirah, p183.

CHESED חסד

LOVINGKINDNESS

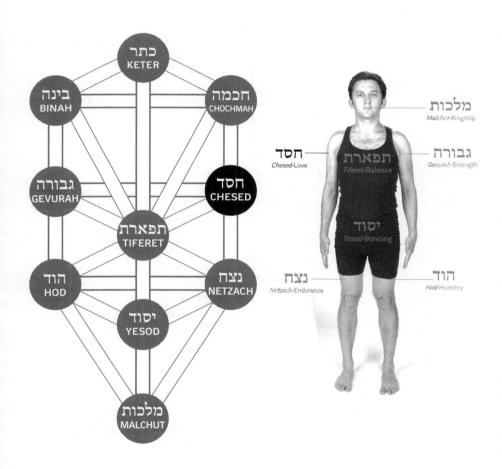

WEEK 1

CHESED INTRODUCTION: ENDLESS LOVE חסד

Five hundred twenty five thousand six hundred minutes
Five hundred twenty five thousand moments, so dear
Five hundred twenty five thousand six hundred minutes
How do you measure, measure a year?
....How about love?
Measure in love
Seasons of love — *"Seasons of Love",* Rent

Love is a tricky business. If you give somebody too much of it you might smother them. If you give them too little, they may feel neglected. If you are too compassionate then things can get out of balance. If you push too hard they may be driven away, and if you are too easygoing they may walk over you. If you rush the connection then you go too fast for the relationship, and if you don't get a handle on the relationship then it is doomed to failure.

This is the essence, at least one interpretation, of the Kabbalistic view of *Chesed*-lovingkindness. *The Kabbalah Sutras* does not attempt an over-intellectualised approach because our aim is to enlighten our lives and help improve the world rather than increase our powers of analysis. For those who are already familiar with the basic terms, here is the same paragraph again, with a Kabbalistic commentary. Don't worry if you don't understand it yet - we will be exploring this in far more depth during the following seven essays:

Love is a tricky business - *this is Chesed, our theme for the week.*

If you give somebody too much of it you might smother them - '*Chesed*-love in *Chesed*-love' = *how we love.*

If you give them too little, they may feel neglected. - '*Gevurah*-discipline in *Chesed*-love' = **the discipline with which we love.**

If you are too compassionate then things can get out of balance. '*Tiferet*-balance in *Chesed*-love' = *the compassion and balance we bring to our love.*

If you push too hard they may be driven away, '*Netzach*-endurance in *Chesed*-love' = *the way we sustain and endure through our relationships.*

and if you are too easygoing they may walk on you. '*Hod*-gratitude in *Chesed*-love' = *the amount of humility we bring to our loving connections.*

If you rush the connection then you go too fast for the relationship, '*Yesod*-bonding in *Chesed*-love' = *the way we connect and bond to others. This also includes our intimate relations.*

and if you don't get a handle on the relationship then it is doomed to failure. '*Malchut*-mastery in *Chesed*-love' = *the amount of mastery and nobility we bring to the way we love ourselves and others.*

EXTERNAL *CHESED*

And so, our journey begins with the Sefirah of *Chesed*, which is love-in-action[1]. Often translated as "loving kindness", *Chesed* is the way that we show our love to others. It is the act of giving within a relationship, whether it is a parent to a child, a wife to a husband or the sharing of friends.

Rabbi Matis Weinberg described *Chesed*-love as "existence expressing itself" in the way that human beings naturally want to give to one another and that sense of loving kindness is hard-wired into our DNA[2]. At its most gross level this comes out in the desire to procreate, for the human race to keep on multiplying.

On a genetic level, *Chesed*-love might be seen as the way that we *just want* to recreate as an in-built human drive. It is the way that a parent *just wants* to look after their child, or the way that you *just want* to care for certain people such as your partner.

---

[1] According to Chassidic teachings, the inner dimension of *Chesed*-lovingkindness is *Ahavah*-love.

[2] Rabbi Matis Weinberg said this in his lectures on *Sefirat HaOmer*, which were recorded in Jerusalem.

INTERNAL *CHESED* & YOUR RIGHT ARM

There is the internal aspect of *Chesed*-love, which is the way that **you** are loving towards yourself. The *Zohar* ("Book of Brilliance" or "Book of Illumination") teaches that *Chesed*-love resides in the right arm[3]. On a very practical level, this relates to the fact that most people are right-handed, and when you give somebody a gift, you will primarily be moving your right arm to complete the action. Rabbi Shneur Zalman of Liadi (1745-1812), the *Alter Rebbe*, connected this with the "acts of charity and kindness" that we do in this world. A primary example would be giving a coin for charity/*tzedakah*, where you reach out with your right arm and give to the needy recipient[4].

The internal aspects we will also explore relate to how we are giving towards ourselves, and our internal relationship to ourselves. Knowing oneself can be underrated but is incredibly important in the path towards self-realisation.

ABRAHAM'S ACTS OF LOVE

"I will sing of the Lord's steadfast love forever...the world was built with loving kindness", wrote King David[5]. *Chesed*-love is the primary quality through which we can understand God, relate personally to the Creator, and bring Light into the world. The Torah describes God as "*Rav Chesed*"[6] or 'Rabbi Chesed'[7], in other words, the master or teacher of Loving kindness.

The patriarch Abraham is seen as the epitome of *Chesed*-love, due to the way that he acted with kindness towards every person, and it is this quality that we are encouraged to emulate.

---

3 [The sefirah] of *Chesed* is [called] the [Supernal] 'right arm'" - Sefer Tanya, Epistle Three, Lessons in Tanya #4 p39, quoting the Zohar.
4 See Tanya #4, epistle 5, p95 and footnote #54 there for connections between the right arm and *Chesed*.
5 Book of Psalms/*Tehillim* (89: 1-3).
6 Exodus 34:6.
7 This observation - God as "*Rabbi Chesed*" was observed by friend Rabbi Dr Raphael Zarum.

We learn from his attributes of welcoming in guests even when it was least convenient, such as three days after his circumcision.[8]

ESOTERIC KABBALAH - FINGERS & TOES

The Kabbalistic masters explain how everything we do on earth has a corresponding reality in a higher world. Just as we can experience *Chesed*-love in our body when we are giving to somebody else, this has resonances in alternate realms. The Kabbalah presents a worldview that our body is a microcosm of the Divine image[9], so anything that happens on a lower world is also happening on a higher realm[10]. This is also practically represented in our body as the 10 represent the 10 *Sefirot* in the upper worlds, while our 10 toes represent the 10 *sefirot* in the lower worlds[11]. (To avoid any confusion, this book is only discussing the lower seven *sefirot* which are directly connected to the body and emotions. The upper three sefirot - *Chochma*-wisdom, *Binah*-understanding and *Daat*-knowing - are more intellectual and conceptual. The Kabbalah Sutras is concerned with teachings that you can immediately use in the gym, on the yoga mat, in relationships and in your workplace!)

HEALING OUR DYSFUNCTIONAL LOVE/*CHESED*

This work is all about healing, both internal and external. The Kabbalistic term for this healing is *Tikkun* and relates to the way that we are attempting to heal the entire universe.[12]

---

8   Genesis 18:1. We learn of the precise timing from Rashi, ad loc.
9   "And God created man in His own image, in the image of God created He him; male and female created He them". Genesis 1:27
10 This is discussed at length in the Tanya and elsewhere. We learn of the *"Upper Sefirot"* and the *"Lower Sefirot"*. This is practically represented in our bodies as the fingers represent the upper sefirot and the toes represent the *lower sefirot*, as there are 10 of each in direct correspondence with the Divine spheres. See *The Bahir*, p125.
11 *The Bahir*, p125 in the commentary of Rabbi Aryeh Kaplan, who wrote: "The Ten Fingers allude to the Ten *Sefirot*".
12 See *The Bahir* p88 where Rabbi Kaplan's commentary discusses how the initial chaos (*Tohu*) and desolation (*Bohu*) of the world relates to the way that we are trying to fix it. The Torah begins וְהָאָרֶץ הָיְתָה תֹהוּ וָבֹהוּ "The world was full of chaos and desolation" (Genesis 1:2). Rabbi Kaplan explains *"Tohu* relates to the first vessels, which were shattered, while *Bohu* relates to these vessels after they were restored and rectified". On a very basic level, when we fix our relationships and heal the way we experience *Chesed*, we are transforming the world in this area.

QUESTIONS TO HEAL DYSFUNCTIONAL RELATIONSHIPS (CHESED)

There are many forms of dysfunctional *Chesed*-love, which is the essence of our work. Here are some questions to ask, to bring about healing (technically we might refer to this as 'healing the sefirah of *Chesed*-love').

Where are all of the areas in my life where I have a deficiency *Chesed*/loving kindness?

1. Am I being stingy and holding back from giving? This could be taking more than I am giving or listening. It could affect surface-level spending - *e.g.* money. Or, it could show up with the way I am eating - am I over-filling my stomach through being too kind to myself?

2. Where am I holding onto things and not letting go out of fear of loss?

3. Am I hoarding energy? Are there things I need to let go of because they are no longer serving me? Am I holding onto keepsakes from a former romantic partner or friend, and keeping their memory and energy present when I know it is bad for me?

4. Where am I not giving enough to people? Are other people giving me gifts or spending time with me and I am not sufficiently reciprocating?

Where are all of the areas in my life where I have an excess of *Chesed*/lovingkindness?

1. Am I giving too much to somebody? This reminds me of the old joke - *"What's the difference between a Jewish mother and a Rottweiler? The Rottweiler lets go, eventually"*. Do you need to give people more space?

2. Am I giving too much and not allowing somebody the space to give back to me in return?

3. Am I generating 'Karmic Debts' through an imbalance? (*e.g.* maybe I am giving too much and not allowing someone to give back to me).

4. Where have I given more than was required and created a problem as a result? (Here is a personal experience of when my own *Chesed*-love created an imbalance: I was asked to do three tasks for a client and I did five. Or I was asked to put 5 teachings on a website and I put 50 up. This act of 'loving kindness' generated many extra hours of work later on. More is not necessarily better. *e.g.* an ocean liner is not better than a speedboat if you want to be able to quickly change course and direction. So giving too much can overbalance a situation and somebody feels like they have to give too much to you. Giving too early on can smother a relationship. *i.e.* If a guy gives a girl too many gifts when they have just started seeing one another, her experience of being overwhelmed may well destroy the nascent relationship.

5. We are told *"you shall not add to the word I have commanded you nor shall you take away from it"* (Deuteronomy 4:2). We can see this as a healthy relationship

CHART #1: DYSFUNCTIONAL *CHESED*

Here is a practical way of looking at *Chesed*, through the mundane example of looking after a pet dog.

Too much *Chesed*-love in *Chesed*-love:

I give my dog too many sweets. My dog is sick.

My business is underpriced because I give to too many people. I go bankrupt.

There are no boundaries to my relationships. Or worse still, I am so giving to the other person that I do not give them any personal space - "I'm all up in your stuff"

Too much *Gevurah*-discipline in *Chesed*-love:

Dog is hungry. Business is overpriced. Relationship is no personal space and suffocating.

Tiferet in *Chesed*-love:

Perfect synthesis. We compromise in our relationship. I compromise with clients. Sometimes there are discounts and sometimes it's full price. I see what is needed and do what is needed (think of Yaakov in *Business Situation, e.g.* with Laban. He paid Laban back and he also took care of himself. Laban as more *Gevurah* = all taking.). *Tiferet* in *Chesed* is not generating Karmic debt.

Too little *Netzach*-endurance in *Chesed*-love:

There is an inconsistent love and lack of trust in my relationships.

Too much *Netzach*-endurance in *Chesed*-love:

In business this might show up as an overload of marketing, or too many contact points with the customer. As one friend put it, "Being persistent to the state of annoying".[13]

Too little *Hod*-gratitude/humility in *Chesed*-love:

I don't remember my place and I step on people.

I am always complaining and lacking gratitude and humility.

Too much *Hod*-gratitude/humility in *Chesed*-love:

I am a doormat. People step on me. I have very little personal power.

Too little *Yesod*-bonding in *Chesed*-love:

I am loving but not connected with the other person. I am showing up, giving, doing the acts, but not **bonding** with them. What does it feel like when we are not bonding? Instead I must ask: *Am I bonding through my giving? Am I balancing Endurance & Humility?*

Malchut-mastery in *Chesed*-love:

Am I continually calibrating all of the different facets & aspects of *Chesed*-love? Giving enough, holding back when necessary, doing it compassionately, sustaining my loving kindness, staying in gratitude & humility, bonding and connecting through my acts...this and more is *Malchut*-mastery.

---

13 Quoting Marissa Leigh Salem!

CHART #2 - COMMUNICATING HEALTHY *CHESED*

I LOVE YOU BUT....I NEED TO GIVE YOU MORE LOVE
(*Chesed*-love in *Chesed*-love)

I LOVE YOU BUT...I NEED BOUNDARIES (*Gevurah*-
discipline)

I LOVE YOU BUT...I NEED MORE COMPASSION (*Tiferet*-
compassion)

I LOVE YOU BUT...I NEED US TO BE TRUTHFUL AND
I NEED THIS TO BE SUSTAINABLE & ENDURE (*Netzach*-
endurance)

I LOVE YOU BUT...I NEED (YOU) TO BE LESS
ARROGANT AND MORE HUMBLE (*Hod*-humility)

I LOVE YOU BUT...I NEED US TO CONNECT MORE ON
DEEPER LEVELS (*Yesod*-bonding)

I LOVE YOU BUT...I NEED TO FEEL SAFE, SECURE
AND THAT WE ARE IN CONTROL OF THIS
RELATIONSHIP (*Malchut*-mastery)

****

Our task is cut out for us...let's get to work!

DAY 1/LOVINGKINDNESS IN LOVINGKINDNESS / ALL YOU NEED IS LOVE / חסד שבחסד

KABBALAH SUTRA: *Chesed She b'Chesed* – Loving kindness in Loving kindness.

INTENTION: To draw endless love and positive energy into your life through boundless giving.

"My bounty is as boundless as the sea,
My love as deep; the more I give to thee,
The more I have, for both are infinite." — Romeo and Juliet (II:ii)

Western culture has a lot to answer for. Unless we stop and question our values, we are told how to eat, how to think, how to love, how to behave and how to show up in every area of our existence. *The Kabbalah Sutras* is intended to reconnect us with an ancient practice to elevate every aspect of our life. Week One begins with healing and reconsidering the realm of love in our lives. Whilst a million love songs proclaim a love that is demanding, needy and ego-centred, a love that asks "how much can I get?", *Chesed*-love asks, "How much can I give?".

Which seems more powerful: approaching relationships from a perspective of "I am looking for X, Y, Z, and I have these expectations of a partner", or being like God and thinking "what is the healthiest way to express my love to the other person and give in a way that will be good for both of us? Naturally this is about healthy balances, but *Chesed*-love is the action of giving and in Week Two we will explore *Gevurah*-discipline which is all about receiving.

GIVING LIKE GOD

The Ramak[14] (1522-1570) is an important early Kabbalist who asked *"How should a person train himself in the attribute of Chesed-kindness?"*. He suggested that we can connect to this trait through considering how the Divine gives to us, saying that *"The main way to enter the secret of Chesed-kindness is to love God so absolutely that one will never forsake His service for any reason...[15]"*.

In the *Tomer Devorah* ("Palm Tree of Deborah"), he listed a series of practical ways that we can perform these loving acts;

> *"1)At the moment of a child's birth, one should provide him with all the necessities of his sustenance... 2)circumcising the child....3)Visiting the ill and healing them. As is known, the Shechinah [feminine presence of God] is lovesick for unification, as the verse states "...for I am sick with love"[16]. Her cure is in the hands of man, who is able to bring her pleasant remedies.. 4)Giving constantly to the poor... 5) Offering hospitality to strangers... 6)Attending to the dead... 7)Bringing a bride to the chuppah [marriage canopy] ...8)Making peace between a man and his fellow...the same explanation applies regarding making peace between a man and his wife...All similar ways of making peace are also acts of benevolence in the higher worlds".[17]*

---

[14]   The Ramak was Rabbi Moshe Cordovero, author of many Kabbalistic works, including *Tomchei Devorah* (*The Palm Tree of Deborah*). As a note of reference, his teachings pre-date the Ari z"l, the Baal Shem Tov and the Alter Rebbe. What this means in practice is that he came before the birth of Chassidut which really "unlocks" the Kabbalistic teachings for practical usage. The first couple of times I learned the *Tomchei Devorah* it was hard to understand much of what was going on, but after I had studied the Tanya, which is a form of "master key", I was then able to "unlock" the earlier work of the Ramak. And yes, I am playing fast and loose with my use of "quotation marks" here, but the aim is not to get approved by the MLA for scholarly genius - although that might be fun - but rather to help you bring Godly light into the world through this work. Hence the need for "emphasis" for today's busy reader! Enjoy! b'H.

[15]   Tomer Devorah, p.85.

[16]   Song of Songs, 2:5.

[17]   Ibid., p85-100.

An eastern society might call this Karma Yoga, the west may call it Good Deeds, and on another level, the Ramak is teaching Practical Kabbalah. This is where the spiritual experience happens - through visiting the sick, welcoming people into our homes, attending weddings and funerals. *Chesed*-Love is being involved in the flow of life and helping it flow more smoothly for others.

INTERNALISING ABRAHAM

The attribute of *Chesed*-love is attributed to the patriarch Abraham, and is the first kabbalistic quality through which we can understand God. *Chesed* is central to the beginning of any relationship, the building of any community and the creation of peace. One way of internalising the principle is to read and learn the stories about Abraham but imagining the "Abraham" part of ourselves. When Abraham is giving to guests, I can think about how I am giving to guests. When he is arguing with God to save the lives of the people in Sodom, I can think about how I might argue to save other people's lives (and by "lives", this might mean protecting people's reputations, their jobs, their place in the community, or helping people save themselves from destructive behaviours).

This also demands a more creative reading of the Torah and *midrashim* (rabbinic stories) but is in line with the kabbalistic approach that deeply associates all of these principles with our body; we are told that "*Chesed*" lives in our "right arm"[18], and it is the dominant characteristic of Abraham. In a sense, Abraham is part of us. But that is all theory; the question is, how are you going to change your life with this information?

DO YOU EVER GIVE WITH STRINGS ATTACHED?

Have you ever received a gift from someone that left you feeling uncomfortable or guilty, perhaps as if you owed them something? They appeared to be giving to you but were actually taking in the process?

---

[18] The Tikkunei Zohar teaches: "*Chesed* - the 'Right Arm', *Gevurah* - the 'Left Arm', *Tiferet* - the 'Trunk' *Netzakh* and *Hod* - the two 'Thighs', *Y'sod* - the trunk's 'Extremity'; sign of the Covenant most holy. - *Malchut* - the 'Orifice'; the oral Torah we call it." (Translation by Rabbi Zalman Schachter-Shalomi, originally posted at his website http://www.jewishrenewalhasidus.org/wordpress/reb-zalman-resources/)

The Kabbalah talks of the idea of *Tikkun*, or "rectification" and we are trying to rectify all of the ways that our giving or kindnesses are impure. Much like a jeweller would polish a diamond to remove flaws, we are trying to polish our personality and soul. The true self-reflection may sting a little at first but the results can be beautiful. If your love is "boundless like the sea", then now is the time to start removing any blockages so that the course of your love may run smooth.

TODAY'S PRACTICE

YOGA PRACTICE GUIDELINES:

Karma is central to Indian philosophy and can be understood as the process of cause and effect. You perform an action out of love and you will receive love (although not necessarily from the same source). The sage Patanjali taught that *"all is suffering for the sage"*[19] and the process of karma, acting with a loving intention, helps us transcend this earthly pain[20]. This in effect is Karma yoga.

Becoming kind in the way that we give demands intelligence and sensitivity, and the type of gift will differ according to the needs of the recipient. This is a call for flexibility in our yoga practice (no pun intended). Whilst there are huge benefits to regularly practicing major postures and having a flowing sequence, today's challenge is to notice: *what does your body need on this particular day, and can you choose extra postures that will fulfil that need. Is your back tight after a bad night's sleep? Do you have shoulder ache from carrying heavy bags? Are your feet sore from an evening out on the town?* Guide your practice with *Chesed*-kindness.

GYM PRACTICE GUIDELINES:

Notice how you are giving to yourself through your gym practice this week. Many people cause themselves damage by pushing too far. This is an example of unkind giving, like the friend who 'gives' you a present that leaves you feeling uncomfortable and obligated to return

---

19 Yoga Sutras 2:15.
20 *Bhakti Yoga*, the yoga of loving devotion, was another path to overcoming this challenge of day-to-day pain.

something. One might say "that's fine: I won't push myself at all; I'll just stay in bed or take a very easy workout so as to avoid any remote possibility of injury". This doesn't work either, so strive to achieve a healthy balance for your body and soul.

QUESTIONS FOR MEDITATION

RELATIONSHIPS:

- Where am I not loving or giving, and how is it costing me? How am I not stepping into my true loving potential?
- How do I feel when I receive something from somebody who expects something in return?
- Can I give 'cleanly', from a place of 'no karma' that is, giving without wanting to receive anything in return?
- Can I give something to someone that they especially need today? Is there something that only I can give?

BUSINESS & CAREER:

- How can I give more to co-workers and/or clients?

SPIRITUAL GROWTH:

- Where can I experience Divine love? Where do I experience it in different areas of my life?

GYM SEQUENCE, DAY 1/BICEP CURL

3 x 8 repetitions of Bicep Curls, with a short rest between each one.

YOGA SEQUENCE, DAY 1/COW POSE (GOMUKHASANA)

Note: All yoga poses are to be performed with equal amounts of breath on both sides of the body. *e.g.* if you are raising your left leg for 5 breaths, then switch sides and raise your right leg and breathe for the same amount of time.

If you need to, modify the pose by wrapping a strap around your upper wrist and hold it with your lower hand. Keep your torso straight and draw your shoulder blade downwards.

חסד
Chesed-Love

חסד
Chesed-Love

DAY 2 / DISCIPLINE IN LOVINGKINDNESS - THE ART OF A HEALTHY "NO" - גבורה שבחסד

KABBALAH SUTRA: *Gevurah She b'Chesed* – Discipline in Lovingkindness

INTENTION: To draw endless love and positive energy into your life through boundless giving.

"How obvious it is now--the gift you gave him. All those letters, they were you... All those beautiful powerful words, they were you!.. The voice from the shadows, that was you... You always loved me!"

Roxanne in *Cyrano de Bergerac*

Gevurah-discipline in *Chesed*-love can be simply illustrated as follows: A child picks up a knife and starts playing with it. The parent shouts to protect the child *"PUT DOWN THAT KNIFE!!"*. The child might cry and become upset or angry but love was expressed through the filter of discipline and the child was protected.

Too much love can suffocate a relationship, while too little can starve it. *Gevurah She b'Chesed* is getting that balance just right, knowing when to give and when to hold back. "Discipline in Love", it is the power of saying a healthy "no".

HOLDING BACK DESIRES

The patriarchs Abraham and Isaac represent *Chesed*-love and *Gevurah*-discipline. As we shall explore later, there were several ways that Isaac withheld his own independence and, to follow the path of his father Abraham, quite literally going into his father's business. *"And Isaac returned and he dug the wells of water which they had dug in the days of Abraham his father and which the Philistines had stopped up after Abraham's death; and he called them by the same names that his father had called them"[21].* There are many deeper meanings within this passage, with the "wells of water" representing the Divine flow of *Chesed*-love and the

---

[21]   Genesis 26:18.

35

"Philistines" representing the *kelipot* or negative energy shells that prevent that flow, but on a straightforward level we can consider the areas where we might benefit from holding back our own desires to serve someone else in a relationship. This might apply to a child holding back their desires to help a parent, or a husband foregoing watching a football match to help his wife.

TOO MUCH DISCIPLINE

Cyrano De Bergerac is a beautiful and tragic play about someone who holds back from truly expressing his love, and both potential lovers suffer as a result. Just as a relationship will suffer if it is exposed to too much discipline (*Gevurah*), there will also be problems with no boundaries at all. Every successful relationship must discover the balance between giving and receiving, and *Gevurah She b'Chesed* is the combination of disciplining the way that we love.

Our principle of Discipline in Love is key to having balanced relationships. "Healthy love must always include an element of discipline"[22] teaches Rabbi Simon Jacobson, and we might call this The Healthy 'No'.

We see this in relationships where one person smothers another with too much love, too many questions, and does not hold back or give them space. This might be seen as an over abundance of *Chesed*-kindness. Too much love can be suffocating. It is easy to create a bad feeling through our giving if it is out of balance - if you buy a friend dinner once or twice that is one thing, but if you always pay for them on every occasion then perhaps something is out of balance. You take them out for dinner 100 times and nothing is coming back - this is a problem.

IN YOUR BODY

In the relationship with ourselves, this might look like over-eating (too little *Gevurah*-discipline) or anorexia (too much *Gevurah*-discipline). A fitness fanatic who works out too much can cause themselves injury - this is certainly something I have experienced in the past with my yoga

---

[22]   *The Counting of the Omer: Forty-Nine Steps to Personal Refinement According to the Jewish Tradition*, by Rabbi Simon Jacobson. (Vaad Hanochos Hatmimim, 1996: Brooklyn, NY).

practice - while someone who has no discipline at all may spend their life sitting in front of the television eating junk food.

The same principle is true everywhere else: if you give too many gifts to your partner and lavish them with too much attention it could eventually destroy the relationship, while ignoring them would also create the same effect. A painter who indiscriminately throws paint at a canvas will eventually cover the canvas in a huge mess (too little discipline) while a painter who is pure-discipline might at best be able to create a straight line with no additional artistic 'love'[23].

THE KABBALAH OF YES & NO, or, HILLEL & SHAMMAI

A famous story is brought by the Talmud about the great sages Hillel and Shammai (also referred to as "Beit" Hillel and "Beit" Shammai, referring to the House of Hillel and the House of Shammai):

> *"It happened that a certain gentile came before Shammai and said to him: "Make me a convert, on the condition that you teach me the whole Torah while I stand on one foot."Thereupon Shammai pushed him away with the builder's cubit that was in his hand. When he went before Hillel, Hillel said to him, "What is hateful to you, do not to your neighbour. That is the whole Torah, while the rest is the commentary; go and learn it"[24].*

This passage is normally taught from the perspective of Hillel, in that we can all be more loving to ourselves and others as the basis of spiritual practice, although I would like to offer an alternative perspective. Beit Shammai's approach is equally valid. Sometimes trite questions demand sharp answers, to train people to ask better questions! Or maybe Beit Shammai's approach was to push him with a builder's measuring tool because it was teaching the potential convert that spiritual growth is about building foundations and building structures - a *bayit*/house (We might go into a Kabbalistic discourse about how the

---

23 My painter example is a development of an idea originally mentioned by Rabbi David Aaron in *Endless Light: The Ancient Path of Kabbalah*.
24 Babylonian Talmud, Shabbat 31a.

first letter of bayit - Bet - is the first letter of the Torah (*Bereishit*/In the Beginning)...but we are getting off-point.

In short, maybe Beit Shammai was offering a healthy "no" or maybe he was disciplining the convert. King Solomon spoke of the importance of discipline as part of love - *"He that spares the rod hates his son, but he that loves his son is careful to discipline him"*[25]. We often require teachers to be tough with us.

The Tanya explains how our souls must incorporate both *Chesed* and *Gevurah*, and *"at times you must use one attribute and at times the other"*. It goes on to explain how Beit Shammai's soul *"was rooted in the supernal 'left' [Gevurah-discipline], which is why they decided stringently as regards all the prohibitions of the Torah, whereas Beit Hillel, who derived from the Supernal 'right' [Chesed-lovingkindness] would find arguments for leniency in order to render permissible the things prohibited by Beit Shammai"*[26].

There is no "getting there" in this lifetime. Part of the reason this 49 day practice is repeated on a yearly basis is because we continue to understand the nuances more deeply as we progress in life. Refining the way we love is a lifetime project.

TODAY'S PRACTICE

YOGA PRACTICE GUIDELINES:

Today we might practice The Yoga of Love and Discipline. A deep asana practice where we hold postures for a long period of time, can be remarkably challenging as the body sends messages saying "stop! Enough! I don't want to do any more". When we apply a principle of fiery discipline (*Gevurah*) to our practice, what the yogis called *tapas*, and 'burn through' a posture as we begin to sweat and perhaps the muscles give a little tremor, we suddenly realise that we are capable of much more than we previously thought possible. The next time we visit the posture, it is much easier to be at one with it and stay in the position for a longer period of time.

---

[25] Proverbs 13:24.
[26] Iggeret HaKodesh, Epistle 13.

The notion of asana as being *sthira sukham* – 'firm and pleasant'[27] – is a challenge for any novice. Everybody may find at least some of the postures uncomfortable at the beginning but by learning to sit still in an asana, we can begin to overcome our human limitations. A former gymnast who has physical flexibility may find the positions physically easy but mentally challenging when it comes to achieving meditative stillness, whilst an accomplished meditator may find challenges in certain physically demanding postures. Similarly, our comfort with certain asanas can change as our bodies get older.

Pain is the obstacle that stops us reaching our limits but this isn't always a good thing. The pain of minor discomfort is ego-driven and wants us to feel more comfortable. The inner voice might be counting down the minutes until a class is going to end, or thinking of what we are going to eat for dinner, convincing us that we are tired and shouldn't be exercising, or thinking of anything that allows us to mentally escape from being in the posture. The other type of pain is your knee screaming out because it has been forced into a position that is actually damaging the joint. These two types of pain might be seen as two types of love that we practice in our life. The first is the disciplined love that causes a parent to send their child to school, even though the child is nervous and possibly even crying, whilst the second is the type of love that encourages a parent to give their child as much chocolate as they desire, even though the child is becoming horribly overweight.

GYM PRACTICE GUIDELINES

Gevurah is also "strength", so consider where you can strengthen your good intentions today. If your intention is to improve your physical health, consider how you can lock down your discipline and be more focused on this path.

---

[27] Yoga Sutras 2:46.

RELATIONSHIP PRACTICE

Be disciplined in your love, and loving in your discipline.

QUESTIONS FOR MEDITATION

RELATIONSHIPS:

- Where am I not holding back in my giving and how is it generating a negative effect?
- Where do I love too much?
- Where am I holding back too much in my giving?
- Where do I need to be more disciplined in my giving?
- Where am I smothering the other person or making them feel guilty because I am always giving and they are not able to reciprocate? (*Gevurah*-discipline is the balance to this)

YOGA/BODY/GYM:

- How can I be stronger in the way that I give to my body (*i.e.* in my resolve to meditate, exercise more, or practice yoga?)

BUSINESS:

- Where can I be more disciplined in the way that I am giving to clients and colleagues?

SELF:

- How do I express kindness towards myself? Where do I give too much towards myself (*e.g.* a chocolate binge or watching too much television), and where do I give too little to myself?

GYM SEQUENCE, DAY 2/FRONT RAISE

3 x 8 repetitions. Raise the dumbbell to shoulder level and bring it all the way back down.

.01 חסד
Chesed-Love

.02 גבורה
Gevurah-Strength

YOGA SEQUENCE, DAY 2/WARRIOR ONE (VIRABHADRASANA)

Keep the front leg bent whilst maintaining a strong line of energy from your back foot.

גבורה
Gevurah-Strength

חסד
Chesed-Love

DAY 3 / BALANCE IN LOVINGKINDNESS: LOVE ME TENDER
תפארת שבחסד

KABBALAH SUTRA: *Tiferet She b'Chesed* – Balance in Lovingkindness.
INTENTION: To share your love with balance and harmony.

"The greatest thing you'll ever learn is just to love and be loved in return"
Eden Ahbez, Nature Boy

We have all experienced relationships that are out of balance. Maybe you feel that you are giving too much and feel slightly resentful of the other person. Or your partner or friend might suddenly explode with anger because they feel that they have been giving and things are out of balance. Today's principle is *Tiferet* (balance, beauty, harmony, compassion or justice)[28] in *Chesed* (giving, kindness, love or lovingkindness).

On one level, the focus for this entire week is how we give. Now we consider how we do it with balance. *"Tiferet is beauty, the golden mean"* explained Rabbi Aryeh Kaplan. "This is the concept of measured giving"[29].

CONNECT HAND & HEART

The Tikkunei Zohar teaches that the energy of *Tiferet*-beauty corresponds to the trunk of the body[30], while *Chesed*-love connects to the right arm. Perhaps it is a cliché to discuss "giving from the heart", but this is a helpful visualisation. Rather than just reaching out and giving to someone with our hand, an optimum level would be to give with intention from our entire being. This will certainly make an energetic imprint on the recipient even if they are not consciously aware of it.

---

[28] I make no apologies for the multiple translations of these sefirot. They may continue to change throughout the book. My recommendation is not to try and pin them down in a masculine manner. Rather, see each Sefirah as a beautiful woman: sometimes she will feel one way, at other times she will feel another emotion. Give her the space, respect and be prepared to receive her powerful feminine energy. If you approach it from a masculine perspective, *i.e.* "I just want one simple translation!", then you will limit the power and beauty that can flow through these teachings. This pedagogy demands a flexible and intuitive approach rather than a linear restrictive approach.

[29] Commentary to *Sefer Yetzirah*, p87.

[30] *Tikkunei Zohar*, Introduction II. For more explanation, see Rabbi Moshe Cordovero, *Pardes Rimonim, Shaar 4.* Chapter 5-6

SPIRITUAL ENERGY IMBALANCES & KARMIC DEBT

One of my teachers writes about how we can benefit from reviewing all of our relationship to see where there is any imbalance between giving and receiving. His essay is titled "Karma: A Fancy Word For Spiritual Energy Imbalances"[31]. What might be called "Karmic Debt" is really another term for the imbalance you feel when you have given so much to someone and they have not given you anything in return. This is not to say that we should give with the expectation of receiving - absolutely not - but we can at least be aware of trying to maintain balance[32].

THE BALANCE

The reason that *Tiferet*-balance will always come in third place after *Chesed*-love and *Gevurah*-discipline is because it is the centre point. First the giving (*Chesed*), then the receiving (*Gevurah*) and then the balancing (*Tiferet*). Certain relationships are impossible to truly balance out, for example that of a parent to a child when the parent has been giving for many years. In this case the "debt" can be settled in other ways, for example looking after a parent in their old age, or "paying it forward" to one's own children, or other people you are responsible for (employees, relative's children, neighbours etc).

DIS-EASE

Our bodies are continually aiming for homeostasis so that we can live in a healthy and harmonious balance. When we eat food, our liver and kidneys will extract waste material while the rest of our body assimilates the nutrients. When we get hot our sweat glands will release moisture to keep the temperature balanced. When cells divide (mitosis), old cells will naturally die off.

---

[31] "Karma: A Fancy Word For Spiritual Energy Imbalances", by Eric Sander Kingston. http://ericsanderkingston.com/w011_karma-a-fancy-word-for-spiritual-energy-balances/

[32] The discussion can quickly edge into complicated territory, for example - what about the Karmic debt accrued by someone who cannot pay back, such as a beggar who is always receiving money? There are various ways to answer it - most beyond the scope of this book - but 1) it can be paid forward to others when the time is right, 2) It can be paid back in other ways if agreeable to the recipient (even in prayers and blessings, if they agree), and 3) From a truly esoteric standpoint, it can be paid back in another lifetime. But for all practical wordily purposes, we are looking to ensure that we do not create an imbalance with others.

When the body's processes for harmonising (*Tiferet*) get out of balance, we fall into dis-ease. If cells do not die but keep on growing and multiplying, we see the disease known as cancer. From a Kabbalistic perspective, this is *Chesed*-love out of control, as too much giving will ultimately kill the person in question. We can emulate this in the way that we give to the world, using a rhythm that is measured, paced and regular and not giving too little or too much.

JACOB & THE AMAZING SPECKLED SHEEP

The forefather Jacob is associated with *Tiferet*-harmony because of the way that he walked the middle path of balance. Even whilst being ill-treated by his father-in-law Laban, Jacob was able to find balance in the situation. After Laban tricks Jacob into working for 14 years rather than 7 years, Jacob agrees that his payment will be that he can keep certain animals: "in the future [my wage will be]..speckled or dappled among the goats, or brownish among the sheep". Laban replies "Yes! If it is exactly what you say [by those precise criteria]!"[33].

Laban thinks that he will get the better of Jacob once again, but Jacob's middle-path produces a different and better result. Jacob performs alchemy which determines that the first new animals will be born speckled, ringed and spotted, thus becoming part of Jacob's flocks, while the later-born animals will be plain and go to Laban. Thus Jacob gets rich but Laban also gets a fair return.

We might object with "but I can't do alchemy on sheep!", but there is a core principle here that we can apply directly in business or relationships. When negotiating a situation, we must look for a way of giving to the other person that is balanced. One of my business mentors is a former pawnbroker and explained that he will often have debts repaid before anyone else because he always looks for a way of giving business to the recipient so that they are treated fairly[34]. This is *Tiferet* in *Chesed*.

---

33   Genesis 30:33-4
34   To learn more about his philosophies of Portable Wealth, visit http://www.
     stevelawrence8.com.

Shakespeare even summarised this by means of his favourite Jewish businessman[35] in *The Merchant of Venice*.

> *"SHYLOCK: No, not take interest—not as you would say*
> *Directly interest. Mark what Jacob did:*
> *When Laban and himself were compromised*
> *That all the eanlings which were streaked and pied*
> *Should fall as Jacob's hire, the ewes, being rank,*
> *In the end of autumn turnèd to the rams.*
> *And when the work of generation was*
> *Between these woolly breeders in the act,*
> *The skillful shepherd peeled me certain wands.*
> *And in the doing of the deed of kind*
> *He stuck them up before the fulsome ewes,*
> *Who then conceiving did in eaning time*
> *Fall parti-colored lambs—and those were Jacob's.*
> *This was a way to thrive, and he was blessed.*
> *And thrift is blessing, if men steal it not."* [36]

What are you able to give to the world on a regular basis? Whether it is teaching children, serving clients at a restaurant or preparing tax returns, we can always strive to improve the balance. Harmonious living is our intention and this is one path towards *Shalom*-peace and *Shalem*-wholeness.

---

35 I am using "favourite" somewhat ironically. Here is a modern translation of the speech. "No, he didn't charge interest—not in your sense of the word. But listen to what Jacob did. When he and Laban agreed that all the spotted lambs would be Jacob's pay, it was the end of autumn, when the sheep were starting to mate. Because newborns look like whatever their mother sees during mating, he stuck some spotted branches into the ground right in front of the sheep, who saw them while they mated. The mothers later gave birth to spotted lambs, all of which went to Jacob. That was his way of expanding his business, and it worked. My point is that profit is a blessing, as long as you don't steal to get it." Courtesy of http://nfs.sparknotes.com/merchant/page_32.html.

36 The Merchant of Venice, William Shakespeare, Act 1, Scene 3.

TODAY'S PRACTICE

YOGA PRACTICE GUIDELINES:

A flowing vinyasa is based around the rhythm of the breath and similar to the flow of a river. As we breathe using the *ujiya* 'ocean breath', inhaling and exhaling through our nostrils whilst making a gentle 'ssssh' sound, we emulate the smoothness of flowing water. The term vinyasa is usually applied to sun salutations which are obviously moving the entire time, but it is relevant throughout all supposedly still postures. Our continual aim in a yoga practice is to keep a smooth rhythm of the breath inwards and outwards, gentle deepening into a posture on every exhale and maintaining these small but regular movements. As we smooth our movements, we smooth our breath and smooth our thoughts. We move towards harmony and balance in the way that we give our body this gift of increased life, and prepare to share with others this gift of balance in lovingkindness with others.

GYM PRACTICE GUIDELINES:

Focus on keeping your body balanced and harmonious today. Notice where you might be out of balance, perhaps with too many weights or too much cardio.

RELATIONSHIP PRACTICE GUIDELINES:

Pay keen attention to where your relationships may be out of balance and see where you might give more (*Chesed*) or hold back (*Gevurah*) to get things back in harmony.

QUESTIONS FOR MEDITATION

RELATIONSHIPS:
-   Where am I being too loving (*e.g.* giving too many gifts?)?
-   Where am I being too stingy? (*e.g.* holding back too much)?

YOGA/BODY/GYM:
-   Where am I going too easy on my body (Not exercising enough)?

- Where am I over-exercising or driving myself into the ground?

BUSINESS:

- Where am I giving away too much to my clients and undercharging?
- Where am I overcharging and holding back too much?
- Where would my business benefit from giving more?

GYM SEQUENCE, DAY 3/SIDE LATERAL RAISE

3 x 8 repetitions with a short rest between sets. For a greater challenge, perform the lifts more slowly.

.01

.02

חסד
Chesed-Love

תפארת
Tiferet-Balance

YOGA SEQUENCE, DAY 3/TRIANGLE (TRIKONASANA)

3 x 8 repetitions with a short rest between sets. For a higher challenge, perform the lifts more slowly

DAY 4 / ENDURANCE IN LOVINGKINDNESS: WATER & ICE
נצח שבחסד

KABBALAH SUTRA: *Netzach She b'Chesed* – Endurance in Lovingkindness.

INTENTION: Sustaining Long-term relationships through constant and enduring love.

"The world is sustained through… acts of lovingkindness"
(Ethics of the Fathers 1:2)

One of my father's favourite jokes is one of my mother's least favourite jokes: *"What is the difference between a Jewish mother and a Rottweiler? The Rottweiler lets go, eventually"*. Is it better to be deprived with love or overwhelmed with love? *Netzach* is sustainability and endurance, an essential component of loving that needs to be kept in balance like everything else. Just as too little love can be harmful, too much giving can be suffocating. My mother is proof-reading this book so I will categorically state that she has perfectly refined this balance.

The question I have often meditated upon when finding myself in this position, is "what part of me is giving beyond the boundaries of what is healthy or harmful?". Sometimes we might want to give out of anxiety rather than what is needed, perhaps as seen with a parent who smothers their child's freedom out of the parental fear. This can limit the child's growth and often instills anxiety in the child which might not otherwise have been there.

There is an art to appropriate giving, and *Netzach* is the drive to endure, move forwards and keep moving forwards with our giving. Rabbi Aryeh Kaplan explains that *"The word Netzach comes from Menatzeach, meaning "to conquer" or "overcome". One can see this implication in a male-female relationship. Some men in a relationship feel that they must totally overwhelm the woman, who is not left with much personality of her own. Some women also have a Netzach relationship with their husbands, where they have to dominate them in every way*[37]. Rather, this is about finding the balance in the way that we relate: "If I am dealing with another person, it is not just a question of giving or holding back, because essentially, the more I give (*Chesed*), the more I am changing this person, the more I am overwhelming him (*Netzach*)"[38].

THE SORCERER'S APPRENTICE

The 1955 Disney movie *The Sorcerer's Apprentice* shows how the young apprentice, in this case played by Mickey Mouse, enchants his broom to sweep and fetch buckets of water. Because the spell is so successful, he cannot stop it and there are too many buckets which flood the room until the wizard returns to remove the spell. This is essentially a reworking of a story of Rabbi Judah Lowe's Golem of Prague[39], and demonstrates the problem with too much giving. (Ironically, this has a deeply kabbalistic root because the Sefer Yetzirah, a classic work of Kabbalah which we will often refer to here, is considered the handbook for how to create a Golem).

ICE & FIRE

As with each of these essays, we are trying to do *Tikkun*, to rectify one aspect of our soul and how it manifests in the world. There is the concept that *Chesed*-giving is connected with Water, while *Netzach*-endurance is represented by ice. Whereas water is flowing, and *"has the connotation of change and free will…Ice is frozen water and indicates the concept of water when it is transformed into a state of permanence. This is related to Netzach–victory, since the word Netzach also has the connotation of permanence and eternity"*[40]. We try to balance these elements within ourselves.

APPLYING THIS IN YOUR WORKPLACE & BUSINESS

Endurance in giving is a fine line. People can be overwhelmed with too many marketing emails, but if you do not send anything then

---

37 Innerspace, p65.
38 Ibid.
39 "The Golem - Jewish Origins and German Renditions", p23, in The Golem in German Social Theory By Gad Yaᵭir, Michaela Soyer.
40 Rabbi Aryeh Kaplan, commentary to The Bahir, p116.

there is no opportunity to grow your business. We have all experienced people and companies being persistent to the point of annoying[41]. Equally, some new entrepreneurs can be reticent about reaching out to potential customers and many people have a fear of cold-calling, yet by completely holding back it is impossible to build a relationship.

CAREGIVER BURNOUT

The phenomenon of burnout is known to affect people in the caring profession, whether it is nurses, therapists or family carers. One mental health professional I knew of would get angry after a day of seeing patients and would find it very hard to maintain a stable conversation with their loved ones until they had undergone a major decompression. Another person gave so much to their clients that their personal relationships suffered. These are classic imbalances of *Netzach*-endurance in *Chesed*-kindness which we all need to find and heal within ourselves.

NUTSHELL: KEEP IT REGULAR

The principle is about keeping it regular: regularly giving to partners, to colleagues and clients and even giving regularly to charity. Rabbi Shneur Zalman of Liadi describes this regulated giving as similar to creating a coat of chain mail: *"And He garbed himself with tzedakah as with a coat of mail, and a helmet of salvation upon his head"*[42]. From a spiritual perspective, he explains that each coin we give builds up a form of protection much like a coat of armour, and *"just as the mail is made of scales covering gaps, and these shield one against any arrow entering through the gaps, so it is with the act of charity"*[43].

ENDURING KINDNESS

This attitude of constant and enduring lovingkindness applies to the way we treat our bodies, the way we treat others. We can practice this principle at all times, whether it means being kind to friends and family

---

[41] "Being persistent to the point of annoying" - thank you to Marissa Leigh Salem for this phrasing of *Netzach She b'Chesed*.
[42] Joshua 59:17.
[43] Tanya, Iggeret HaKodesh, Epistle 3.

even when they don't seem to deserve it. Perhaps that is the time for us to remove judgement and show our love more than ever before.

TODAY'S PRACTICE

YOGA PRACTICE GUIDELINES

A regular practice is essential for anybody who is looking to get fit, lose weight, deepen their meditation practice or develop as a human being. Five short daily yoga sessions are always better than one long weekly practice because the body has more time to attune and develop. The same is true with the gym and other forms of exercise. Also if we miss our weekly session then we might not do anything for a fortnight, but if you have a daily practice then a lost day will be made up on the following day.

As *Netzach* is the quality of endurance, we can see how regular and enduring kindness can only be good to our bodies. The value of a regular yoga practice cannot be underestimated as it allows us to heal our body and soul in a way that would be impossible if we only did yoga when we felt good. This means stepping onto the mat even when you are feeling slightly ill, overtired, hung-over, jet-lagged and finding time when work seems busier than ever. It has been said that 'repetition is the mother of skill'[44] and the rabbis emphasised the notion of having a regular practice with regards to Torah learning (*makom kevuah*), which applies equally to our meditation and prayer. On some mornings I feel like I'm 15 years old and on others I'll feel like I'm 90, but my body appreciates the frequent activity as long as it is practiced with kindness (*Chesed*). The Yoga Sutras mentions how we are trying to achieve a 'secure steadiness' in our mind and body[45]. We see minute changes in our physicality, as we gradually become more flexible and expand our physical capabilities.

---

44 Said by Anthony Robbins in his talks on transforming behaviour and mindset.
45 Yoga Sutras 1:13.

GYM PRACTICE GUIDELINES

Play with the notion of endurance today and see where you would benefit from a more sustained workout practice. Cardio would be a good example of this, but continue to exercise kindness as you exercise your body.

RELATIONSHIP GUIDELINES

Go out of your way to perform random acts of lovingkindness, even though you may not be in the mood. See where you sustain your giving in one area of your life.

QUESTIONS FOR MEDITATION

RELATIONSHIPS:
- How have I given so much to another person that I have overwhelmed them?
- How has this damaged the relationship?
- What part of me is wanting to give beyond the bounds of what is needed am I trying to take through my giving?
- Where do I give up too easily in my loving and giving, and how am I selling myself short/not reaching my potential?
- Where do I need to give more to my partner?
- Where can I be more regular with the way I give to others, whether it is regularly buying flowers for my spouse or "showing up" more for my children, parents or friends?
- Who can I be kind to today, even though I might not be in the mood?

YOGA/BODY/GYM:
- Are you consistent in your physical exercise practice?
- Where can you be more giving to yourself without giving too much?

BUSINESS:
- Where can you be more regular in your client contact?
- Are you giving consistently to your co-workers?

COMMUNITY:

- Where can I be more sustained in my charitable giving? (*Netzach*)

PRACTICE FOR YOGA & THE GYM:

- Establish a regular practice with a sense of giving to yourself, and holding an enduring lovingkindness towards your body and soul.

GYM SEQUENCE, DAY 4/LUNGE

8 lunges with each leg. Continue performing until exhaustion.

.01

חסד
Chesed-Love

.02

נצח
Netzach-Endurance

YOGA SEQUENCE, DAY 4/EXTENDED SIDE-ANGLE (UTTHITA PARSVAKONASANA)

Stretch your fingertips and outside blade of your straight-leg foot in the opposite direction, lengthening your side.

DAY 5 / HUMILITY IN LOVINGKINDNESS: BEHAVE LIKE A GUEST/ HUMBLE LOVE הוד שבחסד

KABBALAH SUTRA: *Hod She b'Chesed* – Humility in Lovingkindness.

INTENTION: To increase and expand your love and remove your ego limitations.

"Why are spiritual teachings compared to water? Just as water comes from a high place to a low one, so too are the spiritual words of Torah received by the humble"

Babylonian Talmud[46].

The art of giving involves deep listening. Think of a time when somebody gave you a gift which they were excited about but it was not what you wanted, needed or even liked. This could be as simple as being given a cup of tea with honey in it when you find the concept an anathema (as an Englishman, this custom took some getting used to when first moving to Los Angeles), or it might be your birthday present of a gaudy and almost unwearable item of clothing bestowed upon you by a well-meaning relative.

Hod She b'Chesed is Humility in Giving. Considering how we are humble in the way that we give, giving with humility, loving other people whilst creating space for them. *Hod* may be understood as humility, gratitude, or the traditional 'splendour' (because when we have all of these elements in place, there is a sense of spiritual splendour). It is also associated with integrity and being reactive[47].

Lovingkindness works both ways and by receiving you can also be giving. When you *allow* somebody to give to you, such as when you receive a gift that you do not necessarily want, you can be giving respect, gratitude, space, honour and more to the well-meaning giver. This is non-linear thinking - again, because our *sefirot*/Divine Spheres are feminine and circular rather than masculine and linear - so the energetic circle of giving really does work in both directions.

---

46   Ta'anit p7a.
47   As discussed in Love like Fire & Water (Kuntres Avodah), p142.

GOOD GIVING

A lesson I have learned the hard way is to build *Hod*-humility in the way that I give (*Chesed*). When I rush to help somebody out of my own need to give or connect, it can be a form of dysfunctional giving and can even cause damage. Working quickly to complete a client project without fully understanding the brief can create more problems than solutions as I may have to re-do a lot of the work afterwards if it is not correct.

FUNCTION & DYSFUNCTION

With too little humility in my giving, we do not remember our place and step on people. We are always complaining because there is not enough gratitude. On the other hand, too much humility allows people to step on us, and we give away our personal power. This can be disastrous in relationships as we lose respect for ourselves, as does the other person.

BODY FEEDBACK

Havoc can ensue when we take our bodies for granted, whether it is through physical exercise or substance abuse. Our bodies are highly sophisticated organisms that provide multiple warning signals for both health and dis-ease, which may include: Skin feedback (*e.g.* rashes), muscle pain, joint ache, eye irregularities (iridology), breathing irregularities, pulse irregularities (Traditional Chinese Medicine has tools for interpreting health issues through your pulse), discharge differences (*i.e.* reading urine discolouring or stool samples according to the Bristol Stool Scale) and so much more. None of this is possible to interpret without close listening to the body.

HOD IS SPACE & LISTENING

The Zohar associates *Hod*-humility with the left leg and one way to understand this is that the left leg and hip create space for the right because most of us will start to walk with our right leg first[48]. In this sense *Hod* can be seen as humility and gratitude because the left leg is

---

[48] Obviously we then change polarity and the right leg and hip create room for the left leg but we are looking at the core energetic principle here.

taking second place to the right leg. A lack of humility in relationships shows up as excessive arrogance, haughtiness and a lack of space for the other person.

LESS EXPECTATION, MORE APPRECIATION

I was taught that we should have "less expectation, more appreciation" as a path to greater happiness[49]. This essential humility enables us to enter situations with an open mind and an open heart, being in a state of receptivity (which also relates to *Hod*/humility) rather than demanding the situation to meet our expectations. The Talmud compares spiritual teachings to water because it is impossible to truly receive them with an arrogant head or a closed heart. We lower ourselves as an act of love, creating room for the other person and for God. We do of course benefit as a result, but it is up to us to take the first step – backwards.

HOW TO IMPROVE THE RELATIONSHIP WITH YOUR PARENTS FOREVER

Many adult children have conflicts with their parents and these often continue for the rest of their lives. Both parties are wont to complain; the grownup children might say "my parents are difficult [and/or] still speak to me like a child" or similar words. Here is the principle I was taught: When Visiting Your Parents, Behave Like a Guest, Not Like You Own The Place[50].

This is both simple and revolutionary. Rather than mentally behaving like a teenager, full of expectations and demands, visit your parents' house with the intention that you are there as a guest, and respect their space as such. I began practicing this principle over a year ago, ensuring that I continually reminded myself of it until it was embedded as a new behaviour, and experienced a complete transformation in the relationship with my parents.

---

49 Taught to me by Eric Sander Kingston, quoting his late mother Arlene Gail Kingston z"l (1941-2013).
50 Thank you to my teacher Eric Sander Kingston for instilling this principle. More at www. ericsanderkingston.com

The alternative is to see your family through the eyes of your inner teenager, making demands, getting upset with them for old habits, and staying in cycles of verbal arguments or silent resentments. "Behave Like A Guest" is one path to peace, and invokes the principles of *Hod*-humility in *Chesed*-lovingkindness. There is a tremendous amount of peace and love you can give to your family through this simple shift. Transformations can be achieved through Acting Like A Guest in our relationships.

PHYSICAL PRACTICE

When I take my body for granted and lack humility in this internal relationship, there is a price to be paid. This can be in the foods we eat, the substances we might imbibe and the way we exercise. Years of fatty and sugary foods take their toll, and even years of medications will have their impact on the liver and kidneys. When I party too hard, there is a price to be paid, but I try to hold a continual awareness of having gratitude for my body and humility in the way I treat it. The principle of "Behave Like A Guest" is equally true of my relationship with my body, after all, my soul/*neshama* is just a temporary visitor in my physical body.

THE YOGA OF *HOD* IN *CHESED*

Humility is essential in our physical practice, but not to the extent that we are so humble we forget to be kind to ourselves. All yoga is a practice of love, and as we are kind to our body we need to show a degree of humility in the way that we move through postures and in the demands we make of ourselves. There is a continual negotiation between wanting to push ourselves further whilst respecting the current state of our joints and muscles. Without humility in the action, we can push our bodies further than they want to go, and this initially 'kind' approach causes injury and pain.

THE COST OF ARROGANCE

Life goes quickly and some people will turn 80 years old and realise that life has passed them by. We want to avoid reaching an elderly birthday and say "I had it all. Looks, possibility, resources, skills, talent and opportunity..I wasted it all and now it is too late". Continual gratitude (*Hod*) in the way we give to ourselves and create our life (*Chesed*) can be a remedy to this. By continually focusing on what we are creating (*Chesed*) and how we are giving to others, whilst doing this in a state of gratitude and humility, we can experience life far more moment-to-moment and make these brief years count.

TODAY'S PRACTICE

YOGA PRACTICE GUIDELINES:

Move into the posture without forcing yourself, but choose an attitude of humble love for yourself and your body. You may not achieve the full extension of the posture, but the important thing is to go as far as you can without any sense of arrogantly forcing it. Our entire yoga workout can be enhanced by showing a sense of humility towards God, and feeling this surrender (*Hod*) to the greater power as we breathe through the postures.

GYM PRACTICE GUIDELINES:

Maintain this attitude of humility and gratitude (*Hod*) for your body, whilst focusing on what you want to create (*Chesed*) with your exercise practice, *e.g.* Fitness goals, weight-loss or stress relief. Stay in a state of gratitude throughout your workout.

YOGA/BODY/GYM QUESTIONS FOR MEDITATION:
- Where do I inadequately give to my body, *i.e.* Where am I not listening to what my body needs?
- Where am I not being grateful for my relationship and/or taking things for granted with my body (*e.g.* overworking or underworking it)?

RELATIONSHIP PRACTICE:
- Where do I give too much or in a way that is not humble enough?
- Where do I lack humility in the way that I give?

- Where can my giving be more considerate and "listen" more to the recipient of my gifts?
- Where am I not being grateful for my relationship and/or taking things for granted in my relationship/marriage?
- Where are am I lacking humility in the way that I give?

BUSINESS & WORKPLACE PRACTICE:

- Where am I not being grateful for my relationship and/or taking things for granted?
- How can I be more humble (*Hod*) in the way that I give (*Chesed*) to colleagues and clients?
- What I am trying to create (*Chesed*)today?

SPIRITUAL GROWTH:

- Where am I not being grateful for my relationship and/or taking things for granted in my spiritual life am I taking things for granted with God?

GYM SEQUENCE, DAY 5/SQUAT

Lower yourself as far as possible before straightening your legs.

.01

חסד
Chesed-Love

הוד
Hod-Humility

.02

YOGA SEQUENCE, DAY 5/STANDING LEG RAISE (UTTHITA HASTA PADANGUSTASANA)

Maintain a steady balance in this posture.

חסד
Chesed-Love

הוד
Hod-Humility

DAY 6 / BONDING IN LOVINGKINDNESS: STRENGHTENING RELATIONSHIPS יסוד שבחסד

KABBALAH SUTRA: *Yesod She b'Chesed* – Bonding in Lovingkindness.

INTENTION: To deepen you loving connections through a firmly grounded love. The power to strengthen relationships through the bonds of love.

"Joseph's looks and handsome figure/ Had attracted her attention/ Every morning she would beckon "Come and lie with me, love"
Joseph & the Amazing Technicolour Dreamcoat

"Those who are together when they should be apart will be apart when they should be together".
Rabbi Menachem Mendel Schneerson

Yesod-bonding in *Chesed*-love can be a remedy for healing dysfunctional relationships. There are few things more exciting than the flurry of new love but fast connections can sometimes fizzle and burn despite the initial highs. A lasting relationship demands bonding so that, like a tree that has its roots burrowed deep into the ground, the relationship can weather the natural storms and gusts that life brings along. Only by being deeply connected and bonded towards another person can the relationship grow.

BIBLICAL BONDING

The Zohar connects *Yesod*-bonding to the reproductive organs[51] and to the *Brit Milah* (circumcision) in Jewish males, and we can understand *Yesod* as 'bonding', 'connecting' and 'grounding'. The Biblical figure of Joseph represents *Yesod*-bonding because he was seen to have mastered

---

[51] Although *The Zohar* connects this explicitly to the male reproductive organs, elsewhere there are teachings that women are considered 'already circumcised', hence not needing a physical circumcision. Other teachings suggest that the idea of circumcision is a principle as much as a practice as it talks about four types of circumcision: the foreskin, circumcising the heart (Deuteronomy 30:6 - "The LORD your God will circumcise your hearts and the hearts of your descendants"., the lips (Exodus 6:12 - "If the Israelites will not listen to me, why would Pharaoh listen to me, since I speak with faltering lips?) and even the ears").

his physicality when he resisted the attempted seduction by the wife of his employer:

> *"After a time, his master's wife cast her eyes upon Joseph and said, "Lie with me". He said to his master's wife, "Look, with me here, my master gives no thought to anything in this house, and all that he owns he has placed in my hands. He wields no more authority in this house than I, and he has withheld nothing from me except yourself, since you are his wife. How then could I do this most wicked thing, and sin before God?". And much as she coaxed Joseph day after day, he did not yield to her request to lie beside her, to be with her"*[52].

We see dysfunctional relationships everywhere. *Yesod*-bonding is the spiritual quality of bonding and connecting with another. When we rush to bond with someone in a romantic situation before fully knowing them, ties can be created which are then painful or complicated to break. The Lubavitcher Rebbe famously taught that *"those who are together when they should be apart will be apart when they should be together"*[53]. Rushing into physical intimacy is rarely the basis for lasting and knowing relationships.

BINDING PRINCIPLES/ BINDING FOREVER

Jewish men begin morning prayers with a romantic act with the Divine. It starts with practice of tying the leather *tefillin* straps onto the left hand, whilst saying Biblical verses that describe the eternal nature of the spiritual relationship: *"I will bind you to Me forever, I will bind you to me with righteousness, justice, lovingkindess, and mercy. I will bind you to me with fidelity, and you will know God"*[54]. There is a beauty in beginning the day by making such a bold statement to God.

---

52 Genesis, 39:7-10. JPS Translation. The commentators understand that on one level Potiphar's wife was acting on prophecy that Joseph's line would continue through her, although she misunderstood the intuitive messages she was receiving because in actuality Joseph was later to marry her daughter, who would give birth to Ephraim and Manasseh.
53 I could not find a source for this but have heard often it quoted in his name.
54 Hosea, 2:21-22.

THE BUSINESS OF HEALTHY CONNECTIONS

This principle applies directly to your business, in the way that you connect with other people. When a salesperson is clearly interested in only selling us a product rather than finding out what we really need, that is a form of dysfunctional *Yesod*-bonding in *Chesed*-lovingkindness – it is all about connecting and trying to give us something without really finding out who we are or what we want. If we apply this idea in all of our work relationships, whether it is with colleagues or clients, we firstly focus on genuinely connecting with the other person (*Yesod*) and then finding out what or how we can give to them (*Chesed*). It feels far nicer from the recipient's perspective as the energy is kinder and lacks neediness.

TODAY'S PRACTICE

YOGA PRACTICE GUIDELINES:

Stay grounded in your yoga practice today, rooting into your groin ("*Mulah bandha*" if you are familiar with it) and rooted to the floor. Use this grounding practice (*Yesod*) as a basis for the postures that you are creating (*Chesed*).

The yogic ideal is described as *"Sthira Sukham Asanam"*, or *"Yoga pose is a steady and comfortable position"*[55]. Another way to translate this would be "a yoga pose should be grounded and joyful"[56]. A purpose of yoga is to reach a state of oneness between our body, soul and creator, and as a result we embody a feeling of love. It is no coincidence that the way of creating a child is for a man and woman to join together in a state of physical oneness, and the Rabbis explain that this physical oneness is representative of the unity of God.

The same principle is at work within our bodies. It is all well and good to try different diets in a bid for weight loss, to flirt with different sports in a bid to find one that is exciting and engaging, or to occasionally meditate to reach a sense of internal balance. But any occasional activity

---

[55] Yoga Sutras 2:4, Mukunda Stiles translation.
[56] This is my translation, as the sanskrit "sukha" also means pleasant, easy or joyful.

will only yield occasional results. Regular practice, on the other hand, leads to regular results.

GYM PRACTICE GUIDELINES

Stay connected with your intention today. Remember what you are trying to create (*Chesed*) with your practice.

QUESTIONS FOR MEDITATION

RELATIONSHIPS:
- Is there a block in my relationship? Are we lacking emotional intimacy? What can I do to get closer?
- Are we being physically intimate (*e.g.* Giving to each other in this realm) but we are not bonding through this?
- If I am not connecting to my partner through my giving, where am I not connected in my relationship?
- How can I appreciate friends and family and build my personal relationships through building stronger connections?
- What is one thing I can do for someone else that will help strengthen our relationship?

YOGA/BODY/GYM:
- Am I giving to my body in a way that is grounded?
- Am I rushing through my practice or can I stay connected to my deeper intention?
- Are my thoughts rushing around in my head or can I feel my feet and feel connected to my whole body?

BUSINESS:
- Where am I giving to clients and not getting any business?
- Where is there a breakdown in communications? Where are we speaking but somehow it isn't "gelling"?

GYM SEQUENCE, DAY 6/SEATED OVERHEAD PRESS

Ensure you take your dumbells as low as possible before straightening
your arms to full extension: This will help you get the best results.

YOGA SEQUENCE, DAY 6/HEADSTAND (SALAMBA SIRSASANA)

Push your forearms into the ground, relax your neck and press through the balls of your feet.

.01

.02

יסוד
Yesod-Bonding

חסד
Chesed-Love

DAY 7 / **MASTERY IN LOVINGKINDNESS**: THE ROYAL PATH OF LOVE מלכות שבחסד

KABBALAH SUTRA: *Malchut She b'Chesed* – Mastery in Lovingkindness.

INTENTION: To love with dignity and elevate others through your lovingkindness.

"I had forgot myself; am I not king?
Awake, thou coward majesty! thou sleepest.
…Say, is my kingdom lost? why, 'twas my care
And what loss is it to be rid of care?
…For God's sake, let us sit upon the ground
And tell sad stories of the death of kings;"

Richard II, Act 3 Scene 2.

Our first week has taken us on a journey through various aspects of love: compassion, discipline, balance, endurance, humility and bonding. The seventh day brings together of all of these elements into the energy of *Malchut*, which might be understood as kingship, leadership, mastery, nobility and sovereignty. *Malchut* is a sense of wholeness and completeness and brings a final dimension to the way we love ourselves and others. There is the wisdom of all of the other six elements combined with a noble, complete approach.

Malchut-mastery is also an aspect of the Divine Feminine[57]. The Zohar associates *Malchut* with the hands, feet and mouth. This makes perfect sense on reflection, as these are the organs that we can use to master ourselves and to complete the relationship with others, depending on the words we speak and the way we interact (*e.g.* Who we are giving to or walking towards and away from). In this sense, *Malchut*-mastery also comprises communication. It asks us: how are you using communication as a tool for giving and creating? Are you using your

---

57   This is beyond the scope of this book, but the Divine Feminine is represented by *Malchut* for various reasons. The Kabbalists consider this entire world as a place of *Malchut*, or Feminine receptivity. it also relates to the final "heh" in the four-letter name of God. For more information on this, see Rabbi Aryeh Kaplan's writings in *The Bahir*.

feet to walk towards situations where you can be more loving, and are your hands creating a kinder world?

YOU ARE THE KING

Chassidic teachings explain that King David's *"sovereignty was based on the trait of kindness"*[58] and refers to *"David's faithful kindnesses"*[59]. This is the essence of *Malchut*-sovereignty in *Chesed*-kindness.

- Whilst we may not be King David, we do all have positions where we are the 'King' or 'Queen' in certain aspects of our lives. There will be positions where you are a leader, be it with children, students, employees or even friends. In these cases, are you leading (*Malchut*) with kindness (*Chesed*)? Are your leadership vessels your mouth, hands and feet being used for loving ends? Most of all, are you holding yourself with dignity? It isn't easy being king!

WEEK IN REVIEW

We can take this opportunity to review all seven aspects of *Chesed*-lovingkindness that we have learned during this last week. Am I continually calibrating all of the different facets and aspects of *Chesed*? Giving enough (*Chesed*-lovingkindness in *Chesed*-lovingkindness)

- Holding back when necessary (*Gevurah*-discipline in *Chesed*-lovingkindness)
- Giving compassionately (*Tiferet*-compassion in *Chesed*-lovingkindness) Sustaining my lovingkindness (*Netzach*-endurance in *Chesed*-lovingkindness)
- Giving with gratitude and humility (*Hod*-humility in *Chesed*-lovingkindness)
- Bonding and connecting through my acts of giving (*Yesod*-bonding in *Chesed*-lovingkindness)
- And have I mastered my giving? (*Malchut*-mastery in *Chesed*-lovingkindness)

---

[58] Derech Mitzvotecha, p246.
[59] Isaiah 55:3.

CALIBRATE YOUR GIVING

All of these Kabbalistic concepts need to have a practical aspect to them lest they remain in the realm of pure theory. *Malchut*-mastery in *Chesed*-Lovingkindness asks: how can you master your giving? This question makes me consider all the aspects of how I am giving to others, whether it is through my charitable (*tzedakah*) donations, how I am giving my time and energy in relationships? How I am giving to my clients and students, and where I might be holding back from giving or reinvesting in my business and personal development?

MASTERY IN RELATIONSHIPS

Malchut is also a kind of nobility, or mastery, that can only exist in relation to other people and the Kabbalah refers to the way that a king can only be effective if there is someone to rule over. During the celebrations of the Jewish New Year there are various prayers that proclaim God as King, and these remind us of the spiritual relationship that is going on the whole time. Our time on earth is limited, we can elevate our lives by being thankful for what we have, and we are aware that our life can be taken away at any moment, however indestructible we feel. Just as the Creator has been kind to us by giving us life, so too can we be kind to others. In maintaining our nobility and kindness we strive towards *imitatio dei*, to act and behave in the image of God.

TODAY'S PRACTICE

YOGA PRACTICE GUIDELINES:

Yoga is a form mastery of ourselves, in that we are applying this principle of *Malchut*-mastery to our own bodies as we overcome our desires to sit back and relax and take ourselves through the discipline of asana and vinyasa. Be aware of how you express this lovingkindness towards yourself, and whether you need more or less physical movement today.

Most of the book's *Malchut*-mastery postures are going to be seated postures, for two initial reasons. Firstly, there is a value to taking one day off per week and either doing a lighter yoga sequence or just a simple meditation, in order to allow the body some rest and recovery time. Secondly, God is often referred to as sitting on a metaphorical 'throne of glory'[60] and in the seated posture we can meditate on this aspect of nobility whilst embodying all of the elements we have looked at this week.

GYM PRACTICE GUIDELINES

Stay focused on the intention of your exercise. Remember what you are trying to create (*Chesed*) with your practice. *Malchut*-mastery in *Chesed*-Lovingkindness also implies a kind of responsible love. We have sovereignty over the way we are treating our body and can choose whether the lovingkindness we show to ourselves is appropriate, and whether we are being too strict or lenient with ourselves. The balance is not always going to be easy because different things are needed at different times, but part of the essence of a regular gym or yoga practice is to increase the sensitivity towards our own body and to keep the instrument finely tuned so that our soul can fulfil its potential.

QUESTIONS FOR MEDITATION

RELATIONSHIPS:

- Which of my current relationships would benefit from a more noble, responsible kind of love?
- Where can you give more to your partner? Or to your colleagues and clients?
- Where are you being stingy in relationships?
- Where are you out of balance with your giving?
- Where are you not giving enough to yourself?
- Where are you compromising your dignity in the way you give?
- When have you given to someone and left them feeling bad? Or when has somebody given to you and made you feel bad?
- Am I behaving with dignity towards my parents or partner?

---

[60] This appears in the prayer Nishmat Kol Chai, 'The Soul of All Living Things' or 'The Breath of All Life' .

YOGA/BODY/GYM:

- How can you give more to your body? What is your body asking for? (This could include giving it more rest!).
- Hands, Feet and Mouth are the organs of *Malchut*-mastery. How are you using them to be more loving?

BUSINESS:

- Where are you not giving enough to your clients and colleagues? Where are you giving too much?
- Where are you holding back from reinvesting with your business?
- Am I behaving with dignity towards my clients and colleagues?

BONUS JOURNALLING EXERCISE

- In my relationship, do I have too much love/boundary/ compassion/endurance/
- Humility/connection/nobility *i.e.* Am I out of balance? Where am I out of balance? Make a checklist of all of these things.

GYM SEQUENCE, DAY 7/KNEE PUSH-UP

Modified push-ups or full push-ups. Perform in sets of 8 with short breaks and keep going until you cannae do no more.

.01

חֶסֶד
Chesed-Love

מַלְכוּת
Malchut-Kingship

מַלְכוּת
Malchut-Kingship

.02

YOGA SEQUENCE, DAY 7/EASY (SUKHASANA)

Steady your mind, release tension from your forehead and jaw, and steady your breath.

מלכות
Malchut-Kingship

חסד
Chesed-Love

מלכות
Malchut-Kingship

מלכות
Malchut-Kingship

מלכות
Malchut-Kingship

GEVURAH גבורה

STRENGTH TRAINING

WEEK 2

GEVURAH INTRODUCTION: STRENGTH TRAINING גבורה

"Who is strong? One who overpowers his inclinations. As is stated [1]*,
'Better one who is slow to anger than one with might,
one who rules his spirit than the captor of a city'"* — Ethics of the Fathers [2]

*"You, me, or nobody is gonna hit as hard as life. But it ain't about how hard
you hit. It's about how hard you can get hit and keep moving forward; how
much you can take and keep moving forward. That's how winning is done!
Now, if you know what you're worth, then go out and get what you're worth.
But you gotta be willing to take the hits, and not pointing fingers saying you
ain't where you wanna be because of him, or her, or anybody. Cowards do
that and that ain't you. You're better than that!"* — Rocky Balboa

Gevurah-strength is the power that comes through conserving and
directing our energy. Just as we build muscle through lifting weights
that restrain us and weigh us down, *Gevurah* channels energy through
restriction and holding back.

Our intention with this work is achieving a healthy balance in our body,
mind and soul. Where *Chesed* is all about giving, loving and saying
"Yes!", *Gevurah* is the ability to say "No", or "Not right now". *Gevurah*
represents contraction, discipline, restraint and strength. It is essential
to any relationship and the part of us that holds back to strike a healthy
balance.

As children we begin life surrounded in a state of overflowing *Chesed*-
lovingkindness, able to express ourselves freely without the need for any
restrictions. The next stage of development is heralded by the quality
of *Gevurah*, of strength and restriction, which makes us more aware

---

[1] In Proverbs 16:32.
[2] *Ethics of the Fathers*/Pirkei Avot 4:1.

of others, enables us to have an impact on the world around us and to create sustaining healthy relationships.

EXPANSION & CONTRACTION

We see the expansion-contraction principle alive in nature and our bodies. The sun rises (*Chesed*) and then sets (*Gevurah*)[3]. Our lungs expand (*Chesed*) and then contract (*Gevurah*)[4]. Our bodies are continually aiming for homeostasis and a balanced pH level in the blood; if we eat acidic foods that are expansive (e.g. sugar, sweets, caffeine, salty processed foods), our body will aim to expel toxins through its proper channels. Too much of these expansive foods will literally cause the body to expand and grow fat. Alkalising foods bring a healthy balance through the process of contraction. Eating raw green vegetables and drinking green juices are an excellent way to alkalise your diet[5].

So I wonder if this principle is happening the entire time on an energetic or spiritual plane. For example, when you are giving to someone, you are taking from somewhere else. There are obvious exceptions to this rule, with Love and Light. If you give love to someone then it is quite possible to receive it at the same time, and this would make sense because Love is *Chesed* incarnate. The same with Light - when you take a match and light a candle, and that candle lights another candle, there is not 'less fire' or 'less light' on the first candle (although a counter-argument would be that as a candle gives off light (*Chesed*), there is less wick and diminishing fuel (*Gevurah*).

---

3   Although in reality there are interlocking/interweaving/multiple cycles going on simultaneously - eg Sun sets (*Gevurah*) as Moon rises (*Chesed*), Moon and stars disappear (*Gevura*h) as sun rises (*Chesed*).
4   Interestingly, our lungs contain both principles simultaneously depending upon your perspective. As you inhale it is *Gevurah* because your mouth is receiving air rather than expelling it, however you are also 'giving' to your lungs and performing an act of *Chesed* towards them. When you exhale you are 'giving' breath from your mouth which is an act of *Chesed*, but you are contracting your lungs, which is an act of *Gevurah*.
5   An excellent book on this is *Food is Your Best Medicine* by Dr Henry Bieler.

MENTAL & SPIRITUAL STRENGTH

Gevurah is often translated as 'strength' and it is[6] used to describe God in the *Amidah* prayer. Genesis teaches that we are all made in the image of God and as such, we all have power in different ways with varying degrees of application and influence. Physical strength allows us to lift heavy objects, defend ourselves against possible attack, gather food and even make love. Mental strength enables us with the ability to make new discoveries, organise our lives, and perform certain tasks. Emotional strength gives us the ability to withstand challenges, build families, grow companies and sustain communities. Spiritual strength is the force that has enabled many people to survive for a lot longer than they would have done otherwise, as the power of belief helps people through difficult situations. Nelson Mandela's long imprisonment on Robben Island, Victor Frankel's internment in Auschwitz and many recovering addicts on 12-step programmes have all been helped, motivated or even saved by the power of their beliefs.

TRUE STRENGTH

What then is *Gevurah,* true strength? Rabbinic masters asked this question and the answer was *"the person who restrains their true desires"*[7]. *Gevurah* is therefore much more than just strength, but rather the ability to restrain, to hold back, to apply self discipline. *Gevurah* is power with responsibility, having the ability to punish someone who has harmed or wronged us and choosing restraint when appropriate. *Gevurah* is having a plate of chocolate gateaux in front of us and holding back from eating it. When we have the opportunity to perform some sort of indiscretion, even though nobody will know and we will probably never be found out, *Gevurah* is what helps us decide not to go ahead. Rather than asking 'lead us not into temptation', *Gevurah* is the Divine energy that keeps us grounded and allows us to apply inner strength.

---

6 From the Hebrew words *Gever* and *Gibor.*
7 *Ethics of the Fathers/*Pirkei Avot 4:1.

OVERCOMING YOURSELF: THE POWER OF ISAAC

Gevurah is also the power to overcome yourself and take back personal power when you are lacking. This *middah* (personality trait) is connected with the forefather Isaac who was physically bound to an altar by his father Abraham. This act of holding back goes deeper than just the body, as it also relates to his inner essence: *"Gevurah-restraint ..relates to Isaac. The paradigmatic event in Isaac's life is where he totally nullifies his own will and allows himself to be bound to the altar. He is in complete control of himself. Not only is he physically bound but mentally bound as well. You see a person totally held back. Gevurah is thus the ability and the strength to overcome one's self"[8]*. Whilst restraint is not necessary in every situation, as with each of the *sefirot* it is a power that can be called upon when needed.

SPIRITUAL ECONOMICS

Rabbi Shneur Zalman of Liadi explained how each of our souls has a specific root, and that the great Rabbi Shammai was primarily connected to *Gevurah* because of the way that he tended to be more conservative and restricted in approach, while his colleague Rabbi Hillel was more connected to *Chesed*-lovingkindness.[9] He taught that each of our souls contain both elements within it:

> *"Now, every one of Israel needs to comprise both these traits, for "There is no thing that has not its place." Thus we find various matters that are of the leniencies of Bet Shammai and 'of the stringencies of Bet Hillel. This comes to teach us that Bet Shammai, the root of whose soul is of the category of the supernal left – [that is why they always decided stringently as regards all the prohibitions of the Torah; but Bet Hillel, who were of the supernal right, would find favourable arguments to be lenient and to permit the injunctions of Bet Shammai so that these should become muttarim from their issur , and able to ascend upwards. Nevertheless]– in several matters, even Bet Shammai are lenient. This is so because of the inclusiveness of their soul's root, which compounds the right as well. And, likewise, the root of Bet Hillel's soul compounds the left also".*

---

8   Rabbi Aryeh Kaplan in Innerspace, p.62.
9   From *Tanya*, Epistle 13.

Neither one of these qualities is better than the other, but by recognising which trait we are lacking, we can engage in *Tikkun*, which is the fixing and rectifying of our souls and personalities.

THE YOGA OF *GEVURAH*

The Yoga Sutras teach that "by frequent repetition of restraint, an undisturbed flow of tranquility results"[10]. The attitude of restriction is central to yoga as we apply internal strength, or *Gevurah*, to our mind and body. Pranayamic breathing is achieved restricting the flow of breath through our nostrils which consequentially restricts the direction of energy within our body. There is also a sense of moral restriction through the disciplines of the yamas and niyamas. The attributes of ahimsa (non-violence), asteya (non-stealing), aparigraha (non-jealousy) and brachmaharya (non-lusting/retention of vital fluids) are all about holding back our impulses and applying internal strength. When entering a posture we are aiming for economy of movement which focuses our energy, and this too is an application of the energy of *Gevurah*.

THE QUEST FOR EDWARD'S HANDSTAND

My yogic journey began in September 2002 when I saw a move that literally took my breath away. I was studying acting at the Webber Douglas Academy for Dramatic Art in London and one of our acting teachers would precede each class with a yoga session; little did I realise at the time that he was a world-class yogi. My teacher Edward Clark took a deep inhale, folded forwards and gracefully lifted his feet into the air on the exhale. He executed an Olympic-worthy perfectly-refined handstand. I was determined to learn this and tried copying by kicking my legs into the air, flailing up and using my strength to "get" the handstand.

"This is a breathing exercise", explained Edward. It was a long time before I could let go of my ideas and learn what he was teaching. By focusing the breath and only using the muscles that were needed, I eventually managed to find my own handstand. It took me many

---

10   Yoga Sutras, 3:10, Stiles translation.

months to reach that point, but when I did, it was a spectacular experience.

QUESTIONS TO HEAL DYSFUNCTIONAL DISCIPLINE (*GEVURAH*)

Where are all of the areas in my life where I have a deficiency of Gevurah/ strength?

1. Where do I lack discipline?
   - Have I promised myself to diet and broken my diet?
   - Have I promised myself that I will exercise more, but fallen short?
   - Have I promised myself to do creative or building projects and not followed through?
2. Where do I lack self-control?
3. Where have I not pursued the goals that are truly important to me?
4. What are the important things in my life to which I have not given time?
5. Where is my generosity restrained? Where did I plan to give more gifts? (i.e. To charity/*tzedakah*?)

Where are all of the areas in my life where I have an excess of Gevurah/ strength?

1. Am I too strong with my dieting or self-control? Does it cause me to miss out on certain aspects of life? (As it says in the Talmud, *"R. Chizkiyah said in the name of Rav: You will one day give reckoning for everything your eyes saw which, although permissible, you did not enjoy"*[11].

2. Where have I been too disciplined with other people, or over-used my power?

---

[11]   Jerusalem Talmud, Kiddushin 4:12.

GEVURAH/STRENGTH CHECKLIST

Gevurah is the way that I hold back and direct my energy, and an aspect of God, *or* channeling Divine Energy. It is *strength and and an aspect of God, or channeling Divine Energy. It is strength and discipline, but is it balanced?*

Am I loving in the way I hold back? Is my personal discipline coming from a place of lovingkindness? (***Chesed*-love** in ***Gevurah*-discipline**)

Am I able to be strong when I need it? Am in touch with my true self-discipline and strength? (***Gevurah*-discipline** in ***Gevurah*-discipline***)*

Am I balanced and just in my discipline and control? Do I know when to exert it and when to hold back? (***Tiferet*-compassion** in ***Gevurah*-discipline**)

Can I routinely exert my discipline and control (e.g. With regards to my diet, my relationships, the goals I am pursuing and the things I am trying to avoid)? Is my strength sustainable? (***Netzach*-endurance** in ***Gevurah*-discipline**)

Am I humble in my discipline? Can I apply it with a sense of gratitude and graciousness? (***Hod*-humility** in ***Gevurah*-discipline**)

Do I bond with myself and others through my strength? Is it deeply grounded and connected? (***Yesod*-bonding** in ***Gevurah*-discipline**)

Have I mastered my own strength? Do I wear it in a noble manner? (***Malchut*-mastery** in ***Gevurah*-discipline**)

DYSFUNCTIONAL GEVURAH

There is no love when I exert my strength. I am mean or hard-hearted (lacks ***Chesed*-love** in ***Gevurah*-discipline**)

I cannot be self-disciplined and controlled when I want to be (lacks ***Gevurah*-discipline** in ***Gevurah*-discipline**)

There is no balance when I exert discipline. I am unfair with myself and others (lacks ***Tiferet*-compassion** in ***Gevurah*-discipline**)

I cannot stick to my diet or exercise plan, and have trouble with long-term projects (lacks *Netzach*-**endurance** in *Gevurah*-**discipline**)

I get arrogant and irresponsible with my strength (lacks *Hod*-**humility** in *Gevurah*-**discipline**)

My strength pushes people away rather than draws them closer and bonds relationships (lacks *Yesod*-**bonding** in *Gevurah*-**discipline**)

I lack discipline, get weak when I should be strong, give when I should receive and do not have a handle on my inner strength (lacks *Malchut*-**mastery** in *Gevurah*-**discipline**)

ADVANCED ADDENDUM: A SPIRITUAL DEEPER-DIVE WITH *GEVURAH*

Here are some deeper thoughts about *Gevurah*-strength, based on Kabbalists' teachings.

SPIRITUAL RESISTANCE TRAINING: The Bahir teaches about the balance between giving (*Chesed*) and restraining (*Gevurah*): *"even though giving is higher than restraint, that which is withheld is always greater than that which is given"*[12]. We might apply this directly to the idea of resistance training, whether internal or external. Resistance training is the idea that we lift or push against a heavy weight which causes microscopic damage to muscles, stimulating them to grow back stronger than before. 'Catabolism' is the breakdown and 'Anabolism' is the repair (similar to the anabolic steroids used by weightlifters[13]. Consider that *Gevurah* allows us to get stronger by holding back.

JUST GIVING: The Zohar explains how *Gevurah*-strength comes after *Chesed*-lovingkindness because it is about balancing the experience of love. For example if a parent has two children but lavishes all of their attention on the younger child, then the older one may become neglected; *"Gevurah, the power of restraint, is often referred to as din, law and judgement, for it demands that Chesed be distributed justly, i.e. in*

---

[12] *The Bahir*, p123.
[13] Information courtesy Dr Richard Weil, MD., http://www.emedicinehealth.com/ strength_training/page2_em.htm#how_does_resistance_exercise_work.

proportion to the recipient's merit"[14]. This might prompt us to consider how we are distributing our affections.

EXPANSION IN OUR SOUL: The Tanya deeply explores how some people's 'soul-root' is based in *Chesed*-love while others lean towards *Gevurah*-discipline. Neither is intrinsically better as all are expressions of God, but by understanding our soul-root, we get a clearer picture of our mission in life and the particular soul-attributes we need to repair and correct[15]; *the soul's root in the Supernal "left", in the attribute of Gevurah, will lead one to act in a manner consistent with its character trait of limitation; so that he will only give as much tzedakah, study only as much Torah, and perform the mitzvoth only to the degree that he is obligated*"[16].

LIVING IN ABUNDANCE:

The counter to this is to live in abundance and expansion. In this area we can look at how our generosity has been restrained with ourselves and others. This may show up as neglecting to get a medical treatment we need, or repairing that item that would make a qualitative improvement in our life. On a spiritual level, it is looking at where we are spiritually holding back, to the detriment of all. The Tanya explains[17]; *"as it is written, "And I will walk about expansively"*[18] *and without any contraction or limitation whatever. There is no restraint to the spirit of his generosity, whether it be with respect to charity, the study of Torah or other commandments. He is not satisfied with merely discharging his obligation but [continues] "to the extent of never saying Enough!"*[19]".

LOVE & FEAR:

We have the option to live life out of love (*Ahavah*) or fear (*Yirah*). There are few other choices. The global battle for higher consciousness aims at a planet that is flowing with love, but the negative forces of media will fight this by continually trying to install fear (e.g. Through

---

14   *Zohar*, Vol. II, pp175b, 51b.
15   This is the idea of 'Tikkun', repairing, and understanding our soul-root is discussed in the early chapters of Tanya.
16   Epistle 13, Iggeret HaKodesh.
17   *Lessons in Tanya*, Epistle Thirteen, pp223-224.
18   Psalm 119:45.
19   Malachi 3:10.

daily reports of terrorism and pain). Fear is connected to *Gevurah*, as Rabbi Yitzhak Ginsburg explains: *"The spiritual state identified in Chassidut as corresponding to the sefirah* [Divine sphere] *of Gevurah is that of yirah (fear)"*[20].

Chassidic teachings often speaks of these as the two forces that motivate our actions, and we can choose which we will use as a motivating factor. E.g. Do I want to stop eating sugary foods because they will make me fat (Fear) or because I want to be healthy (Love)? In the language of NLP[21], this might be seen as motivating towards something (Love) or away from something (Fear).

Finally, *Yirah* (fear) is related to the word *Roeh* (seeing). *Yirah* can also be translated as awe, because it is the sense of awe we feel when we 'see' the supernal nature of God and the Universe. This is the 'Grand Canyon' feeling when we stand in front of a massive piece of nature or in the subtle murmur of a sleeping baby. Enlightenment is everywhere and available at all times; we just have to see it.

---

[20] http://www.inner.org/sefirot/sefgevur.htm
[21] Neuro-Linguistic Programming, discovered and developed by Richard Bandler and John Grinder. See their introductory book, *Frogs Into Princes: Neuro Linguistic Programming*.

DAY 8 / LOVINGKINDNESS IN DISCIPLINE/ WHEN LOVE MEANS SAYING "NO" / חסד שבגבורה

KABBALAH SUTRA: *Chesed She b'Gevurah* – Lovingkindness in Discipline.
INTENTION: To develop personal strength, inner power and ongoing discipline and to achieve all of this through lovingkindness Strengthen the way you love and make yourself a stronger lover.

"Being deeply loved by someone gives you strength, while loving someone deeply gives you courage." — Lao Tzu

"Chesed-Love and Gevurah-Restraint can thus also be seen as representing master and disciple. The master has to be the one who gives; the disciple is the one who totally annuls his ego to receive. Together they represent the perfect Chesed-Gevurah relationship" — Rabbi Aryeh Kaplan[22]

"Love means never having to say you're sorry" — Love Story

The tagline for the 1970's film *Love Story* was 'Love means never having to say you're sorry'. Tosh and balderdash! Love can often demand giving apologies when we overstep our boundaries. *Chesed* in *Gevurah* is the aspect of discipline (*Gevurah*) that is applied with love (*Chesed*). Healthy relationships need healthy boundaries. To understand this idea we will first look at the polar opposite: what happens when love knows no boundaries.

WHEN LOVE MEANS SAYING "NO"

Unrestricted giving might initially sound like a wonderful quality but would soon turn to disaster. If a homeless person asks you for money you would give them all of your funds, if your child asks to drive your car then you would immediately say yes, and if you desired someone other than your spouse then you would head to a nightclub and take your

---

[22] Innerspace, p163.

pick. Similarly, when my then-one-year-old nephew reached to pull a telephone off the wall, or grab the food from my plate, I had to gently move him away even though this sometimes resulted in tears. There was discipline underpinning this love even though he was upset that I stopped him sticking his fingers into an electrical socket.

There needs to be an element of *Gevurah* - restraint or discipline - in every healthy interaction we have. We may occasionally need to hold back information from people we love to avoid unnecessarily hurting them. When it is more helpful to remain silent about an issue for the sake of a friendship, both parties benefit from the *Gevurah* of not speaking.

HEALTHY GROWTH

There has to be a balance of expansion and boundaries for any organism to grow healthily: "*Plants were created on the third day. A plant grows, so that you have the element of Chesed. Yet, a plant is enclosed; it has a barrier between itself and the outer world, which is the element of Gevurah. A plant is like a controlled, aesthetic growth*"[23]. Human beings are frequently compared to trees[24] and the whole Tree of Life that we are studying - the structure of the *sefirot* (Divine spheres) in this book - is intrinsic to the human body[25]. These principles are directly relevant to the way that our relationships develop; you fall in love and your relationship grows (that element represents the *Chesed* phase) and then you place a boundary on the relationship by publicly pronouncing your exclusivity by getting married (that is the *Gevurah* phase)[26].

---

[23] Rabbi Aryeh Kaplan in Innerspace, p163.

[24] "Man is a tree of the field" (Deuteronomy 20:19).

[25] We have discussed this principle in the earlier chapters, where the Tikkunei Zohar connects each of the *Sefirot* to the body. This section's theme, *Gevurah*, is connected to the left arm.

[26] The other elements of the *Sefirot* will also apply to this model: *Tiferet* would represent the blending of the two people in the relationship as you go from individuals to a couple, *Netzach* would be the long-term energy needed to sustain the relationship, *Hod* would be the humility that is needed to make space for each other, *Yesod* is the deeper bonding with one another to create a child, *Malchut* is the full coalescence of the relationship as the child is born... and then the cycle begins again with a new relationship as you give *Chesed* (love) towards your child. The next stage is to teach your child boundaries (*Gevurah*) and help them understand justice and balance and compassion (*Tiferet*). And so this goes on ad infinitum! It is a perfect sphere so there is no beginning and no end to the cycle. As the Kabbalists teach "the end of the action is contained in the beginning thought" ("*Sof Ma'aseh B'Machshava Tehilah*" - from the song '*Lecha Dodi*').

TRANSFORM YOUR RELATIONSHIPS BY BIBLICAL PROPORTIONS

Abraham represents lovingkindness (*Chesed*) through the way that he continually reached out to people and welcomed in guests even when he had just been circumcised[27]. Isaac represents restriction (*Gevurah*) and boundaries for many reasons, as Rabbi Aryeh Kaplan explains:

> *"...Isaac's life becomes a perfect parallel of Abraham's life. He digs the same wells that Abraham dug[28]; he goes down to the Philistines and calls Rebecca his sister[29], just as Abraham had done with Sarah[30]. The reason for this is that Isaac is a person who totally gives up his ego. Abraham is the initiator; Chesed is essentially initiating a new idea. Whereas Abraham initiates the new movement, Isaac sees himself as a transmitter. He is a perfect disciple. Chesed-Love and Gevurah-Restraint can thus also be seen as representing master and disciple. The master has to be the one who gives; the disciple is the one who totally annuls his ego to receive. Together they represent the perfect Chesed-Gevurah relationship"[31].*

This principle is essential for helping us grow and transform our relationships as we consider how we can allow our love to grow through restricting our ego and will. The more we make our relationship about the other person, the more the bond can strengthen. When husband looks out for wife and vice versa, the relationship has a far greater chance of success and harmony.

IN YOUR BODY

My yoga teacher Edward used to say words to the effect of "the hardest part of yoga is putting on your shorts and getting to the front of the mat". There are days when we have no interest in doing our practice, be it meditation, yoga or gym. It could be too cold, too hot, too tiring,

---

[27] Genesis 18:1.
[28] Genesis 26:18.
[29] Genesis 26:7.
[30] Genesis 20:2.
[31] Innerspace, p.63.

too *anything*, but that is the time to apply discipline. *Chesed*-love in *Gevurah*-discipline is a loving discipline which asks "how can I do my practice with love, even though I might not be feeling it?". One remedy for this is to stay connected to your higher goal, e.g. To get into better shape and stay fit, and then get started with love as your fuel. This is different from "no pain, no gain", which is all discipline (*Gevurah* in *Gevurah*). More of that tomorrow.

TODAY'S PRACTICE

YOGA PRACTICE GUIDELINES:
Physical yoga - *asana* and *vinyasa* - is a practice of love and discipline, performing postures that will be heal our body whilst remaining within the boundaries of correct alignment and consciously-applied breath.

GYM PRACTICE GUIDELINES:
Can you stick to your disciplined practice today but do it with a sense of love and warmth?

QUESTIONS FOR MEDITATION

RELATIONSHIPS:
- Where do I experience challenges through not giving loving boundaries?
- Where am I not loving in the way that I set my boundaries? Where am I too rough?
- Today's meditation is to approach our friendships and relationships with a degree of healthy boundaries, and restraint. When can I remain silent rather than saying something that is going to be unhelpful?
- How can I strengthen a relationship through being more disciplined?
- Where can I hold back (*Gevurah*) and give more as a result (*Chesed*)?

- Where am I creating a Karmic Debt by taking (*Gevurah*) without giving (*Chesed*)?
- Where am I giving to someone without giving them the opportunity to give back to me?

YOGA/BODY/GYM:

- Where am I lacking discipline? Where can I apply more?

BUSINESS:

- Where do I need to be more boundaried with my clients and colleagues?
- Where do I need to be more disciplined in my work practice?
- Can I work harder but with a 'softer heart', e.g. to do the practice while connecting to a Higher Source?

ADVANCED PRACTICE: SPIRITUAL DEEPER DIVE

STAY CONNECTED TO GOD WITH ALL OF THIS...

When we are giving towards someone else, or trying to be kind within a relationship (*Chesed*), we might cultivate strength by restraining (*Gevurah*) our passions and bad attitudes by not answering back.

The Ramak taught that *"a virtuous man should emulate [is] tolerance. Even when he is insulted to the degree mentioned above he should not withdraw his benevolence from those upon whom he bestows it"*[32]. This is our challenge.

---

[32] Tomer Devorah, p6.

GYM SEQUENCE, DAY 8/PUSH UP

3 x 8 repetitions. If necessary, modify into the 'Knee Push up'. Other variations include doing your push-ups with your hands on the side of a sofa.

.01

גבורה
Gevurah-Strength

חסד
Chesed-Love

.02

YOGA SEQUENCE, DAY 8/CHAIR (UTKATASANA)

Keep your legs pushed together and lower your hips as far as possible. Release any unnecessary tension in your jaw and focus your eyes on your thumbs.

חסד
Chesed-Love *(Right arm)*

גבורה
Gevurah-Strength

DAY 9 / **DISCIPLINE IN DISCIPLINE** / GOAL SCORING / גבורה שבגבורה

KABBALAH SUTRA: *Gevurah She b'Gevurah* – Discipline in Discipline. INTENTION: To realise your potential and accomplish important goals through strong discipline. Achieve a strong body and strong mind.

"Better is one slow to anger than a strong man, and one who rules over his spirit than a conqueror of a city" — The Book of Proverbs[33]

"We are only as strong as we are united, as weak as we are divided."
Professor Dumbledore in
Harry Potter and the Goblet of Fire

"The weak can never forgive. Forgiveness is the attribute of the strong."
Mahatma Gandhi,
All Men are Brothers: Autobiographical Reflections

Gevurah-discipline in *Gevurah-discipline* is a power day of focusing on where we need more strength, discipline and boundaries in our lives. This can take some discernment as it is not always immediately apparent. The Kabbalah teaches of the "dark side" of *Chesed*-Lovingkindness[34], that is, there are occasions when it is not good to keep on giving. Although you may love your child, if you see that they are terrorising other children or writing graffiti on the walls, then it is senseless to continue giving them toy weapons and painting implements.

SELF-DISCIPLINE: STOP FEEDING ISHMAEL

There are character traits that we may be looking to kill off that may require exactly this sort of discipline. Just as an alcoholic may choose to stop drinking, we can look at the parts of ourselves that house their

33 Proverbs 16:32.
34 The *"kelipah"* (husk, shell or dark side) of *Chesed*. Iggeret HaKodesh, Epistle 2.

own addictions, especially when these addictions are taking energy away from our true goals. This might include harbouring negative thoughts, wasting time on the internet or eating fattening foods.

Rabbi Shneur Zalman of Liadi phrases this in more classical terms, speaking of the relationship between Abraham and his wayward son Ishmael, explaining that *"the more kindness"* shown to Ishmael, *"the more he grows in pride, arrogance and self-satisfaction"*[35]. On an internal level, we can consider our 'inner Ishmael' - the parts of us that are not in harmony with our highest goals, and on an external level this may include choosing to distance ourselves from certain people whose energy is detrimental to what we are trying to achieve.

DEEP INNER STRENGTH

Referring to more than just physical musculature, *Gevurah* is seen as deep inner strength, and specifically the power to restrain ourselves: *"Ben (the son of) Zoma said: Who is wise? He who learns from all people, as it is said: 'From all those who taught me I gained understanding'*[36]. *Who is strong? He who conquers his evil inclination, as it is said: 'Better is one slow to anger than a strong man, and one who rules over his spirit than a conqueror of a city'"*[37]. Conquering ourselves and really bringing our will under control leads us towards our highest potential, because gaining master of over our passions is often the hardest battle of all..

MISDIRECTED STRENGTH: YOGA WITH THE ANOREXICS

The Yoga Sutras hint towards what can be achieved through self-control, explaining that *"strength arises by performing self-control, such as the very strength of an elephant"*[38]. We have great potential within our bodies. It was whilst working in an Eating Disorders' Unit that I first saw the results of too much personal discipline. Teenagers who decided that they wanted to lose weight had implemented extreme

---

[35] He continues: A Jew must thus be on guard against the *"Chesed of kelipah,"* and ensure that G-d's acts of kindness will lead him to cultivate the traits of Abraham and Jacob, the *"Chesed* of holiness," so that his response will be humility rather than pride". Iggeret HaKodesh, Epistle 2, Lessons in Tanya.

[36] Psalms 119:99.

[37] Proverbs 16:32

[38] Yoga Sutras 3:25.

diets and kept to them with iron rigidity. These behaviours were usually accompanied by extreme exercise regimes, and before entering the clinic a typical day might have included an intake of 500 calories and a workout that burned many more calories each day.

My role was to teach English Literature and Drama to the patients so that they could continue their school studies whilst in residence at the clinic and undergoing treatment, and they also became my very first yoga students as I had just begun teaching at the time. They were generally very dedicated students, and because there was so much discipline in their lives, they tended to be highly academic super-achievers who would get through vast amounts of schoolwork in a short period of time. If they were getting more ill (which rarely happened under the close supervision of the unit's watchful staff) their discipline would eventually wane and because when they were severely underweight, there was such an insufficient flow of blood to their brain that they would find it hard to concentrate. Another aspect of discipline was displayed by several obese children who were also being treated in the same unit. They were grossly overweight as a result of having too little discipline (*Gevurah*), which created a different set of problems. Whilst self-control is a powerful quality, it is entirely a question of how we direct it.

SERVING WITH JOY

We see religious fanatics who are so excessively disciplined that their religion becomes a tool of oppression rather than liberation, and the yoga world is equally guilty of certain systems that are undisciplined in their application of discipline. King David's maxim of *"serving the Divine Spirit in joy"*[39] cannot apply when we are slavishly keeping to a system that is ultimately detrimental. The principle of *Gevurah*-discipline in *Gevurah*-discipline is about finding moderation and balance in the way that we restrain our desires and keep to a certain regime, with 'balance' being the operative word. Too little discipline and we become metaphorically (or even literally) obese, and with too much

---

39   Psalms 100:2.

discipline we can starve ourselves. We need to be disciplined in the way we dish out the discipline, and that will differ on a daily basis depending on where we are at. Although there are generally applicable principles, such as doing a physical exercise practice at least once a day, there is no system that is going to be right for everyone all of the time. A flexible approach is essential, no pun intended, if we are going to provide and nourish our physical, mental and spiritual health. As a growing organism, we have continually changing needs, but at the same time it is essential to have some form of regular discipline if we are to grow rather than atrophy.

MORE OR LESS DISCIPLINE?

Today's challenge is to become more aware of the areas in your life that could benefit from more or less discipline. Are you spending too long at work at the expense of your family? Do you spend too long on the internet or telephone at the expense of work and relationships? Would you like to improve your fitness regime and general wellbeing, but just can't get to the gym? What about finishing – or at least starting – that novel you have been planning to write for the last five years?

NOW DO SOMETHING

Gevurah-strength in *Gevurah*-strength is about taking action. If your yoga or gym practice is currently non-existent (beyond sitting and reading this book), then now is the time to go and do 10 minutes' movement. If on the other hand you have done three hours of extreme yoga and have damaged your hips and knees so badly that it hurts to walk or sit down, then take a long hot bath, a couple of days off and go back to yesterday's essay about compassionate discipline.

TODAY'S PRACTICE

YOGA PRACTICE GUIDELINES:

As you go through your series of sun salutes and today's posture, pay attention to the type of discipline you are applying and whether it is too much or too little. Really focus on channelling strength through your practice today, in your mental, emotional and physical strength.

GYM PRACTICE GUIDELINES:

Focus on a strength-building practice today, paying attention to the muscles that you do not usually work, and any areas of your body which seem weak or underdeveloped.

QUESTIONS FOR MEDITATION

MEDITATION:
- Where do I need to strengthen my mind?

RELATIONSHIPS:
- How is my lack of boundaries causing problems in relationships?
- Where do I need to develop more healthy boundaries?

YOGA/BODY/GYM:
- How frequent is your yoga practice? Are you doing it regularly enough, or is it even too much for your own good? This is not a call to guilt, but a call to Liberation!
- Where do you need to develop strength in your training?
- How is my lack of strength costing me?
- How different would my life be if I had more strength?

BUSINESS:
- Where would I benefit from applying more discipline in my work or career?
- Where can I hold back more in order to create space and help other people?
- Where do I need more boundaries or discipline with my clients and colleagues?

MONEY:

- Where can I watch my spending and hold back? Where is my money-relationship out of balance?
- Is there an area where I need strength to give more? Perhaps in my charitable giving?

GOALS & SELF-DEVELOPMENT:

- Is there a goal that is completely within my reach but hasn't yet happened because I haven't fully applied myself?

GYM SEQUENCE, DAY 9/ALTERNATE SHOULDER TAP

Maintain your balance as you tap alternate shoulders. Keep your breath going and your abs strong.

.01

גבורה
Gevurah-Strength

.02

YOGA SEQUENCE, DAY 9/WARRIOR 2 (VIRABHADRASANA II)

Bend your front leg until your thigh is parallel with the ground, straighten your back leg and keep the energy flowing through both arms.

גבורה
Gevurah-Strength

DAY 10 / COMPASSION IN DISCIPLINE / SOFT FOCUS
תפארת שבגבורה

KABBALAH SUTRA: *Tiferet She b'Gevurah* – Compassion in Discipline.
INTENTION: To bring healing for oneself and others through practicing
compassionate discipline.

For our relationships to be healthy and nurturing, sometimes we need
to exert discipline. Occasionally we need to even create distance with
people we love, such as with a highly dysfunctional friend or partner.
Creating healthy boundaries in a compassionate manner is one aspect of
Gevurah-discipline in *Tiferet*-compassion. Can we do it kindly, and can
we utilise our strength with mercy and compassion? This can include
reprimanding children, setting boundaries with our partners, or firing
an employee who you like but who just isn't suited to the job.

Tiferet in *Gevurah* can also be understood as Balance in Judgement,
as we make sure that our way of judging people and situations is
not weighted too much on the side of love (*Chesed*) or harshness
(*Gevurah*), but somewhere in between. "If you don't have balance in your
judgement, you can become Hitler" explained my martial arts teacher
Eric, stressing the importance of finding this *Tiferet*-Compassion/
Balance at all times.

Shakespeare presents a heart-wrenching moment in *Henry IV, Part
II* when Prince Harry gets crowned King Henry V and cuts off the
relationship with his old friend Jack Falstaff, despite the fact that
Falstaff had earlier pleaded[40] to be accepted as part of King Henry's
court;

---

[40] The pleading was done with subtle theatrical irony, as part of a play-acted conversation in
the Boar's Head pub when the then Prince Henry was pretending to banish Falstaff when
he became king. The reality played out when Prince Henry became king and banished
Falstaff. There are two exceptionally moving renditions of this I have seen on film where
Falstaff is played by Orson Welles and Simon Russell Beale.

"If sack and sugar be a fault, God help the wicked! If to be old and merry a Sin,
then many an old host I know is damned: ...But for sweet Jack Falstaff......old Jack Falstaff, banish not him
thy Harry's company, banish not him thy Harry's Company: banish plump Jack, and banish all the world". [41]

Falstaff's wayward antics - including drinking, thieving and wenching - are not conducive for a stately king and he imposes a permanent boundary with this speech.

THE SURGEON'S KNIFE

When a doctor makes an incision, one hopes it is the perfect balance of discipline and compassion. There is the harsh blade of steel that cuts into your flesh but it is done with a deep compassion and desire to restore the body to its natural state of harmony. Without the compassion, it is just a blade cutting into a skin. We can treat our words and thoughts in the same way, seeing them as knives which can cut or heal, and should be wielded with care. Indeed, the Kabbalists taught the danger of having negative thoughts and how our intentions can create angels of different degrees. Rabbi Chaim Vital explained that *"all angels are possessed of matter and form"* which is to say that on a spiritual plane, every thought is tangible. [42]

REBALANCING RELATIONSHIPS

Compassionate boundaries help our relationships stay healthy. When relationships are out of balance, they are a rollercoaster ride, and not the fun kind of rollercoaster. Either you are in love and things are fantastic, or you are arguing and it feels awful. *Tiferet*-Compassion in *Gevurah*-Discipline is a harmonious blending, finding the balance between expansive love and restrictive boundaries.

---

[41] Henry IV, Part i, Act 2, Scene 4.
[42] In Chapter 40 of Likutei Amarim, Sefer Tanya, the Alter Rebbe quotes Rabbi Chaim Vital and explains that spiritual study which is done for selfish reasons, "She'lo lishmah", "as, for example, for the purpose of becoming a scholar and the like, does not ascend on high at all, not even to the "chambers" or to the abode of the holy angels, but remains instead below, in this physical world, which is the abode of the *kelipot* (negative energy constructs). From Lessons in Tanya, Vol II, pp560-561.

The Alter Rebbe taught that the inner aspect of *Tiferet*-compassion is *Rachamim*-Mercy because it is the compassion that frees someone from a harsh judgement[43]. In this sense we are continually trying to be merciful towards ourselves and others.

BEAUTIFUL BLENDING

Tiferet is also called "beauty", compared to a "*beautiful garments which are dyed with many colours blended in a way that gives rise to beauty and decoration. To a garment dyed in one colour, however, one cannot apply the term Tiferet,* which implies the beauty of harmony"[44]. Here Rabbi Shneur Zalman of Liadi is teaching us that when two opposites come together, a third stronger force can result, as it says in Ecclesiastes, "*Two are better than one; because they have a good reward for their labour. For if they fall, the one will lift up his fellow; but woe to him that is alone when he falls, and hath not another to lift him up. Again, if two lie together, then they have warmth; but how can one be warm alone? And if a man prevail against him that is alone, two shall withstand him; and a threefold cord is not quickly broken*".[45] We are continually bringing together opposing forces and trying to find balance and harmony between them.

It is easy to fall into the trap of being too strict about something. Perhaps there was a work colleague who failed to meet a deadline and you reprimanded them. Maybe it was a friend who arrived late for a meeting and you then proceeded to remind them of their lousy timing and the fact that they kept you waiting. Or maybe it was your partner who was too lazy to do the dishes after you asked them for the hundredth time. Ultimately, the whole system of the *sefirah* energy is about love, liberation and connecting to God, and this week's theme of *Gevurah* is all about expressing love through restraint and discipline.

---

43 "Rachamim-Mercy is the mediating attribute between *Gevurah*-Discipline and *Chesed*-Love". From Lessons in Tanya, Iggeret HaKodesh #15.
44 Ibid.
45 Ecclesiastes 4:12.

YOGA OF BALANCED DISCIPLINE

The Yoga Sutras says that *"self-control on the heart brings knowledge of the mind"*[46]. A Kabbalistic reading of this could be 'self-control i.e *Gevurah*) on the heart (e.g. *Tiferet*)[47] brings knowledge of the mind'. Through the experience of exerting healthy boundaries on our desires, we can get to a deep knowledge of ourselves.

INTERNAL COMPASSION

One of the biggest challenges for combining compassion with discipline is for ambitious people who hold high expectations for their own level of achievement. We can reprimand ourselves when we do not keep up with our daily goals and disciplines, but this is the time to practice some compassion towards ourselves. Even the 'every-morning-without-fail-before-breakfast' yogi can find it hard to practice on those days following a late night and an early meeting when it is difficult to keep to their regular morning practice session.

Tiferet-compassion in *Gevurah*-discipline is the antidote to the "Jewish mother syndrome", as it is the freedom from guilt. Whilst it is important to recognise boundaries and to accept or communicate when boundaries have been crossed and discipline has been imposed, today's energy is a softening of the reprimand. But more than just being a passive freedom, it is continuing to impose restraint and discipline but doing it in a way that is balanced and sensitive.

KING HENRY'S CONCLUSION

My heart still aches at the site of the elderly Falstaff being banished by his former drinking buddy the new King Henry, but there is still *Tiferet*-compassion within King Henry V's *Gevurah*-discipline. He hints that if Falstaff changes his ways then there will be the possibility of re-establishing his place at the court: *"And, as we hear you do reform yourselves/ We will, according to your strengths and qualities/ Give you*

---

[46] Yoga Sutras 3:53, Swamij translation.
[47] Technically the heart is connected with the sefirah of Binah-understanding as in the Zohar's phrase "Binah liba" - "the heart is understanding" - but as *Tiferet* is connected with the torso, hence my explanation here.

advancement"[48]. Let us too be compassionate in all the areas where we exert our power and influence.

TODAY'S PRACTICE

YOGA PRACTICE GUIDELINES:

Begin by establishing the *Gevurah*-discipline in your yoga practice. Know the correct footing for your asana-postures and correct breathing where applicable. Strengthen your posture and then soften your heart. Apply compassion within the discipline of the pose. This is an especially important quality to develop for the longevity and good health of your practice.

Explore the edges of today's posture, ensuring that you are able to go to the limits with the correct discipline (i.e. foot alignment, spine alignment, directed breath and focus) and then soften away from the edge. Initially go to 90% of your capacity, back to 50% of what you are capable of, go to 100% and then settle around 75% of your potential with this posture.

In your yoga sequence, pay special attention to the demands of each posture and keep within these boundaries, for example, the vinyasa flow should be smooth and unstilted with the breath as regulated and even as possible. When entering standing positions such as warrior, keep the strictures of the posture – i.e. straight back leg, hands held high – whilst keeping your face soft and your gaze gentle. Maintain the posture and step slightly back from the edges whenever you feel hardness setting in. This hardness can often happen in the process of breathing, particularly with the exhale as the air hits the back of the throat. By being aware of the beginning of the exhalation and allowing the air to gently leave our body, we can avoid hardening of the breathing mechanism and even a sore throat.

---

[48] Henry IV, Part i, Act 2, Scene 4.

GYM PRACTICE GUIDELINES:

Practice *Tiferet*-compassion in your *Gevurah*-strength. Focus on building strength in your gym practice, but do it with a sense of harmony and balance. If you are going too strongly, ease off a little. If you are easing off too much (i.e. An excess of *Chesed*-lovingkindness) then go a little stronger. Play with the edge until you find your balance. This balance may change from day to day. Bring balance, harmony and softness to all of the boundaries within your relationships. There may be places where you have to say 'no' to your partner, but do this with a quality of softness.

THOUGHT PRACTICE GUIDELINES:

Can I stay compassionate and disciplined with the way I think, shunning the negative thoughts that do not serve me? When challenging thoughts arise that may throw me off-purpose, can I stay on track?

QUESTIONS FOR MEDITATION

RELATIONSHIPS:

- Where can I show more compassion for other people?
- Where have I been too disciplined in relationships, and at what cost?

YOGA/BODY/GYM:

- Where do I need to be more compassionate with my body where I was previously too disciplined?
- Where have I injured my body or mind by being too strong and rough with myself?

BUSINESS:

- Where can I be more balanced in the way I am approaching my work discipline? i.e. Am I too boundaried with clients and can I give them a little more?

- Am I being disciplined with my colleagues and lacking compassion?
- Am I being hard on myself and my behaviour without cutting myself some slack and self-compassion?

GYM SEQUENCE, DAY 10/SAXON SIDE BEND

Keep your arms in a fixed position whilst moving into the bend.

.01

.02

גבורה
Gevurah-Strength

תפארת
Tiferet-Balance

.03

YOGA SEQUENCE, DAY 10/PYRAMID (PARSVOTTANASANA)

Keep your hands pressed together, hold your elbows or a strap between your hands. Keep your legs straight and hips in alignment as you fold forwards. Stay connected to your breathing.

.01

תפארת
Tiferet-Balance

גבורה
Gevurah-Strength

.02

DAY 11 / ENDURANCE IN DISCIPLINE / MARATHON MAN
נצח שבגבורה

KABBALAH SUTRA: *Netzah She b'Gevurah* – Endurance in Discipline.
INTENTION: To transform limiting patterns and behaviours through
sustained discipline. Sustainable power and achieving long-term goals.

*"Courage isn't having the strength to go on – it is going on when you don't
have strength."* — Napoléon Bonaparte

*"Some people believe holding on and hanging in there are signs of great
strength. However, there are times when it takes much more strength to
know when to let go and then do it"* — Ann Landers

We begin with two simple questions: Where are you suffering through
giving up and becoming weak? If you could keep going with more
strength, how would it change your life?

The crescendo of Deuteronomy ends by telling us that *"Never again
has their arisen in Israel a prophet like Moses, who God had known face
to face"*[49]. These words are written at the tomb of The Rambam, Rabbi
Moses Maimonides at his resting place near the Sea of Galilee[50].
Moses represents the quality of *Netzach*-endurance in the way that he
fully embodied this quality through his lifelong mission that involved
beginning a slave revolution in Egypt, liberating the entire people,
communing with God on Mount Sinai and helping the Jews live
through 40 years of harsh desert conditions. *Netzach*-Endurance in
Gevurah-Discipline combines the long-term sustainability of Moses
with the restrictive ego-less nature of Isaac who represents *Gevurah*.
Isaac could harness his strength and put other people's desires before

---

[49] Deuteronomy 34:10.
[50] Maimonides, Rabbi Moses ben Maimon, is best known as the author of the Yad Hazaka,
     the 14-volume codification of Jewish law, and the Moreh Nevuchim, the Guide for the
     Perplexed. He also wrote a number of treatises on health, wisdom and wellbeing,
     including a guide to correct intimate conduct which have been translated as Sex Ethics in
     the Teachings of Moses Maimonides, translated by Fred Rosner.

his own; if we can sustain these qualities over the long term we can draw upon the power of *Netzach* in *Gevurah*.

In simple terms, we can meditate on where we can continue to draw strength, and continue to channel our passions without giving up. Persistence is essential when we feel ourselves weakening, as President Calvin Coolidge underscored when he said that *"nothing is more common than unsuccessful people with talent"*. Talented people do not have to undergo the sufferings of Mozart or Van Gogh, but they do need to do the work, and that is the combination of endurance and strength.

Shakespeare's comedy *Love's Labours Lost* begins with the King of Navarre and his three friends who set the intention to highly develop their mind and souls by spending three years in complete abstinence and restriction of physical pleasures, including intimate relationships. The King introduces the Jedi training:

> *"Therefore, brave conquerors,–for so you are,*
> *That war against your own affections*
> *And the huge army of the world's desires,*
> *Our late edit shall strongly stand in force"*[51].

One scene later, by pure coincidence, a French princess arrives at the estate with three beautiful handmaidens in tow. The shenanigans begin, the labours of love are lost and the plans go awry. But Shakespeare's would-be heroes are driven by *Netzach*-endurance in *Gevurah*-strength, trying to refine their souls through continued and sustained effort. In Kabbalistic metaphors this is sometimes described as how we try to refine our souls just like a jeweller might cut and polish a diamond to get it looking its finest: it takes much effort and can be painful if you are the diamond[52].

NAME YOUR MARATHON

Sustaining discipline is key to achieving any long-term goal. *Netzach*-Endurance in *Gevurah*-Discipline is the ability to succeed with a diet, running a marathon, finishing writing a book or completing any major

---

51   *Love Labour's Lost*, I:i. It is a gem. See it!
52   I have heard this example taught by various teachers.

115

project. When we lack it, we fall through. As Steven King allegedly said, "writing equals bum on seat"[53]. You have to sit down and do it. Not "I will end procrastination tomorrow".

REPETITION IS THE MOTHER OF SKILL

The energies of *Netzah* of *Gevurah*, or Endurance in Discipline, are the combination that lead to fulfilment. It is the girl who practices her musical scales every day and grows up to be a concert cellist, the boy who spends hours on the golf course and thrills his hometown by bringing back the PGA cup, or the scholar who completes five years and 100,000 words' worth of research material to attain the coveted PhD. It has been said that "repetition is the mother of skill"[54] and *Netzach*-endurance in *Gevurah*-discipline is the energy of pursuing success through enduring discipline.

FUTURE PACING

There is an NLP[55] technique called "future pacing" where you begin imagining yourself having achieved success in a particular goal you are working towards. For example, a writer may imagine their book being published, holding it in their hands, seeing it for sale, and really try to tap into the different modalities of this experience: how the book feels, what it looks like, what it sounds like when you turn the pages, what tastes are associated with the feeling, what it smells like. We can trick our brain into feeling the emotions as if it has already happened. Today step into your future self. Although we do not have to emulate the achievements of Moses, we can question why our soul is on earth and how we can step into our highest potential.

The legendary Reb Zushia of Hanipol[56], famously taught that at the end of our life we will be asked why we did not fulfil our personal potential. He explained that you will not be asked why you did not fulfil the destiny of Moses, but why you did not fulfil your own destiny. This

---

53 No source for this. In American it was probably 'butt'.
54 I heard this from Tony Robbins.
55 Neuro-Linguistic Programming.
56 1718–1800 brother of Rebbe Elimelech of Lizhensk and student of the Maggid of Mezeritch.

may a question that many spend a lifetime avoiding, but all may have to answer when the time comes.

TODAY'S PRACTICE

YOGA PRACTICE GUIDELINES:

Set up a strong practice today. Be firmly established in your groundwork, breathing, footwork.

Today's focus is having a strong practice and sustaining it. You might choose and internal strength, or an external strength, or both. Internal could focus on building your strength through breath and constantly energising your postures, even if you are just standing up straight - e.g. It is not about an external display of strength. This is also about the strength of your mental focus.

The external strength can focus on the way that you are executing your postures. Notice where your body is weak, and notice where you are lacking endurance (i.e. a deficiency in *Netzach*-endurance *in Gevurah*-discipline). Begin by establishing the *Gevurah*-discipline in your yoga practice. Know the correct footing for your asana-postures and correct breathing where applicable. Strengthen your posture and then soften your heart. Apply compassion within the discipline of the pose. This is an especially important quality to develop for the longevity and good health of your practice.

GYM PRACTICE GUIDELINES:

Today is a strength-based practice and we would benefit by focusing on both the inner and outer aspects. Inner strength is the ability to keep going despite psychological obstacles - "it's cold", "I am tired", "it is my birthday" [fill in your excuse here]. The external aspect of strength is really working on building your muscles, whether it is weight-based interval training or even reviewing your fitness goals and focusing on where you want to build strength…and taking action.

QUESTIONS FOR MEDITATION

RELATIONSHIPS:

- Where do I need to be more enduring in my discipline? Do I need to stay stronger for longer in certain aspects of my relationship?
- Where are you weak in your relationship and not able to keep to your new resolutions?

YOGA/BODY/GYM:

- How can I sustain a longer practice? Where can I endure more through practice?
- Where is there weakness in my mental, inner approach? How can I build this up to sustain it over time?

BUSINESS:

- Where do I require more endurance with my discipline in business? Is that summoning greater strength when picking up the phone to drum up business and cold-call new potential customers? Or to stay longer at the office or be more productive during the hours I am at my desk?
- Do I need to endure with my discipline to not check personal emails or social media during the working hours? What structures can I introduce to make this happen? (e.g. switching off my mobile phone, installing software that blocks social media during timed periods?).

PERSONAL DEVELOPMENT:

- Where are you not sustaining your goals? Where are you setting new boundaries and guidelines for yourself and then not keeping to them? (i.e. a deficiency of *Netzach*-endurance in *Gevurah*-discipline).
- What do you want to accomplish in life, and where are you paying the price for not enduring?

ADDITIONAL JOURNALING:

One way to improve any skill is to keep a journal of progress, and this can also apply to a yoga practice or gym workout. You might make a note of how often you practice and see where you can do a little more. Another approach is to explore some key postures, such as hip openers, headstand and triangle, and note how far you have progressed since you began doing yoga. For example, can you open your hips wider than before or touch your foot in Triangle pose where it was previously impossible?[57]

When we can note our genuine achievements whilst still being aware of our room-for-improvements, there is space to feel satisfaction, especially when you notice that your hands are closer to the ground in your forward bend, and that the old pain has completely disappeared from your right shoulder when you reach back to grab your left ankle.

---

[57] Mukunda Stiles' excellent book Structural Yoga Therapy has some superb examples, charts and ways of measuring physical progress through asana work.

GYM SEQUENCE, DAY 11/DUMBBELL LUNGE

Slowly lower yourself into the lunge. 3 x 8 repetitions on both sides.

.01

גבורה
Gevurah-Strength

נצח
Netzach-Endurance

.02

YOGA SEQUENCE, DAY 11/DOWNWARD DOG (ADHO MUKHA SVANASANA)

Experiment in this posture, bending one leg and then the other, before placing your feet in a still position. Play with bringing your chest closer to the ground and deepening the stretch in your back. Keep your neck relaxed.

נצח
Netzach-Endurance
(Right Leg)

גבורה
Gevurah-Strength

DAY 12 / HUMILITY IN DISCIPLINE / THE HUMBLE LEADER
הוד שבגבורה

KABBALAH SUTRA: *Hod She b'Gevurah* – Humility in Discipline.
INTENTION: To remove ego and improve self-esteem and relationships through disciplined humility. Develop subtle strength to face difficult situations.

I used to be a bad boy, and not in a good way. I didn't respect other people's rules. It seemed like a good idea at the time but was damaging to relationships and often required cleaning up messes. There are many facets to strength and discipline, to our inherent power that is the *sefirah* (Divine sphere) of *Gevurah*-strength, but we can cause damage when this gets out of control. If we are too strong in a relationship it can overpower the other person, and if we are too weak then we may get walked over.

Hod is the Divine quality that translates as humility, gratitude, surrender and even splendour in the sense that it provides room and sensitivity towards others. "*It is clearly recognising your qualities and strengths and acknowledging that they are not your own*"[58], explains Rabbi Simon Jacobson, and can be demonstrated by forming a healthy relationship to our own power that can help us keep a healthy balance.

VULNERABILITY & LEADERSHIP

Surrendering and staying vulnerable is difficult at the best of times, especially for men who are taught not to show weakness, and extra-especially for Englishmen who are trained from a young age to keep a 'stiff upper lip'. Yet without *Hod*-humility/surrender/vulnerability, our *Gevurah*-power cannot be complete. If you are in a leadership position and continue to believe exclusively in your own strength, it is inevitable that there will be some challenge which cannot be overcome without

---

[58] Rabbi Simon Jacobson in his introduction to Hod in *A Spiritual Guide to The Counting of the Omer: Forty-Nine Steps to Personal Refinement According to the Jewish Tradition.*

humility. Leaders who lack humility, for example Moses' cousin Korach who fell at the first hurdle due to his arrogance.

HUMILITY AS A PATH TO SELF-REALISATION

Although we can feign humility or let other people know how terrifically humble we are, it is hard to actually do it. *Hod*-humility in *Gevurah*-strength allows us to get to a more powerful place through harnessing the yin, or feminine energy that is required to be vulnerable[59]. As the Yoga Sutras explains that *"the state of yoga"*, which can be understood as oneness, unity with the Divine, or self-realisation *"is attained by complete, instant, dynamic, energetic and vigilant surrender of the ego-principle to God"*[60]. This surrender is, in theory, achieved by the regular practice of standing at the front of the yoga mat and recognising that we stand before a Higher Power.

GRATEFUL POWER & THE POWER OF GRATITUDE

Our strength is also compromised when we lack gratitude to the source of our power. In saying 'thank you' to the Universal One for all that I have been given, I humble myself in gratitude. Relationships are strengthened as we recognising and respect their boundaries.

The Hebrew word *hodaya* means thanks, and *Hod*-energy is the power to express thanks, and be humble before the gifts of others, and express humility towards God. Everyone has their own boundaries in life that they do not want other people to transgress. Whether these are physical boundaries such as refusing to touch, kiss or shake hands with a member of the opposite gender, personal boundaries such as avoiding lending money or books to friends, emotional boundaries within relationships, or spiritual boundaries such as telling people what you really believe in. There is a beauty in all of these boundaries, and it by

---

[59] The structure of *sefirot* places *Hod* on the left side of the body which is the 'feminine' side in the sense that it is holding back rather than driving forwards into the world. The right-side qualities include *Chesed*-Lovingkindness and *Netzach*-Endurance which are considered masculine qualities in the way that they push forwards. On a basic biological level, these are represented in the reproductive organs; the male pushes forwards whilst the feminine receives. Nonetheless, we are told "Male and female he created" the primordial human (Genesis 1:27). We have all of these qualities within us regardless of our gender.

[60] Yoga Sutras, 1:23, Venkatesananda's commentary.

having laws and regulations that we are able to keep society functioning. The energy of *Hod*-Humility in *Gevurah*-Discipline - is that which allows us to recognise, appreciate and grow through the beauty of these boundaries. Human beings have always found it difficult not to test boundaries, i.e. "You can eat the fruit of any tree in the garden except for THAT ONE!"[61], but we still strive to keep to them. The ultimate human boundary we can create is a marriage, marking the two people romantically off-limits for the rest of the world.

TRUE HUMILITY

True humility strives for a balance and the ability to live with the paradox. You are created in the image of God but you are not God. You have the power to create things but you are not The Creator. The Kabbalah differentiates two kinds of creating; making something from nothing - "*Yesh M'Ayin*" and making something from existing material "*Yesh M'Yesh*"[62]. There is a Hasidic story about the man who had a piece of paper in either pocket, one saying "you are nothing" and the other reading "the world was created for your sake alone"[63]. In finding this balance, we tap into the power of being a human who is made in the Divine image and learn how to wield our strength.

TODAY'S PRACTICE

YOGA PRACTICE GUIDELINES:

Today's practice should be governed by a form of humble strength. When I get arrogant with my ability, injury sets in. An easy form of reacting to injury is to sit back and recuperate and to completely abandon our practice. Instead, today is about working with limitations.

Keep focusing on the strength aspect of your postures and keeping your muscles firmly engaged, but do this with a sense of humility. Be aware

---

61 "Of every tree of the garden you may freely eat, but of the Tree of Knowledge of Good and Bad, you must not eat thereof; for on the day you eat of it, you shall surely die" (Genesis 2:16).
62 *Yesh M'Yesh* literally means creating "something from something", i.e. a pre-existing material.
63 Mishna Sandhedrin 4:5 states that "the world was created for my sake".

that your soul is a guest in your body. Stay within the boundaries of the posture and become aware of the space around your yoga mat. When you find ego arising within you, breath more deeply and turn your attention to God, who is far greater than you or I.

GYM PRACTICE GUIDELINES:

Continue with your strength-building practice but do it with a sense of gratitude and humility. Be careful with your muscles rather than forcing or harming your body; the complete opposite to a 'no pain, no gain' mentality. Experience your body with a sense of humility towards it.

Also bring this attitude towards other people you may meet at the gym. Still stay strong but be gracious, non-judgemental and forgiving towards others.

QUESTIONS FOR MEDITATION

RELATIONSHIPS:
- Where have I strong-armed people in relationships? Where have I exerted my discipline and strength and done it without a sense of humility, and what was the price I paid?
- Do I sometimes lack discipline and become arrogant as result?
- Have I become complacent with my relationship? Am I taking the other person for granted, rather than being immensely grateful to be in a relationship with them?
- Where do I need to be stronger for the other person? If I stay focused on being grateful for this relationship, can I use that as a source of deeper strength?
- Where do I need to be stronger for myself in this relationship?
- Where am I arrogant with my strength and what is the damage it causes?
- Where do I disregard other people's requests and boundaries? Where do I overstep their limits?

YOGA/BODY/GYM:

- Where have I injured my body through too much discipline?
- Where am I suffering in my body as a result of too little discipline?
- What are the boundaries of my body today?
- Where do I need to be a little more humble?

BUSINESS:

- Where have I lacked humility in the way that I use my power?
- How can I be more grateful and gracious with my power? (e.g. the way that I manage other workers, or behave towards clients and colleagues who rely on me?)
- Where am I too pushy (*Gevurah*) and not allowing things to happen organically (Hod)? , i.e. am I too pushy with sales?
- Where am I going in too strong?
- Where could I make some space for clients and co-workers? Do I need to step back and make more room for other people's ideas and requests?

PERSONAL DEVELOPMENT & GOALS

- Where do I lack strength and discipline? (e.g. this might be in the realm of pursuing goals and completing projects). Can I apply more discipline but do it with a sense of gratitude and humility?
- Where does my arrogant strength cause me to step on others and cause self-injury?

A BONUS LESSON FROM YOUR ACTUAL YOGA MAT

Although most people tend to use a yoga mat for the grip and comfortable surface, the shape of the mat is often overlooked. The four edges of a standard mat represent boundaries that we keep within whilst doing our practice. These are valuable tools as they allow lots of people to practice in the same studio without crowding one another, even when pushed up close together. When walking across a yoga studio we take care not to step on or cross someone else's mat, and many studios insist that people bring their own mats, albeit for hygienic purposes. Although some of these boundaries can be annoying at times, they also provide us with the potential to practice comfortably with other people and these disciplines ensure that we maintain a degree of humility at all times. The world is here to share with other people and successful living comes through establishing effective boundaries, and maintaining our humility within them.

GYM SEQUENCE, DAY 12/DEAD LIFT

Keep your back straight as you do the Dead Lift.

.01

גבורה
Gevurah-Strength

הוד
Hod-Humility

.02

YOGA SEQUENCE, DAY 12/DANCER (NATARAJASANA)

Firmly root your standing leg into the ground and deepen your backbend in this posture, whether you are holding your ankle or a strap (in the modified version)

.01

גבורה
Gevurah-Strength

הוד
Hod-Humility

.02

DAY 13 / BONDING IN DISCIPLINE / STAY GROUNDED
יסוד שבגבורה

KABBALAH SUTRA: *Yesod She b'Gevurah* – Bonding in Discipline.
INTENTION: To develop personal strength, inner power and increase emotional fortitude through being firmly grounded. Become more disciplined and more grounded.

"It is easier to build strong children than to repair broken men".

Frederick Douglass

Strength can be a formidable force but it can quickly turn into a destructive energy when it is not grounded and being used to connect with others. The Zohar regularly uses sexual imagery when explaining our relationship with God and Rabbi Moshe Cordovero (1522–1570) wrote that sexual desire should be specifically directed towards one's spouse[64]. Similarly, *Yesod*-bonding in *Gevurah*-strength asks whether we are using our strength to improve physical and spiritual relationships at all times, rather than serving our own wants and desires.

Gevurah energy is a form of restraint and discipline with which we might connect to the Divine, and it is a channel for directing the flow of the Light during our interactions with others. We have begun to explore how in human terms the power of restraint and discipline enables our relationships to become safe and strong, and these boundaries give us both peace of mind and emotional wellbeing.

Yesod-energy is the essence of being both grounded and bonded to another, and of being centred and grounded in our foundation. It can be the laser-beam of focused sexual energy and the power of creative energy that is channelled in a healthy manner.

---

[64] "All types of desire deriving from the Yetzer Hara [the 'negative inclination') - they should be used mainly for the benefit of the wife God has chosen as his "compatible helper" (Genesis 2:18). Afterwards, he should redirect all of them to his service of God, binding them to the right". Tomer Devorah, p.106.

STRENGTH WITHOUT CONNECTION

We have all met people who are in love with rules for their own sake, like the vindictive school prefect who enjoyed enforcing regulations and publishing offenders at every possible opportunity. The megalomaniac disciplinarian may be acting this way for a number of reasons - low self-esteem, lack of purpose or just having a negative disposition - but we do not warm to them because of the way that they wield their power. If we find we are irritated by somebody who uses their discipline in a way that is unbalanced, we might ask how we are doing the same thing, even in some small way.

HEALING RELATIONSHIPS

As we discussed earlier, *Yesod*-Connection is the energy of Joseph the *Tzaddik* (Righteous One), and the Kabbalah connects this energy with the sexual organs[65]. If we take this as a metaphor for interpersonal relationships and how we can connect with others (*Yesod*) through respecting boundaries (*Gevurah*). *Yesod*-Connection is a blending of *Netzach*-endurance and *Hod*-humility; sometimes we exert our will in a relationship (that would be the equivalent to *Netzach*-endurance) and at other times we allow the other person to take the lead (*Hod-humility*). *Yesod* is a healthy connection, within the boundaries of the relationship.

On a deeper level this triad of Endurance->Humility->Bonding/ Connection is also represented in the motion of sexual intercourse itself; *"The motions of the sexual act represent the balancing back and forth between Netzach and Hod, while the final cessation of motion is Yesod"*[66]. The Kabbalistic tradition stresses the importance of being married and over the age of 40 in order study the teachings, partly so that one can fully understand the metaphors and analogies in the text.

When I found myself in a challenging relationship, a friend of mine said *"find your foundation. Go back to your centre. Acknowledge what it really is and what it really isn't"*. This process of re-centering or re-

---

[65] Tikkunei Zohar in Patach Eliyahu passage.
[66] Rabbi Aryeh Kaplan in Innerspace, p66., quoting Ben Porath Yosef, Noach 19d, quoted in Sefer Baal Shem Tov, Noach 2; Keter Shem Tov 16; Torath HaMagid, Hanhagoth (p.14).

grounding is the essence of *Yesod*-bonding that gets us connected to our foundation so we know where to place our energy.

This principle is evident on a yoga mat. We strengthen our stance and get connected to our foundation (*Yesod*) so that we stand strong (*Gevurah*). Far more than just a gymnastic pose, this is an attitude and an energetic principle that can inform our day. Get centred, get grounded, get connected and use that a source of your strength for the day.

TODAY'S PRACTICE

YOGA PRACTICE GUIDELINES:

Today's focus is finding a firmly rooted energy. Staying strong and disciplined but keeping grounded, rather than floating up and away with our ego. We are off track if we start revelling in our strength and our abilities. *Yesod*-foundation in *Gevurah*-strength is the ability to keep our strength directed so that we stay deeply connected to our own body, mind and soul and this enables us to connect with others. A misdirected example of this would be that are over-bearing with our strength and this breaks relationships with others rather than improving them.

GYM PRACTICE GUIDELINES:

Continue your strength-building practice whilst staying connected to your goals. We see people at the gym whose minds are completely disconnected from their bodies, as they sweatily run on the treadmills like hamsters on a wheel, their minds absorbed in the nearest television screen and their intentions disconnected from their bodies. Rather, stay grounded and rooted in your body by using your breathing throughout your practice, and keep your mind and heart focused on your overall goal.

QUESTIONS FOR MEDITATION

RELATIONSHIPS:

- Where do I want to strengthen a relationship in my personal life or business? What can I do to be more disciplined in this regard (e.g. writing to people more frequently, more client phone calls etc.)?
- Where do I misuse my strength so that it pushes away my partner rather than helps me bond with them?
- Where can I use more discipline to connect with my loved one(s)?
- Is my show of strength/discipline creating bonding with others?
- How can I improve the relationship with my partner/family through more grounding and deeper connections?

YOGA/BODY/GYM:

- Where can I use my strength and discipline to calm my mind?
- Where does my discipline disconnect me from my body? (i.e. perhaps I am so applied in the gym that it bloats my ego).
- How can I improve the relationship with my body through more grounding and deeper connections?

BUSINESS:

- Where do I need to connect with my customers (*Yesod-*connection) and how can I apply more discipline?
- How can I bond more with my immediate colleagues, and how can I achieve this through more discipline? (e.g. perhaps I need to spend more time to listening to them so that they feel more heard? Do I need to exert more discipline so that I speak less and listen more? How would this practice improve my client relationships?).
- Can I spend more time listening to what my clients want, and be of greater service? Do I need to improve my practical listening skills?

BONUS: ADVANCED KABBALISTIC YOGA PRACTICE

Yoga postures allow us to appreciate the ground even if we are subtly playing with the notion of gravity and lifting ourselves up into a balance. We still need to stay grounded in all postures, aware of our relation to the floor beneath us, and in moments of low energy we can often use it to reinvigorate ourselves. This can be as simple as knowing the correct placement of our feet in a posture such as Warrior I, pushing into our feet and lifting ourselves higher.

Why are there such clear disciplines and firm guidelines about foot placement, skeletal alignment and moderated breath when moving in and through yoga positions? Because by being grounded in this discipline we are able to move towards a path of physical and mental liberation. This is one aspect of *Yesod*-Connection in *Gevurah*-Discipline. Following on from this, a well-aligned posture allows us to open our breathing mechanism, achieve a grounded and controlled breath which in turn leads to stillness of mind, inner calm and a general sense of peace. By aligning the arms and upper chest we are able to deepen the breath and all of this will heighten the meditative experience. Most importantly perhaps, correct alignment helps the body heal from existing ailments and enhances our chances of preventing future injury, as well as increasing our physical vocabulary for self-diagnosis of problems.

Stay within the boundaries of the posture, bringing your awareness to your feet and rooting into the ground, whilst remaining connected to your breath and experiencing the full alignment of the posture.

GYM SEQUENCE, DAY 13/ONE ARM DUMBBELL EXTENSION

Maintain a steady stance as you alternate sides, fully extending your arms. 3 x 10 repetitions.

.01

גבורה
Gevurah-Strength

יסוד
Yesod-Bonding

.02

YOGA SEQUENCE, DAY 13/TREE (VRKSASANA)

Visualise rooting yourself into the ground and imagine your energy going in two opposite directions as the crown of your head reaches towards the sky.

.01   .02

גבורה
Gevurah-Strength

יסוד
Yesod-Bonding

DAY 14 / **NOBILITY IN DISCIPLINE** / MASTERING YOUR POWER מלכות שבגבורה

KABBALAH SUTRA: *Malhut She b'Gevurah* – Mastery in Discipline.

INTENTION: To become stronger and create healthy boundaries in all areas of your life, reaching your higher purpose and enabling others to do the same. Become stronger.

"You have power over your mind – not outside events. Realise this, and you will find strength". — Marcus Aurelius, Meditations

"You are focusing on the negative, Anakin. Be mindful of your thoughts"[67].
Obi-Wan Kenobi

What does it truly look like to master our power? To have the luxury to be able to use our strength when we need it and as we need it? We saw earlier how the Rabbinic view of *Gevurah*-strength is not an action hero who wields immense physical power and can destroy cities with a single blow, but rather, someone who can restrain their desires and control their passions[68]. Mastering your strength, *Malchut* in *Gevurah*, is a quality that allows you to reach maximum effectiveness, whether it is in your relationship with your body, your partner, your clients and colleagues, or with God.

A JEDI EMERGES: ELIJAH THE VISION-BRINGER

When Elijah the Vision-Bringer[69] meets God on Mount Carmel he does not see an overwhelming force but experiences God in the form

---

67 Star Wars Episode II: Attack of the Clones (2002).
68 We learn from Ethics of the Fathers/Pirkei Avot 4:1 - "Who is strong? One who overpowers his inclinations. As it is stated, "Better one who is slow to anger than one with might, one who rules his spirit than the captor of a city"(Proverbs 16:32)".
69 Usually translated as "Elijah the Prophet", here I am employing the term "Vision Bringer" as translated by Gershon Winkler in Magic of the Ordinary: Recovering the Shamanic in Judaism. He interprets Navi/Na-Vee as "Vision Bringer" which is more illustrative than the traditionally-used "Prophet".

of tremendous restraint. The Divine is not revealed in a firestorm, an earthquake or a raincloud, but in a voice of silence, the *Kol Demama Daka*[70].

> *"And, behold, the LORD passed by, and a great and strong wind rent the mountains, and broke in pieces the rocks before the LORD; but the LORD was not in the wind; and after the wind an earthquake; but the LORD was not in the earthquake; and after the earthquake a fire; but the LORD was not in the fire; and after the fire a still small voice. And it was so, when Elijah heard it, that he wrapped his face in his mantle, and went out, and stood in the entrance of the cave. And, behold, there came a voice unto him, and said: 'What doest thou here, Elijah?'[71]".*

At this point Elijah is effectively reborn, emerging from the cave with his cloak around his head like a Jedi, understanding that true power is in the subtleties. It is reminiscent of Obi-Wan Kenobi's warning to Anakin Skywalker when his passionate feelings start clouding his judgement; *"You are focusing on the negative, Anakin. Be mindful of your thoughts"[72]*.

INNER MASTERY

The yogis wrote that *"when inner discipline is mastered, wisdom arises"[73]*. This *Malchut*, mastery of self, combined with *Gevurah*-discipline, goes beyond the physicality of a yoga posture and results in a sense of deeper wisdom. According to most spiritual traditions, wisdom is more valuable than physical wealth

---

[70] Kings 1 19:12.
[71] Kings 1 19:11-13.
[72] Star Wars Episode II: Attack of the Clones (2002).
[73] Yoga Sutras 3:8.

MASTERING SILENCE: A RABBINIC ZEN MASTER

Pure *Gevurah* creates a space through restriction, and this is epitomised in silence, a space of no-speech. Elie Weisel tells of the Hasidic kingdom of Worke where their Rebbe held space of silence, akin to a Zen Master:

> *"It happened during a Shabbat meal. Our holy teacher, the Tzaddik of Worke, was presiding. Lost in thought, he looked at us and at the twilight looming behind us, and said nothing; and we, at his table, listened and said nothing. For a while we could hear only the buzzing flies on the walls; then we didn't even hear that. We heard the shadows as they invaded the House of Study and brushed the burning faces of the Hasidim; then we stopped hearing even them. Finally, we heard only the silence that emanated from the Rebbe united with our own; solemn and grave, but passionate and vibrant, it called for beauty and friendship. We had rarely experienced such communion. We lost all sense of time...*"[74]

In this silence we create a space for God, a space for others, a space for ourselves and a space for new possibility. We cannot hear God if we are filling the space the entire time, yet this is what we tend to do in our modern age of 24/7 news, social media updates and endless pings. Yet the *Kol demama daka*, the "still, silent voice" of the Divine, can only be heard when we make room for it.

GEVURAH REVIEW CHART

- Have I mastered all of the different aspects of *Gevurah*-strength?
- Do I know when to hold back (e.g. when to hold back from giving? (*Chesed*-Lovingkindness in *Gevurah*-Strength), or when to hold back from Taking/Receiving (*Gevurah*-Strength in *Gevurah*-Strength)?
- Do I know when to apply firm boundaries to my relationships, e.g. when to really get a client to step up and buy another product or service level because I genuinely & deeply believe it is better for them? (*Gevurah*-strength in *Gevurah*-Strength)

---

74 *Somewhere a Master: Hasidic Portraits and Legends* by Elie Wiesel, p175-176. Thanks to Matisyahu Miller for sharing this teaching with me.

- Do I know when to hold back my compassion, when it would damage someone (*Tiferet*-Compassion in *Gevurah*-Strength, being cruel or apparently distant to be kind, e.g. when breaking up a relationship and trying to sever an attachment)?
- Do I know when to really apply endurance with my boundaries, e.g. when to keep on saying "No" even though I might want to say yes (e.g. the child really, really, really wants more ice cream… or I really, really, really want to eat chocolate and watch TV even though I've got a weight-loss/fitness target and a book to write). (*Netzach*-Endurance in *Gevurah*-Strength)
- Do I know when to ease off with my discipline and strength training, and give back a little? (*Hod*-Gratitude in *Gevurah*-Strength)
- Do I continually remember to connect with people and stay grounded even when I am saying "No" (*Yesod*-Connection in *Gevurah*-Strength)? Can I give a connected but disciplined "No" to clients?
- Can I be strong and be a great communicator even though I am saying "No" or taking back some self respect?
- The *Malchut*-mastery question - DO I RETAIN NOBILITY WHILST IMPLEMENTING DISCIPLINE & BOUNDARIES?

TODAY'S PRACTICE

YOGA PRACTICE GUIDELINES:

Master your discipline. Notice where you are lacking or if your discipline is off-centre. Consider all of the elements of the week; do you need more love, strength, balance, endurance, humility or grounding to find the power in your postures?

Use your discipline for a higher purpose. The goal of your yoga is mental liberation and unity with the Fabric of the Universe with the Universal Energy. By using the techniques being offered by the postures we can find freedom within these boundaries, and begin to experience the nobility of God through our bodies which are strong, powerful and invigorated.

GYM PRACTICE GUIDELINES:

Develop your strength with *Malchut*-nobility. Be clear on why you are developing your strength, and embody this with every step you take and every action you do.

SPIRITUAL PRACTICE GUIDELINES:

The pursuit of a higher cause can be channelled through *Malchut*-Mastery in *Gevurah*-Discipline. Boundaries can be oppressive or they can form structures that provide the path to liberation. Some religious societies use laws to suppress peoples' will, but it is the successful ones that use laws – often the same ones – to help people reach deeper and higher points of connection. Today consider how you are using these qualities in your spiritual practice, to reach a higher end?

WORKPLACE PRACTICE GUIDELINES:

Look for opportunities to embody *Malchut*-mastery in your *Gevurah*-discipline, bringing that quality to all of your interactions during the day. How can you stay strong in your boundaries while staying balanced and aware?

QUESTIONS FOR MEDITATION

RELATIONSHIPS:
- Have you mastered healthy boundaries in your relationship? Where do you need to improve those boundaries?
- Where have you broken commitments you make to yourself (e.g. to lose weight, write a novel, fulfil a Bucket List goal), and how can you find the strength to master these?

YOGA/BODY/GYM:
- Our hands, feet and mouth are the organs of Malchut-Nobility. How are you using them to be more disciplined?
- How are you using communication, the direction you are "walking" in to become stronger?

BUSINESS:

- Where do you need more strength in your leadership capacity?
- Where can you benefit from more healthy boundaries with those who look up to you?
- How would my business benefit from more strength and boundaries? Can I do it in a way that is loving, disciplined, compassionate, enduring, humble and with the intention of bonding?

GYM SEQUENCE, DAY 14/40 PUNCHES

Put your weight into it as you do 40 punches, alternating sides. One breath per punch.

.01

גבורה
Gevurah-Strength

מלכות
Malchut-Kingship

.02

.03

YOGA SEQUENCE, DAY 14/EASY (SUKHASANA)

If necessary you can modify this position by placing cushions beneath your knees. Just do not modify it too much by lying down on a sofa.

מלכות
Malchut-Kingship

גבורה
Gevurah-Strength

מלכות
Malchut-Kingship

TIFERET תפארת

COMPASSION

WEEK 3

TIFERET INTRODUCTION: COMPASSION / THE PATH OF JACOB תפארת

Tiferet is the middle path, the way of compassion, justice and balance. It translates as 'beauty' but can also be interpreted as 'balance', 'compassion', 'harmony'or even 'justice'. The beauty aspect is logical, as the more symmetrical a person's face, the more we consider it beautiful[1], because everything is in balance. The Kabbalah refers to *Tiferet* souls as "Masters of the Torah" because it represents people who are deeply balanced[2].

The idea of justice and balance is built into the fabric of the Universe. We are continually trying to get into balance, whether it is to eat when we are hungry, discharge waste when we are full, heal when we are ill, get our minds clear when they are foggy, or to reach stable land when things are shaky (literally and metaphorically).

Tiferet asks where our lives are out of balance and where we can retune. Where are we too giving (*Chesed*) or taking too much (*Gevurah*) and where might we find some equilibrium?

Jacob, *Ya'acov*, is considered the epitome of *Tiferet*-Compassion. He combines the loving elements of his grandfather Abraham (symbol of *Chesed*-Lovingkindness) with his father Isaac (*Gevurah*-Discipline) and finds his own path. Jacob is sometimes loving, such as when he gives Joseph the famous coat, "*now Israel loved his son Joseph…*"[3] and strict when dealing with his dishonest father-in-law Laban; "*And Jacob swore by the Dread of his father Isaac*"[4]. He is able to form a military strategy when faced with the uncertainty of approaching his long-estranged brother Esau and facing possible death -"*And Jacob became very frightened…So he divided the people with him*"[5] - and abundantly bestowing blessings at the end of his days -"*Gather yourselves and*

---

[1]　This theory is discussed more extensively in *The Human Face* by Brian Bates and John Cleese (yes, that John Cleese), by DK Publishing, 2001.
[2]　I learned this from Rabbi Yitzhak Gaines.
[3]　Genesis 37:3.
[4]　Genesis 31:53.
[5]　Genesis 32:8.

listen, O sounds of Jacob, and listen to Israel your father"[6]. We see Jacob
for a more extended period than any other person in Genesis, perhaps
because there is so much to learn from him. He takes on the name
'Israel', a title shared by the Jewish people for eternity. There is much to
be learned from the path of Jacob.

The intention of this book is to give you tools to immediately apply
this information to improve your life and bring more Light into the
world. A simple question to ask when learning these Biblical examples
is "Where am I like this?". For example, Jacob is able to be loving at one
time and disciplined at another. *Where am I like this?*

The Kabbalistic notion of *Tikkun*-repair might ask us another variation
on the question; "Where do I need to become like this?", that is, Where
do I go out of balance? Where do I get too loving and lack boundaries
to my own eventual chagrin, or where do I get too strict and lack
compassion?

The *Sefer Tanya* explains that the internal aspect of *Tiferet*-Compassion
is *Rachamim*-Mercy: *"[Rachamim-mercy] is the mediating attribute
between Gevurah-Discipline and Chesed-Lovingkindness, the latter of
which would diffuse benevolence to all, even to a person to whom compassion
is not at all appropriate"*[7]. Thus it works as an internal thermometer
telling us when to stop giving to a person because it is going to start
harming them. A simple example might be to know when to stop
feeding your child ice-cream because it will make them sick, even
though they want more, or forbidding your five-year-old from exploring
your gun collection even though he demonstrates great enthusiasm.

Another analogy for *Tiferet*-Compassion/Beauty is that of a perfect
harmonious blend, e.g. *"beautiful garments which are dyed with many
colours blended in a way that gives rise to beauty and decoration. To a garment
dyed in one colour, however, one cannot apply the term Tiferet-beauty, [which
implies the beauty of harmony]"*[8]. The beautiful, strong person is the one
who achieves harmony in their personality and way of being.

---

6   Genesis 49:2.
7   Sefer Tanya, Iggeret Hakodesh, Epistle 15.
8   Ibid.

TEACHING WITH BALANCE

This also applies to the way that we speak and *Tiferet* contains a sense of economy, only giving people as much information as is needed. At the time of teaching, according to Sefer Tanya,

> *"it is necessary to deliberate how to diffuse in such a way that the recipient will be able to absorb the effusion. For example, when one wishes [and this is a powerful desire] to convey and teach an intellectual subject to his son: If he will tell it to him in its totality, just as it appears in his own mind, the son will be unable to understand and to absorb it. This could happen either (a) because the concept as understood by the father is too abstract and subtle for the son, and needs to be lent a more tangible garb, such as a parable; or (b) because the concept is too comprehensive and too diverse, and needs to be broken down into digestible segments, only some of which will be presented to the son)*[9].

If you start teaching advanced physics to a 9 year old who is learning basic mathematics, your lesson will be not be well received (that would be the equivalent of too much *Chesed*-Giving). Equally if you patronise them and insist on teaching them how to count to 10 when they have already learned it, and really restrict the information you are giving them (i.e. *Gevurah*-restriction), that also will not work.

THE BIRTH OF EVIL

Worse still, we can quickly see the birth of evil when there is a lack of *Tiferet*-compassion. Professor Daniel Matt explains;

> *"Ideally a balance is achieved, symbolised by the central sefirah, Tiferet (Beauty), also called Rachamim (Compassion). If judgement is not softened by love, it lashes out and threatens to destroy life. Here lies the origin of evil, called Sitra Ahra, the Other Side... Tiferet is the trunk of the sefirotic body.*

---

9   Ibid.

He is called Heaven, Sun, King, and the Holy One, blessed be He...[10].

A parent who gives their child a special treat of chocolate may be seen as a good parent, but if they *only* feed their child chocolate, each and every day, the parent may get branded neglectful, punished as such, and the child will end up with social services to be placed with new parents who will feed them a balanced diet. Achieving balance is not an option if we want to enjoy a happy and healthy life.

IN YOUR BODY

It is no coincidence that when the *sefira* attributes are shown on a physical chart in the way that they correspond to the limbs and sections of our bodies, *Tiferet* is located around the heart and solar plexus.

The love expressed through *Tiferet* is a unique balance between selfless, endless lovingkindness and the lessons learned through restraint and discipline, e.g. a combination of the *Chesed*-Love of Week One with the *Gevurah*-Discipline of Week Two. *Tiferet*-Compassion is the culmination of a long-standing relationship where you are able to be perceptive about your friend's needs, know when to step forward to help them and when to stand back and make yourself scarce. It is the compassion balance that allows us to be sensitive towards another.

BEAUTIFUL FRIENDSHIPS

The word *Tiferet* may also translate as 'beauty' because a nurturing and balanced relationship is an essential part of human life, as King Solomon wrote: *"There are companions to keep one company, and there is a friend more devoted than a brother"*[11]. This beauty is an internal quality that becomes externalised when we are able to act with love, balance and compassion. It has nothing to do with external aesthetics, the kind of good looks and sharp features that may wither and fade with age[12]. *Tiferet* is the deep beauty that makes people increasingly attractive as they grow older, compelling to be near and even magnetising to watch.

---

[10] Daniel Matt in *The Essential Kabbalah - The Heart of Jewish Mysticism*, p8-9.
[11] Proverbs 18:24.
[12] 'Good looks are fleeting, external beauty is false', (Proverbs 31:30).

But it can only be achieved through having a 'good' heart and carrying out positive actions that help others.

Our keywords for the week are therefore balance, beauty, centredness, compassion, harmony, mercy and truth. Now to explore the theme through our body and the rest of our life.

QUESTIONS FOR MEDITATION

- Where are your relationships out of balance?
- Where is your business out of balance?
- Where is your body out of balance? (e.g. illness etc).Where do you go out of balance on a regular basis? Where do you get too loving and lack boundaries -later having to pay the price -or where do you get too strict?

TIFERET & COMPASSION

We can think of *Tiferet* as learning to walk the centre line and leading a balanced life.

Can I be compassionate towards others with a sense of love? (*Chesed*-Love in *Tiferet*-Compassion)

Can I be compassionate towards others whilst maintaining boundaries? (*Gevurah*-Discipline in *Tiferet*-Compassion)

Can I be compassionate towards others with balance and justice? (*Tiferet*-Compassion in *Tiferet*-Compassion)

Can I be compassionate towards others with endurance? (*Netzach*-Endurance in *Tiferet*-Compassion)

Can I be compassionate towards others with humility? (*Hod*-Humility in *Tiferet*-Compassion)

Can I be compassionate towards others while increasing my bonding and connection to them? (*Yesod*-Bonding in *Tiferet*-Compassion)

Can I be compassionate towards others while maintaining nobility? (*Malchut*-Mastery in *Tiferet*-Compassion)

TIFERET & JUSTICE

Can I pursue justice (*Tiferet*) whilst staying kind? (*Chesed*-Love in *Tiferet*-Justice)

Can I pursue justice (*Tiferet*) whilst maintaining boundaries? (*Gevurah*-Discipline in *Tiferet*-Justice)

Can I pursue justice (*Tiferet*) whilst with staying balanced and compassionate? (*Tiferet*-Compassion in *Tiferet*-Justice)

Can I pursue justice (*Tiferet*) with endurance? (*Netzach*-Endurance in *Tiferet*-Justice)

Can I pursue justice (*Tiferet*) whilst maintaining an attitude of humility and thankfulness? (*Hod*-Humility in *Tiferet*-Justice)

Can I pursue justice (*Tiferet*) through my bonding and connection to others? (*Yesod*-Bonding in *Tiferet*-Justice)

Can I pursue justice (*Tiferet*) whilst maintaining nobility? (*Malchut*-Mastery in *Tiferet*-Justice)

TIFERET & BALANCE

Our lives go out of balance the entire time. We spend too long at work or too much time socialising, eating and drinking too much or even denying ourselves affordable pleasures. *Tiferet* is the drive to continually restore harmony and balance.

***CHESED*-LOVINGKINDNESS**: Restore balance through kindness: How can I achieve a better balance through love, giving, kindness and creativity?

***GEVURAH*-DISCIPLINE:** Restore balance through discipline: What strict changes do I need enforce to do to get things into harmony?

***TIFERET*-COMPASSION/BALANCE:** Restore balance through harmonious practices: How can I tune in with the harmony of the Universe to let things get restored the easy way?

***NETZACH*-ENDURANCE:** Restore balance through sustained drive.

HOD-**HUMILITY:** Restore balance through gratitude and humility.

YESOD-**BALANCE:** Restore balance through getting our own stuff/opinions/judgements/projections out of the way, becoming focused on the other person and getting into gratitude!

MALCHUT-**MASTERY:** Becoming a master of balance and harmony. Fine tuning our balance through love, discipline, compassion, endurance, gratitude and bonding. Doing what is needed to restore, retune and repair this sefirah.

DAY 15 / **LOVINGKINDNESS IN COMPASSION** / LOVING BALANCE / חסד שבתפארת

KABBALAH SUTRA: *Hesed She b'Tiferet* – Lovingkindness in Compassion.
INTENTION: To achieve internal harmony, become centred and find the perfect balance in all areas of our life. Bring a loving balance to your life.

"Reuben, my firstborn, you are..unstable as water, you will no longer excel"
Jacob[13].

Love can be ruthless at times. We may love someone but realise that they can no longer be in our lives; an abusive partner, an alcoholic friend, an employee who has a charming personality but who is not suited to the job at hand and it is damaging if you keep them around. *Chesed*-Lovingkindness in *Tiferet*-Balance is the pursuit for justice that comes from a place of love. *Tiferet* is often translated as beauty because it is the sense of beauty that comes with harmony, like a perfectly still lake in all its natural glory.

I LOVE YOU, BUT...

Love-in-Balance is the "I love you, but-" that may force a couple to separate. It is Jacob, the personification of *Tiferet*-Balance when he gathers his sons for a final deathbed blessing and begins by addressing his eldest son Reuben to tell him that he is *"unstable as water"* and therefore will not be receiving the firstborn blessing. There is still a hidden blessing in that Reuben can still see how he can step into his own greatness, namely by stabilising the stormy waters of his life and emotions, but he has nonetheless lost his firstborn privileges as a result of his earlier behaviour.

An internal *Chesed*-love in *Tiferet*-balance might look like identifying which skills you are better at and prioritising which ones you will pursue professionally and which you will keep for hobbies. Although

---

13   Genesis 49:5.

you may love playing football and dream of being a soccer star, if you are completely honest you may see that your real strengths are as a chef, so you will make that your livelihood and keep the football for a fun Sunday game. As you apply this to your life, consider where you may need to start making cuts in your life in order to maintain the balance. Personally, for example, there are a number of creative projects I want to work on at the moment but I have prioritised completing this book for publication, lest I go out of balance by having too many projects incomplete at once.

THINKING ABOUT OUR THOUGHTS

The Kabbalist Rabbi Moshe Cordovero (1522-1570), the "Ramak", suggested we turn attention to our thoughts and begin by getting to a space of truthfulness within:

> "*The most important thing of all is to purify one's mind by scrutinising his thoughts and examining himself in the course of debate. If he finds even a trace of impure thought, he must retract his words and always admit the truth in order that Tiferet, the quality of truth, be found therein*"[14].

This sounds deceptively simple because as humans we have the ability to lie to ourselves. We can complain that something is wrong in our lives and there is a massive problem, blame that problem on an external factor and yet not take responsibility. A simple example of this would be a husband who is complaining that his wife is cold and unresponsive when he is not paying her any attention and not giving her any reason to display love, or a business owner who laments the downturn in profits and blames "the economy" when she is not doing the marketing that she knows is necessary. When we audit our thoughts, see what behaviours we need to change and take action, we can create different results. The truth will set you free, but only if you seek out that truth and then do something about it.

The motivational teacher Jack Canfield writes that success in business is dependent upon self-scrutiny, self-honesty and taking responsibility:

---

14 Tomer Devorah p.114.

"If you want to create the life of your dreams, then you are going to have to take 100% responsibility for your life as well. That means giving up all your excuses, all your victim stories, all the reasons why you can't and why you haven't up until now, and all your blaming of outside circumstances. You have to give them all up forever"[15]. Similar to the Kabbalah of Rabbi Cordovero, our purity of thought is an essential to achieving success in life.

ADMIT THE TRUTH WITH LOVE

The drive of *Chesed*-Lovingkindness is to restore *Tiferet*-balance through love, giving and creativity. If we need to admit a truth, make changes in our life, or complete a relationship, our first modus operandi is to use the positive energy of love. This is less about the words and more about the energy and intention[16].

CULTIVATING FRIENDLINESS

A key tenet of self-development is that we are taking responsibility for our own growth. Depending on our soul-root we may be more inclined towards lovingkindness and giving to others, or be more natural at exerting discipline and holding back. Knowing our soul root and natural tendencies helps reveal where we have a weakness, explains Rabbi Shneur Zalman of Liadi: *"the soul's root in the Supernal 'left', in the attribute of Gevurah [restriction], will lead one to act in a manner consistent with its character trait of limitation: so he will give only as much tzedakah… to the degree he is obligated"*[17]. A helpful starting point is to know our "soul root", or at least our natural inclination. Some people are easily drawn towards giving and sharing their resources [*Chesed*] whilst others among us are more naturally held back [*Gevurah*].

RESHAPE YOUR BRAIN

Scientists have shown how we can change our brain's neural pathways through repeated behaviours and thoughts as it creates new synaptic

---

15   *The Success Principles: How to Get from Where You Are to Where You Want to Be*, p5.
16   On higher spiritual levels, *everything* is about intention (*kavannah*). This is a recurring theme in the Sefer Tanya which teaches about how our intentions and thoughts have substance in spiritual worlds and other dimensions.
17   Sefer Tanya, Iggeret HaKodesh, Epistle 13.

pathways though this repetition. The Yoga Sutras explains: "*by cultivating friendliness towards happiness and compassion towards misery... the mind becomes pure*"[18]. We are not always in the mood for rebalancing our diet and want to eat a burger and fries, or not in the mood for rebalancing our body and avoid the gym, or we might avoid making necessary changes to our relationship. This train can be cultivated, according to the Kabbalists and the yogis, but it is a case of regular and active practice.

The *Tikkunei Zohar* locates *Tiferet*-Balance in the torso[19]. This is the home of our major organs, which are continually trying to keep our body in perfect balance through regulating the heartbeat, the pH of the blood, the oxygen/carbon dioxide process, the digestive process and so much more.

COMPASSION: AN INTELLIGENT LOVE

Tiferet is also the action of compassion. It differs from *Chesed*-Lovingkindness in that pure *Chesed* can be giving-without-limit. To "kill with kindness" is an overdose of *Chesed*. *Tiferet* is a more intelligent, nuanced giving which knows when more giving will be achieved by holding back. In this sense, it is a compassionate giving.

When we combine *Tiferet*-Compassion with C*hesed*-Lovingkindness, the result is a sensitive and caring interaction. We've heard the phrase "it's the thought that counts", but it rings hollow. The thought doesn't count without action.

As we open our heart and take action, we complete the impulse by doing something for someone else and change their world. *Chesed*-lovingkindness demands both a giver and a recipient, so our focus is on extending balance in relationship to others. Compassion on its own is not always enough, but it goes a long way to getting our house in order.

---

18 Yoga Sutras 1:33, Swamiji translation.
19 Introduction II to Tikkunei Zohar, reproduced in Siddur Tehillat HaShem, pp. 125-6.

TODAY'S PRACTICE

YOGA PRACTICE GUIDELINES:

Begin by listening closely to yourself, and notice which parts of your own body need some compassion. Are there any joints or limbs that would benefit from special attention and localised healing? Do you have a tight lower back? Sore neck? Aching calf muscles? Using any postures you feel are appropriate, gently stimulate the parts of your body that are in need of attention and hold the position for 10-15 slow, long breaths, so that you can intensify the benefits for the muscles. The longer you are able to hold the posture, the deeper the meditation and the greater the benefits. If nothing is hurting in particular, pay attention to the smoothness of your exhalation and be as 'kind' as possible in the way that you are filling your lungs with air, and expelling it at the end of the breath. Try to soften the breath as if you were presenting your lungs with a gift and exhale smoothly.

GYM PRACTICE GUIDELINES:

Focus on getting your body into balance and do it with a sense of ease and grace. If you are too tight you may need to stretch more. If you are tired you may need to wake up and do some aerobic exercise. If you have been going full-force and overworking, you may need to bring a softness to your physical workout. Ensure your thoughts are kind and loving as you do your workout, and strive for the internal balance while keeping a sense of deep flow.

RELATIONSHIP PRACTICE GUIDELINES:

Today's focus is on being compassionate and doing something about it. Listen closely to those around you and discover where there are opportunities to help or give to them. Sometimes that giving will take the form of just being present and silent. It doesn't necessarily mean actually handing them a solid object (this is certainly the cheapest way of doing it). If in doubt, buy flowers for your Mother.

METAPHYSICAL REFLECTION:

Become aware of the water element within your body and how your cells and entire being is made up primarily of water. See yourself as a body of water like a lake and visualise the surface of this water being calm.

QUESTIONS FOR MEDITATION

RELATIONSHIPS:

- Where are my relationships out of balance and how can I restore this through being loving and giving?
- How am I not loving and giving in the way I express compassion? What is the cost? Where am I going through the motions but not caring enough?
- How is my lack of lovingkindness to others and myself causing a lack of compassion?
- Where are my relationships out of balance and how can I restore this through love?

YOGA/BODY/GYM:

- Where can I be more loving in the way I try to rebalance my body? Do I eat food with a good attitude?
- Where are things out of balance in my body? Where am I suffering as a result? Am I exercising too much or too little, eating too much non-nutritious food or being too austere with my diet? Can I restore this balance (*Tiferet*) with a deep sense of *Chesed*-Lovingkindness? (If you are stuck, try visualising the Divine flow of *Chesed* through your body, and use that energy to help you get back into balance?)

MIND:

- Where are my thoughts out of balance? Am I judging myself too harshly? Can I see myself as a *Beinoni*[20], the middle way?

---

[20] "Rabbah declared "I am a Beinoni" (e.g. neither wholly righteous nor wholly evil), BT Brachot 18b., as quoted in the first chapter of *Sefer Tanya* which urges us to choose the middle path.

- Can I get my thinking back into balance with a sense of love for myself as an emanation of the Divine? Can I connect to God within me and the higher flow of *Chesed*-Lovingkindness and use this to get my thoughts back into balance?

BUSINESS:

- Where are things out of balance in my business and how can I restore balance with a sense of love, giving and creativity?
- Where is there some injustice in my business, and how can I heal this through giving? For example, am I spending enough time with my clients and colleagues, and can I do it from a place of *Chesed*-lovingkindness?

GYM SEQUENCE, DAY 15/AB WHEEL

Steadily roll the Ab wheel back and forth. If you don't have an Ab wheel, one hack is to use a dumbell with a free weight. If neither are available, do Sit-ups. 3 x 8 repetitions.

.01

.02

חסד
Chesed-Love

תפארת
Tiferet-Balance

YOGA SEQUENCE, DAY 15/CAT-COW (MARJARASANA)

Place your hands and knees in parallel position and play with curling and uncurling your spine. As you look upwards, sink your chest towards the ground and push your tailbone to the sky, before reversing the position.

.01

חסד
Chesed-Love
(Right Arm)

תפארת
Tiferet-Balance

.02

DAY 16 / DISCIPLINE IN COMPASSION / ALL IN THE BALANCE/ גבורה שבתפארת

KABBALAH SUTRA: *Gevurah She b'Tiferet*– Discipline in Compassion.
INTENTION: To achieve internal harmony, become centred and find the perfect balance in all areas of our life. Achieve discipline in your balance and become strongly centred.

"Strength does not come from winning. Your struggles develop your strengths.
When you go through hardships and decide not to surrender, that is strength"
Arnold Schwarzenegger

The second stage to restoring balance in our lives is to use discipline. *Gevurah*-discipline is using our firepower, but directing it towards our intended goal. At times we need to enforce strict changes to get things into harmony, and sometimes this means reigning in our actions when we are out of control.

If we are too compassionate to our body and continually comforting ourselves through food (i.e. too much *Tiferet*) we will push the scales out of balance in one direction. If we are too compassionate and stay within our comfort zone at work or in business then it is difficult to grow and earn more. Musicians can suffer from "that difficult second album" because they want to play it safe and recreate the safety of their first successful results; all of these are an overabundance of self-compassion. This is where *Gevurah*-discipline is required to make important cuts and changes.

Relationships demand continual fine tuning but few interpersonal connections are free from dispute. When arguments come up, explains the *Sefer Tanya*, we can subdue our passions (*Gevurah*-disicpline) to seek the balance that is epitomised by Jacob (i.e. *Tiferet*-Beauty):

> *"Rather.. Subdue [your] spirit and heart before every man*
> *according to the attribute of "truth unto Jacob" with humility,*

with "a soft answer [that] turns away anger"[21], and with a
restrained spirit. And through all that perhaps G–d will put
[a conciliatory and loving response] into the heart of [your]
brethren, for "as waters [reflect] one's face,[22] [so too does the
heart of one man reflect the heart of another]"[23].

This teaches us to elevate the potential when we approach a conflict
situation. Rather than blindly holding on to our point of view in a
disagreement we aim to see Divinity in the other person, to restrain our
spirit and to find a mutually beneficial agreement.

BINDING YOUR PERSONALITY

There are times when we need to hold back certain personality traits to
restore order. Restraining our essential nature might mean choosing *not*
to say something to a friend, *not* to take up somebody's time or goodwill
and making more room for others. An extreme example of holding back
is shown in the Biblical conversation between Isaac and his son Jacob,
who respectively represent *Gevurah*-Discipline and *Tiferet*-Beauty.
Isaac, now elderly and suffering from poor eyesight[24], is preparing
to give the firstborn blessing. Jacob is dressed up in the clothing of
his older brother Esau and *"Jacob said to his father, "It is I, Esau your*
firstborn""[25]. Isaac's assessment of the situation is *"The voice is Jacob's*
voice, but the hands are Esau's hands"[26] and he proceeds with the blessing,
much to Esau's later regret.

Although there is much going on beneath the surface, there is this clear
sense of *Gevurah*-restriction that Jacob performs, almost completely
absenting his own personality from the situation, indeed, changing
everything except his voice. Just as Isaac was fully withdrawn and
restricted when bound to the altar by his father Abraham[27], Jacob
is about to "bind" these aspects of his personality. We withhold
judgements from whether it was wrong or right for Jacob to further

---

21 Proverbs/Mishlei, 15:1.
22 Proverbs/Mishlei, 27:19.
23 Lessons in Tanya, Iggeret HaKodesh, Epistle 2.
24 Genesis 27:1.
25 Genesis 27:19.
26 Genesis 27:22.
27 Genesis 22:9.

"bind" Esau in that he stopped Esau from getting the first born blessing (although Esau technically sold it in the first place), but perhaps it was this blessing which enabled Jacob to eventually become known as Israel, father of the Jewish people, whose mission is to pursue the paths of balance and justice; *"justice, justice you shall pursue"* [28].

HEALER, HEAL THYSELF

Did you hear about the healer who needed healing? I once had a friend who was a holistic therapist who was so dedicated to her work that she would try to fix everyone, but the task became so great that healing other people sometimes came at the expense of personal relationships and friendships, because she did not know when to stop to protect herself. The issue of boundaries – *Gevurah* – is crucial if we are to be compassionate in a way that is healthy and balanced. *Gevurah-Discipline in Tiferet-Compassion* asks us to find the right balance.

Does any of this sound familiar? Have you ever given time to a stranger at the expense of someone close to you? What about caring for the needs of others at the expense of looking after yourself? Parents do it the whole time. The parent who works all hours to put their children through college, desperately trying to be a 'good parent', causing themselves stress, anxiety and an early heart attack, will find it hard to be a good parent if they make themselves unwell in the process.

THE YOGA OF FRIENDSHIPS

Relationships cannot function healthily if there is no discipline, even when it comes to being friendly. The Yoga Sutras teaches that *"by performing self-control on friendliness, the strength to grant joy arises"* [29]. *Gevurah*-discipline in *Tiferet*-compassion is the motion of restrained and boundaried compassion. The healthy doctor is the one who is able to say to her patients, "it is now time for me to go home and be with my family", and who is able to put their work down at the end of the day. There are no fixed rules with this and the feminine nature of life is that circumstances and emotions can change regularly; we are experiencing

---

28 Deuteronomy 16:20.
29 Yoga Sutras 3:22.

the spherical nature of *sefirot (Divine spheres)* rather than direct masculine lines which demand unbending rules.

KNOWING WHEN TO SAY "NO"

The 12th century philosopher Rambam/Maimonides taught how we need discernment when giving charity, including knowing when not to give if it is going to overwhelm someone or give them too much luxury[30]. People are not supposed to bankrupt themselves by giving too much charity (although this is rare). Overflowing compassion can actually become toxic and destructive if it is not focused and kept in check.

TODAY'S PRACTICE

YOGA PRACTICE GUIDELINES:

Finding the balance inside our own body is the challenge. *Gevurah*-discipline in *Tiferet*-compassion can be applied by choosing a yoga practice that is correct for our bodies, which may mean forgoing a vigorous session and replacing it with restorative postures that will allow our bodies to refresh themselves. Alternatively it may mean not pampering ourselves, getting to the front of the mat and going through a full-on workout.

Tiferet is about beauty, compassion, harmony and balance, and is located in the heart-centre. Practice today's posture and sun salutes in a way that is most appropriate for your body. Ask yourself whether you need a stronger or softer practice today. Where do you need to focus your *Gevurah*-firepower to get harmony in your body?

---

30   Maimonides, Laws of Gifts to the Poor, 7:3, *"One is commanded to give to a poor person according to what he lacks. If he has no clothes, they clothe him. If he has no utensils for a house, they buy [them] for him. If he does not have a wife, they arrange a marriage for him. If [the poor person] is a woman, they arrange a husband for marriage for her. Even if it was the custom of [a person who was rich but is now] a poor person to ride on a horse with a servant running in front of him, and this is a person who fell from his station, they buy him a horse to ride upon and a servant to run in front of him, as it is said, (Deut. 15:8) Sufficient for whatever he needs. You are commanded to fill whatever he lacks, but you are not commanded to make him wealthy".*

GYM PRACTICE GUIDELINES:

Focus on introducing restrictions and discipline to get your body into harmony and balance. This may mean working harder or doing a more gentle workout.

RELATIONSHIP PRACTICE GUIDELINES:

Which of my relationships need more compassionate giving, and which need more *Gevurah*-restriction? *Gevurah* has the multiple meaning of strength, boundaries and discipline, so decide which aspect you need to apply to your friendships and relationships today. This could mean being stronger and more giving, or perhaps you will need to hold back.

QUESTIONS FOR MEDITATION

RELATIONSHIPS:

- Where are my relationships out of balance and how can I restore this through being more disciplined in the way I show up?
- Where am I not showing enough compassion towards your my parents/siblings/partner?
- Where do I have too little compassion? Where do I have a compassion deficiency? Where are my relationships suffering?
- How am I not disciplined in my compassion?
- Where am I inconsistent and what problems is this causing?
- How is my lack of discipline and boundaries causing disharmony in my relationships?

YOGA/BODY/GYM:

- Where are things out of balance in my body? Where am I suffering as a result? Am I exercising too much or too little, eating too much non-nutritious food or being too austere with my diet? Can I restore this balance (*Tiferet*) with a deep sense of *Gevurah*-Discipline? (If you are stuck try visualising the Divine flow of *Gevurah* through your body, and use that energy to help you get back into balance?)
- Where am I not showing enough compassion towards my body?

MIND:

- Where are my thoughts out of balance? Am I judging myself too harshly? How can I achieve the middle way? Can I get my thinking back into balance with a sense of strength and discipline for myself as an emanation of the Divine? Can I connect to a sense of Godliness within me and the higher flow of *Gevurah*-Discipline, and use this to get my thoughts back into balance?
- Where can I pull back on negative thinking to get myself back into balance?

BUSINESS:

- Where are things out of balance in my business and how can I restore balance with a sense of discipline?
- Where is there some injustice in my business, and how can I heal this through being stronger?
- Where is there some injustice in my business, and how can I heal this through being more balanced, making cuts if necessary?
- Where am I not showing enough compassion towards my clients and colleagues?
- Where have I been too compassionate in my business, e.g. listening SO MUCH to what other people think that it is slowing me down to the point of stopping? (e.g. In my own life at times I have listened so much to the criticism of others that I shut down my own creativity).

ADVANCED KABBALISTIC BONUS:

A place to refine this quality is in the area of giving charity "*Tzedakah*". For many people this will be training yourself to give money to a charity where you would not usually, but for some it will mean giving less because you are suffering. The Sefer Tanya explains how more Divine Flow is brought down through the repeated act of giving coins to charity, explaining: "*[regarding] the act of charity which is performed numerous times, thereby eliciting the supreme [form of] life, (i.e. life that derives from the Infinite Fountainhead of Life,) by repeated bringing about the Supreme Unification (of Kudsha Brich Hu [The Masculine Divine Presence] and His Shechina [i.e. The Feminine Divine Presence]. Every act of tzedakah [charity] draws [the Divine] –Kudsha Brich Hu and Ein Sof downward to His Shechinah– down into the lowest levels of the world'*[31].

GYM SEQUENCE, DAY 16/SPEED ROTATIONS

Keep your body straight as you continue this for 3 sets of 45 seconds, with a short break between each one.

.01

.02

חסד
Chesed-Love

תפארת
Tiferet-Balance

.03

---

[31]   Lessons in Tanya, Iggeret HaKodesh, Epistle 21, pp12-13.

YOGA SEQUENCE, DAY 16/QUARTER-DOG (ADHO MUKHA SVANASANA)

Push into the ground with your straight arm and aim for the backbend you experienced in Downward Dog, whilst reaching underneath and across with your other arm.

.01

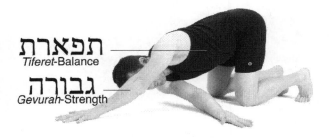

תפארת
Tiferet-Balance

גבורה
Gevurah-Strength

.02

DAY 17 / COMPASSION IN COMPASSION / HEALER, HEAL THY WORLD / תפארת שבתפארת

KABBALAH SUTRA: *Tiferet She b'Tiferet* – Compassion in Compassion. INTENTION: To bring deep healing to oneself and others through compassionate compassion. Live with centredness, balance and harmony.

"Tiferet is called "humanity" (Adam)" — Tikkunei Zohar 6a[32]

Tiferet-compassion in *Tiferet*-compassion is the truest, most balanced version of yourself. It is the ultimate vision of Israel, although you don't have to be Jewish. The *Tikkunei Zohar* calls it *"Adam"*, reminiscent of the yiddish word 'mentsch', meaning to be a good person, a decent person, a kind, giving, and balanced person.

BATTLE YOUR DEMONS

Jacob only gets called 'Israel' after many years, when he has undergone various trials and spent a night wrestling with an angel, after which he is told *"No longer will it be said that your name is Jacob, but Israel, for you have striven with the Divine and men and you have overcome"*[33]. The angel he has wrestled may have been the spiritual force of his brother Esau[34] or the dark side of Jacob's own personality. When you have wrestled with your own soul, when you have purged the thought processes and behaviours that hold you back, and when you have purged your personal 'demons', what is left? That is the truth of *Tiferet*, which is called "beauty". Your beautiful self is finally revealed.

THE BOOK OF INTERMEDIATES

The *Sefer Tanya* was a crucially important work of Kabbalah because it finally unlocked the esoteric mystical teachings and made them

---

32 Translation courtesy David Solomon, from Tiqqunei haZohar, Qushta 1740: An English Translation, p18 (from as-yet unpublished MS).
33 Genesis 32:29.
34 Rashi commentary on Genesis 32:25.

practical, and its opening chapter stresses the importance of finding a balance and choosing the middle path. "*Rabbah declared "I am a Beinoni" (e.g. neither wholly righteous nor wholly evil)*"[35]. Although we might certainly aim for perfection, it is considered reasonable if we at least find a balance in our way of being. The example of the teacher Rabbah (c.270-330) is given because he was known to be an almost-perfect saint, but called himself a *Beinoni*, an "intermediate" so that we have something to aspire to. Indeed an alternative name for the book is *Sefer Shel Beinonim*, "The Book of Intermediates".

START WITHIN

The process of refining the world ("*Tikkun Olam*" in Kabbalistic terminology) begins within. Maimonides (12th Century) taught that "*Anyone who sees a poor person begging and averts his eyes from him and does not give him tzedakah (charity money)*"[36] is in violation of a negative commandment, as taught from Deuteronomy; "*When one of your brethren will be needy ... do not harden your heart and do not close your hand from your needy brother. However, open your hand and give him as much as he lacks, whatever he is lacking*"[37]. The ease or difficulty of this practice will depend upon the individual and relates to "the middle path".

KNOWLEDGE IS NOT ENOUGH

A key part of the integration of *Tiferet* is action. The Torah and the *Tikkunei Zohar* use the language of 'fear' when using our knowledge. Rather than just keeping spiritual facts in the intellectual realm, it is essential to feel it with our emotions. The Hebrew phrase most frequently used is *Yirah* ('fear') or *Yirat Shamayaim* ('fear of heaven') although it a more accurate translation might be 'awe' or 'seeing the Divine and feeling it in your *kishkes*/guts', because *yirah* is a derivation of *ro'eh* which means 'seeing'. It is as if you are seeing God with your entire body. Thus, the Tikkunei Zohar[38] teaches that:

---

35   Babylonian Talmud, Brachot 18b, as quoted in Sefer Tanya Chapter 1.
36   Laws on Gifts for the Poor/Hilchot Matanot Ani'im, 7:2.
37   Deuteronomy 15:7,8.
38   Tiqqunei haZohar, Qushta 1740: An English Translation, p18.

> *"Anyone who prioritises his fear over his wisdom, his wisdom endures...'*[39]*. But everything is truth. Tifereth is called 'humanity' (Adam) – and in like fashion was [the first] Adam – the lower Hei – upon which they determined: 'First in thought and last in deed*[40]*. And because of this, the Rabbis established: 'Israel arose first in thought to be created*[41]*. For it is stated upon them: ...you are man..."*[42]*.

There are many more lessons within this, such as connecting these qualities to the Divine name of God (hence "the lower Hei"), but for our purposes let us focus on the additional light shed upon the essence of *Tiferet and* the nature of Israel. This is about being human and sharing this humanity with the world.

WHEN PRAYER DOESN'T COUNT

The Biblical prophets were generally not the most popular bunch of people because of the directness with which they spoke, and the harsh truths that they often conveyed. Every *Yom Kippur* (Day of Atonement) the striking words of Isaiah are read:

> *"Can such be the fast I choose, a day when man merely afflicts himself? Can it be bowing his head like a bullrush and making a mattress of sackcloth and ashes? Do you call this a fast and a day of favour to Hashem? Surely this is the fast I choose: open the bonds of wickedness, dissolve the groups that pervert [justice], let the oppressed go free and annul all perverted [justice]. Surely you should divide your bread with the hungry, and bring the moaning poor to your home; when you see the naked, cover him; and do not ignore your kin'. Then your light will burst forth like the dawn and your healing will speedily sprout; then your righteous deed will precede you and the glory of Hashem will gather you in. Then, when you call the LORD will answer; When you cry, He will say: Here I am/Hineni"*[43].

39 Ethics of the Fathers/Mishnah Avot, 3:9.
40 Bereishyt Rabbah 8:1.
41 Bereishyt Rabbah 1:4.
42 Ezekiel 34:31.
43 Isaiah 58:5-8 (mainly Artscroll translation but the last line is from the JPS Tanach).

To reach the higher levels of repairing our world, it is not enough for us to pray or fast, but we need to change our essential nature and embody this compassion.

THE YOGA OF MERCY

Tiferet is the part of ourselves that is compassionate and merciful, as Maimonides asked us not to walk past a poor person without opening our heart and ideally our wallet. This asks of us: Am I capable of *Tiferet* in *Tiferet*, endless and unreserved compassion? When I give to other people, can I do so freely, with pure and absolute commitment to the act of giving and no expectation for reward of any kind?

The Yoga Sutras says that we can *"overcome distractions of the mind"* and achieve peace of mind by being friendly *"towards those who are pleasantly disposed to oneself"* and by practicing *"compassion for the sorrowful"* [44]. Accordingly we can induce a state of compassion through following in these steps.

LIVING IT

Everyone certainly likes to think of themselves as caring and compassionate, but this trait demands cultivation and development, much like any other skill. When I see a new person at a party or a communal gathering and they are standing by themselves looking uncomfortable, can I be compassionate towards them in a way that isn't self-serving? I may go and start a conversation with them even though I'd rather stand and talk with close friends who are already at the party, but can I go and have the conversation in a way that will be purely giving, rather than trying to suss out whether they are going to be a potential business contact, yoga client or useful to me in some way?

OVERCOME YOUR DARK SIDE

Have you ever visited a lonely elderly relative in the secret hope that one day they will remember you in their will? (Ok, this is an especially dark example…). What about going out of your way to assist a friend in distress, only to remind them of your selfless good deed at a later date?

---

44 Yoga Sutras 1:33, Ventakesha translation.

Tiferet in *Tiferet* is compassionate compassion, the pure unadulterated desire to help and give without any sense of expecting something in return. It is totally focused on the present-moment awareness because there is no other agenda being followed. It is giving done for the sake of giving, completely free from guilt or ulterior motive.

Getting to the cleanest and purest version of ourselves is an ongoing process that continues throughout life. This is something that cannot be gleaned from a book or a teacher but is a path that has to be walked alone, facing your 'demons' and exorcising them. *"And Jacob was left alone and a man wrestled with him until the break of dawn"* [45]. The path may not be easy and you can only walk it by yourself, but most of us are on a similar journey.

TODAY'S PRACTICE

YOGA PRACTICE GUIDELINES:

As you engage with today's yoga postures, focus on opening your heart space, finding balance within and spreading compassion into the world. Be merciful and compassionate to your body and practice out of love and joy rather than from a place of guilt and fear. Watch your thoughts carefully.

GYM PRACTICE GUIDELINES:

Balance your gym practice with a sense of compassion. Centre your breathing (*Tiferet* is called "body"). Keep balancing the left and right sides of your body, acutely noticing if one side needs more attention than the other (thus achieving the balance that is *Tiferet*).

GIVING CHARITY/*TZEDAKAH*

Notice the thoughts that arise when you pass someone begging on the street. When you give them some money, try to do this with a pure heart and trying to connect with Divine balance; still use your discernment as to how much to give and whom you are giving to, but visualise that you are helping restore order in the world and merely passing on some of the blessing that has been channelled through you.

---

45   Genesis 32:25.

QUESTIONS FOR MEDITATION

RELATIONSHIPS:
- Where are my relationships out of balance and how can I restore this through extra compassion?
- Where can I be more compassionate towards my friends and family?
- Where do my relationships suffer through a lack of compassion? Where am I too strict or lacking mercy with people?

YOGA/BODY/GYM:
- Where are things out of balance in my body? Where am I suffering as a result? Am I exercising too much or too little, eating too much nonnutritious food or being too austere with my diet? Can I restore this balance (*Tiferet*) with a deep sense of *Tiferet*-compassion? (If you are stuck try visualising the Divine flow of *Tiferet*-compassion through your body, and use that energy to help you get back into balance?)
- Am I compassionate towards my body?

MIND:
- Where are my thoughts out of balance? Am I judging myself too harshly? How can I achieve the middle way? Can I get my thinking back into balance with a sense of deep compassion for myself as an emanation of the Divine? Can I connect to God within me and the higher flow of *Tiferet*-compassion and use this to get my thoughts back into balance?

BUSINESS:
- Where are things out of balance in my business and how can I restore balance with a sense of compassion?
- Where is there some injustice in my business, and how can I heal this through being more balanced, making cuts if necessary?
- Where does my business suffer from a lack of compassion?

EARTH & ECOLOGICAL BALANCE

- Restore balance through harmonious practices: How can I tune in with the harmony of the Universe to let things get restored the easy way?

FURTHER PERSONAL DEVELOPMENT:

- When someone is in need, how do I respond?
- Who is the most compassionate person I know, and why? What is that quality within them that I would like to emulate?
- Is my compassion "clean"? Do I give to people whilst expecting something in return? Am I keeping 'accounts', waiting for them to give back to me after I have given to them?
- How is my lack of balance/compassion to others and myself causing a further lack of compassion? (e.g. a double-dysfunction of *Tiferet* in *Tiferet*).
- Am I capable of *Tiferet* in *Tiferet*, endless compassion?
- When I give to other people, can I do so freely, with pure and absolute commitment to the act of giving, with no expectation of reward of any kind?

GYM SEQUENCE, DAY 17/SUPERMAN STRETCH

Stretch to your maximum capacity, hold and relax. 3 x 8 stretches.

.01

תפארת
Tiferet-Balance

.02

YOGA SEQUENCE, DAY 17/SPHINX

Push into the ground with your hands and forearms and draw them towards your waist, as you bring your spine forward and arched upwards in the opposite direction.

תפארת
Tiferet-Balance

DAY 18 / ENDURANCE IN BALANCE / THE FIGHT FOR JUSTICE / נצח שבתפארת

KABBALAH SUTRA: *Netzach She b'Tiferet* – Endurance in Compassion. INTENTION: To bring long-term harmony and balance to oneself and others. Restore balance through sustained drive. Sustain your ability to balance – achieve centredness and keep it.

"Only in the challenges before us do we see what we truly are. If you say to all you are kind, it will be when you don't feel kind that will define the internal soul part of you" [46]. — Eric Sander Kingston

The New Age sold us a lie which was that we can easily "manifest" something simply by thinking about it and raising our "vibration". Although that might be 100% true and possible on a spiritual plane, and perhaps at some point when human consciousness is more evolved, for now most of us need to work!

When we have a dream but do not do anything about it, nothing happens on the physical plane. If you want to grow carrots but have not planted any seeds, it is a guarantee that you will not be reaping carrots at the next harvest. *Netzach*-Endurance in *Tiferet*-Balance is the fight for justice, to continue to get a balance in our own lives; balancing our income with our spending, balancing our dreams with reality, balancing our love with our discipline, balancing who we want to be with who we are. On a deeper and simpler level, it is the drive to unify our thoughts, speech and actions (Hebrew: *machshava*, *dibur* and *ma'aseh*) [47].

THE BUSINESS ETHICS OF JACOB

Netzach-Endurance in *Tiferet*-Balance is not the behaviour of a workaholic whose work ethic can produce results but at the expense of family and friends. Rather it is the balanced approach of Jacob (*Tiferet*) who expends tremendous effort over an extended period (*Netzach*),

---

46 'Mantras for Transformation' in How Far to The Place of Enlightenment?, p8.
47 This is discussed in Sefer Tanya by the Alter Rebbe at the beginning of Chapter 4. Lessons in Tanya, Vol 2, p74.

despite the lies and manipulation of his father-in-law Laban, and only gets pushed to upset when he is falsely accused:

> *"Then Jacob became angered and he took up his grievance with Laban; Jacob spoke up and said to Laban, "What is my transgression? What is my sin, that you have pursued me? These twenty years I have been with you, your ewes and she-goats did not miscarry, nor did I eat the rams of your flock. That which was mangled I never brought you –I would bear the loss, from my hand you would exact it, stolen by day, or stolen by night. This is how I was: By day heat consumed me, and snow by night; my sleep drifted from my eyes. This is for me twenty years in your household: I worked for you fourteen years for your two daughters, and six years for your flocks; and you changed my wage ten countings. Had not the God my father –the God of Abraham and the Dread of Isaac –been with me, you would surely have now sent me away empty handed"* [48].

Rather than living an easy life to build his wealth, name and large family, Jacob worked incredibly hard and had to contend with negative forces as he found his own balance, whether it was the dishonesty of Laban, the threat of his brother Esau or the Divine fear that he referred to as *Pachad Yitzhak*, the *"Terror of Isaac"* [49].

LIFE IS WHAT HAPPENS WHILE YOU'RE BUSY MAKING OTHER PLANS

How often do we give up too easily on a project, a relationship or even a thought process? We will return to this theme later but we might consider the 14 years that Jacob works in order to marry his wife Rachel. He agreed to the initial seven years as part of the contract with Laban but was tricked into a second term when duped into marrying the less attractive sister Leah; *"he said to Laban, "What is this you have done to me? Was it not for Rachel that I worked for you? Why have you deceived me""* [50].

---

48 Genesis 31:36-42.
49 Genesis 31:53.
50 Genesis 29:25.

Perhaps this is to teach us that things do not always go according to plan, and sometimes veer substantially away from our expectations, but with a determined mindset we can achieve our goal, or die trying.

WHERE HAVE YOU GIVEN UP TOO EASILY?

At this point it would be appropriate to ask: What goal have you given up on through a lack of persistence? *Tiferet*-energy goals are those which are grounded and balanced, rather than the more extreme "I-wanna-be-a-rockstar" type of goal. They are the ones that we gave up on through a lack of persistence and our life is noticeably lacking as a result. I certainly have plenty of my own that I am working on rectifying and rebuilding.

ENDURING COMPASSION

The Kabbalists teach that the inner aspect of *Tiferet* is *Rachamim*-mercy, which is why Tiferet is often translated as compassion. *Netzach*-endurance asks us to sustain our compassion over a long period of time. When we are giving, we consider how we can give consistently for the duration, such as from parent to child. We also look at how we are treating ourselves, and when to allow for extra compassion. The goal is harmony, balance and beauty, so take the opportunity to see how you are able to help people on their terms, especially when you do not feel like displaying compassion -that could be when it is needed most of all.

When we endure and use compassion to find balance for ourselves and the world around us, we touch on the aspect of *Tiferet* that is "Beauty", or as the Romantic poet Keats said *"Beauty is truth, truth beauty, -that is all Ye know on earth, and all ye need to know"*[51].

TODAY'S PRACTICE

YOGA PRACTICE GUIDELINES:

The Yoga Sutras says that *"continuous practice [e.g. Netzach-endurance] helps to achieve liberation"*[52]. The implication is that this regular practice

---

[51] Ode On a Graecian Urn by John Keats, written in May 1819.
[52] Yoga Sutras 2:26, Swamij translation.

is applied with compassion towards ourselves. How do you treat your body? Yoga is about growing in love for humanity and being compassionate towards ourselves and others. But how do you approach your practice? Is it a once-in-a-while, punctuated with fast food binges, television-watching marathons or heavy drinking sessions in between? Do you end your day being kind to yourself even though you have not achieved your full potential?

Today's practice is more about being compassionate towards yourself and others, but also about the process of ongoing love, even when you are not in the mood for it. Continue in the process of being kind towards your body, but above all, aim for consistency in today's yoga practice. Remember the mantra – better to do just 10 minutes than nothing at all – and continue with this yoga of love and compassion.

GYM PRACTICE GUIDELINES:

Endure with your gym practice today and practice a longer cardio workout than usual. Set the intention for internal balance.

QUESTIONS FOR MEDITATION

RELATIONSHIPS:

- Where are my relationships out of balance and how can I restore this through extra compassion?
- Where do I give up too easily in my compassion?
- Where do I allow my relationships to go out of balance and what is the cost?
- Where am I not consistent in my compassion? (i.e. where am I not showing up on a regular basis?)
- Am I consistently balanced and compassionate in my personal relationships?
- How do I lack commitment towards my loved ones?

YOGA/BODY/GYM:

- Where are things out of balance in my body? Where am I suffering as a result? Am I exercising too much or too little, eating too much non-nutritious food or being too austere with my diet? Can I restore this balance (*Tiferet*) with a deep sense of *Netzach*-Endurance? (If you are stuck, try visualising the Divine flow of *Netzach*-Endurance through your body, and use that energy to help you get back into balance?)
- Am I consistently balanced and compassionate in my yoga/gym/meditation practice?

MIND:

- Where are my thoughts out of balance? Am I judging myself too harshly? How can I achieve the middle way? Can I get my thinking back into balance with a sense of deep endurance, coming from a Higher Power? Can I keep this going? Can I connect to God within me and the higher flow of *Netzach*-Endurance and use this to get my thoughts back into balance?
- Where do I lack clarity in my thinking and how could I be more consistent about getting my thoughts stable?

BUSINESS:

- Where are things out of balance in my business and how can I restore balance in a way that is enduring?
- Where is there some injustice in my business, and how can I heal this in a way that will be sustainable?
- Am I consistently balanced and compassionate in my customer relations and workplace?
- Where do I lack clarity in the vision for my career or business and how can I achieve a clearer, stronger and more far-reaching vision?

BEING A MENSCH

- Where could I be more consistent in my compassion?

GYM SEQUENCE, DAY 18/JACKKNIFE CRUNCH

Keep your arms and legs straight as you Jackknife. 3 x 8 repetitions.

.01

תפארת
Tiferet-Balance

נצח
Netzach-Endurance

.02

PARSVAKONASANA

Perform whichever version of this is within your capability and lengthen your spine on the inhale as you twist on the exhale.

.01

תפארת
Tiferet-Balance

נצח
Netzach-Endurance

.02

.03

185

DAY 19 / HUMILITY IN BALANCE / A FINE BALANCE
הוד שבתפארת

KABBALAH SUTRA: *Hod She b'Tiferet* – Humility in Compassion.
INTENTION: To stay in humble gratitude and achieve a sense of internal harmony, become centred, finding the perfect balance in all areas of our life. Restore balance through gratitude and humility. Be humble in our compassion for others.

"Greed, for lack of a better word, is good. Greed works"
Gordon Gekko, Wall Street.

Arrogance and greed have often been mistaken as virtues in the business world. Films like *Wall Street* accompanied the explosions of wealth in the 1980's that led to a stock market crash, and financier's greed was blamed as the cause for further crashes in the early 2000's. There are even theories that the Wall Street crash of 1929 was deliberately engineered[53]. Recent years have seen financial crises around 'toxic' loans and a series of scandals relating to corporate financiers' greed.

THE HUMBLE BALANCE

Hod-humility in *Tiferet*-Balance questions how we are being arrogant or single minded and how this is damaging the compassion and balance in our life. This is not to say that we should be over-humble, but rather it is striking a balance; *"The idea of Netzach [endurance] and Hod [humility] is a question of asserting your identity on the one hand, or total compliance with the other person's identity, on the other"*, taught Rabbi Aryeh Kaplan[54]. This is a continual process within our life, which is why *Netzach* and *Hod* are often mentioned together, and their counterparts are the brothers Moses and Aaron. Sometimes we need to push,

---

53 See The Money Masters documentary (1995, available on YouTube), produced by attorney Patrick S. J. Carmack and directed and narrated by William T. Still. The topic is, however, highly contentious.
54 Rabbi Aryeh Kaplan, Innerspace, p66.

sometimes we need to pull. We continually calibrate between driving and allowing. A car does this, accelerating to a certain speed (*Netzach*) and then cruising (*Hod*), before it is time to accelerate again (*Netzach*) and so on.

WRITTEN IN STONE

A recurring question with this spiritual development is; how far are we committed to our growth? We might see each of the Divine Spheres (*sefirot*) as vessels for movement. We explored earlier how the Kabbalah connects *Netzach*-endurance and *Hod*-humility with the right and left legs, and how they correspond to Moses and Aaron. The *Tikkunei Zohar* goes deeper with this, suggesting how they correspond to truth and to the tablets which had the Ten Commandments written upon them. Just as our legs drive us forwards, these Divine qualities represent the forwards motion: "*These are the two thighs, two prophets of truth netzach and hod*[55]...*these are the two prophets of truth. And from the aspect of the Middle Pillar they are called prophets of truth*"[56]. When we walk to a fixed point there is an aspect of 'truth' that we are no longer at the place we started. The quality of *Hod*-humility may be a more humble form of movement but it will take you to a deeper and higher place if you allow it.

SURRENDERING

Hod is also the energy of 'surrendering' or 'allowing' and these qualities help us become more compassionate, refining any arrogance in our personality. When the Yoga Sutras introduced the idea of God into yoga practice, they taught that yoga is achieved through "*surrender to or worship of the indwelling omnipresence*" or "*persevering devotion to God*"[57]. This can only come about through having a humble approach as if we are giving ourselves, or at least giving our breath and dedicating that particular moment, without expecting any reward.

---

55 Tiqqunei haZohar 7a, Qustha 1740: An English Translation.
56 Ibid., 11b
57 Yoga Sutras 2:32, Swamij translation.

HEIGHTENED LISTENING

As human beings we feel the need to be seen, heard and acknowledged. We like to be listened to. When we can give someone else that space to be recognised, we are using *Hod*. Where *Netzach* is the right foot stepping forwards, *Hod* is the left leg that holds back and creates room for the 'driver'. When we consider the people who make us feel great, it is generally those who really see us for who we are. They are the ones who withhold judgement and create space for us to grow.

Jacob's encounter adult encounter with his estranged brother Esau shows *Hod*-humility in *Tiferet*-compassion. Jacob understands that Esau may be harbouring a lifetime of resentment because of what happened when they were younger[58].

> *"And Jacob became very frightened and it distressed him. So he divided the people with him, and the flocks, and the cattle, and the camels into two camps. And he said "If Esau comes to the one camp and strikes it, then the remaining camp shall be a refuge"*[59].

Rabbi Shlomo Yitzhaki (Rashi, 1040-1105) explains that Jacob's fear was that Esau was going to kill him and his family. He reasoned that he would at least save half of his family if Esau attacked one of the camps[60].

There may have been other options available to Jacob. Perhaps he might have turned and faced the other direction and simply run away. But this was not the path of somebody committed to truth and restoring balance within his family and his own soul, perhaps out of a sense of responsibility for buying the birthright from the then-ignorant Esau and then impersonating him at the time of the blessing. As such, Jacob approached the road to justice with a sense of humility.

---

58   When Jacob purchased the first-born blessing from Esau.
59   Genesis 32:8-9.
60   See Rashi commentary ad loc.

FINDING OURSELVES IN JACOB'S DILEMMA

When pursuing our truth, whether it is making the decision to change our career and pursue the path we have always dreamed of, or to finally face a dark truth that we have been avoiding, there is some natural fear and trepidation. We feel that we might lose everything, just like Jacob. But when we have reached the point of "I cannot go on any longer without making a change", and we feel ready to commit to those changes, it would be wise to take this humble approach of "splitting our camp", that is, going forwards with precaution but still making the decision to move forwards to pursue truth. The other option is to stay in darkness, to be like Jacob if he had *not* wrestled with the angel and had *not* become Israel and not fulfilled his destiny. We have the choice at any given moment.

HUMBLE COMPASSION

Another expression of today's sefirah combination is *Hod*-humility in *Tiferet*-compassion. This asks us to be compassionate to other people but to maintain an air of humility. When we are giving to somebody else, can we do it without leaving them under any sense of obligation? Can we be compassionate to someone and not be 'right' about our position? Can we offer advice from our heart and really be ok with somebody ignoring our advice, and not feel the need to defend or maintain our position?

Truly humble compassion is shown by the thankless tasks; the young mother or father who is changing their child's nappy (USA: *diaper)* in the middle of the night, the dustbin men (USA: *trash collector)* who are picking up your rubbish (USA:*garbage*) at 6 am, or the wise schoolteacher who is giving someone life skills but faces disrespectful students. Our challenge of *Hod*-humility in *Tiferet*-compassion is to give graciously and be compassionate for its own sake, so that we can be compassionate givers without any sense of needing something in return.

LIFT YOUR EYES

A position of true, endless compassion might be one of abundance which states that the Universal Spirit will always take care of my every need and that I have all of the resources I need at this very moment. This way my compassion can come from a place of purity rather than one of negativity or in need of something in return. In the words of King David we might "lift our eyes to the mountains"[61] and elevate our minds so that we can banish negative thoughts and complaints, and see the goodness of God that is bestowed upon us at every moment.

TODAY'S PRACTICE

YOGA PRACTICE GUIDELINES:

One method to connect with the energy of *Hod*-humility in *Tiferet*-compassion is by recognising and appreciating everything you have. Begin your yoga practice by using every fibre of your being as you work through sun salutes noticing the space around you, how your fingers feel in the air and the sensation of the ground beneath your feet. Take some moments to appreciate how your body moves and functions, and that it is mobile and flexible enough to allow you to do this. The next stage is to take the focus towards the great unknown. As you inhale the breath that keeps you alive, feel a sense of gratitude towards God. Thanks for having the ability to even say 'thank you' is a good place to start. The Hebrew word *Hod* forms the root of the word *Hodu*, meaning 'we give thanks'. As you move towards today's postures, feel the sense of humility as you stand in awe of this amazing body you have been given. We still do not know exactly where this life force comes from and despite all the advances of modern science, there are still many mysteries about the human body. Humility in Compassion is therefore a way to connect with the Divine Spirit. Just as we have received, so shall we give.

---

61   Psalm 121:1.

GYM PRACTICE GUIDELINES:

Approach your gym practice with a sense of surrender and humility. Notice the energy of people at the gym, where they lack this quality and how it manifests in their body. As you workout, strive for balance in your body and mind. As a secondary practice, count several things you are grateful for in your body.

QUESTIONS FOR MEDITATION

RELATIONSHIPS:

- Where are my relationships out of balance and how can I restore this through being more humble?
- Where am I not humble in the way I strive for balance?
- Where do I go in too strong with my compassion and what is the price that I pay as a result?
- How is my lack of gratitude to others and myself causing a lack of compassion?
- Be aware of your giving today and aim to give without need for anything in return.

YOGA/BODY/GYM:

- Where are things out of balance in my body? Where am I suffering as a result? Am I exercising too much or too little, eating too much non-nutritious food or being too austere with my diet? Can I restore this balance (*Tiferet*) with a deep sense of *Hod*-humility/gratitude? (If you are stuck try visualising the Divine flow of *Hod*-humility/gratitude through your body, and use that energy to help you get back into balance?).

MIND:

- Where are my thoughts out of balance? Am I judging myself too harshly? How can I achieve the middle way?
- Can I get my thinking back into balance with a sense of deep gratitude for all I have been given? Can I keep this going? Can I connect to God within me and the higher flow of *Hod*-humility/gratitude and use this to get my thoughts back into balance?

BUSINESS & SUCCESS:

- Where are things out of balance in my business and how can I restore balance with a sense of humility?
- Where is there some injustice in my business, and how can I heal this through being more humble and grateful?
- Where have I been lacking in gratitude to the extent that it has led to a lack of compassion? (e.g. I lack gratitude for my talents and material resources so I give myself a hard time about not being more materially successful, i.e. am I lacking compassion towards myself?)

MONEY

- Do I maintain gratitude for the money in my pocket and seeing that money as an extension of God? In this way can I show compassion for the beggars who I might otherwise be judging (e.g. for being unkempt, rude, 'fragrant', or some other judgement)?

ADDITIONAL SELF-DEVELOPMENT EXERCISE

Make a gratitude list and focus on transforming it into compassionate and balanced behaviour.

GYM SEQUENCE, DAY 19/FLUTTER KICK

For increased intensity you can attach ankle weights.

.01

.02

YOGA SEQUENCE, DAY 19/CAMEL (USTRASANA)

If easier, you can do this in front of a wall which you may use to provide stability and support against the front of your thighs. Lift your chest as high as possible and reach down with your hands to deepen the backbend.

.01

תפארת
Tiferet-Balance

הוד
Hod-Humility

.02

DAY 20 / BONDING IN COMPASSION / THE EDGE OF GLORY / יסוד שבתפארת

KABBALAH SUTRA: *Yesod She b'Tiferet* – Bonding in Compassion.
INTENTION: Restore balance through getting our own stuff/opinions/
judgements/projections out of the way, becoming focused on the other
person and getting into a state of Gratitude! To become grounded and
achieve internal harmony, finding the perfect balance in all areas of our life.

*"Be nice to people on the way up, because you never know who you're going to
meet on the way down"* [62] — Gillian Freed

I have just realised that my mother is a secret Kabbalist and I attribute
today's teaching to her. She would often remind me that whatever
success or accomplishments we may enjoy, we should still be kind
and considerate to other people. The trappings of power, wealth and
celebrity will magnify people's inner essence, so it makes sense to refine
this quality lest we reach that triumvirate of glory. We all know people
who have power and lack kindness, and we have a choice not to be like
them. It is not enough to be rich and famous; we also need to be *nice*[63].

Our spiritual development should lead us to us being compassionate
as we connect with others. Rabbi Chanina ben Dosa (1st Century
CE) taught: *"If the spirit of one's fellows is pleased with him, the spirit
of the Omnipresent is pleased with him; but if the spirit of one's fellows
is not pleased with him, the spirit of the Omnipresent is not pleased with
him"*[64]. There are two components here; *Yesod* is connection, *Tiferet* is
compassion, and their combination makes for healthy relationships and
a good reputation. We connect with other people, rather than being
aloof. The aim is for us to connect (*Yesod*) with compassion (*Tiferet*),
and similarly our compassion (*Tiferet*) should help us connect (*Yesod*)
with others. All clear? Good!

---

[62] There are three main candidates for authorship of this phrase: playwright Wilson
    Mizner, gossip columnist Walter Winchell, and comedian Jimmy Durante. New evidence
    uncovered by top researcher Barry Popik in December 2014 points to Mizner as the
    originator (Footnote research courtesy of my mother!).
[63] 'Nice', that insubstantial blamange of a word that my secondary-school English teacher
    Mr Fynes-Clinton forbade us from using. Although here it seems appropriate.
[64] Ethics of the Fathers/Pirkei Avot 3:13.

RELATING WITH KINDNESS

On the Tree of Life diagram [please see page 2], *Tiferet*-compassion is shown in the central column, while *Yesod*-bonding is directly beneath it. This represents a conceptual relationship and an energetic relationship. In simple terms, we are kind and just (*Tiferet*) and that strengthens our bonds (*Yesod*) with others. A person who is considered spiritually evolved but lacks kindness is not spiritually evolved.

ADVANCED: THE COMPLEXITIES OF DIVINE JUSTICE

On the other hand, if they are showing tough love and fulfilling Divine justice (*Tiferet*) -like Elijah the Prophet -then that is also a form of Divine compassion, although it might be far harder to understand at a surface level. From a Kabbalistic perspective, a soul might be reincarnated to fulfil a specific mission that only takes 8 days (such as the commandment of *Brit Milah*, circumcision)[65], and that soul may be spared the pain of a difficult, long life on earth. But from the earthly perspective, there may -God forbid -be young parents who have just lost their eight-day old son, and all they can see is Divine tragedy and perhaps feel anger towards God. Here we begin to glance at the incredibly complex depths that Kabbalistic wisdom uncovers. At its purest and most simple level however, it asks us to have faith (*Emunah*) and continue to seek ways of connecting to The Light.

THE UGLY ELIJAH & KINDNESS TO THE POOR

As we refine this trait of improving relationships through our compassion, there is a story of how Elijah the Prophet appeared in disguise to teach this very lesson and demonstrate the Kabbalistic principle. The *Tomer Devorah* relates:

> *"Elijah the Prophet appeared to Rabbi Shimon ben Elazar as an ugly, despicably, loathsome pauper in order to enlighten him. For in his elation [and self-satisfaction/ self-aggrandisement] with his learning, he insulted the*

---

[65] The complexities of reincarnation are explored at length in Sha'ar HaGilgulim, The Gates of Reincarnation, translated from the teachings of Rabbi Isaac Luria 1534-1575 (Thirty Seven Books Publishing: Malibu, CA, 2003).

poor fellow, who then rebuked Rabbi Shimon profusely for this character defect. Such a man who exalts himself over the poor, causes Tiferet-compassion to remain aloof from Yesod-connection"[66].

We can now see how a powerful figure can cause a spiritual and emotional blockage if they cannot be compassionate towards others who are in a less successful position. I see this regularly with a spiritually-inclined man called Joel who has been homeless for nearly 20 years and lives on the street a few blocks from my apartment, on the edge of Beverly Hills. He relates how many so-called successful people are rude to him and judge him for his position rather than reaching out with kindness. It is not their lack of giving money that causes pain, so much as their attitude.

The *Tomer Devorah* continues to explain how we can heal this spiritual blockage: "if a sage pays attention to the poor, *Tiferet* will flow into *Yesod*". In other words, compassion (*Tiferet*) will lead to connection (Yesod). "For this reason, sages should highly esteem the poor and draw them closer. This way, *Tiferet*-compassion will greatly value Yesod-bonding and bind to it"[67].

We see that this is not about whether we give money to charity but *how* we give it. Beneath the surface-level action of reaching out to another person is the attitude, intention and energy with which we infuse our action. When the Alter Rebbe (1745-1812) discussed aligning our *"thoughts, speech and action"*[68], we see the importance of this. If someone gives you a gift but has a bad attitude, how does it make you feel? Even the most rational of non-believers will admit they can 'sense' somebody's intention. Like it or not, we are highly advanced spiritual beings beneath the surface of our skin. As someone once said, "We are not human beings having a spiritual experience but spiritual beings having a human experience"[69].

---

66 Tomer Devorah (The Palm Trees of Deborah), p110.
67 Ibid., p110.
68 This is a recurring theme in Sefer Tanya.
69 This has been variously attributed to the French philosopher Pierre Teilhard de Chardin (1881 – 1955) and also to G. I. Gurdjieff.

TODAY'S PRACTICE

YOGA PRACTICE GUIDELINES:

Connect with your body in a way that is gentle and loving, becoming aware that this organism is purely on loan to you for a relatively short period of time. Notice the little quirks, the twinges, the parts that work well (in your opinion) and the weaker areas that could do with some improvement. But above all, breathe mindfully. Regardless of your shape or size, move beyond issues of body image and grow in love for this amazing gift.

Yesod-bonding connects to the reproductive organs because they are the place where we bond to another human[70]. For the yogis this would correspond to *mulah bandha*, the root lock, which literally binds all of our body together. If you are familiar with this practice, engage your *mulah bandha* whilst keeping a sense of compassion throughout your practice.

GYM/PHYSICAL PRACTICE GUIDELINES:

Bring your attention to your body, and connect with it (*Yesod*) with a sense of compassion (*Tiferet*). Love and appreciate your body, listen to what it needs and respond with compassion. It may require more exercise or more rest. *Tiferet* also relates to beauty, so get present to the beautiful parts of yourself!

RELATIONSHIP PRACTICE GUIDELINES:

Yesod also corresponds to pleasure, so we might ask: Are we enjoying our connections to others? Is our compassion pleasurable? Am I compassionate at the deepest level of my marital and interpersonal relations?

---

[70] The feminine counterpart connects with Malhut because it is through the union of male and female that a new being is created.

PRACTICE GUIDELINES: FOR TEACHERS (OR ANYONE WHO IS TEACHING SOMETHING TODAY)

A compassionless (*Tiferet*-less) attitude will prevent you from connecting (*Yesod*-less) with other people and really helping them grow through your teachings. Be aware of how your improved attitude will vastly transform and increase the impact of what you are saying and how other people hear and process your words.

QUESTIONS FOR MEDITATION

RELATIONSHIPS:

- Where are my relationships out of balance and how can I restore this through getting more deeply connected to the other person?
- How can I be more compassionate so that it strengthens the bonds in my relationships?
- How can I improve the connection with someone else through increased compassion?

YOGA/BODY/GYM:

- Where are things out of balance in my business and how can I restore balance in a way that brings us closer and strengthens our bond?
- Where are things out of balance in my body? Where am I suffering as a result? Am I exercising too much or too little, eating too much non-nutritious food or being too austere with my diet? Can I restore this balance (*Tiferet*) while staying completely grounded and rooted in my foundation?[71] (If you are stuck try visualising the Divine flow of *Yesod*-Grounding through your body, and use that energy to help you get back into balance?)

MIND:

- Where are my thoughts out of balance? Am I judging myself too harshly? How can I achieve the middle way? Can I get my thinking back into balance with a sense of deep bonding to myself

---

71 Foundation/Grounding/Rooting are other aspects of *Yesod* that we are exploring elsewhere in this book.

and my soul and the Divine? Can I connect to God within me and the higher flow of *Yesod*-Grounding and use this to get my thoughts back into balance?

BUSINESS:

- Where are things out of balance in my business and how can I restore balance in a way that truly connects and bonds to others?
- Where is there some injustice in my business, and how can I heal this through being more connected to the goal and mission, and being more grounded?

ADDITIONAL KABBALAH

Yesod in Tiferet connects the Joseph aspects of Jacob. When Joseph sends messages from Egypt up to his father Jacob in Canaan, that can be seen as the story of these two *sefirot*, as if the Divine Spheres are being acted out: *"And to his father [Jacob], he [Joseph] sent in like manner ten asses laden with the good things of Egypt, and ten she-asses laden with corn and bread and victuals for his father by the way"* (Genesis 45:23). A simple Kabbalistic reading would be that the two sets of ten asses being sent upwards represent two complete sets of fully-rectified *sefirot*, masculine and feminine, being elevated from the pit of Egypt to the heights of Israel. In other words, Joseph had achieved a sense of perfection in that moment. This, however, is my personal interpretation.

On a practical level, *Yesod* is the sexual energy, because the sefirah 'resides' in the reproductive organs. So when the sexual energy is raised upwards towards the heart-centre (*Tiferet* is the trunk of the body), this is another version of the same story. If sexual energy is kept at a root level -e.g. it is purely for pleasure and not being used for spiritual purposes such as to raise you and your partners' consciousness or to bring holy children into the world -in those cases, *Yesod* is not being raised up. A non-sexual version of this is as follows; are we keeping all of our relationships and conversations (*Yesod*) at a self-serving level (e.g. talking about the weather or gossiping for the sake of it) or are we using them to increase our compassion and bring more justice and healing into the world (*Tiferet*).

A specific Biblical passage where we might learn more about *Yesod* in *Tiferet* is when Jacob is manipulating the reproductive patterns of Laban's sheep, causing some to be spotted and some to be speckled[72].

GYM SEQUENCE, DAY 20/SIT-UPS

3 x 8 repetitions

.01

תפארת יסוד
Yesod-Bonding *Tiferet*-Balance

.02

---

[72] Genesis 30:37-43.

YOGA SEQUENCE, DAY 20/BACKBEND (URDHVA DHANURASANA)

Take care as you raise yourself into the classic Wheel posture, and aim to bring your chest above your hands. For advanced practitioners, begin in standing pose, raise your hands and drop back into the Wheel before raising yourself back to standing without touching the ground. Try 10 drop-backs and return to standing position.

תפארת
Tiferet-Balance

יסוד
Yesod-Bonding

DAY 21 / **NOBILITY IN COMPASSION** / RAISE YOUR GAME:
מלכות שבתפארת

KABBALAH SUTA: *Malchut She b'Tiferet*– Nobility/Mastery in Compassion.
INTENTION: To elevate ourselves, become centred and find the perfect balance in all areas of our life. Gain control and command over our emotions.

"Everyone has the right to a standard of living adequate for the health and well-being of himself and of his family, including food, clothing, housing and medical care and necessary social services, and the right to security in the event of unemployment, sickness, disability, widowhood, old age or other lack of livelihood in circumstances beyond his control."

The United Nations Declarations of Human Rights[73]

At this point in human evolution you may think we could have mastered compassion, using the resources at our disposal to solve hunger and poverty in the world. Once a year Jewish communities read the portion of the prophet Isaiah that questions religious ritual that is not explicitly directed towards improving the world around us:

> *"Is such the fast that I have chosen? The day for a man to afflict his soul? Is it to bow down his head as a bullrush, and to spread sackcloth and ashes under him? Wilt thou call this a fast, and an acceptable day to the LORD?..Is it not to deal thy bread to the hungry, and that thou bring the poor that are cast out to thy house? when thou seest the naked, that thou cover him, and that thou hide not thyself from thine own flesh? Then shall thy light break forth as the morning, and thy healing shall spring forth speedily; and thy righteousness shall go before thee, the glory of the LORD shall be thy reward"*[74].

---

73   The United Nations Declarations of Human Rights, 25:1 (10 December 1948).
74   Isaiah 58:6-8.

Malchut-mastery in *Tiferet*-compassion demands us to fight for balance and justice, using all of our resources to do it. These qualities are on the centre line in the "Tree of Life" (*Etz Chaim*) diagrams because they relate to us becoming thoroughly grounded and centred. The famed 20th Century Kabbalist Rabbi Yehuda Ashlag explained how these qualities relate to the 'lowest' two spiritual realms that directly affect our plane of existence[75]. He asks: is there more we can do to become compassionate, mastering every aspect of our being: using love (*Chesed*), discipline (*Gevurah*), compassion (*Tiferet*), endurance (*Netzach*), gratitude (*Hod*) and bonding (*Yesod*)? Are we leaving the world better than we found it? What do we need to do to restore, rebalance, retune and repair this Divine Sphere?

The New Age teaches the power of setting intentions, but that is not enough without action. The purpose of this realm of existence is to effect positive change. Theosophers ask why our souls need to be born into a physical plane at all, and the Kabbalistic model teaches that we can affect the highest realms of spiritual reality through actions in this world. Every *mitzvah* (good deed/commandment) has a spiritual impact. Dead people can no longer do this work, but we can do the work for them to elevate their souls. Conversely, because it is so incredibly easy to get lost in the ecstatic delights of the spiritual realms, there are many warnings for seekers to go slow with their Kabbalistic exploration.

REGAINING OUR CENTRE

Martial arts teaches the importance of being able to keep your centre, as opposed to giving it away if somebody knocks you over. This principle is true in all aspects of our lives, such as when somebody says a comment that can throw us "off-centre". In my early years as a playwright and actor, I would give away my centre far too easily, listening to the feedback and critiques of anybody who offered them. This had a significant effect at times, once causing me to completely

---

75 Chapters 47-48 of Rabbi Ashlag's Introduction to the Zohar, as quoted in A Tapestry for the Soul: The Introduction to the Zohar by Rabbi Yehudah Lev Ashlag, compiled by Yedidah Cohen.

stop performing a play rather than taking the feedback in my stride and go back to the rehearsal process to workshop various improvements. We all do this at times, giving away our centre and allowing others to direct our thinking.

There is a powerful energetic quality to somebody who is deeply confident and it is noticeable when they step into a room. The deeply balanced soul knows when to give (*Chesed*), when to hold back (*Gevurah*), when to be forthright (*Netzach*), when to be humble (*Hod*), when to get more connected and *shmooze* (*Yesod*) and when to step into a leadership position (*Malchut*) - "*in a place where there is no leader, strive to be a leader*" [76].

When Jacob is preparing to finally leave the home of his father-in-law Laban with his new family and newly-amassed wealth in tow, he calmly explains to his wives Rachel and Leah: "*I see your father's countenance, that is not toward me as before; but the God of my father has been with me. And you know that with all my power I served your father*" [77]. These are the words of a man who has full confidence in his position, knows who he is and is willing to stand for his beliefs.

HOW CENTRED ARE YOU?

How often do we stand for our beliefs? Can we do the same in our lives, and look ourselves in the mirror at the end of the day knowing that we have aligned our thoughts, speech and action, and that we are living in our full power.

NOBLE COMPASSION & THE GIFT OF DIGNITY

This work of repairing each of the Divine Spheres is intended to lead us to live with regality and nobility (*Malchut*). In the spiritual realm we are not connecting financial success with spiritual success, so being noble does not have any connection to the numbers in your bank account. Rather it is measured by your self-confidence, self-control, ability for balance and justice and kindness to others.

---

76   Ethics of the Fathers/Pirkei Avot 2:5.
77   Genesis 31:5-6.

There are two aspects to this, firstly the nobility with which we bring to our compassionate behaviour, and secondly, enabling other people to maintain or regain their own sense of self-worth. We learn this from the Biblical phrase that "*You shall certainly pledge sufficient for his need, that which is lacking for him*"[78]. The sages explain that if somebody has fallen on hard times, we are encouraged to help them such that they can maintain the standard of living they were at before if they were used to two meals of soup a day then we should try and ensure they have these two meals. If they were used to riding on a horse and having a servant run before them, we should try to help them regain that level of financial security: "*It is related of Hillel the Elder that, for a certain poor man who was of good family, he hired a horse to ride on and a slave to run before him. Once, when he could not find a slave to run before the man, he himself ran before him a distance of three mil*"[79].

In our world of abundance there are still people dying of starvation every day, even though the United Nations declaration of human rights declares that every individual has the right to food, shelter, clothing, sanitation, social security and medical care. The UN charter states the importance of "inherent dignity" and how it is the "*the foundation of freedom, justice and peace in the world*"[80]. This dignity is one aspect of *Malchut*-nobility in *Tiferet*-compassion as we confer human nobility and dignity upon another person.

The sages had a powerful vision which was truly remarkable for an age when many of them would have had personal glimpses of slavery and extreme violence at the hands of the Roman Empire. It is not enough to help someone out according to our own judgement (e.g. I will give my homeless friend a space on my couch for the night), it is not enough to give them resources according to their own request (e.g. 'don't worry about me – I will sleep on your floor'), but we have to closely consider somebody's dignity and be compassionate enough to help them restore their lost status.

---

78   Deuteronomy 15:8.
79   Babylonian Talmud, Ketubot 67b.
80   "Preamble" to UN Declaration of Human Rights.

When do you have the opportunity to give the gift of restored nobility through your compassion? Elderly relatives are sometimes in the need of 'dignity restoration' when they have long-since retired and been deemed useless by society with nobody interested in their help or advice. By spending some time listening to their stories, asking a few questions -regardless of whether you want to hear the answers – you can give an incredible gift to someone by enabling them to feel worthy, needed and important. More often than not it will result in a humbling experience, and I usually find that when this happens I deeply listen.

The *Tikkunei HaZohar* explains that the energy of *Malchut*-Nobility is communicated through the hands, feet, mouth because these are the parts of the body that relate to other people. On a literal level we'll be looking at how the hands and feet (home of *Malchut*) can be used to open the heart space[81] (*Tiferet*). As we've seen earlier, *Tiferet* is also about balance and harmony, so we will see how we can use our hands and feet to bring both harmony and compassion to ourselves and also to other people.

TODAY'S PRACTICE

YOGA PRACTICE GUIDELINES:

Approach your practice with noble compassion. Respect your body and focus on your potential, moving through limitations with a powerful breath and elevating your physical practice to a new level. This is the final day of the *Tiferet* week, and a chance to incorporate all of the lessons of the week as you graduate to the next stage of the practice. As you take your yoga practice into the rest of your day, maintain the *Tiferet*-balance achieved in your posture, and be aware of opportunities

---

[81] Technically, the heart is directly connected to the Sefirah/Divine Sphere of *Binah*-understanding (*"Binah-Liba"* says the Tikkunei Zohar, "the Heart is understanding"), but I am translating Tiferet as *heart*-space because *Tiferet* is located in the trunk of the body, which houses the heart. Also, if we were going to really start getting pedantic about this, each *Sefirah* contains all of the other *sefirot* (the concept of *Partzuf*, which is not discussed in this book). The focus of this work is to help us rectify, repair, replenish and re-vivify our lives, so whilst the academic nuances are important for authenticity, my focus is on the energetic working principles behind each of these ideas and how we can directly apply them to improve our lives and world.

to help other people regain balance in their lives, with *Malchut*-dignity and compassion.

GYM PRACTICE GUIDELINES:

Bring awareness to your hands and feet and everything they are doing during your workout. Whether you are running on a cardio machine, lifting weights or pulling a resistance band, use these limbs to bring balance to your mind and body. Notice what your body needs today -perhaps more cardio or more weights -and take appropriate action to bring yourself into a finely-tuned balance.

QUESTIONS FOR MEDITATION

RELATIONSHIPS:
- Where am I not in control of my compassion?
- Where do I lack emotional balance and how can I get a handle on this?
- Can I make my speech and words more compassionate? (Speech as a tool of *Malchut*-nobility).
- Where are my relationships out of balance and how can I restore this through an extra compassion?

BODY/GYM/YOGA:
- Where are things out of balance in my body? Where am I suffering as a result? Am I exercising too much or too little, eating too much non-nutritious food or being too austere with my diet? Can I restore this balance (*Tiferet*-compassion) with a deep sense of *Malchut*-mastery? (If you are stuck try visualising the Divine flow of *Malchut*-mastery through your body, and use that energy to help you get back into balance?)
- How might I master my body?
- How can I regain control of my eating habits? Which foods do I currently have that push me out of balance?

MIND:

-   Where are my thoughts out of balance? Am I judging myself too harshly? How can I achieve the middle way? Can I get my thinking back into balance with a sense of deep compassion for myself as an emanation of the Divine? Can I connect to God within me and the higher flow of *Malchut*-Mastery and use this to get my thoughts back into balance?
-   Where have I not mastered compassion? What is the cost?

LEADERSHIP:

-   Where is my leadership challenged through a lack of compassion?

BUSINESS:

-   How can I be more compassionate towards my clients?
-   How can I act with greater compassion when I conduct meetings?
-   How might more compassion and balance improve my career?
-   Where are things out of balance in my business and how can I restore balance by mastering all the different elements (doing this in a way that is loving, disciplined, compassionate, enduring, humble and with the intention of bonding)?
-   Where is there some injustice in my business and how can I heal this through being a stronger leader?
-   Where are things out of balance in my business and how can I restore balance by mastering all the different elements (doing this in a way that is loving, disciplined, compassionate, enduring, humble and with the intention of bonding)?

GYM SEQUENCE, DAY 21/PLANK

Push your forearms into the ground, keep your body straight and maintain your breath. 3 x 45 seconds or until you are exhausted.

מלכות
Malchut-Kingship

תפארת
Tiferet-Balance

מלכות
Malchut-Kingship

YOGA SEQUENCE, DAY 21/EASY (SUKHASANA)

Modify your position as needed so that you may comfortably remain in the pose.

תפארת
Tiferet-Balance

מלכות
Malchut-Kingship

מלכות
Malchut-Kingship

מלכות
Malchut-Kingship

NETZACH נצח

ENDURANCE

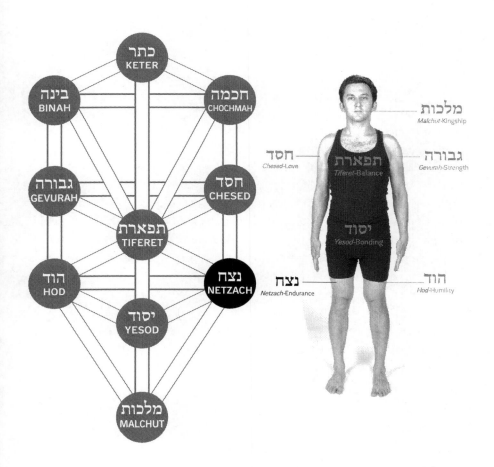

WEEK 4

NETZACH INTRODUCTION: THE BIRTH OF AMBITION נצח

"The moment we begin to fear the opinions of others and hesitate to tell the truth that is in us, and from motives of policy are silent when we should speak, the divine floods of light and life no longer flow into our souls."

Elizabeth Cady Stanton

"Got my first real six-string/Bought it at the five and dime /Played it 'till my fingers bled/ Was the summer of sixty-nine..." — Bryan Adams

Netzach-Endurance is where the rubber meets the road. There are areas of our life where we give up too easily and allow things to be derailed whether these are our relationships, work projects, creative endeavours or life goals. It asks "where do I lose confidence and not follow through?". We can think of *Netzach* as 'flow'. It is a *Sefirah* of action. Where the previous three qualities were located in the upper body - Right arm (*Chesed*-Love), left arm (*Gevurah*-discipline) and torso (*Tiferet*-balance), *Netzach*-endurance is connected with the right hip and leg, as this is the part of the body that drives us forwards. Other translations of *Netzach* include sustainability, fortitude and ambition, or to prevail, to be enduring, to be victorious.[1]

THE WAY OF MOSES

Netzach-endurance is the way of Moses, who epitomised this Divine quality, and repeatedly demonstrated the opposite side of this quality, showing us how to endure when we are overloaded with self-doubt.

At every given opportunity, Moses resisted his mission to lead a people to freedom; "Moses replied to God, *"Please my Lord, I am not a man of words...for I am heavy of mouth and heavy of speech"*. Then God said to him, *"Who gave man a mouth, or who makes one mute or deaf, or sighted or blind? Is it not I, Hashem? So now, go! I shall be with your mouth and teach you*

---

[1] Lessons in Tanya, Vol. 4, Epistle 15, Footnote 40.

what you should say"[2]. In some ways Moses represents an archetype; the part of us that is called to fulfil a mission that we might find scary or overwhelming, but he is able to go ahead nonetheless. He does this by tapping into the Divine power within.

Reverend Dr Martin Luther King was said to be nervous when he began his career preaching before communities, and overcame this *"by putting God in the foreground and Martin Luther King in the background"*[3]. By tuning in to our bigger, Divine mission and not making it about ourselves, we are able to increase confidence through connecting with a higher source.

BE YOUR OWN HERO

Every hero begins their mission by trying to avoid it. In his landmark book *The Hero with a Thousand Faces*, Joseph Campbell analysed the path of mythical heroes. He found that every action figure from Odysseus through to Superman has a story that follows specific points on a cycle. George Lucas famously quoted this as part of his inspiration for *Star Wars* with Luke Skywalker initially resisting his calling. We do the same in many areas of our life, and the focus of *Netzach*-Endurance is healing this spiritual-emotional character-flaw to achieve more in our life. A key part of the hero's journey comes when he or she faces a huge obstacle and considers giving up but overcomes it. He may feel "I am not worthy", whether it is Moses, Luke Skywalker or Neo in *The Matrix*, but even with this sense of humility, the true heroes accept their calling, endure through difficulties and overcome. The people who have enduring success in business and life are those who maintain this humble attitude right through to the end of their journey, although some succumb to an inevitable arrogance that grows as they become more confident in their ability.

FATHER TO SON

The Tanya discusses this in the context of a father teaching his son, and seeing *Netzach*-endurance as part of the flow from father to child; *"the*

---

2   Exodus 4:10-12.
3   I heard this anecdote from my teacher Eric Sander Kingston.

category of Netzach [endurance] also comprises prevailing and standing up against anything, from within or from without, that withholds from his son the transmission of beneficial influence or learning". We can extend this to all the areas of our life where we are blocked in our flow, trying to transmit something, be it an idea, a project, a communication. It goes on to discuss how ultimately this quality taps into our connection with the Higher realms, *"Likewise, by exercising the attribute of Netzach, [a man seeks] to prevail triumphantly against anything that would restrain [him] from the service of God and from cleaving unto Him"*[4].

YOGIC FIRE

The early yogic texts referred to the quality of *tapas* - fire - which we can apply in a yogic practice as we endure and build up heat within the body. This is very similar to *Netzach*, as we find the 'fire in our belly' that helps us drive projects through to completion.

SUSTAINABILITY

We can also think of *Netzach* as "sustainability", applied to relationships when divorce-rates are soaring, or applied to businesses when people's financial health is suffering. Here is a simple overview of how we might apply the *Netzach* model.

SUSTAINABILITY *(NETZACH)* IN BUSINESS
e.g. How can I keep growing my business and expanding my client-base using the following qualities?

SUSTAINABLE BUSINESS THROUGH:
- LOVE (*Chesed*)
- DISCIPLINE (*Gevurah*)
- COMPASSION (*Tiferet*)
- ENDURANCE (*Netzach*)
- HUMILITY (*Hod*)
- BONDING (*Yesod*)
- MASTERY (*Malchut*)

---

4   Lessons in Tanya, Epistle Vol. 4, Epistle 15.

SUSTAINABILITY (*NETZACH*) IN RELATIONSHIPS

e.g. How can I make my relationships stronger and last longer by using the following qualities?

SUSTAINABLE RELATIONSHIPS THROUGH
- LOVE (*Chesed*)
- DISCIPLINE (*Gevurah*)
- COMPASSION (*Tiferet*)
- ENDURANCE (*Netzach*)
- HUMILITY (*Hod*)
- BONDING (*Yesod*)
- MASTERY (*Malchut*)

SUSTAINABILITY *(NETZACH)* IN MY ATTITUDE & THINKING

e.g. How can I transform my attitude so that I hold a different vibrational resonance (think Law of Attraction) and become the person I would like to be?

SUSTAINABLE POSITIVE ATTITUDE THROUGH
- LOVE (*Chesed*)
- DISCIPLINE (*Gevurah*)
- COMPASSION (*Tiferet*)
- ENDURANCE (*Netzach*)
- HUMILITY (*Hod*)
- BONDING (*Yesod*)
- MASTERY (*Malchut*)

SUSTAINING YOUR BIG GOALS AND PURSUING YOUR VISION

e.g. What is the cost of giving up too easily on your goals? Where are you carrying regret for not following-through on a project or vision? How can you rectify this through the different aspects of increased *Netzach*-endurance?

ENDURING WITH THE PURSUIT OF YOUR VISION THROUGH

- LOVE (*Chesed*)
- DISCIPLINE (*Gevurah*)
- COMPASSION (*Tiferet*)
- ENDURANCE (*Netzach)*
- HUMILITY (*Hod*)
- BONDING (*Yesod*)
- MASTERY (*Malchut*

AN INTERSTITIAL DISCLAIMER!

There are cases where we can carry out all of the right actions but things still do not work our way. Earlier we saw the words of Rabbi Shneur Zalman of Liadi (in *The Tanya*) who wrote that *Netzach*-endurance demands *"standing up against anything, from within or from without"*. He was referring to both internal resistance and also external resistance which could be physical or spiritual forces. Ultimately this work demands both physical action but also a spiritual component of prayer, holding healthy intentions and removing the negative energies (*"kelipot"*) that might stand in our way.

INNER CONFIDENCE

Our inner game is as important as our outer actions. There are times when we state a certain intention, such as to launch a project, but our inner thoughts are so full of self-judgement that we prevent ourselves from getting there. A contemporary Kabbalah expert, Rabbi Yitzhak Ginsburg, teaches that *"The spiritual state..corresponding to the sefirah of Netzach is that of 'bitachon' (confidence)"*[5]. This kind of confidence is deceptively simple. It is not a case of putting on the *Rocky* theme tune and going for a run, but finding our confidence day after day, especially when we face criticism, doubts, fears and all of the blockages that stop most people.

---

[5]   See the essay on *Netzach* at Rabbi Ginsburgh's website, http://www.inner.org/sefirot.

INTRODUCTION: THE BIRTH OF AMBITION

START TO FINISH

Netzach-endurance is seeing a project through from start to finish. The world is full of people who have started a 'race' of sorts and given up, whether it is half-finished manuscripts, businesses that were closed when the going got tough, or, tragically, parents who found the pressure too great and neglected or abandoned their own children.

YOUR HIGHER BODY TOUCHES GROUND

How do you know if you are successfully channelling Netzach? When you are in a state of positive action. The word *Netzach* occurs at the beginning of many of the Psalms (*lam'natzeach*), and means "to conduct" or "orchestrate". The first three *sefirot* are located in the upper body - both the upper physical body and the upper 'spiritual body' - whereas *Netzach* has a very grounded energy because our legs touch the ground when we walk. *"Its consciousness is pragmatic by nature, as reflected in its correspondence to the right leg, which is the first limb of the supernal body to "touch ground"*, teaches Rabbi Ginsburg[6].

GETTING INTO FLOW

Dysfunctional *Netzach-endurance* is all about actively pushing rather than passively allowing. *Netzach* is also those times when we are in flow and we just forget ourselves, living in a state of pure being. It is walking the walk. Moving forwards. A forward motion. *Netzach* is Just Doing it.

THE YOGA OF *NETZACH*

From a yogic perspective we can think of *Netzach*-endurance as breaking down the ego through continually working at the body and nullifying our desire. Patanjali wrote that *"this discipline is practiced for the purpose of acquiring fixity of the mind on the Lord, free from all impurities and agitations, or on one's own reality, and for attenuating afflictions. The five afflictions are ignorance, egoism, attachment, aversion and the desire to cling to life"*. The story of Rabbi Akiva's journey to become a great teacher at the age of 40 is the tale of how one man managed to

---

6   http://www.inner.org/sefirot/sefnetz.htm

overcome his limitations, transforming himself from a shepherd into the most prominent rabbi of his generation.

SURRENDER & SACRIFICE

The idea of sacrifices features very heavily in Biblical worship and a key idea behind them is that by relinquishing and burning something valuable to you (e.g. a cow, which was relatively expensive), the worshipper was able to nullify their ego, e.g. the part of them that was focused on wealth and material pleasures. A sacrifice was, and is, about finding a way to elevate yourself to a more spiritual plane through reducing reliance on physical items.

Netzach is holding beliefs and ambitions and pursuing them especially when there is a cost to pay. We can understand it as practicing your golf swing until long after dark, rehearsing piano scales until your hands are sore, waking bleary-eyed to meditate with the sunrise or conscientiously crafting your novel until the thing is written. Through enduring ambition and the diligence to continue applying that ambition, we have the power to overcome our desires, 'burn up' the weaker version of ourselves, and rise, Phoenix-like, from the ashes of our nullified desire. Ambition is one thing but having the diligence to achieve it is another, and repetition is the mother of all skill.

NETZACH RELATIONSHIP MEDITATIONS

-   Where do I give up too easily in relationships? (e.g. dysfunctional *Netzach*-Endurance). How can I heal this through being more loving (*Chesed*) on an enduring basis?

-   Where do I give up too easily in relationships? (e.g. dysfunctional *Netzach*-Endurance). How can I heal this through being more disciplined (*Gevurah*) and keeping it up?

-   Where do I give up too easily in relationships? (e.g. dysfunctional *Netzach*-Endurance). How can I heal this through being more compassionate (*Tiferet*) on a regular basis?

- Where do I give up too easily in relationships? (e.g. dysfunctional *Netzach*-Endurance). How can I heal this through being more enduring? (*Netzach*)

- Where do I give up too easily in relationships? (e.g. dysfunctional *Netzach*-Endurance). How can I heal this through being more humble in my approach and outlook? (*Hod*)

- Where do I give up too easily in relationships? (e.g. dysfunctional *Netzach*-Endurance). How can I heal this through being more grounded and connected to the other person? (*Hod*)

- Where do I give up too easily in relationships? (e.g. dysfunctional *Netzach*-Endurance). How can I heal this through being more humble in my approach and outlook? (*Hod*)

- Where do I give up too easily in relationships? (e.g. dysfunctional *Netzach*-Endurance). How can I heal this through my speech and actions? (*Malchut*)

ILLUSTRATIONS OF THE PRINCIPLES IN ACTION

Here are some solid examples of how these principles might show up in different situations, for better or for worse:

NETZACH-ENDURANCE IN RELATIONSHIPS:

1. "I love you! Let's get married forever! Long-term commitment (*Chesed*-Love in *Netzach*-endurance)

2. "You drive me crazy! I've had enough and want to sleep around and not have these restrictions! (needs *Gevurah*-discipline in this *Netzach*-endurance..)

3. "I am doing this because I feel committed, but not because I'm feeling the love much. I don't like you that much right now, I'm blaming you and you should make me feel better!" (needs *Tiferet*-compassion in this *Netzach* long-term relationship)

4. "Seven-Year Itch! We are in a routine! We are bored! Where are we now?" (needs *Netzach*-endurance in this long-term *Netzach*-enduring relationship..)

5. "Life is amazing. I need nobody. It's all about me. So what if we've grown apart? We can lead separate lives under the same roof. We will make it work! For the kids! For our security!" (may need some *Hod*-humility in this *Netzach*-endurance. Get into Gratitude and Humility.)

6. "We are not feeling connected and our relationship is on the rocks, so LET'S MAKE A BABY!!!" (er..no...find better ways to connect. Get some *yesod*-connection in your Netzach...)

7. "We have a Masterful Relationship. We have corrected each of the imbalances - the love, discipline, compassion, endurance, humility and connectivity. We are Masters of Love" (this would be a positive expression of *Malchut*-mastery in *Netzach*-endurance).

GIVING CHARITY (*TZEDAKAH*) THE *NETZACH* WAY.

There are times when we would like to give money to charity but face internal blocks, whether it is feeling a lack of abundance or facing other obstacles that stand in our way. Here is an example of how we might use the *Netzach* model to in this situation.

1. Connect to the recipient through love (*Chesed*). Consider how you are the recipient of Divine love and how you can pass this on.

2. If I am feeling a lack of abundance and there isn't much money in my wallet, where can I find some strength (*Gevurah*)?

3. If I am not feeling compassion for poor people, or flip between feelings of abundance (*Chesed*) and Lack (*Gevurah*), how can I find some emotional stability? (*Tiferet*)

4. What happens if I am ready to give, but I am tired and my energy is waning? Time to double my endurance (*Netzach*). Keep going: I am nearly there.

5. In the act of giving, can I stay humble (*Hod*) or am I seeking recognition? Am I look for applause or can I have humility towards God who gave me the resources in the first place?

6. I may be giving a lot but am I connected to the recipient? (*Yesod*)

7. Can I master all of these elements and give with nobility? (*Malchut*)

CREATING A CLIENT PROJECT THE *NETZACH* WAY, E.G. BUILDING A WEBSITE

1. Connect with the love and a spirit of abundance (*Chesed*). Why am I doing it? What is my ultimate love/concern? (e.g. I love my family so am earning money to raise them. Or to serve God. Or to be of contribution. Or because I believe in my client's bigger vision. Or because I believe in my company's vision (e.g. elegant design, powerful communications etc.). What is your company's mission statement? What are you standing for? Why are you in this? Know your 'why'.

2. I need to set boundaries (*Gevurah*) and be strong at times, to negotiate well, to hold back from saying some things. I need to be disciplined, to keep to deadlines.

3. Where am I not compassionate to myself or to my client? Or where am I going crazy with my energy and not staying in balance? (*Tiferet*).

4. It is pm and I want to go to bed. But my client is awake in London, my web developer is working in Pakistan - I WILL DRIVE THROUGH!!! (*Netzach*)

5. I am King of the World! I don't make mistakes! I am a Rocket-Ship! (*Hod* - Pride comes before a fall..)

6. I have nailed everything, put a lot of work into this website, but somehow the client is withdrawing from me. Aren't they happy with what I have done? Can't they see all of the hours and great work I have put into this project? (*Yesod* - get connected to the needs of others, and stay connected to their needs)

7. I need to master this project, to walk with nobility, to balance this in all of its aspects (*Malchut*).

DAY 22 / LOVINGKINDNESS IN ENDURANCE / 7-YEAR ITCH
חסד שבנצח

KABBALAH SUTRA: *Chesed She b'Netzach* – Lovingkindess in Endurance.
INTENTION: Maintaining your passion over the long term. Making your love sustainable. To achieving deeply-held ambitions and goals through enduring lovingkindness. To open channels of energy through repeated, boundless giving.

Only Ahava Rabbah (transcendent love), which is love beyond reason and logic, is capable of transforming the essence of the animal soul"

The Rebbe Rashab

People abandon their goals every day, whether it is a new diet, writing a book or launching the business they have dreamt of. When we feel like giving up on a project, it is the strength of our intention that will keep us focused. Arnold Schwarzenegger talked about how he stayed disciplined when training for the Mr. Universe contest and the other bodybuilding championships that he eventually won[7]. It was the power of his intention and staying very clear on the image of what it would look like when he was standing on the winner's podium. He focused on the sense of joy and positive feelings when the goal had been accomplished, which helped him during those times when he did not feel like going to the gym.

LONG-TERM GOALS

Chesed-Love in *Netzach*-Endurance sets the stage for our long-term goals. When we can feel love, creativity and enjoyment to our actions, it will help us sustain our motion even when things get challenging. The Kabbalistic principle that *"the end is rooted in the beginning"*[8] is especially true here. Without love for our goal, our focus can wane. The diet may

---

7   Interview: "Tim Ferris Interviews Arnold Schwarzenegger on Psychological Warfare" http://fourhourworkweek.com/2015/02/02/arnold-schwarzenegger/
8   *"Sof Ma'aseh B'Machshava Tehillah"* as found in the song *Lecha Dodi*, that is sung as part of the Friday night Shabbat service.

well get abandoned unless you can clearly see yourself having met your body goal, and the creative project can get left to by the wayside.

LOVE IN REGULAR DOSES

Relationships suffer without regular expressions of love, whether it is telling your partner you love them, or making those small gestures of love (like taking out the garbage). For a parent to a child it is the parent showing up regularly and being there on a consistent basis. The 1980s brought us the conversation around 'quality time' for families, but the real question came around 'quantity time'. Whilst it is important for a parent to be there at their child's birthday party, their presence is also appreciated on a regular basis for the less glamorous events (dinners, bedtime stories, bath times). Love (*Chesed*) in Regular Doses (*Netzach*) is an essential for any healthy relationship.

CREATIVITY IN REGULAR DOSES

So too with creativity, another expression of *Chesed* is in the sense that it is creativity-in-action. Having the creative thought is not enough - that is the realm of *Chochma*-wisdom and *Binah*-understanding, the ethereal head-based *sefirot* that we are not exploring in this book. Creativity (*Chesed*) in Regular Doses (*Netzach*) looks like the output of the bestselling author Stephen King who said that *"I like to get ten pages a day, which amounts to 2,000 words. That's 180,000 words over a three-month span, a goodish length for a book — something in which the reader can get happily lost in, if the tale is done well and stays fresh"*[9]. The key is to find the rhythm that works for you, but *a* rhythm is essential, whatever it is.

ABUNDANT THINKING IN REGULAR DOSES

The New Age mantras of positive thinking are not enough when they are interspersed with regular negative thinking. The Tikkunei Zohar talks of prayer as being akin to warfare[10] and this is akin to our inner experience of battling negative thoughts. Each of our thoughts has a tangible reality on a spiritual plane, which is why it is so essential to clarify our thinking and keep it pure and focused

---

9   From *On Writing: A Memoir of the Craft.*
10   Tikkunei HaZohar, Tikkun 21.

LOVE YOUR GOALS

The highest expression of *Chesed*-love is on a spiritual level, as we experience pure, overwhelming love, *Ahavah Rabbah*, from the Source of creation. In doing so we can refine our soul and raise our consciousness. Rabbi Sholom DovBer Schneerson, the "Rebbe Rashab" (1860-1920) wrote: "Only *Ahava Rabbah* ("transcendent love"), which is love beyond reason and logic, is capable of transforming the essence of the animal soul"[11]. Our "animal soul" (*"Nefesh Behema"*) can be seen as the parts of ourselves that we are trying to tame, whether it is the drive to overeat, to over indulge, to be lazy and slothful, or to do anything which is not in our higher interests. On a very practical level, this is the part of us that stops us showing up lovingly in relationships out of a desire to be selfish, stops us from writing our books.

ENERGETIC CONSIDERATIONS

There is a serious energetic consideration that more people are becoming sensitive to. One question to ask is: Am I bringing a loving energy to my project? When driving forwards (*Netzach*) am I doing it with a good heart? As King David wrote: *"Who may ascend the mountain of God? Who may stand in His holy place? One with clean hands and a pure heart"*[12]. The opposite of this would be to drive a project forward with a sense of anger or frustration, or any sense of lack. It is certainly possible to just force yourself to do a project. I have certainly done this in the past, but the end results are very different to one which is motivated by love, or a positive motivation. This takes us back to our duality of love (*Chesed*) versus fear (*Gevurah*) - both can be used, but love will be more effective.

Consider when you have received a gift that was given because somebody loves you (*Chesed*), and when somebody has done you a favour because they feel they owe you and they have to do it but don't really want to (which would represent the energy of *Gevurah*). Which one feels better? The answer is obvious, and this is a consideration we would do well to incorporate into our actions.

---

[11]   Love Like Fire & Water (Kuntres Avodah) - A Guide to Jewish Meditation, Essays on the Service of the Heart, by the Rebbe Rashab, p155.

[12]   Psalm 24.

ONGOING GROWTH: BE THE TREE

There is a tree five feet from the window of my apartment and last year I was disappointed to see that the whole tree had been entirely stripped of its foliage. Within months the greenery had grown back stronger than ever. I was inspired watching its force unveil. Now there are several branches pushing up into my window, their leaves pushing through the glass slats and I have to start pruning it. This is *Chesed*-Creation[13] in *Netzach*-Endurance. The force of creativity is so overwhelming that it needs to be trimmed back or the branch provides a pathway for bugs to just walk straight into my apartment.

There is truth behind the hippy custom of hugging trees. The Torah teaches that *"man is a tree of the field"*[14] and we can ask how each of us are like a tree; where we can continue to give and continue to grow, despite apparent setbacks and the obstacles that life presents.

UNBRIDLED AMBITION

And so, for yet another translation of our concept: *Chesed*-Passion in *Netzach*-Ambition! *Netzach* might be seen as ambition in its grasp and reach for long-term growth. In this context, *Chesed* in *Netzach* is the aspect of ambition that is governed by lovingkindness. Unbridled ambition is like a wild animal. When it goes unchecked and unbalanced by considerations of lovingkindness, we see the mettle of political dictators, suicide bombers and chronic depressives. Similarly, parents who don't engage lovingkindness with endurance have the potential to put extreme pressure on their children so that they are forced to pursue goals that may not suit them and live a life that is chosen and often doesn't suit them.

How do you direct ambition when it comes to other people? Spouses, partners, colleagues, parents, children and friends are all subject to our expectations and judgement – the energy of fortuitous *Netzach*. Are you able to keep perspective and maintain your calm even when the people

---

13   I am translating *Chesed* as creation here, because creation and creativity is another aspect of Divine Lovingkindness. As God gives to the world and we give to each other, that is essentially a creative force.

14   Deuteronomy 20:19.

closest to you fall short of the behavioural standards that you would like them to keep?

LONG TERM LOVING

The idea of the "Seven Year Itch" became famous in Billy Wilder's 1955 film of the same name, starring Marilyn Monroe and Tom Ewell, and is apparently alive and strong today. *"The concept of the seven-year itch has been a widely accepted phenomenon. It is based on the belief that many couples start to get antsy and lose interest in their significant others around the seven-year mark"*[15]. Despite the aspersions of popular culture, the power of *Chesed*-Love in *Netzach*-Endurance is love for the long-term. Many lovers can proclaim "I love you! Let's get married forever!", but long-term commitment, *Chesed*-Love in *Netzach*-Eternity, takes effort and work.

✳✳✳

YOGIC AMBITIONS

This week's yoga practice is about holding a focus of *Netzach*–endurance that helps you blast through any exhaustion and keeps you determined and driven through the practice. Your body may well heat up, like small fires burning inside, and these flames can help you to keep going beyond the point when you would normally give up. Today we will balance a yoga of endurance with continual lovingkindness, keeping the face soft and maintaining a gentle and loving practice. There may seem to be an apparent contradiction between lovingkindess and endurance, as if they could cancel out one another. Surely you are pursuing driven ambition or you are being kind? Rather, the energy of *Chesed*-lovingkindness in *Netzach*-endurance is a more sophisticated energetic interplay, a more subtle type of ambition that is sensitive and aware.

If you find yourself becoming tired during the practice, bring your focus back to the breath. Keep going with the sequences and move beyond your mind that might be calling out for you to stop. Burn through and move beyond, but with an attitude of love.

---

[15]   Jennifer Nagy in The Huffington Post, 03/29/2013. http://www.huffingtonpost.com/jennifer-nagy/the-sevenyear-itch-fact-o_b_2443171.html

TODAY'S PRACTICE

YOGA PRACTICE GUIDELINES:

Pursue your practice with a sense of determination and endurance, but keep a soft heart and a sense of deep love the entire time. This might look like doing a longer practice than usual and testing your stamina (that is the *Netzach*-endurance element), but be kind to your body and maintain kind thoughts towards others (that is the *Chesed*-Lovingkindness element). Move into your practice with an attitude of gentle determination. Hold your focus throughout, work through fatigue and difficulty but be kind and benevolent when you reach the edge of your capability.

GYM PRACTICE GUIDELINES:

This week's focus is on building your endurance, be it cardio, weights or otherwise. Today focus on extending your stamina whilst staying connected to a source of Divine Love. There are two modes of operation here: fear and determination (*yirah*) and love. The highest form of love, *Ahavah-Rabba* (the "Great Love") connects us to the source of creation. Reflect again from the quote at the top of the page - *"Only Ahava Rabbah ("transcendent love"), which is love beyond reason and logic, is capable of transforming the essence of the animal soul"*[16].

QUESTIONS FOR MEDITATION

RELATIONSHIPS:

- Where do I fall short on enduring in a loving relationship? Where does my interest wane over time?
- Where do I need to put more effort into a relationship? Can I do it from a place of love (*Chesed*) rather than responsibility or resentment?

---

[16] Love Like Fire & Water (Kuntres Avodah) - A Guide to Jewish Meditation, Essays on the Service of the Heart, p155.

- Where do I give up too easily in relationships? Where do I make promises and not follow through? How would my relationships improve if I applied and lived these principles?
- Where do I give up too easily in relationships? (e.g. *dysfunctional* Netzach-Endurance). How can I contribute through being more loving (*Chesed*) on an enduring basis?
- Is my long-term relationship continuing with a sense of love or am I just staying out of routine?

YOGA/BODY/GYM:

- Where do I lack *Netzach*-endurance? Where do I give up too easily with my workouts or yoga practice?
- Where am I too forceful with my practice and how can I do undertake them in a state of joy and love?
- How do I behave towards the other people in my class, community or at the gym? Where can I be kinder to people on a regular basis?
- Where do I give up too easily with regards to my regular practices, whether it is yoga, the gym or meditation? How can I find a creative and loving solution to this? (*Chesed*)
- Is my long-term physical practice (yoga, gym, meditation) being carried out with a sense of love or am I just doing it out of routine? What about in my personal relationship, or my business?

GOALS & AMBITIONS:

- Can I stay loving when pursuing my long-term goal (e.g. The energy I am putting into writing a book, training for a marathon, staying happily married!)
- When driving or walking/moving forwards, am I doing it lovingly?
- Where am I not giving in the way I endure? Where am I pushing forwards from a place of lack or stinginess? (e.g. pushing someone without giving back, creating Karmic Debts)
- When I am pursuing an ambition, am I going crazy with it or am I maintaining a state of love?

BUSINESS:

- Where have I given up on my goals or long-term plans?
- Where have I blindly and ruthlessly pursued goals without consideration of how it will help and affect others?
- What can I do to make my business more sustainable? (this could be environmental sustainability, getting my cash-flow more regular and sustainable, or it could be maintaining the vision in my company or workplace). How can I do this through acts of creativity and love (*Chesed*)?

HOW TO CONNECT WITH A CLIENT OR PROJECT IN THE SPIRIT OF ENDURING LOVE:

Connect with the love and a spirit of abundance (*Chesed*). Why am I doing this project? What is my ultimate love/concern? (e.g. I love my family so I am doing this to earn money to raise them. Or I want to serve humanity through this sacred commerce. Or I want to serve God. Or I want to make a contribution to humanity. Or because I believe in my client's bigger vision. Or because I believe in my company's vision (e.g. elegant design, powerful communications etc.). What is your company's mission statement? What are you standing for? Why are you in this? Know your WHY.

BONUS SPIRITUAL PRACTICE: HELP SOMEONE ELSE WIN AT THE GAME OF LIFE:

Reflect on the one goal that truly matters to you today and take steps to pursue it whilst being ruthlessly loving. Help someone else along the route to pursuing their goal and remember that life isn't a zero-sum game where we can only win if someone else loses. Similarly, keep your standards high when interacting with friends and family but take a deep breath and remind yourself to be loving and kind when they fall short.

WHEN GIVING CHARITY (*TZEDAKAH*)

Connect to the recipient through love (*Chesed*). Consider how you are the recipient of Divine love and how you can pass this on.

GYM SEQUENCE, DAY 22/ALT ARM & LEG RAISES

Alternate arm and leg raises whilst maintaining your balance.

.01

נצח
Netzach-Endurance

חסד
Chesed-Love

.02

נצח
Netzach-Endurance

חסד
Chesed-Love

YOGA SEQUENCE, DAY 22/TRIANGLE (TRIKONASANA)

Revolve your torso towards the ceiling whilst keeping both legs straight.

.01

חסד
Chesed-Love

נצח
Netzach-Endurance

.02

DAY 23 / DISCIPLINE IN ENDURANCE / GETTING THINGS DONE / גבורה שבנצח

KABBALAH SUTRA: *Gevurah She b'Netzach*– Discipline in Endurance.
INTENTION: To transform situations and break bad habits through disciplined endurance.

"Inspiration without application is fantasy" — Anon.

The world is full of could-have beens. The *someday maybe* projects that never got finished. Ethereal Libraries replete with books that never got written, fantastical jukeboxes of never recorded. What were the important ideas in your life that you never brought to fruition? What do you regret? Most importantly, are you willing to do something about it?

Discipline (*Gevurah*) in Endurance (*Netzach*) is an essential factor in accomplishing goals. On a spiritual level, we are allowing the Divine flow to reach us and removing the blockages that stops Light from getting through. *"Netzach conquers the barriers between the outflow of Divine benevolence and its intended recipients"*[17] explained Rabbi Moshe Cordovero (1522-1570). Our aim is to increase our personal discipline so that we can get things done.

WHERE DO I LACK DISCIPLINE?

We must ask key questions to bring about change, primarily around where we lack enduring discipline, and *how* we are paying the price; the book that never gets written, the film that never gets made, weight that is never lost, or the relationship that never improves. The Marathon runner has the strength to go the distance and it is built through *Gevurah*-discipline in *Netzach*-endurance. A successful author does not wait for inspiration to strike but cultivates it on a daily basis.

---

17   Tomer Devorah introduction, x.

COMPLAINTS ARE THE ENEMY

Often we give up for really good reasons. Parents with young children, a day job that is tiring - there are *always* reasons. We can live from a place of excuses, or we can take action. The question is whether we will be happy at the age of 75 turning around and saying "I never wrote my book but at least I had a couple of extra hours of sleep"[18]. As one of my teachers wrote, *"There is no life without challenges, life may not be a game, but it is called a human RACE"*[19]. Life passes quickly. To kick-start the process, ask the simple question: *What are you trying to achieve and where are you giving up too easily?*

LASER FOCUS

Think back to a time when you were laser-focused on a task and generated results. This may have been a moment of desperation such as cramming for an exam, but if you can locate the memory or even imagine it, you can benefit from this power. *Gevurah* is the power of restraining and focusing your will.

The spiritual master Rabbi Akiva (1st Century) was a 39 year-old shepherd when he noticed a rock with water dripping into the centre, where it had hollowed out a bowl. "Amazing", he said to himself. *"If what is soft (water) can carve out a hard substance (the rock), how surely words of Torah/Spiritual Instruction which are as hard as iron will (eventually) penetrate my heart, which is flesh and blood"*[20]. He recognised the power of this small, consistent action, and at the age of 40 he changed profession, began studying to eventually become the spiritual leader of a generation with over 24,000 students at the height of his career. With a little discipline in endurance, anything is possible.

LEARN FROM YOUR TEACHERS

I have repeatedly seen feats of determination from my teachers that helps them apply this principle to set a powerful example. When my teacher Rabbi Chaim Brovender was living in London during the

---

18 Thanks to Eric Sander Kingston for this teaching.
19 In 'Mantras for Sustained Transformation & Attitude', dedicated to Marcus J Freed, in How Far to The Place of Enlightenment by Eric Sander Kingston, p12.
20 Avot De Rabbi Natan, 6:2.

1990s, he was rushed into hospital for minor surgery but insisted on giving his regular evening class soon after leaving - and that was only a couple of years after he had been driving through an Arab village in Israel and was physically attacked. When I was studying at Webber Douglas Academy of Dramatic Arts in London, my teacher Edward Clarke would routinely fly in from a weekend teaching and performing yoga in the United States, only to travel directly from Heathrow Airport to teach our 9 am Monday morning acting and movement class. My teacher Eric, mentioned earlier, will frequently write through the entire night, sometimes going for days on end with very little sleep in order to compose thousands of poems and songs. Everyone must find a rhythm that works best for them, but the key is to find a rhythm.

OVERCOMING MENTAL LIMITATIONS

So many of our limitations are psychological. The Yoga Sutras says that *"when the agitations of the mind are under control, the mind becomes like a transparent cog that has the power of becoming whatever form is presented"*[21]. By finding stillness and focus within our mind and exercising this sense of internal control, we can actually turn ourselves into clay, with the ability to mold our thoughts at will.

What are the physical habits you would like to break? As we move into the space of disciplined endurance, we begin to restrain and refrain from taking the easy route that stands in the way of our growth. This is the energetic quality of *Gevurah*; it is a word that means strength but is often applied in the context of constraints and boundaries. We learned that true strength is in overcoming one's natural desires, and this is especially true when it is carried out with endurance.

The process of personal spiritual refinement has been compared to the diamond-cutter who receives a rough piece of rock and has to work with care, skill and endurance to reveal the sparkling jewel within. Viewing our soul as the uncut diamond, the spiritual masters encourage us to gradually refine and reveal our true spiritual beauty, using the tools of ethical behaviour to do so.

---

[21] Yoga Sutras 1:41, Swamiji translation.

Most of us have some habit that we would like to break, whether it is nail-biting, smoking, overeating or even gossiping. Stage one is to notice the habit you want to overcome and the second stage is to choose a better habit to replace it with.

Choose your life goals with care. Set the discipline, apply yourself, break the habits that have been preventing you from achieving them up until this point, and the ambitions will be within your reach. Lasting changes can be yours for the taking.

TODAY'S PRACTICE

YOGA PRACTICE GUIDELINES:

Extend today's yoga practice so it lasts for longer than usual. This can be through taking slower breaths, extra breaths in a posture, or doing more postures. Focus on the qualities of *Gevurah*-strength in *Netzach*-endurance, burning through the voice that wants to take it easy and rest, and closely observe your results. There is no right or wrong, and you may find yourself energised or exhausted at the end. Either way, you will experience immense growth if you incorporate this transformative behaviour into your daily routine.

GYM PRACTICE GUIDELINES:

Develop your iron will. Set the boundaries (*Gevurah*) for what you want to achieve (*Netzach*), whether it is a 5-mile run, 40 repetitions lifting 20lb weights or staying on the treadmill for 30 minutes. The magnitude in itself is not important because it is all relative to where you are starting from (if running a half mile is more than you would usually do, then start with that). The principle is the most important; find the limits of your comfort zone and summon the internal will to push through those limits.

QUESTIONS FOR MEDITATION

RELATIONSHIPS:
- Where do you get weak about enforcing boundaries in relationships? Where have you said 'no' to something but you keep allowing it to happen? What is the cost to you?
- Where do you give up too easily in relationships? (Eg *dysfunctional* Netzach-Endurance). How can you heal this through being more disciplined (*Gevurah*) and keeping it up?

YOGA/BODY/GYM:
- Where have you set goals and not kept to them? Where have you let yourself down?
- Where do you give up too easily with regards to my regular practices, whether it is yoga, the gym or meditation? How can I be stronger and disciplined about my practice? (*Gevurah*)

BUSINESS:
- Where do you not go 'start to finish' on projects, beginning something and then not completing it? How does this impact yourself and your business?
- What can you do to make your business more sustainable? (This could be environmental sustainability, getting your cash-flow more regular and sustainable, or it could be maintaining the vision in your company or workplace). How can you do this through acts of strength and discipline (*Gevurah*)?

CREATIVE PROJECTS:
- What is a project that you have begun but not followed through and completed? What are your internal weak points that get you off track? (e.g. Perhaps someone made a critical comment and you stopped pursuing your passion)

AMBITION:

- What is the bigger ambition in your life? Where are you not being disciplined enough in your journey to pursue and achieve it? Where have you "let go of the reins"?

GYM SEQUENCE, DAY 23/RAISED LEG PUSH-UPS

Keep legs raised during push-ups and alternate. 3 x 10 repetitions.

.01

גבורה
Gevurah-Strength

נצח
Netzach-Endurance

.02

YOGA SEQUENCE, DAY 23/EXTENDED SIDE-ANGLE (UTTHITA PARSVAKONASANA)

Stretch your fingertips and outside blade of your straight-leg foot in the opposite direction, lengthening your side.

.01

גבורה
Gevurah-Strength

נצח
Netzach-Endurance

.02

DAY 24 / **COMPASSION IN ENDURANCE** / LOVING THE JOURNEY: תפארת שבנצח

KABBALAH SUTRA: *Tiferet She b'Netzah* – Balance in Endurance.
INTENTION: Bring about permanent change through committing to your spiritual growth. To restore balance to difficult partnerships and relationships through enduring compassion.

"Straighten up and fly right, straighten up and stay right, Straighten up and fly right, Cool down, papa, don't you blow your top" — Nat King Cole[22]

"Happy are they: the masters of the study house" — Tikkunei Zohar

In the quest for happiness, many aspire to develop their spirit. As we try to progress in life we can push forwards relentlessly, driving through blockages with a 'no pain, no gain attitude'. *Tiferet*-Balance in *Netzach*-Endurance offers the wisdom of how to move forwards, to work around the obstacles that are standing between you and your goal, whilst paying attention to the needs of both your body and your soul.

SPIRITUAL DEVELOPMENT

First we must consider the soul. "Spiritual Growth" or "Spiritual Development" are vague terms. Many have come to believe that it is all about learning information; how many ancient sources can you quote, how much information can you recall, or put more simply; how clever are you? Another approach would have us ask an entirely different question; how much have you transformed your life?

The money education expert Robert Kiyosaki teaches that your bank balance is a kind of financial "report card" letting you know how well

---

22 Lyrics from "Straighten Up and Fly Right", Words and Lyrics by Nat King Cole and Irving Mills.

239

you are doing[23], but measuring our spiritual growth demands a different set of criteria. Whilst information and mental understanding is not to be undervalued, the spiritual "report card" might be far simpler: How kind are you to family members when you are stressed? How do you treat poor people? What is the level of your faith when put to the test? Do you greet people with a happy face when meeting them, even if you are not in the mood[24]? Do you stand up for others[25]?

WHEN JACOB MET MOSES

The Tikkunei Zohar refers to *Tiferet*-compassion as "Masters in Torah" which we might understand as "Masters in Spiritual Development". *Tiferet*-Balance in *Netzach*-Endurance conjures up an Biblical meeting which never happened - it is the aspect of Jacob, who represents *Tiferet*-balance/compassion, in the actions of Moses, who represents *Netzach*-endurance. Put simply, as you endure with your personal development, are you spiritually connected and balanced (*Tiferet*)? Or, as you drive forwards with a project (*Netzach* can be understood as 'inner drive'), are you doing this with a state of balance?

STRAIGHTEN UP & FLY RIGHT

The Tikkunei Zohar also hints that enduring with our spiritual development will lead to a state of happiness. The analogy of the bird is used as an expansive metaphor, perhaps for the way that our soul can fly like a bird, and that it takes time to learn how to "fly" in life.

> *"Happy are they: the masters of the study house, the masters of the Midrash, the masters of Torah*[26]*! For even the bird has found a home... A home in which are heard expressions*[27] *of Torah! For in a place where there is Torah - which is the Middle Pillar (amuda*

---

23 See the *Rich Dad, Poor Dad* series of books by Robert Kiyosaki.
24 "Shammai says: *"Make your Torah study a fixed practice; say little and do much; and receive everyone with a cheerful face"*, Ethics of the Fathers/Pirkei Avot 1:15.
25 "Hillel says: *If I am not for myself, who will be for me? And if I am [only] for myself, what am I? And if not now, when?"*, ibid., 1:14.
26 Psalms 84:4.
27 Footnote courtesy of Professor David Solomon's Tiqqunei haZohar, Qushta 1740: An English Translation, p60 in manuscript: "*Pitgamei oraiita* (lit. 'expressions,' or 'words' of Torah); see Targum Yonatan on Exodus 15:26 and Zohar 1, 71a, where the meaning is more 'ordinances of Torah'".

d'emtz'a-ita) - the bird also finds a home there. And because of this, the Rabbis determined: "any house in which are not heard words of Torah will eventually be destroyed". And those in whom [i.e. in whose houses] are heard words of Torah are called: eggs, chicks, and children. Eggs are the masters of Scripture; chicks are the masters of Mishnah; children are the masters of Kabbalah"[28].

The bird metaphor is used in various forms, and also refers to the *Shechina*, the feminine presence of God. In this sense, however, we can directly apply it to the way we are living and strive to integrate spiritual growth throughout all of our practices (the facilitation of which is a major aim of this book).

HOW TO DEAL WITH BLOCKAGES

Obstacles present themselves the entire time. Straight after meditating, perhaps somebody is rude to you and you must choose how to respond. Maybe you have come back from a relaxing vacation and there are work stresses to deal with, or you slept well through the night and your children suddenly wake you with a jolt. One way to deal with our challenges, to borrow from the 'bird' metaphor, is to rise above them; to spread our new-found wings and fly.

We might see the way of Jacob similar to that of a bird - he brings the balance of his father Abraham (*Chesed*-Love) and his father Isaac (*Gevurah*-Discipline) and these are the 'wings' that help him take flight. In another model, he is flanked by the qualities of Moses (*Netzach*-Endurance) and Aaron (*Hod*-Humility) and he keeps the centre path. One message for today is to keep going with your spiritual development and keep applying the teachings. Practice rising above your challenges until soaring and flying is a natural motion.

BURNOUT: WHEN THE BIT HITS THE FAN

Burnout happens easily. Nobody is immune, especially when you are in a job or working on a project for a long time. Religious leaders suffer from burn out, as do doctors, other professionals, factory workers, and

---

28 Tiqqunei haZohar, Qushta 1740: An English Translation, p3.

even (or especially) parents from time to time. *Tiferet* asks us to be aware of compassion and balance when we are in the mode of *Netzach-*endurance. When we monitor our level of balance, we know when to take a break, when to take our foot off the pedal and when to recalibrate our actions.

NO PAIN?

Many of us were raised with the exercise mantra of "no pain, no gain", although this never spoke to me that deeply when I was a teenager and being forced to run around a field for rugby practice on cold winter days in England. There is a value to pushing through a certain level of pain, particularly they pain that our ego experiences when it is resisting growth. But is there a virtue to enduring through real, physical pain? Having experienced yoga injuries from pushing my body too hard, perhaps not. But we are trying to find a balance here, and you will find the balance that is right for you.

ONGOING MEDITATION

The yogis discussed how an ongoing mental focus can be developed through a healthy yoga practice, but continual discipline must be balanced with ongoing compassion to avoid unnecessary pain. *"Unbroken continuation of that mental ability [ekagrata] is meditation"*, wrote Patanjali[29]. The Yoga Sutras' description of this continually applied meditation is the essence of *Netzach*-endurance.

Staying compassionate over the long term (*Tiferet*-compassion in *Netzach*-endurance) sounds deceptively simple. It is the motion of going the distance, sticking with a route, and hopefully enjoying yourself along the way. The marathon runner must be gentle at times, rather than literally running their body into the ground.

There are some instances where pain does lead to gain, and the Kabbalists explain how we do learn from painful experiences as they

---

[29] Yoga Sutras 3:2, Swamij translation.

help us grow[30]. They are essential to growth and the painful contractions that a woman experiences during childbirth are integrally connected to the birth of the new child. The ancient writings prophesise how the emotional and psychological chaos found in contemporary society are the birth pangs of a Messianic era.

We have the opportunity to learn from all of our painful experiences, and if you think back to the times that you went through immense difficulty, it is worth spending a moment to think how you have learned and grown from them. Painful breakups, saying the wrong thing, behaving inappropriately – all of these things can cause difficulty at the time but help refine and improve us at a later date.

Any long-term endurance will bring inevitable frustrations, however worthy the purpose. The pursuit of life goals, careers or relationships is fraught with difficulties, but Compassion in Endurance is the energy of loving the journey rather than being a slave to the destination.

> *"A buzzard took a monkey for a ride in the air,*
> *The monkey thought that everything was on the square.*
> *The buzzard tried to throw the monkey off of his back,*
> *The monkey grabbed his neck and said, "Now listen Jack"*
> *Straighten up and fly right..."*[31]

TODAY'S PRACTICE

AMBITION GUIDELINES:

"Beautiful Endurance": Stay focused on your long-term ambition whilst pursuing it with grace and balance.

GYM PRACTICE GUIDELINES:

Much of this week's focus is on building endurance. As you endure today, be mindful and watch that you are staying in balance.

---

30 As explained by Rabbi Akiva Tatz in the lecture Seven Steps to Greatness, at the Jewish Learning Exchange, London, 2003.
31 See earlier footnote, by Nat King Cole & Irving Mills.

MEDITATION PRACTICE GUIDELINES:

Plan a longer meditation practice today, but value, enjoy and appreciate every movement along the way and focus on having absolute compassion during each part of your breath. Notice the four parts of your breathing; i. the inhalation, ii. a brief pause at the 'top' before exhaling, iii. the exhalation and iv. a short pause after all of the air has been exhaled from your lungs. Allow this meditation to be joyful, revelling in the life-giving oxygen that is nourishing your body and the feeling of relief as carbon dioxide is released from your lungs. Power through your yoga practice giving special emphasis on each breath, listening to the sound of the breathing, and loving every moment or at least treating it with compassion. Even though you might find the overall practice a challenge, by breaking it down into small, individual moments, it can become something deeply restorative and enjoyable.

RELATIONSHIP PRACTICE GUIDELINES:

Set an intention to restore the balance to difficult partnerships and relationships through enduring compassion. Explore compassion in your enduring situations, being kind to competitors at work, loving towards your more testing friendships and being kind with your family when they are getting annoying. What if you get frustrated with your partner? That is fine. Visit each moment with patience and grace, and *Tiferet-compassion* in *Netzah-endurance* will carry you through.

YOGA PRACTICE GUIDELINES:

When committing to a yoga routine, the first stage is to keep it regular and establish a rhythm (*Netzah*-endurance). Balancing that endurance with compassion means that although you need to keep going with what you have started, you are gentle with yourself and others in the process. The inner voice that chastises – "Work harder! You've missed a posture! You've missed a day! McFly, you're a slacker!" – is not welcome. Nor is the voice of envy that looks at another yogi or yogini and tells you that their practice is better than yours, that you are just "not good at yoga" or that you are not doing well. *Tiferet*-compassion in *Netzach*-endurance is keeping with the course, loving yourself and loving the process.

You could also take this principle very literally and try various balance-based exercises (*Tiferet*-balance) for a sustained period of time (*Netzach*-endurance).

QUESTIONS FOR MEDITATION

RELATIONSHIPS:
- Where do I give up too easily in relationships? (e.g *dysfunctional* Netzach-Endurance). How can I heal this through being more compassionate (*Tiferet*) on a regular basis?
- Where am I running myself into the ground? What can I do about it?

YOGA/BODY/GYM:
- Where do I give up too easily with regards to my regular practices, whether it is yoga, the gym or meditation? How can I keep going for longer whilst remaining compassionate towards my body, and keeping a balanced mental state? (*Tiferet)*
- Where am I pushing my body too hard? How can I get back into balance?

BUSINESS:
- What can I do to make my business more sustainable? (This could be environmental sustainability, getting your cash-flow more regular and sustainable, or it could be maintaining the vision in your company or workplace). How can I do this through acts of compassion and rebalancing (*Tiferet*)?
- When I am driving forwards with a project (*Netzach* equals drive), am I doing this with a state of balance?
- Where is my business or workplace out of balance?
- Where am I burning out at work? How can I rejuvenate, restore or revitalise?

SPIRITUAL DEVELOPMENT
- As I endure with my personal development, am I spiritually connected and balanced (*Tiferet*)?

GYM SEQUENCE, DAY 24/LEG RAISES

Alternate leg raises. 3 x 10 repetitions.

.01

.02

YOGA SEQUENCE, DAY 24/WARRIOR 1

You may modify the pose to make it easier by raising your back heel off the ground so that your hips are parallel, in a kind of Runner's Lunge. Alternatively you can intensify your Warrior 1 by holding the pose for longer.

תפארת
Tiferet-Balance

נצח
Netzach-Endurance

DAY 25 / ENDURANCE IN ENDURANCE / DON'T STOP
BELIEVING נצח שבנצח

KABBALAH SUTRA: *Netzach She b'Netzach* – Endurance in Endurance.
INTENTION: To become your ideal self and fulfil your potential through
enduring endurance. Become able to sustain your endurance – to keep
going at all times by discovering the strength within.

"Nothing in this world can take the place of persistence. Talent will not;
nothing is more common than unsuccessful people with talent"

Calvin Coolidge

The problem is that many of us give up too easily. It is as simple as
that. De Niro's *Raging Bull* character bemoaned "I could have been a
contender" and we often do the same, regardless of age. 25 year-olds
moan that they have missed opportunities as do 85 year olds. We have
the power to choose if we want to complain or take responsibility and
give it our best shot. *Netzach*-endurance in *Netzach*-endurance is the
epitome of unleashing our drive to move forwards.

STEP INTO YOUR DESTINY

There is an irony that Moses is the epitome of *Netzach*-endurance when
he is so reluctant to start his mission, as we discussed earlier. Kabbalah
locates *Netzach*-endurance in the right hip, the leg that initially swings
ahead of us, but Moses has to have a Divine commandment to move.
We may receive our "Divine command" in the form of a feeling,
intuition or general ambition, but it is up to us if we listen to the call.

WHERE ARE YOU?

Strangely, Moses' name is mentioned twice, when he is called out of
the Burning Bush: *"[God] called to him from the midst of the bush, saying,*
"Moses, Moses!", and he replied [Hineni] "Here I am""[32]. How often can we
say "Here I am, *Hineni*" when we hear the call? I know this avoidance

---

[32] Exodus 3:4.

well, which is why this book took eight years to get finished and published. Life can be a lot easier if we just say *Hineni*.

The Lubavitcher Rebbe taught that Moses' name is called twice because it represents a call to his spiritual body and his physical body[33]. I would add that he replied with one "Here I am" to represent that he has integrated his soul, mind and body. When we feel disassociated, when we state one intention or ambition but our actions are not aligned, we get nowhere fast, or our results are not what we had hoped for, like the person who refrains "I always wanted to be a writer but now I am a lawyer". We have a far higher chance of achieving success when we align our thoughts, speech and actions.

We might also consider the idea of these two names, or the higher and lower self, being represented in our body: the fingers representing the ten upper *sefirot* and the ten toes representing the ten lower *sefirot* (Divine spheres) - these are the upper and lower worlds in our body.

TRUTH IS REVEALED

There is an element of *Netzach* that we can understand as Truth, e.g. something that endures over the long-term proves to be 'true'. At challenging times we find out who are 'true' friends are and over the passage of time, 'true' lovers are revealed, even if *"the course of true love never did run smooth"*[34].

MENTAL FOCUS

The yogic journey takes us to a place where we *"still the fluctuations of thought*[35]*"* and gain self-mastery. It says that *"mental equanimity may be gained by the even expulsion and retention of energy*[36]*"* and this brings to mind my teacher Rabbi Shlomo Riskin, who taught that it is important

---

33   "Moses soul descended into his physical body via the inner Divine energy of the spiritual worlds, and therefore it was not affected by its descent through these worlds...This indicates that the first "Moses", Moses in his spiritual origin, is the same as the second "Moses", Moses in his physical body" - as quoted on p21 in Torah, Chumash Shemot, The Book of Exodus. With an interpolated English Translation and Commentary based on the works of the Lubavitcher Rebbe (Kehot: New York, 2011).
34   In A Midsummer Night's Dream 1:i Lysander says: *"For aught that I could ever read, Could ever hear by tale or history, The course of true love never did run smooth"*.
35   Yoga Sutras 1:2.
36   Ibid, 1:34, Swamij translation.

to get up in the mornings to *daven*, to pray, *especially when one doesn't feel like it*[37]. By breaking through the barriers, mental blocks and thousand reasons to hold us back, we can achieve greatness purely by turning up to an activity day after day. This is similar to Malcolm Gladwell's theory as expounded in *Outliers*, that by putting an average of 10,000 hours' practice into any activity it is possible to achieve expertise.

Can it be any coincidence that the theme on day 25 of a 49-day programme is Enduring Endurance? If you are still reading this far, you are over halfway there (quite literally).

IT'S ALL ABOUT THE BASS

When I was 12 years old I played trombone in the school brass band but the other trombonists used to annoy me. Actually, I was a little jealous. They tended to get better parts to play and while I was stuck playing the bass line to the *Cagney and Lacey* theme tune, they would get something more closely resembling the tune itself. Why did they get the more fun stuff? Simple. Because they practiced their instruments more regularly, took more music exams and worked harder at it. They may have had more of a natural music ability but they made the most of whatever was there. Of course I practiced on occasion. Maybe two or three times a week. But the players in the First Trombone Section practiced every single day for an hour or more. They endured and succeeded.

FREUD

Human beings have human feelings and in trying to endure in reaching our goals, we are fighting against Freud's pleasure principle which he described as "the path of least resistance"[38]. The father of psychoanalysis observed that our natural inclination is to veer towards pleasurable experiences, and we will take the easiest possible route to get there. Why go to the gym when there is a great film on television? Why do an evening course to improve your mind when your friends are holding great parties at the same time? Why get up early for yoga when you feel

---

37 I heard him teach this during a lecture on prayer in 1997 at Yeshivat HaMivtar in Efrat, Israel.
38 Sigmund Freud writing in The Pleasure Principle.

like extra sleep and your bed is warm? Why learn an ancient language to access obscure texts in their original form when you can just use a translation?

PERSISTENCE POWER

The power of persistence was recognized by Calvin Coolidge, the 30th President of the United States, who said that;

> "Nothing in this world can take the place of persistence. Talent will not; nothing is more common than unsuccessful people with talent. Genius will not; unrewarded genius is almost a proverb. Education will not; the world is full of educated derelicts. Persistence and determination alone are omnipotent. The slogan 'press on' has solved and always will solve the problems of the human race".

It is not necessarily completely true that persistence will always 'solve the problems of the human race' as there are spiritual obstacles that are certainly not manifest in a physical realm. It is also a very masculine view that pushing forwards will get you what you want. However, there is a lot to be said for the principle of what he is teaching. And who wants to be another unsuccessful person with talent? The coffee shops in Los Angeles are full of them.

TODAY'S PRACTICE

YOGA PRACTICE GUIDELINES:

My teacher Edward said that "Yoga can help us learn anything". In learning the various asanas we break things down into their constituent parts: every action has a series of breaths and within the posture there is correct foot placement, skeletal alignment, visual focus, mental focus (usually the breath), and some would argue, direction of energy. In cooking a new meal we follow a very specific recipe and the same is true of pursuing new yoga postures. The recipe relates to breath, alignment and focus. When we master each of these individual stages we can then master the posture. This principle extends to other areas of life because it teaches us that we can endure through difficulties, work around problems, and achieve the results we are looking for.

We can make major physical progress when we work at it over time. Some yoga students give up at an early stage, perhaps in their first one or two classes, simply because they are finding it difficult or feeling a slight twinge in their body. Not every teacher or every style is the best match for all students and it often takes time to find the best solution, which is yet another aspect of endurance.

Use today as an opportunity to work more deeply in your practice and pay attention to five components of the posture; i. correct foot placement, ii. yogic breathing (*pranayama*), iii. mental focus, iv. visual focus and v. the direction of energy through your arms and legs. Allow yourself to take an extra five breaths in the posture, applying enduring endurance.

GYM PRACTICE GUIDELINES:
Today, Just Do It. Take action. Endure.

QUESTIONS FOR MEDITATION

RELATIONSHIPS:
- Where do I give up too easily in relationships? (e.g. *dysfunctional* Netzach-Endurance). How can I heal this through enduring for longer and seeing things through? (*Netzach*)
- Who are the people I can count on in relationships? Those who are *Netzach* who will be there for the long term?
- How can I be there in the long-term for other people? Where have I fallen short as a friend?

YOGA/BODY/GYM:
- Where do I give up too easily with regards to my regular practices, whether it is yoga, the gym or meditation? How can I double my efforts to endure and keep going for longer? (*Netzach*)

BUSINESS:

- What can I do to make my business more sustainable? (This could be environmental sustainability, getting my cash-flow more regular and sustainable, or it could be maintaining the vision in my company or workplace). How can I do this through feats of endurance and long-term planning (*Netzach*)?
- Who are the people I can count on in my business? Who are the long-term colleagues or clients who I could do more for?

AMBITION:

- What is one major goal important to me? What are my next actions towards achieving it?
- Where am I giving up too easily and what is it costing me?

GYM SEQUENCE, DAY 25/DUMBELL SPLIT SQUAT

Step one foot forward, hold dumbell with both hands and bend both knees until your rear leg reaches the ground. 3 x 8 repetitions.

.01

נצח
Netzach-Endurance

.02

YOGA SEQUENCE, DAY 25/WARRIOR 2 (VIRABHADRASANA II)

Bend your front leg until your thigh is parallel with the ground, straighten your back leg and keep the energy flowing through both arms.

נצח
Netzach-Endurance

DAY 26 / HUMILITY IN ENDURANCE / PRIDE & FALL / הוד שבנצח

KABBALAH SUTRA: *Hod She b'Netzach* – Humility in Endurance.
INTENTION: To break the ego and endure to develop inner power. Refine
your ability/capacity to endure.

"I can see his pride/ Peep through each part of him".
All is True (Henry VIII)[39]

"Being so great, I have no need to beg"
The Tragedy of King Richard II[40]

Talent and arrogance are a lethal combination. We may be able to
drive forwards with power, but it can cause endless upsets along the
way. Over-confidence in our position can mean that we do not listen
to the opinions of others, miss potential opportunities in all areas
(work, relationships, friendships and fun) and - more dangerously we
might collide with potentially threatening situations. The Kotsker
Rebbe (1787-1859) advised that a person should have a slip of paper
in each pocket, one reading "the world was created for me alone" and
in the other "I am dust and ashes"[41]. There is an apparent paradox
and humility in this approach, the blending of *Netzach*-endurance/
confidence and *Hod*-humility, yet it is a complex balance that is crucial
to success.

"Being so great, I have no need to beg" said King Richard II in
Shakespeare's powerful tale of how a king lost his power[42]. *Hod-*

---

[39] All Is True, or, Henry VIII (I:i), by William Shakespeare and John Fletcher.
[40] *The* Tragedy of King Richard II (IV:i), by William Shakespeare.
[41] The Kotzker Rebbe never published any works as he had all of his manuscripts burned before he passed away. There are, however, published collections of sayings.
[42] Richard II , Act 4, Scene 1. King Richard is speaking to Henry Bolingbroke, the future King Henry IV who seizes power from Richard. This play is the start of Shakespeare's history cycle, which culminates in the Wars of the Roses between the houses of York and Lancaster - the action-packed trilogy of Henry VI plays - and the entire rift that splits England originally begins in Richard II.

humility in *Netzach*-endurance asks us, 'where we are being arrogant in our ambitions?'. Confidence is essential when pursuing projects, but it is also a *mitzvah* to respect and be kind towards other people..

PRIDE & PREJUDICE

A lack of *Hod*-humility can show itself in pre-judging other people and situations. You decide that the older gentleman in the tatty jacket is some good-for-nothing and brush off his question without a second thought, not realising that he is a multi-millionaire who could hire you and become an incredible client. "Self-judgement is a poison" says my martial arts teacher Eric, as it continually undermines us and our ability to move forwards. People judge their looks and it gets in the way of relationships or they judge their abilities and it stops them from creating projects. Humility also applies to the way we relate to ourselves. *"One who is too self-confident..is a fool, wicked and arrogant of spirit"*[43] taught the sage Rabbi Yishmael. When we avoiding pre-judging (*pre-judice*), we reduce pride and increase opportunity as we begin to see situations more clearly.

TRAVELLING WITH HUMILITY

Hod-humility in Netzach-endurance asks us to progress with humility. Work hard on your body but do so with an air of gratitude. Step up to speak in front of a thousand people but do it with humility. As we explored earlier, the Tikkunei Zohar takes a passage from the book of Proverbs that *"Like a bird who wanders from the nest, so is a man who wanders from his place"*[44] and explains that on one level it is referring to Moses:

> *"'So is a man who wanders from his place...'* [Who is this?] This is Moses. For it is written: *And the man Moses was very humble*[45] - for his spirit was driven after them"*[46].

Moses is referred to as the greatest teacher in the entire Torah, the only one to be known as "Moshe Rabbeinu" - literally, 'Moses our Rabbi' or

---

43   Ethics of the Fathers/Pirkei Avot 4: 9.
44   Proverbs/Mishlei 27:8.
45   Numbers/Bamidbar 12:3.
46   Tikkunei HaZohar, 1b, David Solomon translation.

'Moses our teacher' and yet it also says that his level of humility was "more than any other man on earth"[47].

As we progress (*Netzach*), we aim to leave our pride behind (*Hod*). Moses is seen as the greatest teacher but also one of the humblest people to walk the earth. From this we can take inspiration and edification.

THANKING THE SOURCE

Another aspect of *Hod*-gratitude in *Netzah*-endurance is recognising when we have been successful and thanking the Higher source. Maintaining humility at the peak of our endurance, rather than succumbing to the paradox of fame and fortune. Our cult of the ego is not helped by a celebrity culture where pop singers and actors are encouraged to share their morals and values and to explain the secret of their success, regardless of whether it is just due to natural talent, sheer luck or simply having a great producer. The problem with taking credit for all of your successes is that you will then shoulder all of the blame for the inevitable failures that we all experience.

STAYING IN GRATITUDE

Hod-Gratitude in *Netzach*-Endurance is also the hallmark of a continued gratitude practice. Ancient religions of all kinds would habitually offer sacrifices to their gods of choice as a way of marking success. Today, we tend to take full credit for all of our successes which is not good for our mental health, because it will usually mean that we take full responsibility for all of our failures and blame ourselves as a result. Rather than saying 'this success is from God' or 'this failure is from God', and having somewhere to turn to for spiritual comfort and celebration, we take it entirely on ourselves and look inwards for answers that are not always there. The Hebrew *Hallel* prayer is about sharing the responsibility with God, looking upwards during the good times and saying 'thank you'. Similarly, there are prayers such as *Tahanun* which are themed around seeking solace.

---

47 Numbers/Bamidbar 12:3.

During your yoga practice become aware of where your capacity to endure comes from. Erich Schiffman talks about "channelling the Universe" through our practice as we breathe through asana and vinyasa. As you work through the sun salutations, allow the breath to flow in and out of you and cultivate a sense of awe and Oneness with the Source of All Breath. Visualise the *Ehad*, meaning One, and repeat it as a mantra. Grow in awareness that you are a created being and part of a much larger system. Your breath comes from outside of you, your food comes from outside of you and the decisions about when you were born and when you will die are also made by a power outside yourself. As you become centred with the breath that is within your control, allow a growing sense of humility to drive your enduring practice. Discover your hero inside, go forth and conquer!

TODAY'S PRACTICE

YOGA PRACTICE GUIDELINES:

Practice your yoga with a growing sense of awe and humility, appreciating this amazing machine we call a body, and the power-channel we call 'breath' that connects us to a greater system (which we call 'the world'). As you incorporate *Hod*-humility in *Netzach*-endurance, it will increase your capacity to endure for that much longer, becoming stronger and more balanced in the process.

In the Yoga Sutras, Patanjali described how the *"light of transcendental insight"* can be achieved by meditating on large objects and problems, and that over time we will have the capacity to tighten or focus on increasingly subtle areas. The progression takes place in stages, he explains, *"ranging from meditations on gross material objects to gradually subtler regions"*[48]. When we start on the journey towards a new achievement we have to begin with tackling large problems, the physical issues, such as being able to sit still for five minutes on a yoga mat or to be able to endure a 90-minute class. Over time the problem reduces to more subtle issues such as whether it is possible to get a deeper backbend or reach a certain posture that has been eluding us. Through

---
48   Yoga Sutras 3:6, Stiles translation.

enduring and continuing to pursue our goal we can reduce the size of the obstacles and reduce our egoic self.

GYM PRACTICE GUIDELINES:

Pursue your ambitions today but be very aware of pride or arrogance creeping into your practice. Consider the phrase that King Solomon had engraved upon a ring - *Gam Ze Y'Avor* - *"This too shall pass"*. Our bodies are transient. Can you bring a spiritual awareness into your gym practice and tap into the eternal part of your being?

RELATIONSHIP PRACTICE GUIDELINES:

Focus on your enduring relationships; spouse, partner, children and long-term work colleagues. Observe the areas where you can improve the relationship through applying humility, and through finding the places that you are able to step back and make room for the other person, discover incredible results.

BUSINESS PRACTICE GUIDELINES:

When we move forward with an arrogant spirit, we can miss details, lose focus and it can cost us dearly. When we meet people with a lack of humility they can sense that we are making things more about us than we are about them.

QUESTIONS FOR MEDITATION

RELATIONSHIPS:

-   Where do I give up too easily in relationships? (e.g. *dysfunctional Netzach*-Endurance). How can I heal this through being more humble in my approach and outlook? (*Hod*)

YOGA/BODY/GYM:

-   Where do I give up too easily with regards to my regular practices, whether it is yoga, the gym or meditation? How can I fix this through staying grateful? (*Hod*)

BUSINESS:

- What can I do to make my business more sustainable? (this could be environmental sustainability, getting my cash-flow more regular and sustainable, or it could be maintaining the vision in my company or workplace). How can I do this through more humility and gratitude (*Hod*)?

GYM SEQUENCE, DAY 26/DUMBBELL SQUAT

Maintain the arch in your back and squat as low as possible, engaging your legs as you straighten up. 3 x 12 repetitions.

.01

נצח
Netzach-Endurance

הוד
Hod-Humility

.02

YOGA SEQUENCE, DAY 26/BOAT (NAVASANA)

Lift yourself into Boat Pose for 6 breaths, rest for two breaths and then repeat two more sets. To make it more difficult, perform a half-vinyasa between sets or even lift yourself into a handstand. To modify the pose, bend your knees so that your shins are parallel to the ground.

נצח
Netzach-Endurance

הוד
Hod-Humility

DAY 27 / **BONDING IN ENDURANCE** / THE PLEASURE
SEEKERS/יסוד שבנצח

KABBALAH SUTRA: *Yesod She b'Netzah* – Bonding in Endurance.
INTENTION: Connect to yourself, your goals and achieve them. Solidify
and firmly establish your ability to endure. Strengthen your ability to
endure. To strengthen your Long Game. To Stay Connected To Your Goals
& Stay In Motion.

*"Life isn't about how hard you can hit. It's about how hard you can get hit,
and keep moving forwards…that's how winning is done!!! Until you start
believing in yourself you ain't going to have a life. Somewhere along the way,
you stopped believing in yourself. ..If you know what you're worth, go out
and get what you're worth. But you've got to be willing to take the hits and
not start pointing the finger because of him, or her, or anybody. Cowards do
that, and that ain't you. You're better than that".* — Rocky Balboa

Staying true to our goals can be challenging when there are so many
opportunities for distraction. We can always find something to blame,
whether it is other people, social media, or even being born at the
wrong time and place. Our best chance of success consists of fighting
our way forwards, staying connected to our intentions and following
through on our word. *Yesod*-bonding in *Netzach*-endurance keeps us on
track.

PLEASURE OF THE JOURNEY

Yesod can also be understood as pleasure[49]. We may consider the motion
of finding pleasure as we journey forwards, enjoying the adventure no
matter what. When we are dealing with people who are challenging or
unlikeable we can see them as 'training tools', much in the same way
that you might fight with somebody in a dojo when training for martial
arts. The trainee fighter knows that each of these opponents help them
sharpen his or her skill, and similarly, the disagreeable people in our

---

49   The Tikkunei Zohar connects *Yesod* with the sexual organ, hence this understanding of
Yesod as pleasure.

midst can help train our personality and refine our soul as we increase our skill set in learning how to communicate and work with them.

CONNECT TO YOUR ENDURANCE

The Biblical account of King Saul told of how he was weak in following directions and as a result was going to have the kingship removed to him (it gets passed on to King David). The prophet Samuel said *"The Glory of Israel does not deceive or change His mind, for He is not human that He should change his mind"*[50]. This name for God, the "Glory of Israel" is written in Hebrew as *Netzach Yisrael*. In other words *Netzach*-endurance is another name for God, so the "Endurer of Israel" or "Sustainer of the God-wrestlers"[51]. In staying connected to our goal, we might invoke a divine power in our drive to endure.

LONG-TERM RELATIONSHIPS

Yesod in *Netzach* is also the idea of Bonding in Endurance, of staying committed to relationships for the long term. *Yesod* can mean 'foundation'[52] and is the action of actively grounding ourselves in relationships, rather than continuing blindly and hoping that things will somehow work out for the best. Whilst there is certainly a lot of merit in enduring love and continuing with relationships over a long period of time, if they are not sufficiently bonded, they will eventually fall apart. In this sense, *Yesod* is the glue that keeps people and friendships together.

The Yoga Sutras teach that *"by insight into another's perceptions, one is blessed with the knowledge of their point of view"*[53]. Empathy, intuition and deductive reasoning can help us connect more deeply to another, understanding the challenges that face them and what is being said by the heart, and how it may contradict what is being said with their words.

---

50 1 Samuel 16:29.
51 Israel as "God Wrestler", from Genesis 32:29 - *"Your name shall no longer be Jacob, but Israel, for you have wrestled with God and man and overcome"*.
52 As in the phrase *"the righteous are the foundation of the world"* צַדִּיק, יְסוֹד עוֹלָם (Proverbs 10:25).
53 Yoga Sutras 3:19, Stiles translation.

In general, men do not like to stop the car and ask for directions[54]. If lost in an unfamiliar area we would rather drive for hours and get furious than actually stop and ask a stranger how to get from A to B, thereby admitting defeat. *Yesod*-bonding is what causes us to stop along the journey and – yes – ask for directions or check where we really are. The same is true with our jobs and projects. Although we can all continue doing an action which we do not believe in, such as working a mindless day job to pay the rent or writing a bland term paper to pass an exam, it is our natural inclination to want some kind of emotional or intellectual bond with the fruit of our labours.

FIND BLISS FROM BOREDOM

Many people do jobs that they do not entirely like, but there is usually something about the situation that draws them in. It could be work colleagues, the environment, the goals of the company, or in worst cases, the pay. The happiest people are those who are so congruent with their work that they believe in what they are doing, enjoy being around work colleagues, and get complete fulfilment from the task at hand. In other words, they are completely bonded (*Yesod*) with the object of their endurance (*Netzach*).

We tend to feel naturally bonded at the start of a new relationship, when we are excited by the other person's presence, be it friend, partner or lover. The initial excitement of a new situation can fade over time and although there was a strong motion of *Yesod*-bonding at the start, this gives way to the daily grind as *Netzach*-endurance takes over. How many friends do you take for granted, and do you ever question what you are getting out of the friendship? The real question being raised by *Yesod*-bonding in *Netzach*-endurance is; What are *you* putting into the friendship? This is where the real need for endurance takes over, as we are forced to sacrifice our ego and our own desires, to focus on the other person's needs and to endure through the highs and lows.

---

54 This example will be rendered obsolete by the younger generation who were born after GPS (US) / Satnav (UK) became available in cell phones. Back in the day we had no telephones in our cars and used a foldable paper-based technology called "maps".

Endurance is an important part of yoga and meditation. Today we will apply *Yesod*-bonding in *Netzach*-endurance to ground ourselves, and to stop and ask directions from our body.

TODAY'S PRACTICE

YOGA PRACTICE GUIDELINES:

Begin by sitting quietly and noticing any pain or tightness in your body, and where your body would like to go today. Although your ego might be plutzing for you to leap into the splits or work on your backbend, your body could be yearning for some gentle calf-muscle stretches or spinal twists for the lower back. Try to continually ground yourself during the practice, pushing your feet into the floor beneath you for support and bonding with your body through sensitivity and close observation. Do not worry if you are not being technically correct with the external aspects of your practice, because today's focus on the inner aspects, and achieving the state of oneness that comes through bonding.

GYM PRACTICE GUIDELINES:

Stay focused on your workout intentions, connect to how you would like your body to look or feel when you have reached it, and find pleasure (*Yesod*) in the process.

RELATIONSHIP PRACTICE GUIDELINES:

Today is a space for improving connections with the people around you and for taking action towards the things you believe in. It has been said that "one should never leave the scene of a decision without first taking an action towards realising the goal".[55] Good luck with sustained bonding!

---

55   Heard at an Anthony Robbins lecture.

QUESTIONS FOR MEDITATION

RELATIONSHIPS:
- Where do I give up too easily in relationships? (e.g. *dysfunctional Netzach*-Endurance). How can I heal this through being more grounded and connected to the other person? (*Yesod*)

YOGA/BODY/GYM:
- Where do I give up too easily with regards to my regular practices, whether it is yoga, the gym or meditation? How can I keep this going through staying connected to my goals and internally connected to myself? (*Yesod*)

BUSINESS:
- What can I do to make my business more sustainable? (this could be environmental sustainability, getting my cash-flow more regular and sustainable, or it could be maintaining the vision in my company or workplace). How can I do this through getting more bonded to my vision and connected to what I believe in? (*Yesod*)?

GYM SEQUENCE, DAY 27/GOBLET SQUAT

Maintain the arch in your back and lower yourself until your elbows are inside your knees, then squeeze your knees so you feel it in your legs. If you can't squat that low, go as far as you can whilst keeping your back extended. 3 x 8 repetitions.

.01

יסוד
Yesod-Bonding

נצח
Netzach-Endurance

.02

YOGA SEQUENCE, DAY 27/HERO (VIRASANA)

Sit on a block so that your feet are on either side of your hips. Gently roll your calf muscles outwards as you ease into the position, being careful not to hurt your knees. For a deeper challenge, lay your back down into the reclining version of the pose, Supta Virasana.

.01

יְסוֹד
Yesod-Bonding

נֵצַח
Netzach-Endurance

.02

DAY 28 / **NOBILITY IN ENDURANCE** / MASTERS OF ENDURANCE / מלכות שבנצח

KABBALAH SUTRA: *Malhut She b'Netzach* – Nobility in Endurance.
INTENTION: To endure in your efforts of self-mastery, leading your mind and body to its full potential. The ability to control and command your capacity to endure.

"Sure I am this day we are masters of our fate, that the task which has been set before us is not above our strength; that its pangs and toils are not beyond our endurance. As long as we have faith in our own cause and an unconquerable will to win, victory will not be denied us".

Winston Churchill

We can waste energy in pursuit of our bigger goals. Rather than doing exactly what is needed, we get distracted. This might costs us in time, energy, money or even health. Part of mastery is to become fully economic with our energy. We think of a project, apply ourselves, plan the work, go through the process and complete it. *Malchut* is kingship, nobility, dignity and mastery.

WELCOME THE DIVINE FEMININE: NON-LINEAR & DEEPLY CARING

There is a deep spirituality balanced with profound practicality. *Malchut*-mastery is the *sefirah* (Divine sphere) that represents this world, and it is feminine in the sense that our world is a sphere rather than a straight line or cube, and that our lives tend not to work in a logical order. Nonetheless, *Malchut* is still very practical. *"All revelation ultimately comes through Malkhut-Kingship, which is the Female"* taught Rabbi Aryeh Kaplan[56]. Our life on earth is not logical and things do not always go according to plan, but we are still to stay engaged. *"You are not obligated to complete the work, but neither are you free to desist from it"* says the second-century *Mishna*[57]. Where *Netzach*-endurance is

---

[56]   In Rabbi Aryeh Kaplan's commentary to The Bahir, p129.
[57]   Ethics of the Fathers 2:21.

going the distance, *Malchut*-mastery is completing the actions to get you there, and continually modifying your approach as challenges arise.

DRIVING THROUGH

You want to go for a run but you are tired, your legs ache, an email comes in, your favourite programme is on television, you want to get to bed early - the list continues. Hands, feet and mouth are the organs of *Malchut*-mastery[58]. How are you using them to further your goals and stay in your truth? How are you using communication, the way you are "walking", the direction you are moving in, for long-term ambition and victory? How are you using this for endurance?

DIGNITY

Malchut-mastery also asks us to be dignified and king-like. This does not mean that we cannot doubt ourselves but it is concerned with how we behave on the outside. Moses, the paragon of *Netzach*-endurance, was also a monarch-like figure, effectively becoming first king of the nation of Israel in his leadership role, but the midrashic literature also tells of how he became King of Ethiopia (Hebrew: *Cush)* at the age of 27 where he ruled for 40 years[59]. Moses' life was one of long-term endurance and the question we might ask of our own soul is where are the areas we are looking for to go the distance but are currently falling short.

GOAL SETTING

What is the one activity that you would like to do more of but do not manage to, for a variety of good reasons? The sentence usually begins with "I should" and you can take it from there. A top five of the most popular shoulds would usually include "I should do more exercise, lose more weight, spend more time with my children/ parents/friends, work harder, learn a new skill...". The list is endless and usually stays

---

58 As taught in the Tikkunei HaZohar 17a (*Malchut* as mouth) and Zohar 169, "For the lesser star, the holy *Shechina - Malchut* grew smaller, clothed in impure forces and "her feet descend to death" *(*Proverbs/Mishlei 5:5)*", courtesy of www.kabbalah.info.

59 Yalkut Me'am Loez on Shemot 2:15. With more details: Yalkut Shimoni on Shemot, remez 168. Quoted in "Where Was Moses?" by Chaya Sarah Silberberg at www.chabad.org.

as an unproductive list. Tony Robbins said that we can 'should all over ourself'[60] but it rarely helps us achieve anything or makes us feel good.

THE RUNNING KING

Malchut-mastery in *Netzach*-endurance combines the energy of a monarch with a long-distance runner. This begins on an internal level and many of us keep ourselves in pain and negativity through a lack of internal dignity and self-respect. A king or queen, at least in the kabbalistic sense, is somebody who is in control of a situation and sets the boundaries, but if we let the internal voice take over and reprimand ourselves then we are effectively becoming slaves to an internal taskmaster. Quieting our mind is the goal of all meditation techniques but it can be particularly difficult to get to a state of inner calm. We need to practice and build the 'muscles' needed for effective meditation.

TRAINING OUR MIND

The Yoga Sutras teaches that *"by frequent repetition of restraint, an undisturbed flow of tranquillity results"*[61]. We can gain *Malchut*-mastery over our mind through repeated practice and application, but it means retraining our desires and ego. On the yoga mat we are literally retraining our bodies to stay within the confines of the posture, and gaining self mastery through this enduring attitude (*Netzach*).

The practice of yoga does not seek to force internal quiet or banish certain thoughts, but to initially bring our focus inwards so that we ignore all other extraneous sounds. Patanjali's system uses *pranayama* (breathing), *asana* (posture), and both *dharana* and *dhyana* (forms of meditation) to find this stillness. I will sometimes find that my mind is busier than ever at the start of a midday meditation, prayer or yoga session but by keeping a regular routine it means that my ability to focus becomes stronger over time. The mind works like a muscle and the more accustomed we are to a certain movement, the better we become at it.

---

60   Anthony Robbins in the live lecture series Personal Power.
61   Yoga Sutras 3:10, Stiles translation.

If the mind is a task master that whips us with painful thoughts, then we have a choice. We can become like kings or queens, elevate the *Malchut*-nobility to the forefront and relegate our unhelpful thoughts to a back seat. As we become like a monarch inside our mental and physical palace, the negative thoughts are like the ravings of a madman outside the castle gates. Although we still hear them when the wind is blowing in the right direction, they no longer hold any value and it is that much easier to ignore them. Chassidic stories will routinely compare the human mind to a king and our body to a subject, and recognise the insanity of many of our daily thoughts.

Yoga is a liberation technique and by approaching our practice with dignity we bring the final element to the energy of *Netzach*-endurance, raising our game and creating stunning results.

TODAY'S PRACTICE

YOGA PRACTICE GUIDELINES:

Approach today's practice with dignity and mastery. This affects the way you dress for yoga and interact with others on the way to a class. Most importantly, we are aiming for dignity in our long-term practice.

GYM PRACTICE GUIDELINES:

Consider *Malchut*-mastery in *Netzach*-endurance as 'feminine' or 'soft-edged' endurance. How am I going about my endurance? Am I masterful - slow when I need to be, grounded when I need to be, balanced when I need to be? Am I paced? Marathon-running is a great example - you need to train, be prepared, pace yourself, have a great mental attitude - you need to master each of these seven aspects.

QUESTIONS FOR MEDITATION

RELATIONSHIPS:
- Where do I give up too easily in relationships? Or where do I push too hard? (e.g *dysfunctional Netzach*-Endurance). How can I heal this through my speech and actions? (*Malchut)*
- Am I enduring, successful & truthful in my relationships? (Netzach)

YOGA/BODY/GYM:
- Where do I give up too easily with regards to my regular practices, whether it is yoga, the gym or meditation? How can I keep this going through making declarations, sharing it with others to make myself accountable, and making commitments? (*Malchut*)

BUSINESS:
- What can I do to make my business more sustainable? (this could be environmental sustainability, getting my cash-flow more regular and sustainable, or it could be maintaining the vision in my company or workplace). How can I do this through my speech and actions (*Malchut*)?
- Where am I giving up too easily in my business and how can I fight/work harder in a way that is loving (*Chesed*), disciplined (*Gevurah*), compassionate (*Tiferet*), enduring (*Netzach*), humble (*Hod*) and grounded (*Yesod*) and dignified (*Malchut*)?
- Where have I not mastered "Start To Finish"/Endurance & Sustainability? How am I falling short of my potential?
- Am I enduring, successful & truthful in my communications?
- Where am I giving up too easily in my business and how can I be enduringly compassionate (i.e. *Tiferet* in *Netzach)*, fight/work harder in a way that is more compassionate?
- Where am I giving up too easily in my business and how can I be enduringly driven and goal-focused (I.e. *Netzach* in *Netzach)*, fight/work harder in a way that is more enduring?

ADVANCED KABBALISTIC EXPERIMENTS

This book does not have the scope to cover *partzufim*, the Kabbalistic idea that our body is a hologram and that every sefirah includes every other sefirah. So these spheres can go infinitely deeply, to several levels (see the movie *Inception* for an idea of where this might go). Here is an example of how an advanced practice might look, although it is still a work-in-development at the point of publishing. My thinking is that each day of the week has a particular sefirah (see *Sefer Yetzirah* for more information) - e.g. Sunday is *Chesed*-lovingkindness. When the *Omer* count falls on a Sunday, you may have *Malchut* in *Netzach* (Day 28) fall on a Sunday, so it is really *[Malchut in Netzach]* in *Chesed*. Here are some examples of how we might take *The Kabbalah Sutras* to a deeper level. This is purely based on my own speculation and ideas.

- Where am I giving up too easily in my business and how can I be enduringly loving and creative towards people and work? "Enduringly loving" is *Chesed* in *Netzach*, and there are various ways to apply this principle). Can I fight/work harder in a way that is loving (*Chesed* in *Netzach*)?Can I be more disciplined (the *Gevurah* aspect of *in Chesed* in *Netzach*)? Can I be more compassionate (*Tiferet in Chesed* in *Netzach*), enduring (*Netzach in Netzach*), humble (*Hod in Chesed* in *Netzach*) and grounded (*Yesod in Chesed* in *Netzach*) and dignified (*Malchut in Chesed* in *Netzach*)?
- Where am I giving up too easily in my business and how can I be enduringly disciplined and strong (i.e. *Gevurah* in *Netzach)*, fight/work harder in a way that is loving (*Gevurah* in *Chesed in Netzach*), disciplined (*Gevurah in Gevurah* in *Netzach*), compassionate (*Tiferet in Gevurah* in *Netzach*), enduring (*Netzach in Gevurah* in *Netzach*), humble (*Hod in Gevurah* in *Netzach*) and grounded (*Gevurah in Chesed* in *Netzach*) and dignified (*Gevurah in Chesed* in *Netzach*)?

We might complete this for all of the sefirah and continue to dive deeper.

So you have A = *partzuf* in B = *Sefirah* of week in C = *Sefirah* of week (please note that this theory is a work in progress).

GYM SEQUENCE, DAY 28/BRIDGES

Do several bridges raising your hips on the inhale and bringing them down on the exhale. This differs from the yoga variation where you would hold the pose for several breaths (but if that feels right then do that as well).

.01

נצח
Netzach-Endurance

מלכות
Malchut-Kingship

.02

YOGA SEQUENCE, DAY 28/EXTENDED MOUNTAIN & MOUNTAIN (TADASANA)

Press your feet into the ground, spread your weight evenly into the four corners of your feet, reach your fingertips towards your ankles, drop your chest slightly and raise the sides of your ribs. Breathe deeply.

.01

מלכות
Malchut-Kingship

נצח
Netzach-Endurance

מלכות
Malchut-Kingship

.02

הוד *HOD*

HUMILITY

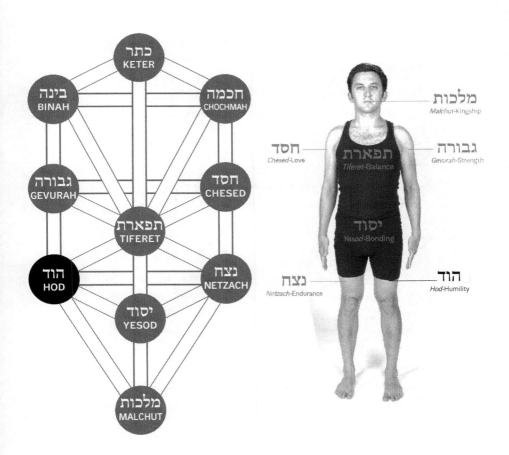

HOD INTRODUCTION: SWEET SURRENDER דוה

"There is a time for everything beneath the sun...a time to weep and a time to laugh, a time of mourning and a time of dancing" — King Solomon[1].

Just as there is a time to weep and a time to laugh, we might say there is also a time for *Netzach*-confidence/endurance, there is also a time for holding back, for allowing, for *Hod*-humility. We need both qualities at the different times and the wisdom to know when each is required.

TWO FAWNS

In *The Song of Songs*, King Solomon wrote *"your breasts are like fawns, twins of a gazelle"* and one major interpretation of this reads *"your two sustainers, the Tablets of the Law, are like fawns, twins of a gazelle"*[2], although elsewhere it also translated as *"your two sustainers, Moses and Aaron, are like fawns..."*. The point is that these qualities of pushing forward and holding back, of masculine-drive and feminine allowing, of yang-fire and yin-water, go hand in hand.

TWO THIGHS

"Netzach-endurance and Hod-humility are the two thighs" according to the *Tikkunei HaZohar*[3], and in order for the right hip to swing someone forward in the action of walking, the left hip has to hold back and create space. The right is associated with Moses, the law-giver and the left with his brother Aaron, the High Priest and peace-maker. Where Moses initiates actions such as climbing Mount Sinai and retrieving tablets of law, Aaron creates space and negotiates harmony between husbands and wives and disagreeing parties; *"Hillel says: Be among*

---

[1] Ecclesiastes 3:4. I have chosen this verse because it relates to the idea of Dominance according to Rabbi Aryeh Kaplan in Sefer Yetzirah p.224, and Dominance is the dominant quality of Hod-humility according to the Gra., (p138 of the same book).
[2] Artscroll Siddur translation, according to Rashi's translation, p304.
[3] Tikkunei HaZohar 17b.

the disciples of Aaron, loving peace and pursuing peace, loving people and bringing them close to Torah[4].

REACHING OUT vs WELCOMING IN

There is a part of us that forces actions, pushing ourselves out into the world, garnering attention, getting clients, bringing about great changes, and there is a part of us that allows things to happen, that makes space for people to come to us. Where Moses/*Netzach*-Endurance is reaching out to someone to pull them close to us, Aaron/*Hod*-humility is the part that opens our arms to welcome someone close to us in a hug.

DISTILLING INFORMATION

There is a time for giving people lots of information and a time for allowing them to digest what they already know. A great teacher has the wisdom to give a student what they need to grow without bombarding them with so much that they will be overwhelmed. This is the same with us and relationships; knowing when to help someone and when to hold back so that they can help themselves. When we 'smother' someone or we ask a person to 'give us some space', that is usually an indicator that things are out of balance and we need to regain the balance.

Rabbi Shneur Zalman of Liadi (1745-1812) taught that "*Netzach*-endurance *and Hod*-humility *are also referred to as "grinders" and "millstones", because they "grind the mannah" for the righteous"*, explaining that "*just as, by way of example, a person who grinds [wheat] with millstones crumbles it into very fine parts, so too does the father need to taper the insight or the intellectual subject he wishes to convey to his son, and to divide them into many parts, relating [them] to him gradually, with devices and discernment"*. This principle is something we are continually asked to bring into balance, at every moment we are in contact with another human being, or even when trying to walk down the street. One part of us drives, another part rides.

---

4   Ethics of the Fathers/Pirkei Avot, 1:12.

GRATITUDE

Hod can be translated as humility, gratitude, modesty, surrender or splendour. It is the root of the Hebrew word for thank you - *Todah*, the prayer for thanks - *Modim* - and other phrases for thanks, such as in the Hallel prayer which reads *Hodu L'Hashem* from the Book of Psalms, *"Give thanks to God for He is good"*[5]. *Hod*-gratitude helps us achieve our potential through showing humility before the power above us, and thanking our way to greatness.

QUESTIONS TO HEAL DYSFUNCTIONAL DISCIPLINE (*HOD*)

Where are all of the areas in my life in which I have a deficiency of Hod/ humility?

1. Where do I lack gratitude and humility?
2. Where am I not grateful? Where do I take without giving? (With my body? With my partner?)

Where are all of the areas in my life where I have an excess of Hod/humility?

1. Where do I allow other people to treat me badly?
2. Where do I treat myself badly?

HOD/HUMILITY CHECKLIST

- *Hod* is the way that I hold back my power, and allow the energy of receiving. It is humble and grateful, but is it balanced?
- Am I loving in the way I express humility? Is my personal gratitude coming from a place of lovingkindness? (*Chesed*-lovingkindess in *Hod*-humility)
- Am I able to be focused and disciplined when I need to stay humble? Am in touch with my true self-discipline and strength? (*Gevurah*-discipline in *Hod*-humility)
- Am I balanced and just in my humility and gratitude? (*Tiferet*-compassion in *Hod*-humility)
- Can I stay grateful and humble in relationships? Can I maintain a mindset of gratitude? (*Netzach*-endurance in *Hod*-humility)

---

5   Psalm 107:1.

- Am I truly grateful or just pretending? Can I count my gratitudes every day? (*Hod*-gratitude in *Hod*-gratitude)
- Do I surrender to the desires of others and allow our relationship to strengthen through my attitude? Is my humility deeply grounded and connected? (*Yesod*-foundation in *Hod*-humility)
- Have I mastered my humility? Can I be a strong leader and be humble at the same time? (*Malchut*-mastery in *Hod*-humility)

DYSFUNCTIONAL *GEVURAh*

- There is no love when I express gratitude. I am strategic rather than genuinely caring (lacking *Chesed*-love in *Hod*-humility)
- I cannot be self-disciplined to stay humble. I am an arrogant idiot at times (lacking *Gevurah*-strength in *Hod*-humility)
- I become too humble and people walk all over me, OR I walk all over others (lacking of *Tiferet*-balance in *Hod*-humility)
- I cannot stay grateful. I become arrogant quickly, do not count my blessings, and become demanding towards others. I ask questions like "why don't I have more abundance in my life?" (lacking *Netzach*-endurance in *Hod*-humility)
- I become arrogant rather than surrendering. I push rather than allowing other people the space they need. I step into other people's space and cause upsets (lacking *Hod*-humility in *Hod*-humility)
- My lack of humility and gratitude pushes other people away rather than drawing them closer, and my relationships and friendships are not closely bonded. (lacking *Yesod*-bonding in *Hod*-humility)
- I lack discipline, push when I should allow space, give when I should receive and do not stay in a space of gratitude (lacking *Malchut*-mastery in *Hod*-humility)

HOD (*HOD* AS MAKING SPACE FOR OTHERS, GRATITUDE & RESPECT)

RELATIONSHIPS

- Where am I growing arrogant and complacent in my relationships? How can I be more loving and creative about the way I stay humble and grateful towards the other person? (*Chesed*-lovingkindness)

- Where do I lack humility and gratitude in my relationships? How can I be more disciplined about transforming this character trait? (*Gevurah*-strength)

- Where am I growing arrogant and complacent in my relationships? How can I increase my humility and gratitude in a way that is compassionate and balanced? (*Tiferet*-compassion)

- Where am I growing arrogant and complacent in my relationships? How can I increase my humility and gratitude on a regular, ongoing basis? (*Netzach*-endurance)

- Where am I growing arrogant and complacent in my relationships? How can I continue to increase my humility, and deepen my gratitude? Where can I truly complement and compliment the other person? (*Hod*-humility)

- Where am I growing arrogant and complacent in my relationships? How can I increase my humility and gratitude in a way that bonds me to another? (*Yesod*-bonding)

- Where am I growing arrogant and complacent in my relationships? How can I express more gratitude through my words and actions? (*Malchut*-nobility)

BODY

- Where am I growing arrogant and complacent towards my body, taking it for granted, being too lazy or even pushing it too hard? How can I be more grateful and humble in the relationship with my body, and do this with a sense of love?

- Where am I growing arrogant and complacent towards my body, taking it for granted, being too lazy or even pushing it too hard? How can I be more grateful and humble in the relationship with my body, and do this in a disciplined manner?

- Where am I growing arrogant and complacent towards my body, taking it for granted, being too lazy or even pushing it too hard?

How can I be more grateful and humble in the relationship with my body, and do this with compassion and balance?

- Where am I growing arrogant and complacent towards my body, taking it for granted, being too lazy or even pushing it too hard? How can I be more grateful and humble in the relationship with my body, and do this on a regular basis?

- Where am I growing arrogant and complacent towards my body, taking it for granted, being too lazy or even pushing it too hard? How can I be more grateful and humble in the relationship with my body, and with deep, fully-embodied gratitude?

- Where am I growing arrogant and complacent towards my body, taking it for granted, being too lazy or even pushing it too hard? How can I be more grateful and humble in the relationship with my body, and get deeply connected through this gratitude and humility?

- Where am I growing arrogant and complacent towards my body, taking it for granted, being too lazy or even pushing it too hard? How can I be more grateful and humble in the relationship with my body, and do this through my thoughts, speech and actions?

MY THINKING

- Where do I live in a space of expectation, and lack gratitude? What love can I be grateful for today?

BUSINESS

- Where do I lack humility in my business? Where have I stopped respecting people, whether these are my clients or colleagues? How can I apply more respect and do it from a place of *Chesed*-love?

- Where do I lack humility in my business? Where have I stopped respecting people, whether these are my clients or colleagues? How can I be more *Gevurah*-disciplined about applying respect and staying grateful for these people and opportunities?

- Where do I lack humility in my business? Where have I stopped respecting people, whether these are my clients or colleagues? How can I have more *Tiferet*-compassion for the people I am working with and the projects I am working on? How can I embody a compassionate gratitude?

- Where do I lack humility in my business? Where have I stopped respecting people, whether these are my clients or colleagues? How can I continue to stay humble and grateful towards them on a daily basis (*Netzach*-endurance)? What new practices or mantras would help me do that?

- Where do I lack humility in my business? Where have I stopped respecting people, whether these are my clients or colleagues? What are all the things I can be grateful for today? (*Hod*-humility in *Hod*-humility)

- Where do I lack humility in my business? Where have I stopped respecting people, whether these are my clients or colleagues? How is this blocking me from connecting with others? How will increased humility or gratitude help me connect (*Yesod*) with people on deeper levels?

- Where do I lack humility in my business? Where have I stopped respecting people, whether these are my clients or colleagues? How can I speak or behave differently today, and truly master these attributes? (*Malchut*)

DAY 29 / LOVINGKINDNESS IN HUMILITY / BLAME & COMPLAINT: חסד שבהוד

KABBALAH SUTRA: *Chesed She b'Hod* – Lovingkindness in Humility. INTENTION: To be more grateful towards the people you love. To create more space for receiving love through humble lovingkindness. Become great through humble acts of giving.

"Our masters taught: Adam was created on the eve of Sabbath, [the last of all created beings]. Why? So that if man's opinion of himself should become overweening, he would be reminded that the gnat preceded him in the order of creation". — Talmud[6]

Most of us know what it is like to be in a situation where the other person does not leave us any room. This feeling can happen at a dinner party where someone is taking up all of the airtime and making the conversation about their views and their opinions, and it feels like there is no space left in the room.

Similarly we also know people who are continually complaining about their life and totally lack perspective. These ingrates lack thankfulness for all of the blessings that have come their way, whether it is food in their fridge, the roof over their heads, the money in their bank account or the loving friends and family - instead they regularly moan about the things that are not going as they would like. They are not fun to be around and will take any opportunity to drag us into their miserable story.

THE KABBALAH OF SELF-ABNEGATION

Hod "implies self-abnegation" explains The Tanya, and ultimately is about *"acknowledging the transcendence of that which defies his mortal understanding"*[7], namely, God. Hence the appearance of the word *Hod*-

---

6   Babylonian Talmud, Sanhedrin 38a, as quoted in Sefer Ha-Agadah p708.
7   Commentary on Epistle 15 in Lessons In Tanya.

humility in the phrase "*[a man seeks] to prostrate himself and to [self-effacingly] praise (L'Hodot) God*"[8].

> "*This [attribute of Hod-humility] also includes the expression of gratitude to God for all the favours that He has bestowed upon us, so that [we] should not be ungrateful, God forbid. This [attribute of Hod] also includes the offering of thanks to God for all His praiseworthy [deeds], and His attributes and His workings in the emanation and creation of the upper and lower worlds, for they are praiseworthy to no end*"[9].

When we become grateful and stay loving about it, that is *Chesed*-love in *Hod*-gratitude. Consider how you are appearing to others. Are you complaining or are you staying thankful about your lot in life? And can you be loving about it at the same time?

LOOKING TO ACKNOWLEDGE OTHERS

Hod-humility/gratitude can also be seen as a sense of acknowledgement, and the *Chesed*-love or creativity aspect would be finding ways to acknowledge others. Get creative about it! Tell your partner or spouse something that you really acknowledge and appreciate about them, whether it is their thoughtfulness or care or anything. Tell your parents, your children, your boss, your clients - just look for ways to acknowledge them. When this sense of gratitude is fuelled by *Chesed*-love, it begins to rectify the 'damaged' sphere in our soul. On a very practical level these are all of the areas in our lives when we have taken people for granted, moaned or complained to them, and not acknowledged them for the blessings they are bringing into our life and the world at large.

FALSE HUMILITY

Pretending to be humble also misses the point, and we know when someone is being disingenuous, obviously lowering themselves for their own gain. Similarly, teachers, managers or religious leaders can easily fall into the trap of becoming too comfortable with their positions

---

8   Ibid.
9   Ibid.

of responsibility, forgetting what it was like to start out and losing all humility in the process. *Hod*-humility is a balance to *Netzach*-endurance and everyone must find the right approach for their individual situation.

By becoming more humble we create space for the other person and it is through this humility that we achieve true splendour.

TODAY'S PRACTICE

YOGA PRACTICE GUIDELINES:

Begin TODAY'S PRACTICE with a sense of humility towards God, holding in mind the name of Nishmat Kol Chai, the "Source of All Breath", recognising that your entire life comes from God. Meditate on the things you love about your body, be it your hair, legs, eyes or even your looks. Perhaps you love certain skills that you have mastered, such as the ability to think clearly under pressure, to be a supportive friend, to be an excellent parent or to play an instrument. Allow yourself to feel a warm glow of love and satisfaction for something you do well. As you sink more deeply into today's posture, hold a sense of surrender and humility whilst balancing it with love.

GYM PRACTICE GUIDELINES:

Treat your body with a sense of gratitude today, still working hard in your gym practice but paying attention to your limbs, muscles, joints, bones, breath and the fact that you have use of your body. Stay creative (*Chesed*) in the way that you are grateful (*Hod*), and continue to work towards your overall health and fitness goals.

RELATIONSHIP PRACTICE GUIDELINES:

Developing a sense of loving gratitude. Finding people you want to connect with and then find ways to express your gratitude. Notice where you are not acknowledging others, and where the way you express love is devoid of humility.

QUESTIONS FOR MEDITATION

RELATIONSHIPS:

- Where do I grow arrogant and complacent in my relationships? How can I be more loving and creative about the way I stay humble and grateful towards the other person? (*Chesed*)
- Do I have the tendency to be arrogant?
- How does my arrogance play itself out?
- Are there any situations where I could be perceived to be arrogant, and other people may view me as such (even though I might be completely genuine and well-meaning in my actions)?
- How good am I at focusing on the needs of others, giving myself to them and improving people's lives.
- Where am I not acknowledging other people for the good they do for me? (e.g parents).
- Where are my loving relationships devoid of humility? How is this damaging my relationships?

YOGA/BODY/GYM:

- Where do I grow arrogant and complacent towards my body, taking it for granted, being too lazy or even pushing it too hard? How can I be more grateful and humble in the relationship with my body, and do this with a sense of love? (*Chesed*)
- How able am I to become humble within my yoga practice, maintaining a sense of surrender?
  How often do I complete a yoga session feeling completely at One, and supremely focused?

BUSINESS:

- Where do I lack humility in my business or workplace? Where have I stopped respecting people, whether it is clients or colleagues? How can I apply more respect and do it from a place of love?

BONUS: IMPROVE RELATIONSHIPS THROUGH ACKNOWLEDGEMENTS

Listen out for what people want to be acknowledged for[10] e.g. if you are spending hours cooking a beautiful dinner, you may want to be acknowledged for the hours you have put in cooking and prepping. Or if you have done a favour for a friend and helped them through a difficult time, you may appreciate an acknowledgement of this. So listen out for what other people want to be acknowledged for - e.g. your parents have helped you out financially, your spouse has bought the food you like, your work colleague has helped you with a project. i) think how you like to be acknowledged and ii) do this for other people, but do it from a place of love (*Chesed*).

---

[10] This is a technique from the Landmark Education's communications course, "Access to Power".

GYM SEQUENCE, DAY 29/PLANK JUMP-INS

Also known as "Squat Thrusts". 3 x 12 repetitions.

.01

.02

YOGA SEQUENCE, DAY 29/STAFF (DANDASANA)

Draw together the lower tips of your shoulder blades and push out through your heels.

.01

חסד
Chesed-Love
(Right Arm)

הוד
Hod-Humility

.02

DAY 30 / DISCIPLINE IN GRATITUDE / CONDITIONED THANKS: גבורה שבהוד

KABBALAH SUTRA: *Gevurah She b'Hod* – Discipline in Humility.
INTENTION: To condition yourself to live a state of gratitude, leading to greater happiness. To reduce your ego through disciplined humility.

Life changes when we condition ourselves into a state of gratitude. Growing up in England we were taught to say our please and thank-you's as a matter of reflex, but the idea of really staying in a space of deep gratitude can positively transform anybody's life. I currently go for a walk each morning and spend three minutes focusing purely on things I am grateful for, such as my nephews, my parents, living in Los Angeles, and by actively looking for reasons to be thankful, I feel better[11].

It takes discipline (*Gevurah*) to stay in a state of gratitude (*Hod*) but it is invariably worthwhile. Even though there is a religious practice to state 100 blessings every single day[12], it is easy to allow this ritual to become a mindless routine with words that are being said while the mind is disconnected. But the power of these words is notable: "*Blessed are You, Hashem, our God, King of the Universe for not having made me a slave*"[13]. Inspiration can be found in any of these blessings - "Who gives sight to the blind", "who gives strength to the weary" - but it does require a mindful approach to continue to stay connected to these words, rather than reeling them off like a bad stage actor who has performed a play many times and allows his mind to wander while speaking the lines that he knows so well.

---

[11] This practice was inspired by Tony Robbins when he discussed his morning rituals in an interview with Tim Ferris - "Tony Robbins on Morning Routines, Peak Performance, and Mastering Money" at www.fourhourworkweek.com.

[12] From the Babylonian Talmud, Menachot 43b. Rabbi Meir said: "A person is obliged to recite 100 blessings every day as it is said, 'What does the Lord your God ask of you?' (Deuteronomy. 10:12). Instead of "ma" (what?), read it as "mea" (the number 100)".

[13] From the morning blessings, as found in the Artscroll Siddur, p18.

FAKE IT 'TILL YOU MAKE IT

There are days when we are grumpy and just not feeling in the mood. But the attitude of gratitude does not require us to feel it, but rather, to do it. On those days we can become very self-centred and lose both gratitude and perspective. One practice is to "empty out" and to consider God who is giving us our ability to be alive and even our ability to complain. Another practice is to try to achieve perspective by becoming acutely aware of people who would love to have our problems. For example, we may be worried about paying our bills, but if we start looking at photographs of children battling cancer, their biggest concern might be turning 10 years old and we can remember that our problems are relatively minor[14].

The aim of the process is to clear the way for enlightenment and more God - so when you get into gratitude and discipline yourself, condition yourself daily, this will i) Make you more happy, ii)Keep you more happy, and iii) Improve your mental attitude, which can lead to better health and relationships, and to receiving more blessings.

DAILY THANKS

We *"should not be ungrateful, God forbid"*, taught Rabbi Schneur Zalman of Liadi. *"This [attribute of Hod-humility] also includes the offering of thanks to God for all His praiseworthy [deeds], and His attributes and His workings in the emanation and creation of the upper and lower worlds"*[15]. As discussed earlier, *Hod* is the root of the Hebrew word *Hodaya*, meaning thanks, and having the ability to say thank you is the first step towards disciplined humility. In thanking God for my physical being, my life, family and possessions, I am able to recognise a power greater than myself. This is a key ingredient of healing and used by all 12-step programmes for recovery from addictions. Some modern meditation instructors employ a gratitude meditation on a daily basis, literally saying "thank you" from the moment of getting out of bed and continuing to express gratitude for the entire first hour of each day. They encourage people to literally say thank you for the ability to stand up,

---

14   Thank you to Eric Sander Kingston for teaching me this important practice around gaining perspective.
15   Tanya, Epistle 15.

for the power to go to the toilet, or even for the mental clarity to be able to say 'thank you'. The Talmud may have recommended this 2000 years ago[16], but it is still as relevant as ever. It does not matter how you interpret or relate to 'God'; if you are just grateful for being able to get up in the morning, it is hard not to feel good.

HUMILITY WITHOUT DISCIPLINE

Humility without discipline goes to one of two extremes. Too little discipline, which is probably the most common, leads to extreme self-confidence and arrogance. By not having boundaries or limits on our humility, we can find ourselves in a place of self-centredness and self-aggrandisement that will eventually repel other people and get in the way of relationships because it is all about us. Too much humility, an undisciplined overdose of it, becomes equally difficult for people to connect with and is a major obstacle in relationships. Think of someone you have known who is excessively modest and self-depreciating – this will usually be the mark of too little self-esteem, this person will often find themselves too yielding to the will of others and will find that others take advantage of them. The ultimate path is the middle way, where there is Discipline in Humility.

We have previously explained how *Gevurah* is a kind of restriction. By holding back our desires and ego, through restricting our will, we can make space for greatness.

YOGIC QUIETUDE

This is clear on a physical plane – when we step back, we make room for someone else – and it is also true with the metaphysical dimension. "*When the mind becomes free from obstruction*", explains the Yoga Sutras, "*all vacillations cease*"[17]. We are only able to set the mind free if we perform an act of *Gevurah*-restriction, and this demands extreme

---

16 From the Babylonian Talmud, Brachot 60b. "*When one awakens in the morning, a person should say 'Elokai Neshama'. Upon hearing the rooster crow, one should recite the blessing 'haNoten laSechvi Binah'. Upon clothing oneself, one should recite the blessing 'Malbish Arumim'. Upon placing one's hands over his eyes, one should recite the blessing 'Pokeiach Ivrim', etc*". As translated by Rabbi Yaakov Beasley. http://etzion.org.il/vbm/english/archive/salt-devarim/47-9reeh.htm
17 Yoga Sutras 1:51, Stiles translation.

humility. The rabbinic sages told us that true strength comes from controlling our desires - *"who is strong? The person who can restrain their desires"*[18] - and this is the ultimate form of humility. Another way to access this is by listing all of the things we have to be thankful for, which also increases our sense of gratitude.

Sanskrit writings talk about the importance of respect for one's guru, and there is an important Hebrew concept of *Kavod HaRav* – reverence for one's teacher. When we continue to consider the idea of the internal teacher, whether it is our emotions, intuition or body, we can start by directing this humility inwards and listening very closely to the internal messages. As we take a moment to recognise and appreciate the teachers around us, whether this is a former schoolteacher, work colleague or family member, we increase our capacity to receive more teachers and to grow splendiferous!

TODAY'S PRACTICE

YOGA PRACTICE GUIDELINES:

There are three approaches for experiencing the energy of Discipline in Humility. As you embark on your daily yoga routine, bring a conscious awareness of gratitude for your physical being. Even if you are in some pain or suffering from a physical limitation or injury, be thankful for the parts of your body that are working well. Enhance this with an awareness of the temporality of life, that we come from the earth and that we will eventually return to it[19]. The body is transient but the soul is eternal, and as we bring a conscious awareness of this fact we can deepen our yoga practice and use our bodies to help us understand and reach a true realisation. Even if you get tired in your asana or vinyasa, by reminding yourself of the transience of your body – that you are not this physical shell – you can transcend physical limitations. TODAY'S PRACTICE should therefore include holding postures for longer than usual, noticing what makes you tired and staying with the postures

---

[18]   Ethics of the Fathers/Pirkei Avot, 1:4.
[19]   For further meditation material, see Ethics of the Fathers/Pirkei Avot, *3:1*

especially when you would like to stop and relax (assuming that you are not in pain).

GYM PRACTICE GUIDELINES:

Apply discipline today but surrender (*Hod*) yourself and in doing so allow the practice to take its own course. If you notice any anger, internal criticism or judgement, that is an opportunity to get back into the space of *Hod*-humility.

GRATITUDE PRACTICE:

Make a list of 10 things you are grateful for in your life, and then repeat this every morning and evening.

QUESTIONS FOR MEDITATION

RELATIONSHIPS:

- Where do I lack humility and gratitude in my relationships? How can I be more disciplined about transforming this character trait? (*Gevurah*)
- Where am I not disciplined in my humility/gratitude and how is this [wrecking] my life? How much better could my life be if I nailed this?

YOGA/BODY/GYM:

- Where do I grow arrogant and complacent towards my body, taking it for granted, being too lazy or even pushing it too hard? How can I be more grateful and humble in the relationship with my body, and do this in a disciplined manner?

BUSINESS:

- Where do I lack humility in my business or workplace? Where have I stopped respecting people, whether these are my clients or colleagues? How can I be more disciplined about applying respect and staying grateful for these people and opportunities?

GYM SEQUENCE, DAY 30/PLANK LEG RAISES

Alternate sides. 3 x 10 repetitions, resting in between sets.

.01

גבורה
Gevurah-Strength

הוד
Hod-Humility

.02

YOGA SEQUENCE, DAY 30/SEATED FORWARD BEND (PASCHIMOTTANASANA)

Keep your back straight for as long as possible and stop before you are about to fold your back. Use a strap if necessary and keep your breath deep.

גבורה
Gevurah-Strength

הוד
Hod-Humility

DAY 31 / BALANCED HUMILITY / BEND LIKE THE REED / תפארת שבהוד

KABBALAH SUTRA: *Tiferet She b'Hod* – Balance/Compassion in Humility.

INTENTION: To create inner harmony and balance through humble compassion to yourself and others. Become great through compassionate humility.

"Our masters taught: A man should always be as yielding as a reed and not as unyielding as a cedar" — Talmud[20]

In a visual and material world it is easy to compare ourselves with the achievements of others and in doing so forget who we are. Part of the challenge of our society is that people either over-aggrandise themselves, including many of the famous "role-models" in the realm of acting and music, or they over-crush themselves with low self-esteem, which is why so many end up with a trail of broken marriages, rehab stories and depression. The truly balanced ones are few and far between.

SKILLS & SHORTCOMINGS

What are your skills and what are your shortcomings? *Tiferet*-balance in *Hod*-humility demands honesty about both. "You are a child of God", wrote Marianne Williamson, *"Your playing small does not serve the world. There is nothing enlightened about shrinking so that other people won't feel insecure around you. We are all meant to shine, as children do"*[21]. Humility does not mean pretending you do not have any skills, rather, it is about being honest and wearing your abilities lightly. Tiferet-beauty invites us to strike the beautiful balance between our confidence in our abilities and humility in the face of them, much like Superman in his guise as Clark Kent.

---

[20]   Babylonian Talmud, Taanit 20a, Sanhedrin 105b-106a in Sefer Ha-Aggadah p710.
[21]   Marianne Williamson in A Return to Love: Reflections on the Principles of "A Course in Miracles".

One of the greatest Kabbalists, Rabbi Shimon Bar Yochai (Second century), taught the following principle;

> *"We have been taught that Rabbi Shimon bar Yochai said: A man should speak of his superiority with a soft voice and of his shortcomings with a loud voice; of his superiority with a soft voice, as may be seen in the confession at tithing [During which one says softly, 'I have not transgressed any of the commandments, neither have I forgotten them'* [22]*; of his shortcomings in a loud voice, as may be seen in the confession of the first fruits".* [During which one is told, "Thou art to speak up and say [loudly] , 'A wandering Aramean was my father'* [23] "[24].

We can apply this directly to our life by asking which skills we are not acknowledging and which parts of our personality are we over-confident about?

HUMBLE SPIRIT:

Benefitting from continual humility is a practice that was recognised by Rabbi Meir (First century). He taught that we should be *"humble in spirit before all people"*[25], a message which has particular resonance in our age of multiculturalism and diversity. At first glance it appears to be asking us to be respectful and gracious towards every person of every culture, regardless of whether we agree with them or not. This is not necessarily the case and although we can be humble in spirit towards someone we disagree with, it is not automatically asking us to spend more time with them than we need to.

INTERNAL HUMILITY:

There are, however, more secrets revealed if we explore the phrase in its original Hebrew. It literally says *Shfal Ru'ach Bifnei Kol Adam* – have a humble spirit before all people – but *Kol Adam* could be read as "all of the body". In other words, we should be humble before each limb and

---

[22] Deuteronomy 26:13.
[23] Deuteronomy 26:5
.[24] Babylonian Talmud Sotah 32b, Sefer Ha-Aggadah p710.
[25] Ethics of the Fathers/Pirkei Avot, 4:12.

sinew in our body, not punishing it and being respectful towards the way we are treating it or the postures we are pushing it into. A further secret is in the word *Ru'ach*, meaning breath as well as spirit, and we might reinterpret the phrase so that it reads "have a humble breath before all of your body parts". This can inform our yoga so that we are grateful for our bodies and careful with the postures we are breathing ourselves into, maintaining sensitivity towards each placement of our hands, feet and so on.

HUMILITY IN THE FACE OF THE UNIVERSE

The ultimate humility we can experience is in our relationship with the Creator. Our yoga practice is a means to creating space so that we can experience the vastness of the creator. Patanjali wrote that *"the end of spiritual practice is only attained by placing oneself in the Lord"*[26]. By achieving this level of trust and humility, *Emunah* (trust in God), we connect with a sense of self which is *"unlimited by time"*[27]. Ironically, by becoming more humble we actually become more expansive. This is a paradox of the ego that cannot be ignored as the ego is clinging to its survival and telling the story that "if you destroy me, there will be nothing left and you will have no honour, glory or compliments". In reality we gain much more through the act of experiencing true humility with the Creator.

TODAY'S PRACTICE

YOGA PRACTICE GUIDELINES:

- Meditate on the verse "be humble in spirit towards all people" or the alternative reading of "be humble in breath towards all of your body" and work on a balanced practice that is considered and consistent.

GYM PRACTICE GUIDELINES:

- Where am I lacking humility with regards to my body? Am I going too easy on one area of my physical exercise (perhaps cardio)

---

26 Yoga Sutras 1:23.
27 Ibid, 1:23.

and too strong on another area (e.g. weights). Pay close attention to your body, humble your ego and listen to what your body truly needs today. Try focusing some exercises on your core (*Tiferet-*balance/torso) and surrendering (*Hod*) to what is most needed.

RELATIONSHIP PRACTICE GUIDELINES:

Whilst it is not always possible to genuinely feel compassion towards the person you are being humble towards – let's say there is a situation at work where you choose to help a colleague who you are **not** that fond of but you can see they will benefit from our assistance – this aspect of *Tiferet*-compassion in *Hod*-humility is asking us to question our motivation. It is about reflecting on our motivations and seeing where we have the capacity for more compassion in our humility.

Today is about learning from other people, learning from each and every one of them. Try finding the most arrogant and dislikeable person you can and see how it is possible to be humble in spirit towards them by focusing on what you are able to learn from them.

QUESTIONS FOR MEDITATION

RELATIONSHIPS:
- What happens when I am not consistently humble? What are the traps that I can then fall into?
- Where do I grow arrogant and complacent in my relationships? How can I increase my humility and gratitude in way that is compassionate and balanced? (*Tiferet*)
- How am I not balanced and compassionate in my humility? Where is it out of balance? Where is too much about me? How can I improve this? How is this lack-of-balance impacting and affecting myself and others?

YOGA/BODY/GYM:
- Where do I grow arrogant and complacent towards my body, taking it for granted, being too lazy or even pushing it too hard?

How can I be more grateful and humble in the relationship with my body, and do this with compassion and balance?

BUSINESS:

- Where do I lack humility in my business or workplace? Where have I stopped respecting people, whether these are clients or colleagues? How can I have more compassion for the people I am working with and the projects I am working on? How can I embody compassionate gratitude?

PERSONAL DEVELOPMENT:

- Which skills am I not acknowledging? Where am I good at something and not focusing or recognising it, or pretending that this is not a personal strength?
- Where am I being over-confident? Which skills am I not so good at but placing too much faith in, and how is that having a detrimental effect on my life? (e.g. income, relationships, happiness).

GYM SEQUENCE, DAY 31/BODY FOLD

A modified sit-up, continue for 3 x 10 repetitions.

.01

תפארת
Tiferet-Balance

הוד
Hod-Humility

.02

YOGA SEQUENCE, DAY 31/INCLINED PLANE (PURVOTTANASANA)

Push your hands into the ground and keep your body straight.

תפארת
Tiferet-Balance

הוד
Hod-Humility

DAY 32 / ENDURANCE IN HUMILITY / GOOD YOGI, BAD YOGI: נצח שבהוד

KABBALAH SUTRA: *Netzach She b'Hod* – Endurance in Humility.

INTENTION: To increase my power through enduring gratitude, acknowledgement and humility. Slow, humble endurance. To develop inner power and the ability to overcome obstacles through enduring humility.

Some people get confused when growing as a leader. They can be too strong, flexing their muscles when it is not appropriate, or too friendly and weak-willed when it comes to asserting their authority. *Netzach*-endurance in *Hod*-humility asks you to stay humble, even when you are growing or in a position as strong as Moses. He was the general of the Hebrew army and yet is known as the most humble person to walk the planet[28]. Humility is an essential tool whether you are developing as a leader or facing a leadership challenge, be it for a company of 5000 people or running your own household, .

EXCESSIVE HUMILITY

Humility does not mean a lack of confidence. Moses could not do his job properly when he was excessively putting himself down and making excuses for why he could not speak with Pharaoh. If we spend our time pretending that we have no skills or lack any discernible talent then we cannot achieve anything. Equally, if we over-emphasise our abilities, we will quickly create enemies. *Netzach*-endurance in *Hod*-humility is an enduring graciousness that makes our actions about other people rather than about ourselves. Be a great teacher, a strong leader, a powerful musician or inspiring boss, but make it about other people and your impact will be all the greater.

---

[28] Numbers/Bamidbar 12:13 - *"Now Moses was a very humble man, more humble than anyone else on the face of the earth".*

EXCESSIVE CONFIDENCE

The sages warned against excessive ego; *"Rabbi Judah said in the name of Rav: When a man boasts, if he is a sage, his wisdom departs from him; if he is a prophet, his gift of prophecy departs from him"*[29]. This was not a threat but an energy principle. Too much self, too much inflated ego will prevent our ability to receive Divine transmissions and reduce our ego. Similarly, *"Rabbi Meir said: Be humble of spirit before all people"*[30].

THE KABBALISTIC PARTNERSHIP

Just as Moses is readily associated with *Netzach*-endurance, his brother Aaron the Priest is the emblem of *Hod*-humility. Kabbalistic teachings continually pair them together. They are described as organs that advise, as testicles that prepare seed to be shared into the word, as "grinders and millstones" which prepare information to be shared.

The basic concept is that *Netzach*-endurance and *Hod*-humility are primarily concerned with affecting and effecting the world. This is why they are located in the hips and legs which physically move us into the world, unlike the arms (*Chesed*-love and *Gevurah*-discipline) and torso (*Tiferet*-compassion) which do not have the power to walk us forwards.

Rabbi Shneur Zalman of Liadi (1745-1812) taught:

> *"Netzach and Hod; These [attributes] are "the kidneys that advise"*[31]*, in a manner similar to their physical counterpart, and they are also (in spiritual terms) the two testicles that prepare the spermatozoa*[32]*. Like their physical counterpart, the attributes of Netzach and Hod adapt the effusion of the concept. i.e. the drop that issues forth from the brain*[33]*. That is, [they adapt] an intellectual subject deriving from the father's mind in such a way that it will not issue unmodified, (as a very subtle concept in his brain and intellect. Netzach and Hod are also referred to as "grinders" and "millstones", because they "grind the mannah for the righteous). Similarly, by way of example, a person*

---

29   Babylonian Talmud, Pesachim 66b, Sefer Ha-Aggadah p711.
30   Ethics of the Fathers/Pirkei Avot 4:12.
31   Babylonian Talmud, Brachot 61a.
32   Zohar III, 296a.
33   Cf. Tanya, Part I, ch. 2.

who grinds [wheat] with millstones crumbles it into very fine parts, so too does the father need to taper the insight or the intellectual subject he wishes to convey to his son, and to divide this into many parts, relating [them] to him gradually, with devices and discernment[34].

Through these qualities of endurance and humility, or confidence and gratitude, we are able to share our love (*Chesed*), strength (*Tiferet*) and compassion (*Tiferet*).

PARTNERSHIP IN LIFE

There is also the ongoing partnership between Moses and Aaron which sees them working together from the initial conversations with Pharaoh in Egypt, to when Moses is descending Mount Sinai and is horrified by with the creation of a golden calf. Their joint journey begins very early on when Moses tries to refuse his calling, saying to God *"Please, O Lord, I have never been a man of words, either in times past or now that You have spoken to Your servant; I am slow of speech and slow of tongue"*[35].

Moses requests, *"Please, O Lord, make someone else Your agent"* and we are told *"The Lord became angry with Moses, and He said, "There is your brother Aaron the Levite. He, I know, speaks readily. Even now he is setting out to meet you, and he will be happy to see you. You shall speak to him and put the words in his mouth – I will be with you and with him as you speak, and tell both of you what to do – and he shall speak for you to the people. Thus he shall serve as your spokesman, with you playing the role of God to him, and take with you this rod, with which you shall perform the signs"*[36].

In considering Moses and Aaron we might think about ourselves; the part of us that is fearful of stepping into a greater leadership role and the part of us that is terrified of the consequences and holds back out of fear. But to be balanced we must also bear in mind the alternative, and that through stepping into our calling, enduring with humility and gratitude for All That Is, we might lead ourselves and others to a place of true liberation.

---

34   Tanya, Epistle 15.
35   Exodus 4:10, JPS Translation.
36   Exodus 4 :14-17, JPS Translation.

TODAY'S PRACTICE

YOGA PRACTICE GUIDELINES:

Today's practice of Netzach-endurance in Hod-humility is to continue working with the postures in such a way that suits your body and to continue enduring with the postures whilst remaining humble and open to inspiration. There is no reason for arrogance because it ultimately makes no difference how proficient we are in relation to other people, and by enduring with humility we can free ourselves from the pain and suffering caused by the ego.

The essence of yoga, as we have learned, is to still the "vacillating waves of perception" that the mind experiences[37] . The entire endeavour is to achieve a place of stillness-in-motion where we are still vitally alive but free from the internal fluctuations, the thousand slings and arrows that flesh is heir to. According to the Yoga Sutras, these psychological waverings can be stilled "through consistent earnest practice" and this is the balance of *Netzach*-endurance in *Hod*-humility. The combination of consistency and humility provides the endurance and earnestness to achieve any goal.

GYM PRACTICE GUIDELINES:

Keep your practice simple today, focusing on modest (*Hod*) goals and staying in a state of emotional surrender, that is, not driving forwards with your ego. Remain humble and grateful to be in your body, grateful for the clothes you are wearing, your surroundings and the gym equipment that you are using (even if it is dragging a sack of rocks and sand). The practice is to stay in continual, enduring gratitude and humility.

RELATIONSHIP PRACTICE GUIDELINES:

Humility with other people may seem like a weakness but the opposite is true. How much respect do you have for the people who lack in humility and how much do you want to be around them? We all know people who are continually talking about their achievements,

---

37   Yoga Sutras 1:12.

and regularly see an untalented reality TV contestant who is seeking their fleeting 15 minutes of fame. The sages say that an honoured and respected person is *"the one who respects others"*[38] and this kind of humble honour is something we can all, in theory, achieve and aspire towards. How? By enduring with it. Practice, practice, and more practice. All is practice.

QUESTIONS FOR MEDITATION

RELATIONSHIPS:

- Where do I grow arrogant and complacent in my relationships? How can I increase my humility and gratitude on a regular, ongoing basis? (*Netzach)*
- Where do I give up in my gratitude?
- Where do I stop being humble?
- Where do I grow weary of my new-found humility and lapse into arrogance or egotism? Even if it is who I really am e.g. deep-down caring, wanting people to improve, what happens along the way?
- Where do I fail to continue to acknowledge people? (see what can happen in a personal relationship when this happens).
- To whom do I need to write thank-you cards?

YOGA/BODY/GYM:

- Where do I grow arrogant and complacent towards my body, taking it for granted, being too lazy or even pushing it too hard? How can I be more grateful and humble in the relationship with my body, and do this on a regular basis?

BUSINESS:

- Where do I lack humility in my business or workplace? Where have I stopped respecting people, whether these are my clients or colleagues? How can I continue to stay humble and grateful towards them on a daily basis (*Netzach)*? What new practices or mantras would help me do that?
- Where have I grown complacent towards clients or my boss or company?

---

38   Ethics of the Fathers/Pirkei Avot 4:1.

GYM SEQUENCE, DAY 32/DUMBBELL FRONT SQUAT

Keep your back straight, elbows forward and parallel, and bend your knees. Ensure you use your leg muscles to smoothly straighten up, and continue to engage your breath.

.01

נצח — הוד
Netzach-Endurance   *Hod*-Humility

.02

YOGA SEQUENCE, DAY 32/HALF-MOON (ARDHA CHANDRASANA)

Raise your foot as high as possible, find your balance whilst facing the ground and then rotate your hip upwards whilst raising your gaze to the ceiling.

נצח
Netzach-Endurance

הוד
Hod-Humility

DAY 33 / HUMILITY IN HUMILITY / RANDOM ACTS OF HUMILITY: הוד שבהוד

KABBALAH SUTRA: *Hod She b'Hod* – Humility in Humility.
INTENTION: Fulfil your glorious potential by reducing ego and embodying the ultimate gratitude.

"It was said that R. Akiba had twelve thousand pairs of disciples, from Gabbatha to Antipatris; and all of them died at the same time because they did not treat each other with respect… A Tanna [teacher] taught: All of them died between Passover and Pentecost. R. Hama b. Abba or, it might be said, R. Hiyya b. Abin said: All of them died a cruel death. What was it? — R. Nahman replied: Croup"

Talmud[39]

We talk of peace and love yet often we walk around with dissatisfaction and disputes in our hearts[40]. There are positive slogans written on people's t-shirts, car bumper stickers or tattooed on their arms, but as long as humans walk around with baseless hatred, it is impossible to raise our consciousness, stop war and improve our planet. Judgement of others is part of the poison, as is self-judgement. The voice that tells you "you are not worthy", "why are you trying to do this task?", or, worst of all, "what will others think of you?".

LAG B'OMER

Today is one of the most critical days for revelation, enlightenment and self-development during the 49-day Omer cycle. Day 33 is known as *Lag B'Omer* as the letters *lamed* and *gimel* - when put together pronounced *lag* - mark a significant moment. Tradition teaches that it was the day that the plague of death ceased from Rabbi Akiva's 24,000 students, and it was also the passing of Rabbi Shimon Bar Yochai, (the

---

39   Babylonian Talmud, Yevamot 62b.
40   I owe this teaching and awareness directly to Eric Sander Kingston.

Rashbi, Second century), who was responsible for profound Kabbalistic revelations, especially at the end of his life. It is a popular day for wedding celebrations, bonfires, and thousands of followers visit the Rashbi's grave in Meron, Northern Israel.

The Talmud teaches that Rabbi Akiva's students essentially perpetrated a form of toxic judgement, disrespecting one another[41], which we may relate to the destruction of the second Temple in Jerusalem that was sacked as a result of baseless hatred. They died as a result of their immense lack of respect for one another. It is no coincidence that today's kabbalistic prescription is *Hod*-humility in *Hod*-humility.

We aim to banish judgement from our lives, whether it is judging other people or ourselves. *Hod* in *Hod* is a humble approach to humility, a simplification of this week's theme and a pure, unadulterated expression of the emotional attribute. When is humility not humble? On a surprisingly regular basis.

FALSE HUMILITY: IF NOT YOU, WHO?

There is a huge danger of false humility, which is actually fear in disguise. Ghandi, Martin Luther King, or Mother Teresa could not have achieved their goals if they had an over-restrictive humility. Rather, it has to be a confident humility in the correct direction. When we humble ourselves before God, as if to say, "I am scared, I don't think I am the best at this, but I recognise you are calling me to do to this. I will give it my best try and I will fully commit". As Rabbi Hillel taught, *"If I am not for myself, who will be for me? If I am only for myself, what am I? And if not Now, When?"*[42].

There are crucial tasks we know that we were born to complete - the book you planned to write, the business you wanted to start, the invention you would love to build, the relationship you would like to grow. Humility is important but when we act so humble that it prevents us from standing up for our beliefs and pursuing important goals, this may really be pride or fear in the guise of humility.

---

41 Babylonian Talmud, Masechet Yevamo*t* 62b.
42 Ethics of the Fathers/Pirkei Avot 1:14.

When we get nervous about following our calling and stepping into a leadership position, we can make all kinds of excuses. Moses did this regularly: *"I am slow of speech and slow of tongue"*[43]. Queen Esther did the same when faced with the opportunity to save an entire people, even though it meant breaking the law and going to see the king without an invitation: *"I have not been called to come in unto the king these thirty days"*[44]. They were both scared. We all get scared. Sometimes we pretend to be humble to hide our fear. But that is just egotistical fear masked as humility.

Dr. Martin Luther King was fearful when he started preaching, but he also managed to get over it by not making it about himself any more: His wife Coretta Scott King recalled : *"In January, Martin was invited to the Dexter Avenue Baptist Church to preach a trial sermon. Martin has said he was rather nervous about being called to preach, in spite of three summers of experience at Ebenezer. But he told himself with sensible humor, "Keep Martin Luther King in the background and God in the foreground and everything will be all right. Remember you're a channel of the gospel, not the source"*[45].

So what is it going to be? Complaints and excuses and blaming others or 'bite the bullet and face your fear'? Queen Esther finally puts her ego aside and commits, saying *"fast for me, and do not eat or drink for three days, night or day; I and my maidens will fast in like manner; and so will I go in to the king, which is not according to the law; and if I perish, I perish"*[46]. Rabbi Hillel taught "in a place where there is no man [i.e. leader], strive to be a man [i.e. leader]"[47]. Now is the time to choose whether or not you want to step up.

DIVINE HUMILITY

We have been around people who lack humility and we like to get away from them because of their attitude. The Talmud teaches a principle about Divine humility that we can take directly into our own lives:

---

43   Exodus 4:10.
44   The Book of Esther/Megillat Esther 4:11.
45   My Life with Martin Luther King, Jr, p96.
46   The Book of Esther/Megillat Esther 4:16
47   Ethics of the Fathers/Pirkei Avot 2:6.

"Rabbi Joseph said: A man should always learn from the reasoning of his Maker. Behold, the Holy One disregarded all mountains and hills, and caused His Presence to abide on Mount Sinai, even as He disregarded all goodly trees and caused His Presence to abide on a thorn bush"[48]. *Hod*-humility does not happen on its own and we might try whatever we can do to keep present to the fact that we are only on earth for a short time and we are not the Creator.

WHO ARE YOU GOING TO HANG OUT WITH?

When we are trying to change a behaviour, it is always easier if we around people who are committed to similar goals. When growing a business I have found it helpful to spend time with fellow entrepreneurs, when working on my acting it is helpful to be around artists, and when trying to hone the six-pack it is useful to be around friends who are also active. The Rabbis considered this question, teaching that "A proverb says, *"Be head among foxes and not tail among lions".* However, Rabbi Matia ben Heresh said: *"Be tail among lions and not head among foxes"*[49]. Nurturing a state of *Hod*-humility does not have to be an accident if we set up the conditions and choose like-minded communities.

Put simply, if you change your attitude about humility and gratitude, you will change your life. Master this and you will master your world. Walk around in a continual state of gratitude and humility - grateful for your body, relationships, needs being met (e.g. the Maslow hierarchy of needs, including food, shelter clothing etc.) and this will change your life.

Lag B'Omer is an opportunity to rectify the actions of Rabbi Akiva's students, by replacing deep disrespect with humility, surrender and trust in one another. Let us begin.

---

48   Babylonian Talmud, Sotah 5a, Sefer Ha-Aggadah p708.
49   Sanhedrin 4:8 (Jerusalem Talmud); Ethics of the Fathers/Pirkei Avot (4:21). In Sefer Ha-Aggadah p709.

TODAY'S PRACTICE

YOGA PRACTICE GUIDELINES:

The action of yoga is to simplify. One breath, one action, one thought. Carry out today's postures with a sense of surrender and giving oneself over. The great irony amongst Rabbi Akiva's 24,000 students was that there was a lack of God-awareness amongst them. If they had truly been able to say "there is something above us, a being greater than us" then they may well have been able to overcome their egos. Awareness of God is threaded throughout the Yoga Sutras, e.g. *"from devotion to the Lord, one is given perfect absorption into the spirit"*[50] and the result is to approach each practice with a sense of tranquility and humility. It is impossible to hold an awareness and thanks to God and still maintain arrogance – there is no surrender without burning away this ego-centred haughtiness.

GYM PRACTICE GUIDELINES:

Surrender to your practice today. Do not force anything but go with the flow. Listen closely. *Hod*-humility is also an action of allowing rather than forcing. You might think of it as a feminine energy rather than a pushing, masculine energy.

RELATIONSHIP PRACTICE GUIDELINES:

The process of humbling ourselves can initially feel like we are being lowered, and that is exactly what is happening to the ego. Our conscious mind may do everything it can to avoid this happening, but we can overcome it by performing random acts of kindness. This is the *tikkun*, the spiritual correction for the students of Rabbi Akiva who died in the plague from a lack of interpersonal respect, and in this way we transcend our pride and vanity. Therein lies one path to enlightenment.

Additionally, as a *Hod*-gratitude practice, go around making blessings today and thank or acknowledge as many people as possible for the light they bring into your life. Write thank you cards after a party and be sure to repair any lasting oversights.

---

50   Yoga Sutras 2:43, Stiles translation.

QUESTIONS FOR MEDITATION
RELATIONSHIPS:

- Where do I grow arrogant and complacent in my relationships? How can I continue to increase my humility, and deepen my gratitude? Where can I truly complement and compliment the other person? (*Hod*)
- Where has my arrogance caused problems in friendships and relationships?
- Where am I deficient in humility? Where am I demanding that life goes according to my own terms ("I want to play baseball and have 4 strikes instead of 3!!") and what is the cost to my friendships and relationships?
- Where do I ignore the wishes of others and just do what I want?
- Where am I getting into trouble through a lack of refined humility? Where does my over-active ego create problems (with my eating, my exercise, my mental faculties, my relationships, my career or business?)
- Where is there baseless hatred (*Tzinat Chinam*) in my soul? Where am I arrogant or insensitive towards others?

YOGA/BODY/GYM:

- Where do I grow arrogant and complacent towards my body, taking it for granted, being too lazy or even pushing it too hard? How can I be more grateful and humble in the relationship with my body, and with deep, fully-embodied gratitude?
- Where has my arrogance caused me to injure myself or others?

BUSINESS:

- Where do I lack humility in my business or workplace? Where have I stopped respecting people, whether they are clients or colleagues? What are all the things I can be grateful for today?
- Where has my arrogance caused me to lose jobs or clients?
- Where am I deficient in humility? Where am I demanding that life goes according to my own terms and what is it costing me? (i.e. "*I want to earn money but I do not want to have to work or play by the rules – I want you to employ me, you to pay my bills, but I want to do things my way*").

GYM SEQUENCE, DAY 33/BOTTOM TO HEELS

This is an Extended Child's Pose, used for gym purposes to stretch your muscles. To deepen it, work your hands forward on the inhale and keep pushing your hips backwards on the exhale.

.01

הוד
Hod-Humility

.02

YOGA SEQUENCE, DAY 33/EXTENDED CHILD POSE (BALASANA)

Place your buttocks on your heels or modify by putting a cushion on top of your heels. The intention is to be fully supported in this position and to be able to rest. To make this a more dynamic stretch, work your fingertips forward with each inhale and push your hips backwards on the exhale.

הוד
Hod-Humility

DAY 34 / **BONDING IN HUMILITY** / HUMBLE SPLENDOUR:
יסוד שבהוד

KABBALAH SUTRA: *Yesod She b'Hod* – Bonding/Grounding/ Foundation in Humility.
INTENTION: Get connected to others through humility and gratitude. Share your light with others and shine ever brighter.

Many people wander through their lives with an attitude of being angry and upset. Life should have treated them better, people should treat them better and the world owes them something. We are all prone to this, whether it is frustration at the Government, our friends or spouses. Would it not be nice to be free from all of this and clear to use our energy for the really important things rather than complaining? Imagine the mental and psychic energy that could be released for us to use on the projects that matter to us.

Yesod is getting grounded, connected, bonded and rooting into our foundation. It is the aspect of *Hod*-humility that helps us to be clear on why we are humble, what we have to be thankful for, and rooting it into the core of our being. When I look at pictures of children on cancer wards, I am humbled and grateful to go through my day knowing that I have many more days to look forwards to even if there is a heavy slew of bills to be paid. When I listen closely to the news and hear of war-torn areas where militias ravage rural villages and leave people dead, mutilated or as refugees, I can stay grateful and keep perspective about my next mortgage payment. This is an art and a skill that needs to be acquired through regular practice. We do not expect to be able to play a sonata on the piano without learning and applying ourselves, and there is no difference when it comes to living in a state of humility and gratitude. But consider how much brighter the world would be if everyone lived in this place.

BATHROOM BLESSINGS:

Whenever I taught Hebrew school classes to younger children, it was always a fun day to reveal that there is a blessing upon going to the bathroom. This blessing is said after washing one's hands and having exited the toilet, and is profoundly connected to *Yesod*-bonding in *Hod*-gratitude because it is about expressing gratitude for the organs which are connected to *Yesod*:

> *"Praised are you, Lord our God, King of the Universe, who with wisdom fashioned the human body, creating openings, arteries, glands and organs, marvellous in structure, intricate in design. Should but one of them, by being blocked or opened, fail to function, it would be impossible to exist. Praised are You, Lord, healer of all flesh who sustains our bodies in wondrous ways"*[51].

The Talmud relates that the Rabbis then disagree on the precise ending of the blessing, questioning *"How does the blessing conclude? Rab said: "[Blessed art Thou] that healest the sick'. Said Samuel: Abba has turned the whole world into invalids! No, what he says is, 'That healest all flesh'. R. Shesheth said: 'Who doest wonderfully'. R. Papa said: Therefore let us say both, 'Who healest all flesh and doest wonderfully"*[52]. Either way, we have the opportunity to stay aware of the miracle of what has just occurred and feel better about life as a result. Few people know that they also considered a meditation before going to the lavatory. The Talmud relates:

> *"On entering a privy one should say: 'Be honoured, ye honoured and holy ones that minister to the Most High. Give honour to the God of Israel. Wait for me till I enter and do my needs, and return to you'. Abaye said: A man should not speak thus, lest they should leave him and go. What he should say is: 'Preserve me, preserve me, help me, help me, support me, support me, till I have entered and come forth, for this is the way of human beings'"*[53].

---

51   Babylonian Talmud, Brachot 60b.
52   Ibid.
53   Ibid.

This one simple awareness can help us stay happier, healthier and even reduce depression and anxiety as we become truly thankful for the miracle machine that is our body.

HEALING RELATIONSHIPS:

Yesod-bonding in *Hod*-humility also relates to our communications and the way that we respect the words of others. Ethics of the Fathers explains that "*One who says something in the name of its speaker brings redemption to the world, as is stated*[54], "*And Esther told the king in the name of Mordechai*"[55]. Tabloid newspapers are less interested in quoting reliable sources, but the more spiritual path is to stay connected (*Yesod*) when quoting something, rather than claiming it as our own[56].

The Academy of Hillel (1 BCE - 1 CE) showed a deeper level of *Hod*-humility in that they would quote the words of their competitors, the Academy of Shammai, demonstrating a deep bond (*Yesod*) to their colleagues:

> "*Rabbi Abba said in the name of Samuel: For three years there was a dispute between the school of Shammai and the school of Hillel, the one asserting, "The law is according to our views" and the other asserting, "The Law is according to our views". Then a divine voice came forth and said, "the utterances of the one and of the other are both the words of the living God, but the law is according to the school of Hillel". But since both are the words of the living God, by what merit did the school of Hillel have the law fixed according to their rulings? Because they were kindly and humble, and taught both their own rulings and those of the school of Shammai. Indeed, they taught the rulings of the school of Shammai before their own. This should prove to you that the man who humbles himself, the Holy One exalts: and the man who exalts himself, the Holy One humbles. From everyone who tries to thrust himself upon eminence, eminence thrusts itself...*"[57].

---

54 In The Book of Esther/Megillat Esther, 2:22.
55 Ethics of the Fathers/Pirkei Avot 6:6.
56 This is a principle I have attempted to build into the fabric of this book, hence the cornucopia of footnotes.
57 Babylonian Talmud, Eiruvin 13b. In Sefer Ha-Aggadah p708-9.

In a world of reality TV stars where people are famous for the sake of being famous, this does seem like a natural sequitur. The Talmud goes to lengths to remind us that Moses' first encounter with the Divine was through the burning bush, which is noted for its "humility"; "*Bush, O bush! Not because you are taller than any of the trees in the field did the Holy One cause His presence to abide on you, but because you are lower than all of the trees in the field did the Holy One cause His Presence to abide on You*"[58]. This applies to our own life to see where we can stop taking credit where it fuels our ego and causes problems such as lack of connection with others or leads to arguments. If the Divine can speak through a shrub then maybe we can 'ground' ourselves to make room for God to speak with us.

SURRENDER & SUCCEED:

The notion of 'surrender' is not a part of everyday reality in the West. Our obsession with social media profiles, 15 minutes of fame and having our voice heard does not easily align with the Eastern notion of surrender. Yet more surrender - another possible translation of *Hod* - can lead to more happiness.

The Yoga Sutras promises that we can achieve oneness and stability through "*complete, instant, dynamic, energetic and vigilant surrender to the omnipresent ever existent reality or God. This is the instant realisation of God as the only reality, when the (ego's) quest of self-knowledge meets its counterpart, ignorance, and stands bewildered in choiceless encounter, and when the ego-ignorance phantom instantly collapses*"[59].

Even with the lofty spiritual goals of pursuing oneness with the Divine, we have work to do on earth; this is the essence of Chassidic and Kabbalistic practice. In other words, humble ourselves, stop complaining, start appreciating, stay grounded and reach the heavens through our actions on Earth.

---

58 Babylonian Talmud, Shabbat p67a,
59 Yoga Sutras 1:23, Ventakesha translation.

TODAY'S PRACTICE

YOGA PRACTICE GUIDELINES:

Get connected to all the things you might be grateful for. Take the quality of *Yesod*-bonding in *Hod*-humility as you enter today's posture, grounding deeply into the position and focusing on your foundation (another aspect of *Yesod*), keeping the posture strong and coalescing all of your muscles and breath together as one.

As you grow in awareness, become more familiar with and gradually master the quality of Hod-humility, an amazing thing will happen through your yoga practice. The flow of *prana*-energy will be increased and the physical element of the practice will gradually feel more powerful. Once you have embodied this sense of humility, it then becomes a useful tool for improving relations with other people. In bonding with humility, humility then becomes a tool for deeper bonding. Your newly mastered skills become a way of enabling other people to feel good, relationships are strengthened and everyone benefits as a result.

Begin your yoga practice by setting an intention that is focused on other people. This might be along the lines of "I would like to increase the healing within myself so that I can go and heal others" or "I would like to raise the level of internal peace and emanate peacefulness amongst everyone I meet". The breath can then be a deeply humbling experience, focused on serving a higher purpose. Stay with this simple practice, gratefully accepting each life-giving breath and faithfully moving through your practice.

ADVANCED YOGIC PRACTICE:

Yesod-bonding/foundation can be understood with regards to the internal connections we make through yoga as we strengthen the bonds with our body, breath and thoughts, and the external bonds that we make with other people as we live more conscious and mindful lives. In terms of the body, the metaphorical location of *yesod* is rooted beneath the genitalia and is the key energy point that the yogis referred to as *mulah bandha*, or the 'root lock'. Begin with internal bonding, focusing *Yesod* inwards towards the connection with your breath and soul. We improve our physical connection as we draw more oxygen into our lungs, giving ourselves more energy in the process, and all of this can be used as a preparation for increasing our connection with others.

GYM PRACTICE GUIDELINES:

Stay grounded in your gym workout. Breathe deeply, notice your feet, and try not to get "in your head". Next, enjoy it! Yesod also can be understood as pleasure. So keep enjoying it.

QUESTIONS FOR MEDITATION

RELATIONSHIPS:

- Where do I grow arrogant and complacent in my relationships? How can I increase my humility and gratitude in a way that bonds me to the other? (*Yesod*)
- Where am I worse off through not connecting to others with my gratitude? What is it costing me?
- Where am I in trouble through a lack of bonding in my humility? (e.g. a self-serving humility that others don't "buy"?)
- Where am I not taking pleasure in my gratitude and acknowledgements?
- *Yesod* as Pleasure and *Hod* as Surrender: Where can I take more pleasure in surrendering? Surrendering to God, to my partner, my children, my boss, my clients?

YOGA/BODY/GYM:

- Where do I grow arrogant and complacent towards my body, taking it for granted, being too lazy or even pushing it too hard? How can I be more grateful and humble in my relationship with my body, and get deeply connected through this gratitude and humility?

BUSINESS:

- Where do I lack humility in my business or workplace? Where have I stopped respecting people, whether it is my clients or colleagues? How is this blocking me from connecting with others? How will increased humility or gratitude help me connect with people on deeper levels?

GYM SEQUENCE, DAY 34/HALF JACKS

A modified version of Jumping Jacks, do these in quick succession.
3 sets of 20 repetitions, with 30 second breaks in between.

.01

יְסוֹד
Yesod-Bonding

הוֹד
Hod-Humility

.02

YOGA SEQUENCE, DAY 34/BOUND ANGLE OR COBBLER (BADDHA KONASANA)

If required you can modify this by placing cushions underneath your knees. Be careful not to over-push your knees or hips in this (or any) posture.

הוד
Hod-Humility

יסוד
Yesod-Bonding

DAY 35 / NOBILITY IN HUMILITY / HUMBLE RULERS / מלכות שבהוד

KABBALAH SUTRA: *Malhut She b'Hod* – Nobility in Humility.

INTENTION: Become truly noble, achieving your vast potential through transcending ego-limits.

"The mass of men lead lives of quiet desperation. What is called resignation is confirmed desperation" — Henry Thoreau, *Walden*

There is an epidemic of not-knowing-oneself. Grown men post questions about basic emotional questions on social media, perhaps because they did not achieve the emotional security to trust themselves when they were younger. Some complain and others drown their sorrows or numb their pain using alcohol, food or their drug of choice. When we know who we are, we know what we are aiming for, what our boundaries are, what we must say "no" to and where we can give a wholehearted "Yes".

WHO ARE YOU?

Although Moses has a series of self-doubts before stepping into his leadership role, he then steps into his position and maintains humility despite immense power. His background as King of Ethiopia[60], and role as leader of the Hebrews and personal intermediary with God is all executed with humility. Similarly his brother Aaron, the symbol of *Hod*-humility is able to fulfil his role as High Priest with a complete lack of pride and vanity. He offers sacrifices on behalf of an entire people, wears a golden headband with the words *"Holy to HaShem"* and communicates with the Divine through the bejewelled breastplate (with the *Urim* and *Tummim* mystical diamonds), but he always knows who he is.

---

[60] This is based on the Midrash Yalkut Me'am Loez on Shemot 2:15. With more details: Yalkut Shimoni on Shemot, remez 168. See: http://www.chabad.org/parshah/article_cdo/aid/1017949/jewish/Where-Was-Moses.htm.

The newspapers are full of people who reach powerful positions and their money and fame magnifies their behaviour, but they frequently get into trouble because they do not know who they are. Who are you? What is your mission? When we know who we are and what we stand for, we can stand up and be counted, but do it with a *Malchut*-mastery of humility and gratitude (*Hod*).

FALSE HUMILITY

Pretending you are not good at something is not humility if it is not true. It is lying. In Kabbalistic terms, you are "crushing" the sphere of *Hod*-humility because this is actually arrogance masked as humility.

IN YOUR BODY

Our hands, feet and mouth are the organs of *Malchut*-mastery. One question we can simply ask is; How are you using them to become more grateful and humble? Consider how this might change your life if you were to run to perform acts of gratitude (e.g. volunteering), to use your hands to write things that thank others, to speak kinder words that acknowledge the contributions of others, and to catch yourself before self-aggrandising words escape your lips.

CONQUERING THE EGO

Malchut-mastery in *Hod*-humility also includes mastering our shadow side, the ever-hungry ego which is desperate for glory. This is a spiritual practice, as taught in various places. "*Rabbi Eleazar said: The Presence wails over a man who has haughtiness within him*"[61]. This makes sense on a basic emotional level as the Divine Presence, the *Shechina*, is a feminine energy (which, incidentally, represents *Malchut*-mastery). If we think of the feminine energy (or *Shechina*) as in our emotional body, the feeling part of us, then arrogance and self-aggrandisement will crush that. We will be so focused on what we think about ourselves (which is a masculine energy) and judging others, that there will be no room left for feeling. So in Rabbi Eleazar's statement, the self-centred thoughts will push out the feelings, emotive capacity and intuitive abilities.

---

[61] Babylonian Talmud, Sotah 5a, Sefer Ha-Aggadah p711.

This is underscored elsewhere in the Talmud; *"He who walks even four cubits with a haughty bearing is as though he had pushed aside the feet of the Presence, of which it is written*[62]*, "The whole earth is full of His glory"*[63]. This is a working energy principle that can be seen in nature, and the Rabbis sometimes brought agricultural analogies so that everyone could understand the idea on a very practical level. *Rabbi Akiva expounded: "he in whom there is haughtiness of spirit will presently be reduced in rank, as it says, "They are exalted, then a reduction [in rank]"*[64] *. What is meant by "They are cut off as the topmost of ears of corn?"*[65]*. A sage in the school of Rabbi Ishmael taught: It is like a man who, entering his field, plucks the topmost ears"*[66]. Mastering humility is clearly an essential task for any spiritual adept.

POINT OF SUPPORT

When we are insulted by others, *Malchut*-mastery in *Hod*-humility might be shown as the art of not allowing comments to affect us by not over-focusing on them. If somebody insults us we can ignore the comment or keep replaying it in our head many times. My Martial Arts teacher, Eric, describes this as giving something a "Point of Support". The more you think about it, the more you are supporting their comment and the more you give them power. So the choice is yours. *Hod* is the humility that allows us to brush off comments and dissolve them into thin-air. If a punch lands on us, we can allow it to roll off rather than resisting it which willcause us more injury. *Malchut*-mastery is the ability to stay dignified and in control of our thoughts and what we do with them.

MASTER HUMILITY IN YOUR BODY

Without humility, we can cause ourselves injury. I know this personally through years of ego-fuelled yoga practices, where I pushed my body harder and harder until it caused repeated injuries. As I emerge from one particular injury that has taken eight years to heal, I know this lesson well. We can learn two things from teachers; how to do

---

62 In Isaiah 6:3.
63 Babylonian Talmud, Brachot 43b.
64 Job 24:24.
65 Ibid.
66 Babylonian Talmud, Sotah 5a, Sefer Ha-Aggadah p711.

something and how not to do something. In this instance I offer the teaching of learning not to follow my example in this regard.

Malchut-mastery in *Hod*-humility teaches a path towards attaining ultimate strength through creating space for others and being aware of our own tendencies to become arrogant. The Yoga Sutras teaches that *"the practical means for attaining higher consciousness consists of three components: self-discipline and purification, self-study and devotion to the Lord"*[67]. Self-discipline establishes our regular practice and helps purify our lazy or deconstructive attitudes, self-study helps us see our shortcomings, and faith (Hebrew: *Emunah*) enables us to elevate our consciousness through the practice.

SINCERELY YOURS

Rabbi Yitzhak Ginsburg teaches that the inner aspect of *Hod*-humility is sincerity[68]. This is the deeply unglamorous aspect of mystical Kabbalistic practice which is firmly rooted here on earth. It means keeping to your appointments, being true to your word and fulfilling the promises you make. An important step to enlightenment, Mastery in Humility, is showing up on time. Check your calendar.

TODAY'S PRACTICE

YOGA PRACTICE GUIDELINES:
Practice in a way that is humble and dignified. Stay grounded and breathe into your feet (*Malchut*). Stay grateful for all aspects of your practice and all of the teachings that are available to you today.

GYM PRACTICE GUIDELINES:
Step into the Kingship of your body - mastering your muscles, your posture, your breathing and your attitude. Do it in a way that maintains gratitude and try offering your gym workout as a 'prayer', dedicating your work to the merit of someone who is ill, or to a spiritual teacher, or to a Higher cause.

---

[67] Yoga Sutras 2:1.
[68] *"The spiritual state identified in Chassidut [or practical Kabbalistically-inspired living] as corresponding to the Sefirah of hod is that of temimut (sincerity)"*, from http://www.inner.org/sefirot/sefhod.htm.

QUESTIONS FOR MEDITATION

RELATIONSHIPS:

- Where have I not mastered humility? What is it costing me? How is my life affected as a result of not having integrated this into the core of my being?
- How have I not mastered gratitude? What is it costing me?
- Where do I grow arrogant and complacent in my relationships? How can I express more gratitude through my words and actions? (*Malchut*)
- How can I express more gratitude for my partner or family through my words and actions?
- Hands, Feet and Mouth are the organs of *Malchut*. How am I using them with a sense of gratitude and humility?
- How am I using communication, the way I am "walking", the direction in which I am moving, to become more grateful and humble?
- How can I express my gratitude to others today, finding reasons to thank and acknowledge them?

YOGA/BODY/GYM:

- Where do I grow arrogant and complacent towards my body, taking it for granted, being too lazy or even pushing it too hard? How can I be more grateful and humble in the relationship with my body, and demonstrate this through my thoughts, speech and actions?
- What can I do today to express gratitude for my body? [*Doing/action* is *Malchut*].

BUSINESS:

- Where do I lack humility in my business or workplace? Where have I stopped respecting people, whether it is my clients or colleagues? How can I speak or behave differently today, and truly master these attributes?
- Where is my humility or gratitude out of balance in my business and how can I restore that through being loving, disciplined, compassionate, enduring, humble, connected and dignified?

LEADERSHIP:

- Have I mastered my humility? Can be a strong leader and be humble at the same time? (*Malchut*-mastery in *Hod*-humility)

GYM SEQUENCE, DAY 35/STANDING TOE RAISE

Keep your balance and connect your breath as you raise and lower.

.01

מלכות
Malchut-Kingship

הוד .02
Hod-Humility

מלכות
Malchut-Kingship

YOGA SEQUENCE, DAY 35/BRIDGE (SETU BANDHASANA)

Place your block beneath your sacrum and allow it to completely take your weight. For a more dynamic stretch, lift your hips as high as possible and focus on opening out the front of your thighs.

.01

הוד
Hod-Humility

מלכות
Malchut-Kingship

.02

YESOD יסוד

BONDING

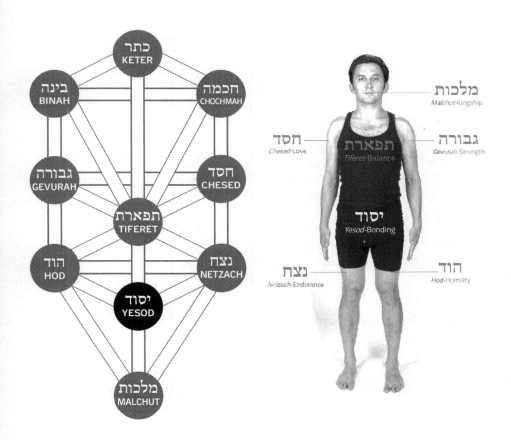

מלכות
Malchut-Kingship

חסד
Chesed-Love

תפארת
Tiferet-Balance

גבורה
Gevurah-Strength

יסוד
Yesod-Bonding

נצח
Netzach-Endurance

הוד
Hod-Humility

כתר
KETER

בינה
BINAH

חכמה
CHOCHMAH

גבורה
GEVURAH

חסד
CHESED

תפארת
TIFERET

הוד
HOD

נצח
NETZACH

יסוד
YESOD

מלכות
MALCHUT

WEEK 6

YESOD INTRODUCTION: WELCOME TO THE PLEASURE ZONE יסוד

"Th' expense of spirit in a waste of shame
Is lust in action; and till action, lust
Is perjured...
All this the world well knows; yet none knows well
To shun the heaven that leads men to this hell".

Shakespeare, Sonnet 129

It is not good for a human being to be alone, but are our connections healthy? The free love 'revolution' of the 1960s led to a generation which suffers from the highest divorce rate in the history of the planet and the use of widespread medications for depression and loneliness. *Yesod* is bonding, profound human connection that is rooted in sexuality, but relates to every aspect of how we connect with others. Whether it is with friends, relatives, spouses, partners, business acquaintances or shopkeepers, *how* we bond with others is as important as *who* we bond with.

Yesod also means 'foundation', as a healthy foundation is the basis for relationships to flourish and grow. Unhealthy connections can cause us spiritual and practical damage, whether these are destructive friendships or uncommitted romantic encounters. The injury caused on a spiritual realm cannot be seen with physical eyes, but the physical results are evident. The so-called *"shidduch* [matchmaking] crisis" spoken of in the Jewish community is prevalent in all communities, where people are finding it harder and harder to find their soul mate and settle into marriage. Is it any wonder, considering that we are bombarded with messages that we have endless choice, we can 'test drive' relationships to see if they suit us, we can physically bond with several partners before getting married? The net result is people become emotionally distanced from themselves, finding it that much harder to healthily bond with another.

ADVANCED KABBALAH: THE SEXUAL CONNECTION

The *Tikkunei HaZohar* connects *Yesod*-bonding with the *Brit Milah* - i.e. the circumcised end of the male organ - because the ultimate human connection happens through sexual intercourse. It is also through this organ that the human essence is "communicated" as sperm travels to (the) womb. On the Tree of Life diagram, *Yesod*-bonding (masculine) would represent the sperm and *Malchut*-mastery (feminine) represents the womb. On a practical level, *Yesod*-bonding is when we take our ideas and thoughts and communicate them into the world (the world is *Malchut* and the act of communication is bonding). The Torah prohibits the sin of wasting one's seed, and gratuitous seminal emission, which is not between husband and wife in the permitted manner.

Yesod-bonding is directly beneath *Tiferet*-compassion on the Tree of Life chart. These qualities are represented by Jacob (*Tiferet*) and Joseph (*Yesod*), signifying the father-son relationship between the two. Joseph completes the spiritual mission that Jacob began. He grew up in Jacob's household, learned his value system and ways of being, and spread that into the world in a massive way, affecting the entire nation of Egypt. We can have great ideas or create great projects but if we do not share them with other people (the act of *Yesod*) then they do not reach their full potential.

INTELLECTUAL BONDING

When we are not "getting through" to someone else, such as a work colleague or with our partner, this can be a deficiency of *Yesod*-bonding. Chassidic teaching explains how *Yesod* is bonding on all levels; physical, emotional, intellectual and spiritual.

> *"The category of Yesod is, by way of example, the bond by which the father binds his intellect to the intellect of his son while teaching him with love and willingness, for he wishes his son to understand", explains Rabbi Shneur Zalman of Liadi. Without this [bond], even if the son would hear the very same words from the mouth of his father [as he speaks and studies to himself]. He would not understand [them] as well as now, when his father binds his intellect to him and*

speaks with him face to face with love and desire, because he desires
very much that his son understand. (The father does not merely want
to enlighten his son; his desire is stemming from Yesod is powerful
because it is driven by pleasure)[1].

So in this sense, *Yesod*-bonding is a healthy approach because the son
wants to learn. When we force ourselves upon someone else, that would
be an unhealthy form of *Yesod*.

PLEASURE

Yesod can also be understood as "pleasure" as it is associated with
the organ that leads to the highest sensation of physical ecstasy.
Nonetheless in our pursuit of spiritual growth and raising our
consciousness, the focus is on healthy pleasure rather than self-
gratifying unhealthy pleasure. Rabbi Shneur Zalman of Liadi brought
a very practical example, explaining that *"to draw a metaphor from [the*
attribute of Yesod-bonding in] the sphere of the truly physical, is the profusion
of spermatozoa that results from heightened desire and delight. This is why
the Kabbalists, (seeking to illustrate the imparting of knowledge out of a sense
of pleasure), used the analogy of a physical union, for there are a number
of similarities between these two expressions of the attribute of Yesod)"[2].
There are many more physical analogies available to us in addition to
the intellectual bonding of the father-son example and the physical
bonding of intercourse, and this goes to illustrate the very practical
nature of Kabbalah in the way that everything can be understood in the
body because almost every spiritual reality has a physical counterpart.

SEXUAL KUNG FU

There is a core inner power that mystics of many traditions identify as
residing within harnessed sexual energy. The Biblical figure associated
with the quality of *Yesod*-bonding is Joseph, known as *Yosef HaTzaddik*[3]
or Joseph the Righteous. In resisting seduction by the wife of Potiphar[4],

---

1   Lessons in Tanya, Iggeret HaKodesh, Epistle 15, p267-268.
2   Lessons in Tanya, Iggeret HaKodesh, Epistle 15, p269-270.
3   This might refer back to the phrase from Proverbs that "the Righteous (*Tzaddikim*) are
     the foundation (*Yesod*) of the world (Proverbs 10:25).
4   Genesis 39:12.

Joseph demonstrated his ability to overcome physical temptation. Had he succumbed, the consequences of sleeping with his Master's wife may have derailed his entire journey to become Viceroy of Egypt, thus saving his entire father's house and people. Many political careers have been derailed by scandals, but this leads to a wider principle that is relevant to all of us; focusing our sexual energy can lead to tremendous power.

On a deeper level, the Kabbalists stress the importance of men not wasting their seed, especially through self-gratification, and Rabbi Nachman of Breslov (1772-1810) discovered the *Tikkun HaKelali*, a General Rectification for the spiritual damage caused through masturbation. A similar view is held by Eastern mystics. In *Taoist Secrets of Love: Cultivating Male Sexual Energy*, Mantak Chia explains that

> *"Wise men of the Orient have from time immemorial sought means of preventing discharge of the seminal fluid.. The sages considered one drop of semen equal in vital power to one hundred drops of blood.. Extraordinary powers, including healing and clairvoyant perception, may evolve when one retains the semen and drives its power back up into the body. Many gifted minds have held that if one could retain these fluids for one's entire life, the body would not decay after death"[5].*

On an energetic level, this applies to all of us, at all times. We have a limited amount of energy and we have to decide how we are going to expend that energy and whether we are going to waste it (e.g. through endless web surfing and social media activity when it does not generate any real return on our energy).

PURPOSEFUL PLEASURE vs LUST IN ACTION

There is a strong purpose to the sexual drive and the Ramak (1522-1570) explained how *"The yetzer hatov [e.g. selfless passion] was created for a person for himself, whereas the yetzer hara [e.g. selfish passion] was created for the sake of his wife"[6]*. His teaching illustrates how there is a purpose for our self-serving desire when it is correctly channelled, and a

---

5   Taoists Secrets of Love: Cultivating Male Sexual Energy, by Mantak Chia, p2-3.
6   Tomer Devorah, p103.

strong libido can be of tremendous benefit within a marital relationship when it is directed towards one's wife. Sex has a powerful and essential place within the conjugal relationship, whether it is recreational or procreational.

YESOD AS YOGA?

Yesod can also be creatively translated as "Yoga", which is traditionally interpreted as "unification". The motion of unifying disparate elements is the action of *Yesod*-bonding as everything is coalesced - our muscles, breath, intention and focus. True bonding can be achieved over an eternity or in a single, unified moment. The physical techniques of yoga are very precise and specific because they are focused on this one-pointed goal of unification. Every posture has a specific focal point for the entire body, as the limbs are placed in certain positions, the muscles pull in certain directions, the eyes are focused on a single spot and the mind is directed to the sound of the breath.

There are three main directions for bonding; with ourselves, with other people and with God. The practice of yoga enables all three of these to happen simultaneously. A powerful inhalation allows us to connect deeply within our body, uniting the breath with our movement and our mind, bringing us to a state of physical oneness. In addition to preparing us for unifying connections with other people in our daily interaction, there is an interpersonal bonding that goes on when we practice yoga in a room with other people. You will have felt that joint energy that comes from a group of people simultaneously moving through a vinyasa yoga sequence at the same time and it is easy to get carried away with the buzz of it all. The notion of *minyan*, the quorum of 10 men needed for communal Jewish prayer services, is the basis of group meditation. Back in the yoga class, there are few experiences that are more *energising* as hearing 100 people breathing in total harmony whilst moving through a practice; it really gives you the feeling that you are part of something much bigger than yourself.

The realisation of *Yesod*-bonding leads us towards more powerful relationships and the opportunity for our personalities to flourish, as we approach and bind with The Source.

YESOD CHARTS

DYSFUNCTIONAL CONNECTIONS

- **Dysfunctional** *Yesod*-bonding: wants to connect with others indiscriminately, wants to bond with everyone and everything, gets involved in other people's stuff and allows them to get involved.
- **Dysfunctional** *Yesod*-bonding is not rooted and does not have a firm base. Does not know what s/he is or what s/he stands for.
- **Dysfunctional** *Yesod*-bonding is Joseph who has a dream and then drops an "energy bomb" by telling everyone about it in a way that was insensitive, regardless of how he might hurt others and hurt himself "*Listen to this dream I had: We were binding sheaves of grain out in the field when suddenly my sheaf rose and stood upright, while your sheaves gathered around mine and bowed down to it." His brothers said to him, "Do you intend to reign over us? Will you actually rule us?" And they hated him all the more because of his dream and what he had said*"[7].
- **Dysfunctional** *Yesod*-bonding is attaching faith to the wrong source Joseph asked the Butler to "remember him to Pharoah"[8] and he got punished for not trusting in God.
- **Dysfunctional** *Yesod*-bonding is attaching to women who are emotionally abusive and cold. Not attaching to healthy souls and God.
- **Dysfunctional** *Yesod*-bonding is directing my energy in places without checking beforehand whether I am welcome.
- **Dysfunctional** *Yesod*-bonding lacks patience.

BUSINESS GOALS

- Where am I disconnected from the mission of my business? How can I reconnect to my vision through creativity? (*Chesed*-love)
- Where am I disconnected from the mission of my business? How can I be more disciplined about reconnecting to my vision? (*Gevurah*-discipline)

---

[7] Genesis 37: 6-8.
[8] Genesis 40:41.

- Where am I disconnected from the mission of my business? How can I use compassion to reconnected to my vision? How can I be more balanced in the way I approach things? (*Tiferet*-compassion)
- Where am I disconnected from the mission of my business? How can I reconnect to my vision for the long-term and not get swayed? (*Netzach*-endurance)
- Where am I disconnected from the mission of my business? How can I really appreciate the size of the opportunity in front of me? (*Hod*-humility)
- Where am I disconnected from the mission of my business? How can I stay more connected to the people I am trying to help and the solutions I am trying to deliver? (*Yesod*-bonding)
- Where am I disconnected from the mission of my business? How can I change the way I talk about things, whether it is my internal thoughts or my external speech? What positive actions can I take differently, to create new and better results? (*Malchut*-mastery)

RELATIONSHIPS

- Where am I emotionally disconnected in my relationships and how can I get more connected through acts of love and creativity? (*Chesed*-lovingkindness)
- Where am I emotionally disconnected in my relationships and how can I get more connected through a more disciplined approach? (*Gevurah*-discipline*)*
- Where am I emotionally disconnected in my relationships and how can I get more connected through more compassion and balance? (*Tiferet*-compassion*)*
- Where am I emotionally disconnected in my relationships and how can I get more connected through being more enduring in my attitude? (*Netzach*-endurance*)*
- Where am I emotionally disconnected in my relationships and how can I get more connected through being humble and grateful towards other people? (*Hod*-humility*)*
- Where am I emotionally disconnected in my relationships and how can I get more connected in as many ways as possible? (*Yesod*-bonding*)*

- Where am I emotionally disconnected in my relationships and how can I get more connected through the way I talk and behave? (*Malchut*-mastery*)

BODY

- Where do I not listen or respond to my body's requests (e.g. To exercise more or differently, or to eat nutritious foods, or to heal an ache), and how can I be more loving towards it? (*Chesed*-lovingkindness)
- Where do I not listen or respond to my body's requests (e.g. To exercise more or differently, or to eat nutritious foods, or to heal an ache), and how can I be more disciplined in my approach? (*Gevurah*-discipline*)
- Where do I not listen or respond to my body's requests (e.g. To exercise more or differently, or to eat nutritious foods, or to heal an ache), and how can I be more compassionate and balanced towards my body, bringing healing where it is needed? (*Tiferet*-compassion*)
- Where do I not listen or respond to my body's requests (e.g. To exercise more or differently, or to eat nutritious foods, or to heal an ache), and how can I take a more sustainable, enduring approach? (*Netzach*-endurance)
- Where do I not listen or respond to my body's requests (e.g. To exercise more or differently, or to eat nutritious foods, or to heal an ache), and how can I relate to my body with more gratitude and respect? (*Hod*-humility*)
- Where do I not listen or respond to my body's requests (e.g. To exercise more or differently, or to eat nutritious foods, or to heal an ache), and how can I stay connected with what my body is "saying"? What deeper listening practice or dialoguing can I do with my body? (*Yesod*-bonding*)
- Where do I not listen or respond to my body's requests (e.g.. To exercise more or differently, or to eat nutritious foods, or to heal an ache), and how can I stay connected with what my body is "saying"? What behaviours do I need to change in my physical practice? (*Malchut*-mastery*)

DAY 36 / LOVINGKINDNESS IN BONDING / THE POWER OF LOVE / חסד שביסוד

KABBALAH SUTRA: *Hesed She b'Yesod* – Lovingkindness in Bonding.
INTENTION: To be more loving so that I can improve my relationships and connections/bonding. To develop a strong and grounded foundation, using the power of lovingkindness. Strengthen self esteem and relationships with others through love.

"God's only purpose in creating the world was in order to give pleasure to His created beings". — Rabbi Yehudah Ashlag

Rushing into deep relationships without a strong foundation can cause problems. Too much Yesod-bonding without a basis of *Chesed*-love, or too much love without a firm foundation can be problematic, whether it is a romantic encounter or trying to bond with a new client and overwhelming them with attention in order to close a sale before they are ready. To keep relationships healthy we must manage our bonding, and build a strong foundation before rushing to connect, like the guy who lavishes a new date too many gifts and smothers her in the process.

DIVINE PLEASURE

The 20th Century Kabbalist Rabbi Yehuda Ashlag (1885—1954) spoke of Divine Love and how God's primary focus is to connect to us through pleasure. He wrote in his *Introduction to the Zohar* that *"Our Sages have taught us that God's only purpose in creating the world was in order to give pleasure to His created beings. It is here that we need to put our eyes and focus our thoughts because it is the ultimate aim and purpose of the creation of the world"*[9]. Rabbi Ashlag elevates pleasure to a much higher level than just the physical by focusing on its Divine aspect.

---

9   Introduction to The Zohar, Paragraph 6. quoted in "A Tapestry For The Soul - The Introduction to the Zohar by Rabbi Yehudah Lev Ashlag - compiled by Yedidah Cohen, p40. Rabbi Ashlag's teachings are the basis of much of the theories taught at The Kabbalah Center (with which I have no affiliation) and this also sounds like the basis of the *Five Levels of Pleasure* classes that were given by the late Rabbi Noach Weinberg, the Dean at Aish HaTorah (http://www.aish.com/sp/f/Five_Levels_of_Pleasure.html). I heard him give these lectures in Jerusalem in July of 1994.

This idea of giving pleasure - *Chesed*-giving/love in *Yesod*-pleasure/ bonding is a powerful aspect to any relationship, as we can aim to uplift the other person's enjoyment through our actions. Both parties benefit, whether the aim is to make a partner husband or wife happy, or to please a client.

HIGHER LOVE

What happens when love seems to disappear from a relationship? Perhaps it is possible to re-cultivate it. The Ramak (1522-1570) spoke of 'training' oneself in our relationship with God, and if we can apply that on a Divine level then we can also apply that with human relationships. He wrote; *"How should a person train himself in the attribute of Chesed-kindness? The main way to enter into the secret of Chesed-love is to love God so absolutely that one will never forsake His service for any reason; for, compared with the love of God, Blessed Be He, no other love has any worth"*[10]. As we strengthen our relationship with the Divine, we can use that experience to strengthen our relationships here on earth.

IMITATING GOD

Another way to get closer to our Divine source is *Imitatio Dei,* the action of imitating God. The *Tanya* speaks of how *"because of one's love of God and because of one's great desire to cleave unto Him, he desires with all his being [to practice] Chesed, in order to cleave to His attributes. This* accords with the teaching of our Sages, of blessed memory, on the verse, "And to cleave unto Him"[11]. "Cleave unto His *attributes*"[12].

Love takes work; giving when we do not feel in the mood and doing what we can to improve a relationship. *Chesed*-love is love-in-action, rather than "it's the thought that counts". In this domain it is action that counts to strengthen relationships and strengthen all aspects of bonding and foundation-building.

---

[10]   Tomer Devorah p86.
[11]   Deuteronomy 11:22.
[12]   *Sotah* 14a, as quoted in Lessons in Tanya Vol 4. p274.

THE CIRCUMCISION of TRUTH & PEACE

The ultimate embodiment of *Chesed*-love in *Yesod*-bonding was when Abraham circumcised himself. He was the physical represent of *Chesed*-love and he affected the organ of *Yesod*-connection. Rabbi Yitzhak Ginsburg (b.1944) explains that "*Yesod-foundiation is the covenant between the two Divine attributes of truth and peace, as the prophet says "and truth and peace shall love"*[13]". This may be literal, suggesting that the covenant with God is to live a life of truth and peace, or it may be a more subtle allusion as 'truth' could correspond to *Netzach*-endurance and 'peace' to *Hod*-humility - these two *sefirot* are variously located in the two testicles, and the circumcision covenant literally sits between them[14]. The central principle remains, that having a strong foundation - foundation being another translation of Yesod - demands being both truthful and peaceful.

There is another literal-metaphorical comment from Rabbi Ginsburg with regards to the way that love 'flows' into bonding connections; "*The origin of love is represented by the soul of Abraham, of whom is said "Abraham, My lover"*[15]. *All of his lovingkindness (chesed) flows down (as water) to become concentrated in Yesod-bonding. There it creates the covenant between the absolute truth of Torah and the peace of mitzvot, good deeds performed with love for Israel*"[16]. Metaphorically, we pray for Divine love to flow into our relationships, and on a physical level, the water-element of love carries the seed to create new life through the organ of *Yesod*.

We can strive to raise our connections through acts and attitudes of love. Jonathan Safran Foer stated it beautifully in *Everything is Illuminated*:

> "*From space, astronauts can see people making love as a tiny speck of light. Not light, exactly, but a glow that could be mistaken for light--a coital radiance that takes generations to pour like honey through the darkness to the astronaut's eyes.*

---

13   Zecharia 8:19. Quoted in http://www.inner.org/sefirot/sefyesod.
14   It is possible that the Kabbalists didn't want this spelled out literally.
15   Isaiah 41:8.
16   In http://www.inner.org/sefirot/sefyesod.

In about one and a half centuries –after the lovers who made the glow will have long been laid permanently on their backs–metropolises will be seen from space. They will glow all year. Smaller cities will also be seen, but with great difficulty. Shtetls will be virtually impossible to spot. Individual couples, invisible.

The glow is born from the sum of thousands of loves: newlyweds and teenagers who spark like lighters out of butane, pairs of men who burn fast and bright, pairs of women who illuminate for hours with soft multiple glows, orgies like rock and flint toys sold at festivals, couples trying unsuccessfully to have children who burn their frustrated image on the continent like the bloom a bright light leaves on the eye after you turn away from it. Some nights, some places are a little brighter. It's difficult to stare at New York City on Valentine's Day, or Dublin on St. Patrick's. The old walled city of Jerusalem lights up like a candle on each of Chanukah's eight nights...We're here, the glow...will say in one and a half centuries. We're here, and we're alive".

YOUR BODY

Physical injury is often caused when we push our bodies too far, too quickly. We might have the best intentions in the world, whether it is to run and catch a bus, have fun on a ski trip or get fit in January as part of a New Year's resolution. When we forget to bring consciousness to our actions or deliberately ignore the body's warning signs, pain and harm can set in. Even die-hard yogis can fall into this trap on occasion, going ahead with a practice session when their bodies are sending out warning signals that perhaps it is time for a day off.

TODAY'S PRACTICE

YOGA PRACTICE GUIDELINES:

The closest yogic equivalent to *Yesod*-foundation/bonding is the notion of '*bandha*'. A bandha is a physical lock that is designed to focus the flow of prana through the body, creating a kind of gateway to direct the stream of energy. The primary bandhas or 'locks' are *mulah bandha* (root lock, around the perineum or anus), *uddiyana bandha* (upward flying lock, engaging the abdomen) and jalandhara bandha (sucking the tongue to the palate). Every *bandha* is an internal bond that deepens our connection with our own body and helps us in the path to unification.

As you connect with your breathing, *Chesed*-lovingkindness suggests a softness and love that you can bring to the breath, as you draw it into the depths of your body, rooting it to your foundation. A softer breath is kinder to the nostrils, throat and lungs, providing a gentle wave that is also more effective for the whole meditative action.

GYM PRACTICE GUIDELINES:

Work on your foundation today and go back to basics. Check that your forms are correct - the way you are lifting, your alignment when running or moving in an exercise. Now add a gentleness and care, and use this as your foundation for the week.

RELATIONSHIP PRACTICE GUIDELINES:

Allow the element of lovingkindness to become the focus of your relationships throughout today. We can easily become complacent with the people around us, and when a friendship or partnership has securely bonded foundations, it is easy to take our friends and relatives for granted. A little love goes a long way.

BUSINESS PRACTICE GUIDELINES:

Connecting with a client from the energy of taking - "can I make a sale?" is not *Chesed*-lovingkindness. Rather, "How can I serve? How can I really be of help to this person?" is the best way to create the relationship - that is in essence rectified *Yesod*-bonding. Today, ask how you can serve others as a way of connecting more deeply.

QUESTIONS FOR MEDITATION

Ask for each day of *Yesod*: Where do I lack grounding? Where do I need stronger foundations? (e.g. I could be advanced in one area but not grounded in others)

RELATIONSHIPS:
- Where am I emotionally disconnected in my relationships and how can I get more connected through acts of love and creativity? (*Chesed*)
- Healthy Bonding. But where am I rushing it, where am I over-connecting where perhaps I shouldn't be?
- Where am I disconnected through a lack of love?
- How is my lack of lovingkindness affecting my relationships and connections?
- Consider where you have dysfunctional *Yesod*-bonding, especially on an energetic level e.g. the times you show up and force your way into someone's space, not listening, not caring what they want? How are you forcing your way into other people's space, and how can you stop doing it and start giving instead?
- Bond to your partner..through love.
- Bond to your body through acts of love.
- Bond to your family and friends through acts of love.
- Capitalise on bonding through love, performing random acts of Lovingkindness.

YOGA/BODY/GYM:
- Where do I not listen or respond to my body's requests (e.g. To exercise more or differently, or to eat nutritious foods, or to heal an ache), and how can I be more loving towards it? (*Chesed)*

BUSINESS:
- Where am I disconnected from the mission of my business? How can I reconnect to my vision through creativity? (*Chesed*)
- Consider how I can bond to my customers/company/boss through giving.

SPIRITUALITY
- Consider how I can bond to God and Divine energy through acts of love?

GYM SEQUENCE, DAY 36/STAR JUMPS/JUMPING JACKS

If necessary you can modify this to Half Jacks.

.01

חסד
Chesed-Love

יסוד
Yesod-Bonding

.02

YOGA SEQUENCE, DAY 36/HORSE STANCE

Tuck your pelvis underneath in 'Cat' position (as in the Cat-Cow stretch). Open your hands on your inhale and allow the movement to last for as long as your breath. The breath is essential to this movement and only touch your palms together as you complete the exhale. Each movement must be tied to a breath.

.01

חסד
Chesed-Love

יסוד
Yesod-Bonding

.02

DAY 37 / DISCIPLINE IN BONDING / CATCHING FIRE / גבורה שביסוד

KABBALAH SUTRA: *Gevurah She b'Yesod* - Discipline in Bonding.
INTENTION: To focus your energy. To improve relationships and pleasure through discipline. To develop your personal strength and groundedness, and protect yourself from damaging relationships through disciplined bonding.

"A man given to excessive exercise of coitus is found on inspection to suffer from (premature) lapses of memory and mental debility". — Maimonides

One day my business mentor was teaching how I might achieve more if I focused my energy. Although he had said this many times, I finally understood it when he gave me the following exercise: *"Take a magnifying glass and focus the sun's beam on a leaf. Then start moving the ray in and out of focus and try to set fire to the leaf. After a few minutes, hold the magnifying glass completely still and then focus the beam. See which of the two methods is more effective"*[17].

We have a simple choice if we want to "catch fire" in a good way. The restriction and focusing of our energy - *Gevurah* - and then how we apply it to the world in connection to others - *Yesod*. First we can begin by identifying all of the areas where our energy is not focused and where we are not achieving the results we would like.

HOW ARE YOU USING YOUR ENERGY?

We might think of our energy as a finite resource (which it is) like money, and consider that we start our day with $1000 in the bank. Our next choice is deciding how we are going to spend it. Do we want to use it create and connect with others, to elevate our soul and bring more consciousness onto the planet, or do we want to use it for self-satisfaction?

---

17   Teaching courtesy of Steve Cohn.

HARMFUL EMISSIONS

Just as we are aware of vehicles wasting energy or expelling pollutants, we can see ourselves in the same way; what are the thoughts we are thinking, the words we are speaking or the actions we are taking? Rabbi Aryeh Kaplan (1934-1983) taught that *"A thought is a spiritual entity, and as such, can only contain a single concept. Since both a thought and an angel are basic spiritual entities, this is very closely related to the fact that an angel can only have a single mission"*[18]. Without delving into angelology, Rabbi Kaplan is making a profound point about the nature of thoughts, in that they are completely real entities on a spiritual realm. Thus, we must be exceptionally careful of what we are creating.

> *"How should a person train himself in the attribute of Yesod-bonding?"* asked *Rabbi Moshe Cordovero*[19]. *"To avoid wasteful emission, he must be extremely careful of the kind of speech that leads to licentious thoughts. Needless to say, he should not use foul language; he should even be on his guard against pure speech that leads to licentious thoughts. This idea can be derived from an examination of the verse "Do not allow your mouth to bring sin to your flesh.."*[20], *that is "Do not let your mouth utter words that bring holy flesh [the Sign of the Holy Covenant] to wasteful emission""*[21].

This is not an easy charge. Spiritual development takes commitment and application. In *Love's Labours Lost*, Shakespeare's reluctant spiritual adept is able to recognise the value of physical abstinence as a path to enlightenment but is extremely reluctant to walk the walk:

> *"I will swear to study so,*
> *To know the thing I am forbid to know:*
> *As thus,--to study where I well may dine,*
> *When I to feast expressly am forbid;*
> *Or study where to meet some mistress fine,*
> *When mistresses from common sense are hid;*

---

18 Sefer Yetzirah, p61. In his footnote, Rabbi Kaplan cites Amuda HaAvodah (Chernovitz, 1863), p.83c.
19 Also known as the Ramak.
20 Ecclesiastes/Kohelet 5:5.
21 Tomer Devorah, pp119-120.

Or, having sworn too hard a keeping oath,
Study to break it and not break my troth"[22].

Nonetheless, Kabbalistic practice does not go to the extremes of Shakespeare's antiheroes, as every Rabbinic scholar has a conjugal duty prescribed in the Talmud[23] (which we will discuss in the next essay), but there are rabbinic warnings against too much indulgence in physicality. Maimonides (1135-1204) warned that *"A man given to excessive exercise of coitus is found on inspection to suffer from (premature) lapses of memory and mental debility, with faulty digestion combined with green sickness, defective vision and bad appearance"*[24]. Although contemporary medical science may not fully attest to this, the essence of Maimonides' teaching still remains true. If we continue to promiscuously expend our energy, there will be a price to pay.

MARITAL RELATIONS

The Torah prescribes extreme focusing of sexual energy within the marital relationship as explained in the Laws of *Taharat Mishpacha*, or "Family Purity". This is pure *Gevurah*-discipline in *Yesod*-pleasure/bonding and an act of elevating one's desires above the physical. The Kabbalists understood that one purpose of sexual union (*Yesod*) is to raise our consciousness through the interplay of masculine and feminine energies, and as such it is essential to stay highly mindful of how we are using our mind and body.

We are here to focus our energies, learning how to channel our desires for the good; *"all types of desire deriving from the Yetzer Hara - they should be used mainly for the benefit of the wife God has chosen as his "compatible helper"*[25]. *Afterwards, he should redirect all of them to his service of God, binding them to the right"*[26]. The "right" in this sense is referring to the aspect of *Chesed*-giving which appears on the right side of the Tree of Life. Once we have used our desires to make our partner happy, we can then focus any remaining energy in creative acts.

---

22   Love's Labours Lost, Act 1, Scene 1.
23   Babylonian Talmud, Ketubot 61b.
24   Sex Ethics in the Writings of Moses Maimonides, by Fred Rosner, p55.
25   Genesis 2:18.
26   Tomer Devorah, p.106.

THE PLEASURE OF RECEIVING

Another interpretation of *Gevurah*-discipline in *Yesod*-bonding is around the pleasure (*Yesod*) of receiving (*Gevurah*). Rabbi Yehuda Ashlag (1885-1954) interpreted the *Zohar* as meaning that we are here to receive as part of our relationship with God, and we can receive for ourself alone or receive so that we can share the blessing with other people;

> *"We need to consider that since the purpose of creation was in order to give His created beings pleasure, it was therefore necessary for God to create within the souls an exceedingly large desire to receive all that He planned to give them. After all, the measure of any joy or of any pleasure is proportionate to the measure of our will to receive it, to the extent that as the will to receive grows larger, in like measure the pleasure received is the greater. Similar, if the will to receive pleasure is lessened, then, in like measure, the pleasure in its receiving is correspondingly reduced.*
>
> *The very purpose of creation itself necessitates the creation within the souls of a will to receive, that is of the most prodigious measure, compatible with the great amount of joy with which God intends to give delight, for great pleasure and a great will to receive it go together"*[27].

This is an interesting interplay of *Gevurah*-receiving in *Yesod*-pleasure but provides a powerful avenue for our relationship to both God and humans.

DELAYED GRATIFICATION & THE STANFORD MARSHMALLOWS

The "Stanford Marshmallow Experiment" found a connection between children's ability to delay gratification and their level of success later on in life. In 1970, Walter Mischel and Ebbe B. Ebbesen conducted an experiment at Stanford University where children sat down in front

---

27 Introduction to The Zohar, Paragraph 6, Rabbi Yehudah Ashlag, quoted in "A Tapestry For The Soul - The Introduction to the Zohar by Rabbi Yehudah Lev Ashlag - compiled by Yedidah Cohen, p41

of a marshmallow. They were told that they could eat it immediately if they chose, but if they waited for 15 minutes they would be given two marshmallows as a reward. Of the 600 children tested, only a third were able to wait[28]. In this simple exercise we can see how people are able to restrict (*Gevurah*) their pleasure (*Yesod*), which can affect somebody's ability to save money for the future, keep their body in a good shape by not over-eating, or achieve all manner of things by modifying their energy.

BOUNDARIED RELATIONSHIPS

Another aspect to this principle is Boundaried Relationships. *Gevurah*-boundaries in *Yesod*-bonding guide us where to say "no" in friendships. The dinner-party dilemma runs as follows; How difficult did you find it to not invite the people who will not blend well with the other guests? Is there someone who you do not want at your table but you find it hard to say no to? At the end of the evening, do you have that feeling that you want people to leave but are not exactly sure of how to usher them on their way? Are you able to find the words to say *"it's been a really lovely night, thank you so much for coming, great to see you, and the cloakroom is the second door on the left and make sure to leave quietly so you don't disturb the neighbours"*?

HIGHER PERCEPTIONS

The Yoga Sutras teaches us how to elevate our mind beyond physical pleasures alone, saying that *"another way to steady the mind is by binding it to higher, subtler sense perceptions"*[29]. At times we can take our physical desire for pleasure and elevate it by focusing the energy up towards God, and connect to a far higher level.

TODAY'S PRACTICE

Ask for each day of Yesod: Where do I lack grounding? Where do I need stronger foundations? (e.g. I could be advanced in one area but not grounded in others)

---

28 "Stanford Marshmallow Experiment", http://en.wikipedia.org/wiki/Stanford_marshmallow_experiment.
29 Yoga Sutras 1:35, Mukunda Stiles translation.

YOGA PRACTICE GUIDELINES:

Today's practice needs to be grounded and rooted in the reality of
the moment. This is the fundamental aspect of *Yesod*-bonding. Take
a few minutes to sit still before your practice, either in a cross-legged
position or a variation of lotus posture. The practice should be focused
on both the foundations of each asana and also on keeping within the
boundaries of the physical choreography, applying strength and power
to each movement. If attending a yoga class there is the additional
benefit of using the boundaries of a yoga mat for applying the
Gevurah-discipline in *Yesod*-bonding, using the four sides of the mat to
demonstrate your respect for other peoples' space.

GYM PRACTICE GUIDELINES:

Where do you push your body too far, either by exercising too much,
resting too much, eating too much or taking any other aspect to excess?
How could you be more disciplined and focus your energy so that you
can better reach your goals?

RELATIONSHIP PRACTICE GUIDELINES:

Approach today's interactions with an awareness of strengthening the
bonds between people, doing things to improve the foundations of
your relationships and exercising discretion as to when you can say 'no'.
It is not always the easiest word to use, but there is immense value in
communicating your boundaries, and this often results in strengthening
bonds with others.

Gevurah-discipline in *Yesod*-bonding is the aspect of discipline and
boundaries in relationships. Take a moment to do a mental health
check of the state of your friendships and relationships. Is there anyone
that you have become too friendly with? Do you have friendships
that are unhealthily close? Are you over-dependent on anyone or have
you – for whatever reason – allowed someone to become too reliant
on your goodwill? Conversely, are you too distanced from people? Has
anyone ever told you that you are hard to get to know? *Gevurah* is about
bringing discipline, which leads to balance and healthy bonding.

QUESTIONS FOR MEDITATION

RELATIONSHIPS:
- Where am I emotionally disconnected in my relationships and how can I get more connected through a more disciplined approach? (*Gevurah*)
- Where is my lack of discipline rupturing connections in my relationships?
- Which of my relationships can be strengthened through being more grounded in reality?
- Do I have a dysfunctional fear of connecting with others? Where am I holding back from connecting?
- Where does my lack of discipline/strength negatively affect my relationships and connections?
- Where else can I hold back to connect on a deeper level? Can I switch off my telephone more often so that I can connect with others? Disconnect in order to reconnect?

YOGA/BODY/GYM:
- Where do I not listen or respond to my body's requests (e.g. To exercise more or differently, or to eat nutritious foods, or to heal an ache), and how can I be more disciplined in my approach? (*Gevurah*)

BUSINESS:
- Where am I disconnected from the mission of my business? How can I be more disciplined about reconnecting to my vision? (*Gevurah*)
- Am I disciplined in writing marketing emails regularly for my clients? Am I disciplined about other forms of connecting with existing and potential customers?

GYM SEQUENCE, DAY 37/JUMP KNEE TUCKS

Bend your knees and jump as high as possible, tucking your knees in. For kids of the 1980's, throw in an occasional "Fame" mid-air splits for variation. 3 x 12 repetitions.

.01

גבורה
Gevurah-Strength

יסוד
Yesod-Bonding

.02

YOGA SEQUENCE, DAY 37/BOAT (NAVASANA)

Lift yourself into Boat Pose for 6 breaths, rest for two breaths and then repeat two more sets. To make it more difficult, perform a half-vinyasa between sets or even lift yourself into a handstand. To modify the pose, bend your knees so that your shins are parallel to the ground.

יסוד
Yesod-Bonding

גבורה
Gevurah-Strength

DAY 38 / **COMPASSION IN BONDING** / BONDS THAT HEAL / תפארת שביסוד

KABBALAH SUTRA: *Tiferet She b'Yesod* – Compassion in Bonding.
INTENTION: To create balanced relationships. To heal someone else's
pain through compassionate bonding and create stronger bonds of
friendship.

*"The times for conjugal duty prescribed in the Torah are: for men of
independent means, every day; for labourers, twice a week; for donkey
drivers, once a week". — Talmud, Ketubot 61b*

We all have blockages to overcome. One symptom is having a project and
not sharing it, and not being able to 'give birth' to that idea. In Kabbalistic
terms, all ideas are 'born' through *Yesod*, because that is the limb -
physically and metaphorically - which spreads new seeds into the world.

When we have created something beautiful and balanced, this might be
likened to *Tiferet*. Just as *Tiferet* is represented by the torso, it is the that
part of the body that gestates and holds a baby prior to birth.

JACOB & JOSEPH

In this light, Jacob represents *Tiferet* and his favourite son Joseph
represents *Yesod*, and both are situated in the middle line of the body in
the Tree of Life. So when the Torah tells us *"Now Israel[30] loved Joseph
more than all his sons"[31]*, we can use the Kabbalistic tools to read it in a
way that will be applicable to our lives.

Joseph was essential to Jacob (Israel) because it was through Joseph
that Jacob's values were communicated to the world and his family was
expanded. If you have a great idea for a novel but never write or share
it, what is it all for? This physical world is about physical creation. Thus
the Tree of Life diagrams place *Yesod*-bonding directly below *Tiferet*-

---

30 The other name for Jacob.
31 Genesis 37:3.

balance because *Tiferet* literally 'flows' into *Yesod* as our plans 'flow' into action[32].

HARNESSING OUR POWER

Tiferet-balance is also the blend between *Chesed*-creativity and *Gevurah*-restraint. The yogis recognised the importance of balancing our desires as a way to strengthen relationships with the self and others; *"self-restraint in actions includes abstention from violence, from falsehoods, from stealing, from sexual engagement, and from acceptance of gifts"*[33]. Balance is critical, as we are careful to not hold back too much, but we can strengthen relationships by exerting discipline in conscious doses.

CONJUGAL RITES

The same is true in marital relationships as there is a positive commandment to *"be fruitful and multiply"*[34] and being married is one of the traditional prerequisites for learning Kabbalah (although there are exceptions). There is an importance for married couples to get the balance right - not too much sex and not too little - and the Talmud has a series of recommendations based upon one's profession. *"The times for conjugal duty prescribed in the Torah are: for men of independent means, every day; for labourers, twice a week; for donkey drivers, once a week; for camel drivers, once in thirty days; for sailors, once in six months"*[35]. These are guidelines rather than a specific prescription, perhaps to remind tired men that they have more than just a spiritual and financial duty when it comes to fulfilling their marriage vows. Interestingly, a woman is permitted to divorce her husband if he does not perform his conjugal duties and *"Rabbi Joshua ben Levi said: Whosoever knows his wife to be a God fearing woman and does not duly visit her is called a sinner"*[36].

---

32 Rabbi Yitzhak Ginsburg teaches a deeper connection between *Yesod* and *Tiferet*; *"In Kabbalah, the third day, tiferet ("beauty"), is the origin of the sixth day, yesod ("foundation"). Tiferet and Yesod totally integrate in the secret of the "middle line" - "the body and the brit are considered one."* - From The Mystical Signficance of the Hebrew Letters: Tzadik, The Faith of the Righteous One, Rabbi Yitzchak Ginsburgh, http://www.inner.org/HEBLETER/tzadik.htm, (Gal Einai Institute, Kfar Chabad, Israel).
33 Yoga Sutras 2:30, Swamij translation.
34 Genesis 1:28.
35 Babylonian Talmud, Ketubot 61b.
36 Babylonian Talmud, Yevamot 62b.

QUALITY TIME

There was some moment in the mid 1980's when we started hearing about "quality time"[37], which was not just spending physical time with family members but spending high-quality focused time with them. It appeared a few years before mobile phones and email were about to start gaining ground, and our current epidemic of being physically present and mentally absent as we spend time on mobile devices. *Tiferet*-compassion in *Yesod*-bonding is the aspect of connected, grounded relationships that are governed by compassion for the other person.

SELFLESSNESS

Compassionate bonding demands empathy and selflessness in a relationship, and this sometimes demands us to go beyond our comfort zone. You may have heard of someone who is reluctant to visit a friend or relative in hospital because the potential visitor is scared or uncomfortable and does not know how to best deal with the situation? Some people are not unwilling to visit elderly relatives who are suffering from dementia or Alzheimers on the basis that it will be difficult or uncomfortable for the person visiting. I have heard people say they did not visit their grandparent in hospital "because they didn't want to remember them that way". Forgive the judgement, but does that not sound a little bit selfish? What about the ill grandparent in hospital? *Tiferet*-Compassion in *Yesod*-bonding, is the blunt reminder that It is Not All About You.

ADVANCED KABBALAH: RAISING *YESOD* TO *TIFERET*

We aim to bring *Tiferet*-compassion "down" to *Yesod*-bonding - e.g. Jacob going from Israel down to Joseph - which represents bringing the flow of goodness into the world. *"Then Joseph brought Jacob, his father to Pharaoh"*[38] is like the action of giving birth (*Tiferet*=Torso *Yesod*=Pelvis) or "giving birth" to an idea as we manifest it in reality. Yet the opposite is also true, as it says *"Joseph harnessed his chariot and went*

---

37   An early recorded source of this phrase was in The Capital (Maryland), January 1973, in the article "How To Be Liberated". Source: Wikipedia.
38   Genesis 47:7.

up to meet Israel his father, to Goshen, and he appeared to him.."[39]. Joseph "harnessing his chariot" might be seen as the way that we can harness our own energy - the wild horses of our own desires - and raise them up for a higher purpose. In this way, every single Biblical story can be read on a Kabbalistic and practical manner, to enhance our life, improve the world and bring more Divine Light into this realm.

TODAY'S PRACTICE & QUESTIONS FOR MEDITATION:

Ask for each day of *Yesod*-bonding: where do I lack grounding? Where do I need stronger foundations? (e.g. I could be advanced in one area but not grounded in others).

YOGA PRACTICE GUIDELINES:

Yesod-foundation can be practiced by grounding and rooting in each posture, keeping the placement of your feet as strong as possible, whilst allowing the energy to emanate outwards through the four limbs. There are asanas which include 'bonding' with the body, when there is the opportunity to deepen an asana by grabbing hold of one's wrist or hand whilst wrapping it around the body. Many of these will literally combine the binding in aspect of *Yesod* with the heart-opening aspect of *Tiferet*, and we can use this as a meditation for opening our heart space and creating stronger relationships. Ultimately the physical bonding is another aspect of consolidating the flow of energy within our bodies and pursuing physical unification, reflecting our intended unity with God. The Bahagavad Gita says that *"when the mind is not in harmony, this Divine connection is hard to attain; but the man whose mind is in harmony attains it, if he knows and if he strives"*[40]. We can read harmony as *Tiferet* and Divine connection as *Yesod*-foundation, giving us a further insight into today's principle.

GYM PRACTICE GUIDELINES:

Balance your energy and ground it. Use as much energy as you need and no more, so that there is no wasted effort. See yourself as a finely-

---

39 Genesis 46:29.
40 Bhagavad Gita 6:36.

tuned jet, burning the right amount of fuel to reach your goals without wasting any of it.

RELATIONSHIP PRACTICE GUIDELINES:
Today is about using the opportunity for engaging the heart and using the balancing energy of *Tiferet*-compassion to inspire meaningful and positive connections with other people. As we rebalance internally, connecting with our core (through the *Yesod*/root lock energy) and opening our heart space, we prepare ourselves for strengthening bonds with those around us and building communities that are governed by care and compassion.

QUESTIONS FOR MEDITATION

RELATIONSHIPS:
- Where am I emotionally disconnected in my relationships and how can I get more connected through more compassion and balance? (*Tiferet*)
- Where does my lack of compassion (*Tiferet*) and balance cause disconnection?
- Am I balanced in my giving and receiving?
- Do I have any outstanding "Karmic Debts"? Do I owe anyone anything? Are there any unpaid debts within my relationships that are within my ability to balance or pay right now?

YOGA/BODY/GYM:
- Where do I not listen or respond to my body's requests (e.g. To exercise differently, to eat nutritious foods, or to heal an ache). How can I be more compassionate and balanced towards my body, bringing healing where it is needed? (*Tiferet*)

BUSINESS:
- Where am I disconnected from the mission of my business? How can I use compassion to reconnect with my vision? How can I be more balanced in the way I approach things? (*Tiferet*)

GYM SEQUENCE, DAY 38/ARCHER LUNGE

Begin with your feet parallel and step one foot forward as if drawing your bow. Then step back and switch sides. 3 x 10 repetitions.

.01

תפארת
Tiferet-Balance

יסוד
Yesod-Bonding

.02

YOGA SEQUENCE, DAY 38/CHILD'S POSE (BALASANA)

If needed, modify with a cushion on top of your heels or under your forehead.

תפארת
Tiferet-Balance

יסוד
Yesod-Bonding

DAY 39 / ENDURANCE IN BONDING / FRIENDSHIP IS GOLDEN: נצח שביסוד

KABBALAH SUTRA: *Netzah She b'Yesod* – Endurance in Bonding.
INTENTION: To create enduring, grounded, healthy relationships.

"For I am the Lord – I have not changed; and you are the children of Jacob – you have not ceased to be" — Malachi 3:6

"All you need is love" — The Beatles

"Ten Sefirot of Nothingness" — Sefer Yetzirah

To build a house we need a firm foundation. To grow relationships we need enduring, long-term connections. Several decades after the "Free Love" revolution of the 1960's, our modern age has proven that *All You Need Is Love* was not a durable mantra. Wars continue to rage, divorce rates grow, millions of people take anti-depressants and we need more than love. *Netzach*-endurance in *Yesod*-bonding is the action of long-term growth within a relationship, like continuing to water your garden on a regular basis. We fine-tune ourselves, fine-tune our communications and fine-tune our relationships so that everything improves over time.

Yesod is also foundation, and we must continue to strengthen the foundations of our 'building', whether it is in the arena of career, business, emotions, relationships, body or spirituality. Rabbi Ginsburg explains that *"Yesod is associated in the soul with the power to contact, connect and communicate with outer reality (represented by the sefirah of Malchut-mastery). The foundation (yesod) of a building is its "grounding," its union with the earth (Malchut)"*[41]. As we create our buildings, we must take responsibility for what kind of structure is being made.

---

[41] The Divine Emanations--The Ten Sefirot: Yesod "Foundation," Rabbi Yitzchak Ginsburgh,http://www.inner.org/sefirot/sefyesod.htm.

FOUNDATION LETTERS

One of the most important works of Kabbalah, the *Sefer Yetzirah – Book of Foundation – begins by describing "Ten Sefirot of Nothingness, and 22 Foundation Letters: Three Mothers, Seven Doubles And Twelve Elementals"*[42]. Rabbi Aryeh Kaplan explains that *"In Hebrew, "Foundation Letters" is Otiot Yesod. This can also be translated "Letters of Foundation""*[43]. The 22 letters are the foundation of thought, speech and action. They help us communicate with others and communicate with themselves. Without the letters we would have symbols and imagery, much like the language of dreams.

In our body, the 22 letters can be understood to correspond to the ten digits on the hands, ten toes, the head and the male organ. In another Kabbalistic model, each of the Hebrew letters corresponds to a different body part.

WHERE ARE THESE LETTERS HIDDEN?

Where are these *Yesod*-foundation letters 'hidden'? In our bodies! *We* are the foundation letters. Now that we have that information, the question is, which words are we going to 'write' with our 'letters', and what are we going to build?

FOUNDATION SKILLS

When we lack long-term endurance (*Netzach*) in our foundation (*Yesod*), it is difficult to continue to produce at a high level. A couple who stops being respectful towards one another will pay the price in their relationship, and a musicians who loses the ability to practicing their scales will suffer in their musical output. Where are the areas where you are missing or dropping your foundational skills?

---

[42] Sefer Yetzirah 1:2.
[43] Sefer Yetzirah commentary, p27. He further explains;" *In the Kabbalah, Foundation (Yesod) is the Sefirah that corresponds to the sexual organ. It therefore has the connotation of coupling and pairing, usually for the purpose of procreation.*
The letters are said to pertain to Foundation (Yesod), since it is only through the letters that Wisdom and Understanding can come together and be coupled…Wisdom is pure non-verbal thought. Understanding, on the other hand, can only be verbal, since if an idea cannot be expressed verbally, it cannot be understood. The only link between nonverbal Wisdom, and verbal Understanding, consists of the letters of the alphabet".

MOSES KEEPS GOING

Netzach-endurance in *Yesod*-bonding might also be understood as the endurance of Moses in strengthening the relationship with God and creating the basis for laws that have affected the whole of humanity. As Moses continues to build the connection, the relationship between God and Israel is compared to that of a husband and wife. The prophet Malachi (420 BCE) spoke of how God continued to be faithful to the Jews, and in a slightly sarcastic voice describes how they continued to be unfaithful, not bringing their correct charitable contributions:

> *"For I am the Lord – I have not changed; and you are the children of Jacob – you have not ceased to be. From the very days of your fathers you have turned away from My laws and have not observed them. Turn back to Me, and I will turn back to you – said the Lord of Hosts, But you ask, "How shall we turn back?"*[44] *Ought man to defraud God? Yet you are defrauding Me. And you ask "How have we been defrauding You?". In tithe and contribution. You are suffering under a curse, yet you go on defrauding Me – the whole nation of you"*[45].

When we find we are suffering in one area of our life, it is appropriate to ask where we are being 'unfaithful' to our original commitments. This is true of our fidelity to the Creator, but also to ourselves and our interests. If you stop getting clients in your business, are you still marketing your services and developing new avenues for revenue? If your relationship begins waning, are you still taking actions to show you love each other or are you just expecting it to happen? If you are unhappy in your social life, are you doing anything about it or just complaining?

CHARACTER DEVELOPMENT

When living in a state of 'blame and complain', criticising the world around us for the problems we experience, there is a lack of connection to where we can take responsibility for the stresses in our life. It is always easy to blame others or blame our teachers when uncomfortable

---

44   This is the essence of *"Teshuva"*, the call for 'return' or 'repentance'.
45   Malachi 3:6-8.

truths are pointed out. Rabbi Ginsburg explains that *"The spiritual state identified in Chassidut as corresponding to the sefirah of yesod is that of emet (truth), in the sense of the power to "verify" one's convictions and emotions in action and to achieve true self-fulfillment in life"*[46].

NETZACH AS TRUTH

We might also understand *Netzach* as a form of truth because it is our long-term truth, the way that we are behaving time after time. Just as we might identify our 'true' friends at a time of crisis as those who are there for us, we can form a new truth by the behaviours that we repeat.

The late business motivation expert Zig Ziglar taught that *"Repetition is the mother of learning, the father of action, which makes it the architect of accomplishment"*, and Anthony Robbins has often taught that "repetition is the mother of skill". Both of these are true when it comes to repeating our behaviours, and when they are applied to greater goals, we can create powerful accomplishments.

FOUNDATION OF THE WORLD

The question is: Who do you want to be in the world? The sefirah of *Yesod*-foundation, is firmly associated with the tzaddikim, the righteous ones, as it says in the book of Proverbs that "the righteous are the foundation of the world" - *tzaddik yesod HaOlam*[47]. Nonetheless, any foundation can only be achieved with the repetition of *Netzach*-endurance.

TODAY'S PRACTICE

Ask for each day of *Yesod*: where do I lack grounding? Where do I need stronger foundations? (e.g. I could be advanced in one area but not grounded in others)

---

46 http://www.inner.org/sefirot/sefyesod.
47 Proverbs 10:25.

YOGA PRACTICE GUIDELINES:

Work on the foundation of your postures today and continue to strengthen and endure with this; your breathing, your foot placement, physical alignment in postures, engaging your muscles, and continuing to breathe.

GYM PRACTICE GUIDELINES:

Endure with your practice today whilst focusing on staying strong in your core and in your legs.

QUESTIONS FOR MEDITATION

RELATIONSHIPS:
- Where am I emotionally disconnected in my relationships and how can I get more connected through being more enduring in my attitude? (*Netzach*)
- Where does my lack of endurance cause disconnection?
- Where do I need to put more work into building my relationships?
- Where do I need to bond more in my friendships and relationships, and strengthen these bonds for the long-term?

YOGA/BODY/GYM:
- Where do I not listen or respond to my body's requests (e.g. To exercise more or differently, or to eat nutritious foods, or to heal an ache), and how can I take a more sustainable, enduring approach? (*Netzach*)

BUSINESS:
- Where am I disconnected from the mission of my business? How can I reconnect to my vision for the long-term and not get swayed? (*Netzach*)
- Where do I need to put more work into building my relationships?
- Where do I need to bond more with clients or colleagues and strengthen these bonds for the long-term?

GYM SEQUENCE, DAY 39/FLY STEP

Begin in a "Ready, Steady, Go" position and step up into your Superman/Fly Step. Then switch sides. 3 x 10 repetitions.

.01

.02

יסוד
Yesod-Bonding

נצח
Netzach-Endurance

YOGA SEQUENCE, DAY 39/FORWARD STRADDLE BEND (PRASARITA PADDOTANASA)

Be careful in this posture. Place your hands on blocks if needed, or stand in front of a wall and push your flat palms into the wall in front of you.

.01

.02

.03

יְסוֹד
Yesod-Bonding

נֵצַח
Netzach-Endurance

DAY 40 / HUMILITY IN BONDING / THIS TOWN AIN'T BIG ENOUGH הוד שביסוד

KABBALAH SUTRA: *Hod She b'Yesod* — Humility in Bonding.

INTENTION: To cradle yourself in the warm Light of God through humble bonding. To increase gratitude and humility in order to attain a state of deep grounding, ultimate strengthening of all your relationships (family, friends, clients/colleagues and God).

"Silence is a protective fence for wisdom" — Rabbi Akiva

Sometimes a room feels crowded if there are only two people present. "This town ain't big enough for the two us" goes the famous trope, being spoken in everything from Western cowboy movies to M*A*S*H and *Toy Story*. One aspect of *Hod*-humility in *Yesod*-bonding is stepping back to create space for the other person and make more room for them. Apart from anything else, this can often be good manners.

SHUDDUPAYA FACE

The Rabbis noted a simple solution for maintaining one's wisdom and keeping relationships on a positive footing; to stop talking. Rabbi Akiva (c.40–137 CE) taught that *"silence is a protective fence for wisdom"*[48] and Rabbi Shimon ben Elazar (two generations later) said *"Do not appease your fellow at the time of his anger, do not console him at the time his dead lies before him, do not ask him [to regret his oath] at the time of his oath, and do not attempt to see him at the time of his downfall"*[49]. In both cases the received wisdom is to use silence as a powerful tool. This may seem at odds with modern living where the chatter of telephones and the internet make silence an ever-scarcer quality.

---

[48] Ethics of the Fathers/Pirkei Avot 3:17.
[49] Ethics of the Fathers/Pirkei Avot 4:23.

MAKE ROOM FOR YOUR FAMILY

At times we find that we have built an identity that no longer suits us. Our ego can take a battering when we decide to change direction or step into a new role, but if this is the truth of our soul then it is essential to express our truth rather than repress it. In the height of his power as viceroy of Egypt, Joseph, the embodiment of *Yesod*-bonding, revealed his true identity in front of his brothers.

> *"Now Joseph could not endure in the presence of all who stood before him, so he called out, "Remove everyone from before me". Thus no one stood with him when Joseph made himself known to his brothers. He gave [forth] his voice in weeping, Egypt heard, and Pharoah's household heard. And Joseph said to his brothers, "I am Joseph. Is my father still alive?" But his brothers could not answer him because they were left disconcerted before him*"[50].

Joseph had nothing to gain from revealing who he was as he could have found out the information about his father through other means - he was the acting ruler of Egypt after all - but by exposing his vulnerability he was able to restore the damaged relationships with his siblings; a relationship which he had been partly responsible for damaging when he initially angered them by revealing dreams that sounded deeply insensitive (even if they were completely accurate prophecies).

CREATING A HUG BY STEPPING BACK

There are two ways to hug somebody. The first is to grab them and draw them in, but the second, perhaps a more refined approach, is to open your arms and create space for the other person. This opening is a passive energy of *Hod* that makes room for the other.

An essential piece of rabbinic choreography takes place at the beginning and end of the *Amidah*, the *Shemonah Esrei* prayer that is said three times a day in Jewish liturgy. The movement is to take three steps backwards and three steps forward. At the prayer's conclusion, during the blessing about how God makes peace in the world (*Oseh Shalom Bimromav*), the choreography directs people to take three steps backwards and bow in three different directions. This lowering of the

---

50 Genesis 45: 1-3.

head and moving backwards is a very deliberate message to ourselves and others. In order to create peace we must create space for the other parties and lower ourselves in humility.

BENDING OUR KNEE

The Bahir speaks of how knee (*berech*) is connected to blessing (*baruch*); *"It is written "For to Me shall every knee bend"*[51]. *[Berachah/blessing can therefore mean] the Place to which every knee bends". What example does this resemble? People want to see the king, but do not know where to find his house (Bayit). First they ask, "Where is the king's house?" Only then can they ask, "Where is the king?". It is thus written, "For to Me shall every knee bend" – even the highest – "Every tongue shall swear"*[52]. Our question is: where can we do the equivalent of bending our knee in our own relationships, be it with ourselves, friends and family or God?

RELEASING JUDGEMENT

Hod-humility in *Yesod*-bonding allows us to create stronger connections through letting go of pride, expectations and judgements. Eastern wisdom has traditionally focussed on the value of non-attachment which is a specific breaking of bonds from the ego – the 'I want' – in order to enjoy a stronger connection with both God and our fellow humans. The Yoga Sutras describes the process by saying that *"by non-attachment even to that comes the dwindling of the seeds of bondage and absolute freedom is experienced"*[53].

There is an unintended play on words with 'bondage' which helps us understand this further. Bonds are the connections that we do not want because they leave us in a form of servitude, which can be both physical and psychological. We often create pain for ourselves by insisting on bonds that are purely the creation of the ego – "that's MY wife...MY car...MY house....MY job..", Or "why isn't that MINE anymore?" – and by loosening these psychological bonds we free ourselves from uncomfortable bondage.

---

51   Isaiah 44:23.
52   Para 4, The Bahir, p2.
53   Yoga Sutras 3:51, Stiles translation.

381

BONDING THROUGH THANKSGIVING

Saying 'thank you' is one of the first skills taught by parents, and a behaviour that quickly becomes second nature. The process of speaking the words can have several effects depending on how it is done. If it is just an unconscious reaction, it will just skim the surface of our awareness, being little more than a polite formality without any great lasting impact.

A conscious, aware expression of thanks has three potential beneficiaries. Firstly, the person being thanked is shown gratitude and appreciation. They are given respect and accorded value for the object or action they have just given. Secondly, the person thanking you is affected, in some ways much more than the person being thanked. Why is this? When I show my thanks for you, I am recognising that I am the beneficiary of your kindness. Saying thank you takes me to a place of humility, as I recognise that in some way, however minor, my life has been enhanced by you. Finally, saying thank you further strengthens the connection between two people. If you are not sure about this, try to remember an occasion when you made an effort or gave a gift to somebody and they completely failed to say thanks, thereby taking you for granted. How did this make you feel? What did it make you think about the other person? How positive was it for the health of your friendship or relationship?

SPLENDOUR

Hod also translates as 'splendour' and comes from the *Hod'a'ah* meaning 'thanks'. As we have discussed, it can also be understood as humility, as the action of thanking leads to humility. In many ways this is the opposite side of splendour, as a person is able to 'shine' when they reach a level of genuine, rounded humility that becomes a cause of inspiration to other people.

TODAY'S PRACTICE

Ask for each day of *Yesod*: where do I lack grounding? Where do I need stronger foundations? (e.g. I could be advanced in one area but not grounded in others)

YOGA PRACTICE GUIDELINES:

Approach today's postures with humility and reverence whilst fully connecting with your breath and root energy point. Genuine humility can be a source of strength and our awareness of the transitory nature of our bodies, as well as the fragility of human life. It can motivate and inspire us, as we draw the energy from our base region and spread it outwards.

The late Mr. BKS Iyengar (1918-2014) explained that yoga *"teaches humility"*[54]. Humility, however, must start within. Forcing our bodies into yoga postures they are not ready for can cause untold damage, whether it is jamming the knees into lotus or surprising the neck with an unprepared headstand. As we increase our humility (*Hod*), we deepen the internal bond (*Yesod*) with our body. Today, approach your asana practice with humility (Hod) and focus on being grounded (*Yesod*).

GYM PRACTICE GUIDELINES:

Cultivate an attitude of gratitude in your gym practice today. Let this be the foundation for your workout, being grateful for your body, your senses, your ability to stand, to breathe and to have the ability to increase your fitness levels. Extend this approach throughout your workout.

RELATIONSHIP PRACTICE GUIDELINES:

The thanks and humility of *Hod* goes to solidify the connections we have with our own bodies, with one another and with the Universal Spirit. *"Let everything that has breath praise the Lord"*[55] wrote King

---

54   Light on Yoga, BKS Iyengar, p.73.
55   Psalms 150:6.

David. We can apply this directly, visualising each breath as an expression of gratitude and appreciation, and savouring the sweetness of every breath as it fills our lungs.

However successful we might become in life, we are all dependent on the air we breathe and there is a powerful humility to be achieved in recognising this fact. When ancient mystics wrote the mantra *"Creator, the breath you placed within me is pure"*[56], they wanted to instill a daily awareness of the breath, so that we could strengthen our bond with God through this daily meditation and use this impetus to strengthen our society.

Pick one friendship/relationship you would like to improve. Today ask the question "What can I give to the other person?" or "how can I become more humble in this relationships and focus on their needs?". Then do something today to put that into practice.

QUESTIONS FOR MEDITATION

RELATIONSHIPS:
- Where am I emotionally disconnected in my relationships and how can I get more connected through being humble and grateful towards other people? (*Hod*)
- Where does my lack of Humility cause disconnection?
- Where does my lack of Gratitude cause disconnection?

YOGA/BODY/GYM:
- Where do I not listen or respond to my body's requests (e.g. To exercise more or differently, or to eat nutritious foods, or to heal an ache), and how can I relate to my body with more gratitude and respect? (*Hod*)

BUSINESS:
- Where am I disconnected from the mission of my business? How can I really appreciate the size of the opportunity in front of me? (*Hod*)

---

56 From the morning blessings, to be found in the Artscroll Siddur pp18-19.

GYM SEQUENCE, DAY 40/STEP UP

Raise your knees as high as possible, and match each movement with a breath. 3 sets of 45 seconds.

.01

.02

הוד
Hod-Humility

יסוד
Yesod-Bonding

YOGA SEQUENCE, DAY 40/TREE (VRKSASANA)

Visualise rooting yourself into the ground and imagine your energy going in two opposite directions, as the crown of your head reaches towards the sky.

.01

.02

יסוד
Yesod-Bonding

הוד
Hod-Humility

DAY 41 / **BONDING IN BONDING** / HARNESS YOUR LIFE FORCE / יסוד שביסוד

KABBALAH SUTRA: *Yesod She b'Yesod* – Bonding in Bonding.

INTENTION: To become emotionally and physically grounded, develop deep inner strength and powerful relationships. Develop ultimate internal grounding and strong foundations for incredible relationships and friendships.

"Speak the speech I pray you as I pronounced it to you, trippingly on the tongue;
..Suit the action to the word, the word to the action, with this special observance, that you o'erstep not the modesty of nature" — Hamlet[57]

"a man should not draw his bow …unless it is directed towards the proper target: his wife" — Tomer Devorah

We aim for energetic efficiency in our cars, houses and life. *Hamlet* talks about bad actors who waste their energy by over-acting and how good actors achieve their art through doing exactly what is needed and no more. *Yesod* in *Yesod* is about pure economy, keeping our thoughts intentional, not wasting energy and unifying our thought, speech and action. The Kabbalah teaches this in a very explicit manner, which is relevant to all of us at most times in our life:

> *"Yesod also corresponds to 'the Covenant of the Rainbow', which is arched above only to shoot arrows to the attribute of Malchut, the target of the arrows. This refers to guarding the seminal drop, which shoots forth like an arrow "to produce branches and bear fruit" (Yechezkel 17:8). Just as the 'bow' in the higher worlds is never drawn except when aimed at the aforementioned target, a man should not draw his bow – that is, cause himself in any way to have an erection – unless it is directed towards the proper target: his wife, when she is in a state of*

---

57   Hamlet, Act 3, Scene ii.

purity, at the time of union. He should never go beyond this limit, lest the attribute of Yesod become flawed, God forbid. This requires great care, mainly in guarding himself from licentious thoughts[58].

The physicality speaks for itself, but the underlying energy principle is not to waste our life-energy where it is not going to be fulfilled. Just as sexual energy - the core of one's life force and some of the most potent energy available to us - should be used in a "correct" manner, so too with the rest of our energy.

SWEET SLEEP

King Solomon wrote *"The sleep of a labourer is sweet, whether he eats little or much"*, recognising that we are exhausted after deeply expending our energy, unlike *"the satisfaction of the rich [whose wealth] will not suffer him to sleep"*[59]. That is not to say that every rich person who works hard cannot sleep, but rather someone who is not using their energy appropriately is not going to enjoy the deeper satisfaction. The Hebrew word for labourer is *Oved* and in the language of King David, we are all encouraged to 'labour' in our relationship with the Divine[60]. Once again this brings us back to question how we are using our life-force.

REMEMBER YOUR LIFE-FORCE...HOW ARE YOU USING IT?

Kabbalistic teachings ascribe a different name of God to each of the *sefirot* (Divine spheres), whilst being very clear that we should not be praying to the *sefirot* as they are 'merely' channels for Divine Light. One name assigned to *Yesod*-foundation is *"El Chai"* as in the God of Life[61]. The Bahir explains that *""Life" indicates the Sefirah of Yesod–Foundation, and denotes the sexual organ when it is "alive", that is, during intercourse"*[62]. Although this energy is clearly located in the pelvic region, the principle applies to every area of our life where we are creating or expending energy in the world, whether it is making telephone calls to

---

58 Tomer Devorah, p123.
59 Ecclesiastes/*Kohelet* 5:11.
60 Psalms 100:2 - *"ivdu et HaShem b'simcha"* - "serve God with joy".
61 Referenced in Sharey Orah, The Gates of Light, by Rabbi Joseph Gikatalia (1248-1323), in Meditation and Kabbalah, p126.
62 The Bahir, Chapter 72, p136.

build your business, arranging community events or putting energy into raising your children. In this context it is clearly not sexual energy but the energy of all creative acts.

THE HIGHEST BOND

Yesod-bonding in *Yesod*-bonding is one of the deepest connections that can be experienced between two people, and is therefore also a metaphor for our relationship with God. Rabbi Aryeh Kaplan explains this and how it is a climactic progression from *Netzach*-endurance and hod-humility;

> *"The idea of Netzach and Hod is a question of asserting your identity on the one hand, or total compliance with the other person's identity, on the other. The perfect Yesod–Foundation relationship is of course the balance between the two. What is important to emphasise here is that this rule holds true both in the relationship between man and God as well as between man and woman. Yesod–Foundation represents the most powerful bond that can exist between two individuals. At the same time it is the ultimate attachment of man to the Divine. In fact, the Baal Shem Tov explains that marital intimacy is the paradigm of man's relationship with God. The motions of the sexual act represent this balancing back and forth between Netzach and Hod, while the final cessation of motion is Yesod. Yesod–Foundation is thus the perfect mean between Netzach–Dominance and Hod–Empathy, the blending of two people in love. It is not only the physical blending, but a psychological and emotional blending"[63].*

It makes perfect sense that *Yesod* is the organ that permits the human the highest level of pleasure, because on a spiritual realm it is point of connection between a person and their creator. As we discussed earlier, *Yesod*-bonding out of balance would represent a brief sexual encounter where someone gets into bed without fully knowing the other person, without knowing what or who they are getting involved with. The spiritual force of *Yesod*-bonding can then be used against this couple,

---

63   Innerspace, p66.

making it harder for them to be together. The Lubavitcher Rebbe was quoted to have said that *"people who are together when they should be apart will be apart when they should be together"*, referring to couples whose physical intimacy reaches a peak before they get married (e.g. together when they should be apart) and how that can work against them once they finally take their marital vows.

TODAY'S PRACTICE

Ask for each day of Yesod: Where do I lack grounding? Where do I need stronger foundations? (e.g. I could be advanced in one area but not grounded in others)

YOGA PRACTICE GUIDELINES:

Today's focus is on the root energy lock and being aware of it at all times in all postures. Be mindful of this, the *mulah bandha*, as the point from which all of your physical energy is emanating outwards. Like the famous Da Vinci picture of Vitruvian Man which has a human being drawn with arms and legs outstretched and the genitals at the centre of the circle, hold an awareness of this energy point in all of your postures, especially the sun salutes.

David Life, co-creator of Jivamukti yoga, describes it as follows; *"mula bandha is a technique for containing and channelling the energies associated with the mula-dara ('root place') chakra...[it] represents the stage of consciousness where basic survival needs dominate"*. The organs of procreation are the natural seat of our survival, but he takes it to a deeper level, explaining that 'on the deepest level of the subtle body, the ananda (bliss) level – applying mula bandha means binding the normally outgoing senses inward. Normally we look outside ourselves for happiness. But any bliss which we find from outside is temporary, even if it can be intoxicating"[64].

Yesod is precisely what the yogis understand as *mulah bandha*, although they disagree over whether *mulah bandha*, the root lock, is a firm idea

---

64 David Life, article on *'mulah bandha'* published on yogajournal.com.

or whether it is specifically invoked by drawing in the anal sphincter[65]. Either way, it is a base point of energy that can be used as a mental root point for all other energy within the body. If you think of how much energy is released after relieving one's bowels – the action of going to the toilet makes you feel lighter, fresher and more able to function, and this release comes from the same point in the body.

GYM PRACTICE GUIDELINES:

Harness your core power. Focus it like a laser-beam and give your workout 100% of effort.

RELATIONSHIP PRACTICE GUIDELINES:

Today's life practice is to increase commitment and bonding with one other person, whether it is a new or established connection. This might mean making an arrangement that you have been meaning to organise for some time now, or demonstrating a spontaneous show of commitment to someone else (if you are single, this is the kind of action that would make your parents very happy...).

Yesod in *Yesod* is also about committing to your beliefs. When have you devoted time to starting something that you have not followed through? *Yesod*-bonding in *Yesod*-bonding is an invitation to stick with a process and see it through to the end. It may not be easy, but the results can be truly magnificent.

GUIDELINES: FOR HEALING FROM PAST RELATIONSHIPS & CUTTING ASTRAL TIES

Dysfunctional *Yesod*-bonding may look like remaining energetically connected to previous lovers, or having indiscriminate one-night stands and promiscuity. In other words, trying to attach to many people through the organ of *Yesod*, or energetically connecting to other people through astral tendrils, or through asking too many questions and getting involved in their "stuff".

---

65 Ashtanga teachers such as John Scott teach that Mulah Bandha is invoked by drawing in the anus, whilst my teacher Edward Clark suggests that Mulah Bandha is more of an idea, a general point of root energy that isn't specifically fixed but is somewhat moveable around the genital region, depending on how the body is positioned and the breath is connected.

Disconnecting our astral ties can be a deep task requiring the assistance of a qualified teacher, but here are some pointers to get started:

1. Make a list of anyone you still feel energetically connected to in a negative way.

2. Purge any and all items in your home that were connected to that person (yes, that means ALL gifts from your ex-girlfriend/boyfriend/spouse).

3. Buy a Selenite wand (approximately $10 online) and wave it around your body to 'cut' astral ties.

4. Closely watch your thoughts to ensure you are not connecting with the other person.

5. Take a salt bath and do any other cleansing procedures that speak to you.

QUESTIONS FOR MEDITATION

RELATIONSHIPS:
- Where am I emotionally disconnected in my relationships and how can I get more connected in as many ways as possible? (*Yesod*)
- Where does my lack of grounding cause disconnection?
- Where does my lack of connection to self cause disconnection to others?

YOGA/BODY/GYM:
- Where do I not listen or respond to my body's requests (e.g. To exercise more or differently, or to eat nutritious foods, or to heal an ache), and how can I stay connected with what my body is "saying"? What deeper listening practice or dialoguing can I accomplish with my body? (*Yesod*)

BUSINESS:
- Where am I disconnected from the mission of my business? How can I stay more connected to the people I am trying to help and the solutions I am trying to deliver? (*Yesod*)

GYM SEQUENCE, DAY 41/SHOULDER QUAD SET

Extend your arms straight in front then bring the dumbells back to your body. Fully extend out to the sides then back in, above your head and back to your shoulders, before leaning forwards and doing the 'Fly' set. 3 x 8 repetitions of the complete routine.

.01

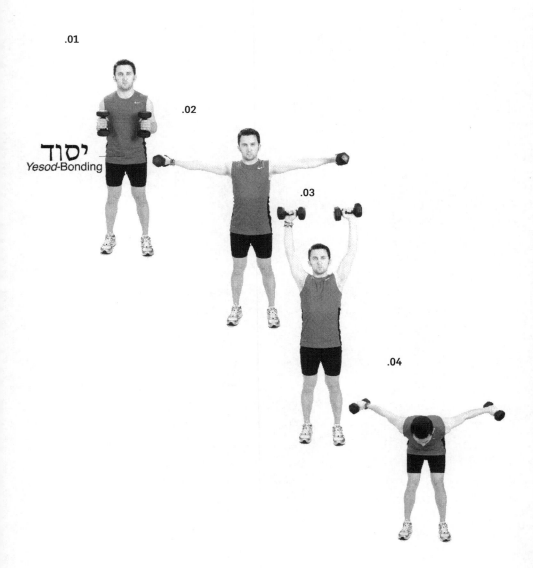

יסוד
Yesod-Bonding

.02

.03

.04

YOGA SEQUENCE, DAY 41/THE GREAT SEAL (MAHAMUDRA)

Place your heel so that it is between your buttocks. Mahamudra means "The Great Seal" and can activate this energy point. Raise your energy up through your back and reach for your foot, whether you are using your hands or strap.

.01

יסוד
Yesod-Bonding

.02

DAY 42 / **NOBILITY IN BONDING** / RELATIONSHIP MASTERY / מלכות שביסוד

KABBALAH SUTRA: *Hod She b'Yesod* – Nobility in Bonding.
INTENTION: To connect with others in a way that is masterful, dignified and healing. Develop a noble approach to friendships/relationships and inner grounding to build the confidence of kings. Achieve deeper grounding and bonding as a pathway to Leadership and Mastery.

"What we do in this life echoes in eternity" — Gladiator

"I call heaven and earth to witness against you this day, that I have set before you life and death, the blessing and the curse; therefore choose life, that you may live, you and your seed" — Deuteronomy 30:19

Every long-married couple will tell you that relationships take work. Love goes through cycles but a relationship cannot survive without being actively nurtured. *Malchut*-mastery is the realm of action of following through on all of our ideas, preparation and well-intentioned plans. As the Kabbalah connects *Malchut*-mastery with the hands, feet and mouth, we might ask the simple question; how are you using these parts of your body to become more grounded and connected to others? How are you using your communication to strengthen relationships? Are you "walking" in a direction that shores up your foundation?

MASTERY

"In a place where there is no leader, strive to be a leader"[66] advises Ethics of the Fathers, and *Malchut*, often translated as "Kingship" is the energy of leadership. *Yesod*-bonding in *Malchut*-Kingship is the way that we are connecting with others as we step into our leadership potential. A leader without any followers is no leader[67]. Just as a politician needs to

---

66 Ethics of the Fathers/Pirkei Avot 2:5.
67 In this manner, Jewish liturgy around the New Year (*Rosh Hashanah*) repeatedly connects God as King/*Melech*.

have the popular vote in order to get elected[68], we need to have strong relationships in order to lead.

LOGIC & EMOTION: CREATING YOUR WORLD

The *Men Are From Mars, Women Are From Venus*[69] hypothesis is based around the observation that men are more logical by nature whereas women are more emotional and intuitive. *Malchut*-mastery is pure feminine energy and is the essence of the world we live in - a world that is two-thirds water (feminine), a planet that is shaped like a sphere (feminine) and we are in bodies that primarily feel before they think (feminine). So *Yesod*-bonding in *Malchut*-mastery can be seen as the connection between masculine and feminine, and the way that we create new life. If we visualise *Yesod* as the male organ and *Malchut* as the female, it is clear that both energies are essential for procreation.

"Yesod-Foundation, however, only functions through Malchut-Kingship", explained Rabbi Aryeh Kaplan. *"Yesod-Foundation parallels the male organ, and, since the male organ cannot function without the female, it is secondary to the female"*[70]. In our conversation this might allude to how relationships (*Yesod*) are important, but they are secondary to how you are using them, what you are creating out of your relationships and how you are making the world a better place as a result (*Malchut*). In this aspect, the feminine is more important than the masculine.

GROUNDING INTO REALITY

Yesod-foundation in *Malchut*-mastery is also the idea of getting grounded in reality. Ideas and plans are fine but if they are not connected, they remain dreams or half-finished projects. Rabbi Ginsburgh explains that *"Yesod is associated in the soul with the power to contact, connect and communicate with outer reality (represented by the sefirah of malchut). The foundation (yesod) of a building is its "grounding", its union with the earth (Malchut)"*[71]. This begs the question; Where are you not connected to reality? Where is there an unfinished or

---

68   Except in the case of the Bush-Gore presidential race of 2000...
69   Men Are From Mars, Women Are From Venus by John Gray, published in 1992.
70   Commentary to The Bahir, p177.
71   The Divine Emanations--The Ten Sefirot: Yesod "Foundation," Rabbi Yitzchak Ginsburgh,http://www.inner.org/sefirot/sefyesod.htm.

unfulfilled goal that you need to ground into reality and get connected to so that you can get it completed?

GIVING BIRTH TO AN IDEA, OR, MAKING A BOILED EGG

Whenever we "give birth" to a new idea - even if it is making a boiled egg for breakfast - we need a combination of masculine *Yesod*-grounding energy and *Malchut*-action energy. There has to be the original desire (e.g. "I want an egg for breakfast!" - this corresponds to the higher sefirah of *Keter*-crown or *Ratzon*-will, the initial idea - *Chochmah*-wisdom, plus an understanding of how to do it - *Binah*-understanding), and eventually it comes to fruition by taking all of the planning - (in this case, sticking an egg in a saucepan of boiling water for five minutes) and putting that into action. The combination of taking the planning and putting it into action is where *Yesod* meets *Malchut*. I mention this basic example as an introduction to the more advanced terminology used by the Kabbalah. At this point we can ask the simple question: "Where am I not putting things into action?"

THE SEVENTH DAY

Rabbi Aryeh Kaplan explains: *"Yesod-Foundation only functions to create souls when it is in conjunction with Malchut-Kingship. Therefore, the main day in which it functions is the Sabbath. Yesod-Foundation corresponds to the sixth day, which is when Adam was created. He did not attain his main aspect of soul, however, until the first Sabbath and therefore, he would have been permitted to eat of the Tree of Knowledge on the Sabbath. His main sin was the fact that he did not wait, but ate of it on the sixth day"*[72] . This paragraph could warrant an entire book in itself, looking at how souls are created, how Adam used the masculine energy of *Yesod* to force his way to eat from the Tree of Knowledge, rather than the feminine energy of *Malchut* to wait until he was given it. Male-female relationships cannot function with a man just taking what he wants until it is offered. Similarly we can look at how we are trying to force things in our own life (*Yesod*/masculine energy) rather than waiting and allowing and being receptive to things when they are offered (*Malchut*/feminine energy). As ever, it is a balance.

---

72 Commentary to The Bahir, Para 158 , p176.

As a point of information, different Kabbalistic systems connect each day with a different *sefirah*, although there is some difference of opinion between the Kabbalists[73]. In the system of the Vilna Gaon (1720-1797), Friday corresponds to *Yesod*-bonding and Saturday/Shabbat corresponds to *Malchut*-mastery).

CHOOSE LIFE

There are different Divine names attached to each of the different Divine spheres and a name for *Yesod*-foundation is *El Chai*, the God of Life[74]. The *Sefer Yetzirah* repeats many times that these *Sefirot* are not God and not to be confused with God - they are "*Ten Sefirot of Nothingness*"[75], but we can "*examine with them and probe from them*"[76], using them as tools to get to know and connect with the Divine.

Rabbi Joseph Gikatalia[77] (1248-1305) taught an advanced method for working with this Divine name to connect to eternity. He begins by explaining that "*One who wishes to perceive Eternal Life should attach himself to the attribute of El Chai (Living God), [which is associated with the Sefirah of Yesod-Foundation]*" and then goes through the method of how to achieve that[78]. Some more of his instruction is in the footnote[79], but we can take the basic principle as follows.

---

73 Rabbi Aryeh Kaplan provides a very useful comparison chart in Sefer Yetzirah pp178-179.
74 One place this is alluded to is in the system of Rabbi Joseph Gikatalia in Sharey Orah, The Gates of Light, translated by Rabbi Aryeh Kaplan in Meditation and Kabbalah.
75 This phrase is repeated many times in Sefer Yetzirah, e.g. see Chapter One.
76 Sefer Yetzirah 1:4, p28.
77 His name is also spelled Gikatilla in some places.
78 Translated in Meditation and Kabbalah, p130. This is an advanced technique which can only be achieved under the guidance of a teacher. Even with a teacher, it can be physically and spiritually dangerous. I have personally experienced this but am not permitted to recount the details. However, I mention this for the protection of all who are drawn to pursue this path b'H.
79 Rabbi Gikatalia writes, "*This means that through his prayers, one should bring El Chai into Adonoy. It was regarding this that King David had passion and desire when he said, "My soul thirsts for God, for El Chai*" (Psalms 42:3). *When the attribute (Yesod), which is called El Chai, is bound to Adonoy (Malchut), then one can draw down all his needs. He can overcome his enemies, and no one can stand up to him..*
We must bind the Sefirot together, attaching all levels through the attribute of Adonoy (Malchut-Kingship). We therefore say "He chooses song of praise, King (Malchut), Life (Yesod) of the world. (This is the end of the "Yishtabach" prayer). If one wishes to seek a good life, he should bind himself to the attribute of El Chai.When a person is attached to Adonoy in purity, then he is also attached to El Chai. It is thus written, "and you, who are attached to YHVH your God, you are all alive (Chai) today"(Deuteronomy 4:4)" Sharey Orah - Gates of Light, pp130-131 in Meditation and Kabbalah.

See the eternity and infinity in your body and your actions. How are you a chain to infinity through your activities? What are you creating that will have ramifications throughout the following generations? Or, meditate upon the part of yourself that is infinite; your body is mostly made of up water that has been circulating on the planet for thousands of years. Consider how your physical body is made of components that have been around for a long, long time and will be around for many moons to come, although these elements will inevitably change form. In the words of *Gladiator*, *"What we do in this life echoes in eternity"*.

TODAY'S PRACTICE

YOGA PRACTICE GUIDELINES:
A powerful *ujiya* breath is the fuel for a sensitive and uplifting yoga practice, and the breath is something that we can also receive with *Malchut*-nobility, as a king might welcome guests into the court. The noble breath clams us, centres us, and grounds us, firming our foundation, stability and sense of self (all expressions of *Yesod*). We can become more regal, less likely to react when provoked and we can become more powerful in the long term.

GYM PRACTICE GUIDELINES:
Master your energy today. Be aware of your feelings and give them a powerful grounding.

RELATIONSHIP PRACTICE
Today's Practice will lead to a noble bonding with tasks in life, and the homework is to take a few moments to pause during the day, reconnect with your breathing, ground your energy and lift up through your spine, allowing energy to flow up to your head and through the crown chakra, which the Kabbalists identify as the sefira-energy of Keter-crown. Walk tall and Choose Life.

QUESTIONS FOR MEDITATION

Ask for each day of *Yesod*: where do I lack grounding? Where do I need stronger foundations? (e.g. I could be advanced in one area but not grounded in others)

RELATIONSHIPS:
- Where am I emotionally disconnected in my relationships and how can I get more connected through the way I talk and behave? (*Malchut*)
- Hands, feet and mouth are the organs of Malchut. How are you using them to be more grounded, bonded and connected?
- How are you using communication, the way you are "walking", the direction you are moving in, to strengthen bonds and relationships?

YOGA/BODY/GYM:
- Where do I not listen or respond to my body's requests (i.e. To exercise more or differently, or to eat nutritious foods, or to heal an ache), and how can I stay connected with what my body is "saying"? What behaviours do I need to change in my physical practice? (*Malchut*)

BUSINESS:
- Where am I disconnected from the mission of my business? How can I change the way I talk about things, whether it is my internal thoughts or my external speech? What positive actions can I do differently, to create new and better results? (*Malchut*)
- Am I sufficiently connecting with my clients and colleagues? Where are things out of balance in my business and how can I restore balance and master all of the different elements (doing it in a way that is loving, disciplined, compassionate, enduring, humble and with the intention of bonding)?

GYM SEQUENCE, DAY 42/SIDE PLANK (VASISHTASANA)

This is the same as the yoga pose 'Vasishtasana'. Hold for 3 breaths and then switch sides. Repeat 5 times.

מלכות
Malchut-Kingship

.01

יסוד
Yesod-Bonding

מלכות
Malchut-Kingship

מלכות
Malchut-Kingship

.02

401

YOGA SEQUENCE, DAY 42/CAMEL (USTRASANA)

If easier, you can do this in front of a wall which you may use to provide stability and support against the front of your thighs. Lift your chest as high as possible and reach down with your hands to deepen the backbend.

.01

יסוד
Yesod-Bonding

מלכות
Malchut-Kingship

.02

MALCHUT מלכות

KINGSHIP

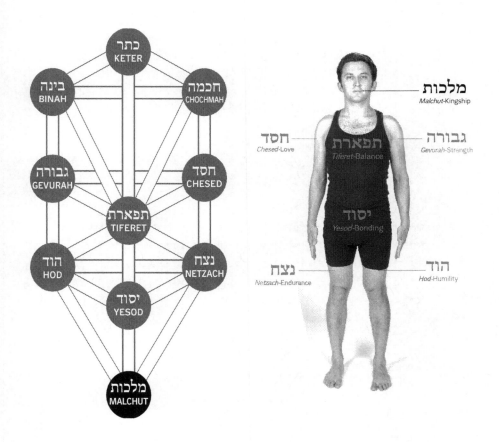

WEEK 7

MALCHUT INTRODUCTION: THE PATH OF ROYALTY מלכות

"For God's sake, let us sit upon the ground
And tell sad stories of the death of kings;" — Richard II

"I have not needed to exert my will on my own behalf, and yet, inwardly anyway, I have lived like a King. Everything comes to me"

Eric Schiffman[1].

There are times in our life where we feel out of control. There are areas in our life where we do not fulfill our given potential. There are occasions when we look at the mirror and are disappointed at what we see. One of Shakespeare's fallen kings bemoans *"sad stories of the death of kings"*[2] but that does not have to be our narrative. If you feel you "could have been a contender" then it is not too late. Whilst there are certain practical considerations, for example, it would be hard to start an Olympic athletics career at the age of 80, there is still much you can do to step into your full power.

Malchut is kingship, sovereignty, leadership, action and potential. Sometimes associated with the mouth[3], other times with the feet[4], this is quite literally the sphere of movement and getting things done. *Malchut*-Kingship is seen to include all of the other sefirah-qualities and is the complete actualisation of them[5].

---

1 Moving Into Stillness, p.xxiii.
2 Richard II, Act III, Sc.ii.
3 *"Malkhut* is the mouth – we call it the Oral Torah." 17b, Introduction to the Tiqqunei HaZohar.
4 Body, Mind, and Soul: Kabbalah on Human Physiology, Disease, and Healing, by Rabbi Yitzchak Ginsburg, p44.
5 "We see *Malchut*-Kingship as the source of all the other *Sefirot*. This may seem to contradict the usual concept of *Malchut*-Kingship, as drawing from all the other *Sefirot*. But as mentioned earlier, with respect to "motivation from above", *Malchut*-Kingship draws from the other *Sefirot* but with respect to "motivation from below, it bestows to the others" - commentary on *The Bahir* 159, p176.

INTRODUCTION: THE PATH OF ROYALTY

The question is asked: are you fulfilling your potential? Where are you falling short and *what can you do to get into your full power?*

PRACTICAL SPIRITUALITY

In our final week of *The Kabbalah Sutras*, the sefirah of *Malchut*-Kingship takes us deeply into the world. We cannot experience spirituality without physicality. The Zohar teaches that

> *"If one wishes to know the wisdom of the holy unification, let him look at the flame rising from a burning coal or from a kindled lamp. The flame cannot rise unless it is unified with something physical"*[6].

The given metaphor is that we are the wick and our spiritual deeds are the flame, but just as every flame needs a wick to 'ground' it to the earth, so too does spirituality need a practical basis. This is why Proverbs says that *"the soul of a person is the flame of God"*,[7] as our role is literally to share light.

Malchut-Kingship can also be understood as *Malchut*-Mastery as we are intending to master all of these different elements of our personality - the way we love (*Chesed*), show strength (*Gevurah*), express compassion (*Tiferet*), endure (*Netzach*), stay humble (*Hod*), remain grounded and connected (*Yesod*). We refine each of these areas in our daily life and aim to do the same within our souls.

THE DIVINE FEMININE SECRET OF THE WORLD

Although the word *Melech* (King) appears many times throughout Jewish liturgy, a largely unknown-fact is that *Malchut*-mastery is an almost entirely feminine concept. The associated colour is blue, it relates to the sea, represents our planet and the way we interact and communicate[8]. *"The Sea is always a female element"*, teaches Rabbi Aryeh Kaplan, *"and usually this is Malkhut-Kingship"*[9]. The water element

---

6   Zohar 1:50b, quoted in Rabbi Aryeh Kaplan's Sefer Yetzirah commentary, p63.
7   Proverbs 20:27.
8   *"This is also the "Sea of Wisdom". The "Sea" is always a female element, and usually this is Malkhut-Kingship. But the "Sea of Wisdom" is the female element associated with Chachmah-Wisdom, and this is Binah-Understanding. This is said to be the blue in the Tzitzit-fringes".* - Commentary to The Bahir, p159.
9   The Bahir, p159.

on our planet, and the intuitive and emotional components of our personalities all fall within the sefirah of *Malchut*. The Sabbath is also identified as a day of *Malchut*[10] - in other words *Shabbat* could be all about tapping into feminine energy, intuition and emotion - although it is rarely taught or experienced this way, at least as yet[11].

WHERE IS GOD HIDING?

Malchut-mastery is also described as *"the final Heh"* in the four-letter name of God[12]. So where is God hiding? Right here on earth. Based on this understanding, *everything* we are looking at it in the physical reality is part of *Malchut*[13].

GIVING AWAY OUR POWER

Malchut-sovereignty asks us where we have been giving away our power. Where are we behaving less like Kings and Queens and more like peasants and serfs? That comes down into all areas of your life - if you feel 'trapped' in a job, city, relationship or situation, what can you do to set yourself free? That can also include freeing your thoughts to interpret events differently.

Communication takes place between ourselves and others but also within ourselves. When we look to the outside to define us, whether that is a partner, therapist or self-help magazine, we are not defining ourselves. The Kabbalah describes this world as *Alma Etgalia* - the 'revealed world' - and this revelation is right here and now is *Malchut*. We live in a world where there is the potential of action to take control of our mind and thoughts.

---

10 This is represented in most systems. In the Vilna Gaon's system, Shabbat/Saturday is associated with Malchut, the colour blue, the Hebrew letter *Tav*, the planet Jupiter and the mouth (Sefer Yetzirah, p183).

11 *"The six Sefirot represent the six directions, while Malchut-Kingship is their centre point. In this aspect, the Sabbath is seen as the middle of the week, preceded and followed by three days"* - The Bahir commentary p176

12 Ibid., p159.

13 Another way of looking at this would be that our bodies represent the "Vav" in God's name, according to the Kabbalists; the Vav is equivalent to the number six, representing the six *sefirot* in the body from *Chesed*-Love through to *Yesod*-Bonding.

WHO'S THE KING?

Now is the time to activate the *Malchut*-sovereignty within ourselves. Think back to a time when you were walking tall, feeling tremendously confident - even in just one aspect or area of your life - and recreate it. How did you breathe, hold your head, hold your back and posture? How did your legs feel? what clothes were you wearing? What thoughts were going through your mind? *Malchut*-sovereignty brings together all of these different elements.

THE FOUNTAINHEAD

Ayn Rand's novel *Atlas Shrugged* explores how people give away their personal power in the face of government and big business, and the third in a series of recent film adaptations has the character John Galt address the nation on telecast that hijacks all of the media channels. He says:

> *"you gave them your power…all evil needs to win is the consent of good people…If you believe that your life is a sacred possession for you to make the most of, if you want to live by the judgement of your own mind, not edicts from the state, then follow our lead. Do not support your own oppressors. Stop letting the system exploit you. Form your own communities on the frontiers of your crumbling world.*

> *Your rulers hold you by your endurance to carry the burdens they impose. By your generosity when you hear cries of despair, and above all, by your innocence which cannot grasp the depths of their evil.*

> *The world you are living in is the world they wanted. leave them to it. Those who have left you have left to build a better world, a world of freedom and opportunity, a world based on mutual respect. In that world you will rise with the spirit you knew in childhood, the spirit of eagerness and adventure and the confidence that the world is what it is and it is there for you to discover. In that world you will not receive alms nor pity nor forgiveness of sins, but honour, respect and justice. Don't let the fire go out, spark by irreplaceable spark and confusion*

and despair. Be sure of your path. The world you desire can be one. it exists, it is real, it is possible. It is yours"[14].

This is not a call for political revolution but it is a call for personal revolution if you feel oppressed, hard-done-by, suffering, wronged or disadvantaged in any way. *Malchut*-Kingship is your birthright, it is getting-it-together, it is mastering the emotional elements within yourself, mastering your desires and bringing things into action to the best of your ability. As Rabbi Tarfon (1st Century CE) used to say *"You are not required to complete the task, but neither are you free to avoid doing it"*[15].

ACTIVATING *MALCHUT*

PUTTING THE PRINCIPLES INTO ACTION

- *Malchut*-mastery in *Chesed*-love: How many ways can you be kind?

- *Malchut*-mastery in *Gevurah*-strength: How many ways can you be strong?

- *Malchut*-mastery in *Tiferet*-compassion: How many ways can you be compassionate?

- *Malchut*-mastery in *Netzach*-endurance: How many ways can you be enduring/victorious?

- *Malchut*-mastery in *Hod*-humility: How many ways can you be humble/grateful?

- *Malchut*-mastery in *Yesod*-bonding: How many ways can you be grounded?

- *Malchut*-mastery in *Malchut*-mastery: How many ways can you be masterful?

---

14 From the screenplay Atlas Shrugged: Who is John Galt? (2014), based on Ayn Rand's novel.
15 Ethics of the Fathers/Pirkei Avot 2:21.

MASTERFUL COMMUNICATIONS

- Am I speaking from love? ? Am I being loving in my communications?- (*Chesed*-love in *Malchut*-mastery)

- Am I speaking from a place of authority? Am I holding good boundaries in my communications?- (*Gevurah*-strength in *Malchut*-mastery)

- Am I speaking with balance and a sense of justice? Am I compassionate in my communications? (*Tiferet*-compassion in *Malchut*-mastery)

- Am I speaking with consistency? Am I truthful in my communications? (*Netzach*-Endurance in *Malchut*-mastery)

- Am I speaking with humility? Am I gracious in my communications? (*Hod*-humility in *Malchut*-mastery)

- Am I speaking with a deep connection to my listener? Am I communicating well? (*Yesod*-bonding in *Malchut*-mastery)

- Am I dignified in my communications? Have I mastered the art of good communication? (*Malchut*-mastery in *Malchut*-mastery)

ADVANCED KABBALAH: A NOTE ON HANDS & FEET

The *Tikkunei Zohar* 17a explicitly equates *Malchut*-Kingship with the mouth (*"Malchut is the mouth - we call it the Oral Torah"*). For the purposes of this book, however, I have also equated *Malchut*-Kingship with the hands and the feet. The Kabbalah teaches that essentially we are in a world of *Malchut*-Kingship: *"Malchut nestles in the world of Assiyah [i.e. our physical realm]"*[16]. In many ways Malchut represents action, and the hands and feet are the key physical proponents for creative action in this world. Our hands create and our feet take us places.

There is, however, a counter-argument. My friend David Solomon suggested that *"equating Malkhut with feet is a bit problematic. Unlike the mouth, or the sexual organ, the feet have no external outlet by which to express physical manifestion of the interiority of intent, except by fulfilling their purpose by standing or walking. Feet can reach new worlds, but they cannot create them"*[17].

Nevertheless, there are other models within the Zoharic literature, and he suggested that there is a passage in *The Tikkunei Zohar* 131b where Isaiah 41:42 is quoted and *"the feet are referred to as a general designation of the location of Malchut"*[18]: *"Righteousness (tzedeq) shall go before him*[19]*.....righteousness (tzedeq) is lower Mother"*. In his translation of the *Tiqqunei haZohar*, Professor Solomon explains in his footnote ad loc *"This verse reads, literally, righteousness He shall call to His foot*; righteousness emerges from *Malchut*, or from below, as symbolised by the feet"*[20].

We might also view the hands and as representative of *Malchut*-Kingship as in some ways it this is the dominant sefirah in our world. Additionally *The Bahir* commentary discusses how the 10 *Sefirot* are represented by the 10 fingers and toes[21] with reference to the Priestly

---

[16]   Sha'ar HaGilgulim (The Gates of Reincarnation), Second Introduction, p28.
[17]   Private correspondence, May 12th 2015. I have preserved David's spelling of the *Sefirot*.
[18]   Ibid.
[19]   Isaiah 41:2.
[20]   Footnote to 131b, Tiqqunei haZohar, Qustha 1740, translated by David Solomon.
[21]   The Bahir, p165.

Blessing and the *Sefer Yetzirah*[22] teaches *"Ten Sefirot of Nothingness in the number of ten fingers, five opposite five"*.

In short, I have included the hands and feet within the *Malchut*-mastery so that we can fully embody the concept and become closer with God as a result, although please bear in mind this is a metaphorical interpretation based on Kabbalistic sources. Thank you, and enjoy!

---

22   Sefer Yetzirah, 1:3.

DAY 43 / LOVINGKINDNESS IN NOBILITY / BEING YOUR BEST: חסד שבמלכות

KABBALAH SUTRA: *Chesed She b'Malchut* – Lovingkindness in Nobility.
INTENTION: To achieve self-control through lovingkindness and to elevate all of your relationships through love. Be a benevolent and loving leader.

"How do I love thee? Let me count the ways
I love thee to the depth and breadth and height
My soul can reach, when feeling out of sight
For the ends of being and ideal grace". — Elizabeth Barrett Browning[23]

There are many occasions when we are acting as a leader, but are we doing it with love? Although we can go through life from a place of reactivity, impulsively dealing with each situation in a state of (possibly unconscious) panic, we have a choice. Is our intention to be noble, to be our highest-level self, to create the best possible version of who we can be. This is, on one level, *Malchut*-nobility - the you when you are at your best.

The first aspect of embodying your best self is to harness the energy of love, creativity and giving, ensuring that your actions are focused on serving others. This is an aspect of *Chesed*-love in *Malchut*-nobility, as you speak lovingly to your children when they are causing stress, to your relatives when they are misunderstanding you, to your clients and colleagues when they do not seem to "get" it. *Chesed*-love in *Malchut*-nobility invites us to be loving leaders, whether we are running a household or a Fortune 500 Company.

CULTIVATING AN ATTITUDE OF LOVE

The emotion of happiness rarely happens on its own without us actively choosing it. Many people spend their lives seeking it from an outside source rather than finding that happiness within. An example of this is: if you are unhappy about your financial situation then go and visit

---

23   How Do I Love Thee? (Sonnet 43) by Elizabeth Barrett Browning (1806-1861)

a children's terminal cancer ward where there are young people who would love to have your problems as they may be dead within a couple of years[24]. This may sound harsh, but happiness can be cultivated if we work at it on a regular basis and train our mind.

THIS TOO IS FOR THE GOOD

The Talmud speaks of Rabbi Nachum who, whenever bad things would happen, would say "this too is for the good" (*Gam Zu L'Tovah*)[25]. *"Such was the habit of Nachum Ish Gamzu [1st century CE], who would always say: This, too, is for the good!"*. Everything was an expression of faith for him and he would actively go looking for the good. We too can look for the good in every situation, or apply faith and trust when we cannot see it, or indeed pray to have the good revealed when it is not apparent. We learn that Rabbi Akiva had a similar practice[26].

When we actively seek the good in the situation, working hard to feel or express love, this is referred to as "binding" in Kabbalistic terminology. The *Tomer Devorah* explains that in Kabbalistic terms,

---

24 I also mentioned this example on Day 30, but personally I find it helpful to have regular reminders!

25 Babylonian Talmud, Masechet Taanit 21a.

26 Rabbi Shlomo Price writes, quoting the Babylonian Talmud, Masechet Brachot 60b, "Rabbi Akiva was accustomed to saying "Everything Hashem does is for the good". Once Rabbi Akiva was travelling with a donkey, rooster, and candle and when night came he tried to find lodging in a nearby village only to be turned away. Although Rabbi Akiva was forced to spend the night in the field, he did not lament his fate. Instead his reaction was "Everything Hashem does is for the best". (It is interesting to note the difference between Rabbi Akiva and us. If for example we were learning for a long time, and we could not find a place to sleep wherever we were, we would have complaints against Hashem that this is the reward we get for learning?! Yet Rabbi Akiva who obviously learned more and better than us had no such feelings). A wind came and blew out his candle, a cat ate his rooster, and a lion came and ate his donkey, and again Rabbi Akiva's reaction was "Everything that Hashem does is for the best". That night a regiment came and took the entire town captive, while Rabbi Akiva who was sleeping in the field went unnoticed and thus was spared. When Rabbi Akiva realized what happened he said, "Didn't I tell you that everything that Hashem does is for the best"?" Rashi explains that if the candle, rooster or donkey would have been around, the regiment would have seen or heard them and would have also captured Rabbi Akiva" -http://www.neveh.org/price/price2.html. This is one of my favourite stories.

> Nachum Ish Gamzu *"always sought to connect everything to the side of Chesed-lovingkindness, which is called 'good', so he would say that even what appeared to be on the left, bound to the side of Gevurah-severity, was in reality only for the good, bound to Chesed-lovingkindness. This way, he would concentrate on the goodness of the attribute of Malchut-sovereignty, concealing its severity. This is an excellent way to constantly bind oneself to Chesed-lovingkindness"*[27].

On a spiritual level there is a great power attached to the idea of thinking positive thoughts, engendering positive feelings and taking positive actions - you are binding yourself to *Chesed*-lovingkindness and transforming reality.

LOVING OF GOD

Feeling love for God is also a practice and the *Tikkunei HaZohar* explains that this is *Chesed*-love in *Malchut*-Kingship because you are loving the Ruler of the Universe. Everyone must find their own understanding of God - whether it is as a Universal Light, a pulsation of Divine Energy flowing through the world - the expressions are endless but as with everything else, it is a practice that can be cultivated. *"And this is primary love, which is the love of God – Malkhut, which is the love of Chesed. Because fear (Yirah) is from the side of Gevurah; and from Chesed it is Malkhut - the love (Ahavah) of God; as has been stated: from Gevurah, She is the fear of God"*[28]. A practical way of applying this might be as simple as going for a walk and actively looking for reasons to feel love for the Divine, whether it is in the fragrance of a flower, the sight of a bird in a tree, or the sound of a baby crying.

HOW DOES GOD BEHAVE TOWARDS US?

Life is full of mysteries and there are many times when we cannot see how something is good. The Kabbalistic world view is that there is an underlying core of goodness beneath everything, although sometimes it can be so shadowed and obscured that we only see it as evil - that is

---

[27] Tomer Devorah, p86.
[28] Tiqqunei HaZohar, 10b (translation courtesy David Solomon).

the *kelipah*-shells that mask the light. The Ramak explained that God sometimes seems to be acting severely, such as with undefinable acts like the death of a child, but there is an underlying flow of *Chesed*-lovingkindness beneath everything, for example, on a spiritual level perhaps that child was housing an incredibly high soul that only needed to visit the earth for a short period of time to complete its mission. He taught that *"Although the secret of Divine conduct, which stems from the attribute of Malchut-sovereignty, may be expressed as severity [din], it is connected to Chesed-Lovingkindness"*[29]. On a deeper level, just as we are considering how we behave towards other people, with love in our leadership, we can also consider how God is behaving in this manner towards us. After all, we are all expressions of God, made in the Divine image[30].

We can experience *Chesed*-lovingkindness in *Malchut*-kingship by reflecting on the sense of God within. By considering how you are receiving love and kindness from above, or how you have been given life opportunities that have been denied to others.

THE INTERNAL RULER

Chesed-Lovingkindness in *Malchut*-nobility is the aspect of nobility that is focused on lovingkindness and noble giving. In yogic terminology we are the 'ruler' of our body, such as when we choose to implement a daily meditation practice. There are many occasions when we choose to relinquish the sovereignty over our bodies, if we are addicted to smoking or drugs, biting our nails, or if we drink ourselves into a state of oblivion. By lovingly re-establishing the *Malchut*-kingship over our own bodies we can maintain a dignity and sovereignty and do those things that are good for our bodies, whether it is exercise, meditation, healthy eating or other wellbeing practices.

---

29   Tomer Devorah, p86.
30   Genesis 1:27.

TODAY'S PRACTICE

YOGA PRACTICE GUIDELINES:

Beginning in a seated position, draw your awareness to your own nobility, sitting on your 'throne'. How can you choose to show lovingkindness to your body today? One way is to experience happiness. Breathe deeply, allowing deep joy and satisfaction to rise within, choosing a positive aspect of your world to marvel about. Become deeply joyous about one aspect of yourself; all has been created by The Source, and is to be appreciated.

GYM PRACTICE GUIDELINES:

Be loving in your practice (*Chesed*) but take action (*Malchut*). Being loving in this context does not mean sitting in front of the television and eating popcorn. See what your body truly needs to meet your goals and do that, but with an attitude of love and creativity.

RELATIONSHIP PRACTICE GUIDELINES:

How can you choose to show lovingkindness to someone else? We all have some position of responsibility or leadership, even if it just finding occasional moments when we have the ability to give something to another person (or, for that matter, withhold it). Today's awareness is towards your own sense of nobility and higher status, and taking opportunities to bestow kindnesses upon others. Be a loving and benevolent ruler.

QUESTIONS FOR MEDITATION

RELATIONSHIPS:

- Where are my thoughts, speech and actions out of alignment with my relationship? Where do I say one thing and do another? Or speak in a way that does not build the relationship? What is one thing I can do today that is more loving? (*Chesed*)
- How do I dominate others and forget to be kind?

- Where in my relationships am I taking more than I am giving? How am I generating an imbalance?

LEADERSHIP & COMMUNICATION:

- Can I be a loving leader?
- Can I be a loving communicator?
- When I say "no" to people, can I do it in a *Chesed*-loving way?
- Can I ensure that the way I behave in the world I is loving?
- Can I tap into my feminine-intuitive love?
- Do I know where to place my affection and where not to place it?

YOGA/BODY/GYM:

- Where have I declared one goal for my body and not acted in alignment with this? How can I get back in line with my stated goals, but do it with love?
- How am I mastering my body but not doing it with a sense of kindness and respect?

BUSINESS:

- Where do I say one thing and do another in my workplace? (e.g. say I want to get lots more business and then not do the appropriate marketing or new business lead-generation?). What creative steps can I take? (*Chesed*)
- How does my lack of love limit my dignity and leadership capacity?
- Where am I leading others but lacking love, or not giving enough?
- Where am I not speaking words of kindness when I am in a position of responsibility?

LEADERSHIP:

- Where am I not fulfilling my leadership potential? How can I be a better leader, and act out of a sense of love?

GYM SEQUENCE, DAY 43/CLAPPING PUSH-UPS

Do your best and aim for some height. Be careful of your wrists and if you experience any pain or strain, stop immediately! Other variations are standard Push Up and Knee Push Up. 3 x 5 repetitions.

.01

.02

חסד
Chesed-Love

מלכות
Malchut-Kingship

YOGA SEQUENCE, DAY 43/CAT-COW (MARJARASANA)

Place your hands and knees in parallel position and play with curling and uncurling your spine. As you look upwards, sink your chest towards the ground and push your tailbone to the sky, before reversing the position.

.01

מלכות
Malchut-Kingship

חסד
Chesed-Love

מלכות
Malchut-Kingship

.02

DAY 44 / DISCIPLINE IN NOBILITY / STRONG HANDS & OUTSTRETCHED ARMS: גבורה שבמלכות

KABBALAH SUTRA: *Gevurah She b'Malhut* – Discipline in Nobility.
INTENTION: To increase our sphere of influence through recognising and respecting limitations. Overcome doubts through disciplined leadership.

"When the blast of war blows in our ears/ Then imitate the action of the tiger" — Shakespeare, Henry V

"A time to love, and a time to hate;
a time for war, and a time for peace". — Ecclesiastes 3:8

We all have the ability to be strong and channel our passion, but many of us express it at the wrong time, at the wrong place or at the wrong people. We get angry with people we love, or become stressed about a telephone bill or parking ticket rather than channelling our strength towards the important goals. When our head is clear and our intentions are well-directed, we can then choose how we are going to apply our strength. There is indeed *"a time to hate"* and *"a time for war"* as King Solomon proclaimed, but the true art is knowing exactly what time that is and what season we are in. The words of Ecclesiastes are deceptively simple and it is only by applying wisdom that we can know whether or not it is a time for love, or a time to build, or a time to destroy. Folly is getting the action right but doing it at the incorrect moment.

KNOW YOUR POWER

Gevurah-strength in *Malchut*-Kingship applies to all of the areas where we come into contact with other people, especially when we are in a leadership position and there are many questions to be asked: Can I be strong as a leader? Where am I asking other people to follow and not doing it myself? Where am I not leading by example? Where am I doubting myself? Where am I making promises to myself and not following through? Where am I saying "this is my intention" and then not following through? Where am I being weak-willed or weak-hearted?

Shakespeare's study of the Kings of England showed strong rulers like Henry V, weak ones like Richard II, evil ones like Richard III, confused ones like King Lear and magical ones like Prospero and Oberon. When it comes to expressing your will, *Gevurah*-strength in *Malchut*-Kingship, Henry V put it most succinctly in his speech before leading the English troops against the French scoundrels of Harfleur:

> *"In peace there's nothing so becomes a man*
> *As modest stillness and humility:*
> *But when the blast of war blows in our ears,*
> *Then imitate the action of the tiger;*
> *Stiffen the sinews, summon up the blood,*
> *Disguise fair nature with hard-favour'd rage;*
> *Then lend the eye a terrible aspect;*
> *Let pry through the portage of the head*
> *Like the brass cannon"*[31].

Often the "war" we need to fight is an inner war, restraining our passions and focussing our energies in that light. When the sage Shimon Ben Zoma (Second Century) taught that the strong person is the one *"who subdues their personal inclination"* or *"restrains their passion"*[32], he quoted the verse from Proverbs that says *"He who is slow to anger is better than the strong man, and a master of his passions is better than a conqueror of a city"*[33]. The war that most of us will face is therefore the internal war, and the battle is against our own passions. Or as Brad Pitt's character Tyler Durden said in *Fight Club*, *"We have no Great War. No Great Depression. Our great war is a spiritual war"*. Whether your show of strength means subduing anger when it is about to rise up or driving yourself out of bed in the morning when you would rather sleep

---

31 Henry V, 3.i.
32 Ethics of the Fathers/Pirkei Avot 4:1.
33 Proverbs/Mishlei 16:32.

a little longer, the true strength lies with our ability to direct ourselves and cannot be measured in the circumference of your bicep.

BEATING GOLIATH

We all have our "Goliath" to face, in the shape of fears that keep us off the "battlefield" of life, not pursuing goals because we are scared of what might happen. We might re-read the story of David and Goliath from the perspective that David represents our potential, and Goliath represents our fear. On seeing the giant Goliath, all the men of Israel *"were terror stricken"*[34], and this is true of life, as most people are living in fear and holding back from pursuing what is truly important because they are scared of what might happen. King David is the symbol of the *sefirah* of *Malchut*-Kingship and we see his *Gevurah*-strength in action:

> *"A champion of the Philistine forces stepped forward; his name was Goliath of Gath, and he was six cubits and a span and a half....David said to [King] Saul, "Let no man's courage fail him. Your servant will go and fight that Philistine!". But Saul said to David, "You cannot go to that Philistine and fight him; you are only a boy, and he has been a warrior from his youth". David replied to Saul, "Your servant has been tending his father's sheep, and if a lion or a bear came and carried off an animal from the flock, I would go after it and fight it and rescue it from its mouth. And if it attacked me, I would seize it by the beard and strike it down and kill it. Your servant has killed both lion and bear; and that uncircumcised Philistine shall end up like one of them, for he has defied the ranks of the living God, The Lord", David went on, "who saved me from lion and bear will also save me from that Philistine". "Then go", Saul said to David, "and may the Lord be with you"*[35].

Too often we fail to trust in ourselves or trust in a Higher power, rather than facing our deepest fear and pushing through. King David repeatedly calls upon the themes of strength and faith in various psalms, such as;

---

34   1 Samuel 17:11.
35   1 Samuel 17:4-37.

"A Psalm of David: The Lord is my light and salvation, whom shall I fear? The lord is the stronghold of my life, of whom shall I be afraid?"[36] *"In your strength The King rejoices"*[37], *"Be exalted, O Lord, in Your strength"*[38], *"I love you, O Lord, my strength. The Lord is my rock, and my fortress, and my deliverer. My God, my rock, in Him I take refuge; my shield, and my horn of salvation, my high tower"*[39].

These psalms continue to bring spiritual comfort to millions of people across many cultures and civilisations and help us develop trust in ourselves and faith in God.

There are places where we are not taking responsibility. We will complain that there is not enough time to do everything and use that as an excuse, forgetting that there are 168 hours in every week and 61,320 hours in a year. Tha is 525,600 minutes[40] which is an awfully long time to get things done![41] Rabbi Hillel (110 BCE-10 CE) taught *"In a place where there is no man, strive to be a man"*[42], which we might interpret as "in a place where nobody is taking responsibility, start taking responsibility!". Where are you avoiding responsibility for your dreams, and using excuses for not having achieved whatever is most important to you?

This week's energy is about deepening and establishing our *Malchut-*Authority. The most dignified people are those who know when to hold back - *"a protective fence for wisdom is silence"*[43]. There is *"a time to keep silent and a time to speak"*[44] but true wisdom is knowing which time we are currently in.

---

36   Psalm 27:1.
37   Psalms 21:1.
38   Psalms 21:14.
39   Psalm 18:3.
40   But the RENT fans already knew that.
41   Thank you to my teacher Eric Sander Kingston for this teaching about time and responsibility.
42   Ethics of the Fathers/Pirkei Avot 2:6.
43   Said in the name of Rabbi Akiva, in Ethics of the Fathers/Pirkei Avot 3:17.
44   Ecclesiastes/Kohelet 3:7.

TODAY'S PRACTICE

YOGA PRACTICE GUIDELINES:

The *Gevurah*-restriction of *pranayama* (controlled yogic breathing and energy management) comes into play through the physical restrictions that are necessary to achieve the yogic breath. The Yoga Sutras reveal an intriguing connection with how *Gevurah* leads to *Malchut*-mastery; *"[through] energy control (pranayama)...the mind becomes fit for concentration...in this way comes mastery over the senses"*[45]. Through beginning with the *pranayamic* energy/breath control, we move towards mental stillness, physical stillness and emotional self-control.

Every yoga posture is replete with the boundaries *Gevurah*-discipline through the 'rules' of how to correctly execute the *asana*. The question is whether we can practice with finesse, grace and dignity. Notice how your prepare for a posture; do you approach it with dignity? Are you in control of your thoughts?

GYM PRACTICE GUIDELINES:

As you increase in sensitivity towards the authority you have over your own body, explore the boundaries and test the limits. Where are you able to do a certain number of repetitions, and when is it going to be too difficult? Notice when you are not working as hard as you are able to, and when you are pushing things too far.

LEADERSHIP PRACTICE GUIDELINES:

Notice the areas when you have authority and the chance to lead others, when it is appropriate to be strong and impose discipline and when it would be wiser to hold back. An excellent practice is to use the tool of silence, to reflect and reconsider and make wise decisions.

---

45 Yoga Sutras 2:51, 53 & 55, Swamiji translation.

QUESTIONS FOR MEDITATION

RELATIONSHIPS:
- Where are my thoughts, speech and actions out of alignment with my relationship? Where do I say one thing and do another? Or speak in a way that does not build the relationship? What is one thing I can do today that will strengthen the relationship? (*Gevurah*)

YOGA/BODY/GYM:
- Where have I declared one goal for my body and not acted in alignment with this? How can I get back in line with my stated goals on a disciplined basis?

BUSINESS:
- Where do I say one thing and do another in my workplace? (e.g. say I want to get lots more business and then not do the appropriate marketing or new business lead-generation?). Where can I be more disciplined? (*Gevurah*)

LEADERSHIP:
- Where am I not fulfilling my leadership potential? How can I be a better leader, and do this with more strength?
- How can I be stronger as a leader?
- Where am I asking other people to follow and not doing it myself?
- Where am I not leading by example?
- Where am I doubting myself?
- Where am I making promises to myself and not following through?
- Where am I saying "this is my intention" and then not following through?
- Where am I being weak-willed or weak-hearted?

GYM SEQUENCE, DAY 44/SEATED DUMBELL EXTENSION

Extend the dumbell above your head before lowering it behind your neck. Keep your feet grounded and your back straight, and breathe through each repetition. 3 x 5 repetitions on both sides.

.01

מלכות
Malchut-Kingship

גבורה
Gevurah-Strength

מלכות
Malchut-Kingship

.02

YOGA SEQUENCE, DAY 44/STANDING FORWARD BEND (UTTANASANA)

You can modify this pose by placing a strap beneath your feet. Ensure your back is flat at all times and that your breath is smooth. Touching the ground does not win you any points if your back is not straight! Also be careful not to overstretch if you have over-flexible glutes.

.01

גבורה
Gevurah-Strength

מלכות
Malchut-Kingship

מלכות
Malchut-Kingship

.02

DAY 45 / COMPASSION IN NOBILITY / THE NOBLE BALANCE / תפארת שבמלכות

KABBALAH SUTRA: *Tiferet She b'Malhut* – Compassion in Nobility.
INTENTION: To experience balance and beauty in your life, through
compassionate nobility. Develop your leadership potential through
compassionate balance. To use justice when leading yourself and others.

Spiritual development is worth very little if we are not kind to people.
What is it all for if we leave a house of worship and ignore the next
homeless person we pass on the street, or if we leave a yoga class and
are rude to the barista in the coffee shop? "Israel" means *"he who has
wrestled with God and man, and overcome"*[46] and that is the mission of
almost every spiritual seeker; to bring more Divine Light. *Malchut*-
Kingship is the world of action and *Tiferet*-Compassion in *Malchut*-
Kingship is the direct application of compassion.

DO NOT CALL PEOPLE DONKEYS

People are not donkeys. They are not to be ignored, treated like animals
or looked down upon. The Ramak explained the kabbalistic implications
of a spiritual devotee who is prideful and lacking compassion;

> *"A man who, by virtue of his Torah knowledge, holds himself
> haughtily over the ignorant – that is, the people of the Lord in
> general, causes Tiferet-compassion to soar above Malchut–kingship
> rather than flowing into it. Instead, a person should be of pleasant
> disposition towards God's creatures, and all civilised people should
> be worthy in his estimation, since they correspond to the secret of 'the
> Land'. If he calls them donkeys, God forbid, he casts them down to
> the external forces, as a result, he will not merit a son imbued with
> the Light of the Torah, as stated in the Talmud"*[47].

My basic understanding of this teaching is that when we feel we are
reaching spiritual heights or making some progress in our personality
and improving ourselves, that is exactly the time we should 'lower' our

[46] Genesis 32:29.
[47] Tomer Devorah, p110.

compassion to help people and connect with them. Referring to, or thinking of people as donkeys - or anything that is lower than us - will cause us not only to disconnect[48] but also prevent us from internalising our so-called transformation. Put into very straightforward terms; if you learn about the value of charity and do not give any, then it has remained an intellectual concept. If you go to a class and learn about Abraham's lovingkindness and do not start being kind to people and giving of yourself, it is merely an academic insight. Your kindness has become 'stuck' in your body rather than flowing down into the world.

THE COMPASSIONATE LEADER

True, dignified leadership is unsullied by bribery and not tempted with the promise of earthly possessions. When put to the test, the best leaders serve their people rather than indulging in their own luxuries. The aspect of *Tiferet*-justice in *Malchut*-Leadership is made explicit at several points in the Torah, especially with regard to judges;

> *"And you shall take no gift, because a gift blinds those that have sight and perverts the words of the righteous"*[49] and *"You shall not judge unfairly: you shall show no partiality; you shall not take bribes, for bribes blind the eyes of the discerning and upset the plea of the judge. Justice, justice shall you pursue, that you may thrive... "*[50].

This demands introspection to consider where we are "taking bribes" and allowing ourselves to go out of balance. There is the explicit form of bribery but also the subtler kind, e.g. if you favour a work colleague for what you will get in return rather than for the good of the company or allow someone to "buy" your goodwill and interest when you are in a position of power.

---

48 This may God forbid cause damage to the sphere of *Yesod*-bonding.
49 Exodus 23:8.
50 Deuteronomy 16:19.

THE IMPORTANCE OF SHARING YOUR GIFTS WITH THE WORLD

Do you have gifts that you are not sharing with the world? Is there an idea within you that will create a benefit for other people that you are not doing anything about? A Biblical illustration of the *Tiferet-compassion* in *Malchut*-Mastery is when Jacob goes to visit Pharaoh in Egypt; *"Then Joseph brought Jacob, his father, and stood him before Pharaoh, and Jacob blessed Pharaoh"*[51]. It is not enough for Jacob to enjoy his spiritual riches of being the grandson of Abraham who has wrestled with an angel and experienced a direct connection to God - he also has to reach out into the world (the domain of *Malchut*) and share that blessing.

Similarly, it is not enough for us to experience the beauty and relative balance of our lives (switch on the foreign news at any point if you want to keep life in perspective), rather it is our task to use our own 'riches' to bring change into the world. This is not about the money in your pocket or bank account, but your ability to improve the lot at others. Volunteering at a homeless shelter or after-school programme has this effect.

When we read *"Then Joseph brought Jacob, his father, and stood him before Pharaoh, and Jacob blessed Pharaoh"*, this can be understood as *"Tiferet-*compassion descending to *Malchut*-Kingship". We can think of it as *Tiferet* as pure spirituality descending to the earthy realms which are *Malchut*, because *Malchut* represents the earth. The challenge is to find these energies yourself so that you can completely experience both of them in your own life and be aware of the places where you may be blocking the flow.

BEAUTY IN ACTION

Tiferet is also 'beauty' and compassionate actions lead to other more intangible forms of beauty, such as beautiful friendships and communities. A person who shows deep compassion for others emanates beauty even if their physical features do not necessarily conform to the textbook definition (to put it politely). Everyone can

[51] Genesis 47:7.

release their inner beauty, and it does not require getting a haircut or botox, but does demand doing something about it.

TODAY'S PRACTICE

YOGA PRACTICE GUIDELINES:

Approach your practice with noble compassion. Respect your body and focus on your potential, moving through limitations with a powerful breath and elevating your physical practice to a new level.

The Bhagavad Gita explains how an individual can master oneself (which is an essence of *Malchut*-kingship) and find this ultimate balance (e.g. *Tiferet*): *"When, happy with vision and wisdom, he is master of his own inner life, his God sublime set on high, then he is called a Yogi in harmony. To him gold or stones or earth are one"*[52]. This is another invocation of the Rabbis' statement in Ethics of the Fathers that the truly wealthy person is the one who is *"happy with what they have"*[53], but gives us even more practical direction towards achieving this golden ideal. Is it possible to really see gold and stones and earth as one?

Rav Matis Weinberg commented that *"to us a sunset is an awareness of the Universe. It talks to us of everything, not just of itself….we have a sense that in a detail, somehow lies, face to face, the nature of existence itself… its tenderness, sensitivity"*[54]. This, I believe, is the essence of why yoga postures work. We are aiming at a visual aesthetic in every pose where there is a clear line of energy emanating through each limb. When we see yogis we admire and watch them in what we consider to be a 'good' posture, it provokes a reaction within us. There is something about beauty that speaks to our soul, whether it is a beautiful movement or a beautiful person.

John Keats recognised this when he wrote that *"Beauty is truth, truth beauty, that is all ye shall know on Earth and all ye shall need to know"*[55]. He could have been speaking about *Tiferet*-compassion or asana

---

[52]   The Bhagavad Gita 6:8.
[53]   Ethics of the Fathers/Pirkei Avot 4:1.
[54]   Middat HaYom lecture series, 'Tiferet She B'Hesed, Day 3', given in Jerusalem.
[55]   Ode On a Graceian Urn, 1819-1820.

practices and the Kabbalistic idea is that we can express this beauty through compassionate behaviour. When we see someone whom we consider to be truly beautiful, we help ourselves but want to be kind towards them and to get close to them.

Finally, bring an awareness to the innate sovereignty you have over your body, and express compassion towards yourself. Even if this means that you cannot attain the posture that you would like to achieve, go as far as you are able to, practice to the edge of your limits whilst maintaining deeper compassion.

GYM PRACTICE GUIDELINES:

- Be aware of the power in your body and see where it is out of balance. Notice where you can become more physically powerful and how you can achieve this goal and bring it into being.

LEADERSHIP PRACTICE GUIDELINES:

Who is a compassionate leader? Usually a sensitive one. The leader who cares about their people, striking the right balance of love and discipline, in a way that is effective and commands respect in return. There are many examples of leaders who are all *Gevurah* – too much discipline – the authoritarian regimes who base their rule on fear and punishment and usually go down in history as tyrants. Conversely, the leaders who are all *Chesed*-love, who want to give everything away, are also destined to failure. Shakespeare's character study of King Lear shows a man whose boundless love hands all authority over to his children, with disastrous results for his kingdom.

QUESTIONS FOR MEDITATION

RELATIONSHIPS:

- Where are my thoughts, speech and actions out of alignment with my relationship? Where do I say one thing and do another? Where do I speak in a way that does not build the relationship? What is one thing I can do today that will make my relationship more balanced? (*Tiferet*)

- Where does my dignity suffer through a lack of compassion?
- How would more compassion improve the way I speak and act? (Mouth and hands as tools of Malchut)

YOGA/BODY/GYM:

- Where have I declared one goal for my body and not acted in alignment with this? How can I get back into line with my stated goals, but do it with compassion and balance?
- How would more compassion improve the way that I manage my eating habits? (Self-management is an aspect of *Malchut*-mastery. Am I eating foods that help me stay in balance?).
- Do I harbour negative thoughts that push me out of balance? Can I master my thoughts differently to achieve inner harmony (*Tiferet*)?

BUSINESS:

- Where do I say one thing and do another in my workplace? (e.g. say I want to get lots more business and then not do the appropriate marketing or new business lead-generation?). Where can I be more balanced? (*Tiferet*).
- How would more compassion increase my effectiveness with clients?
- How would more compassion improve the way I conduct meetings?
- How might more compassion and balance improve my career?

LEADERSHIP:

- Where am I not fulfilling my leadership potential? How can I be a better leader, and act with more compassion towards other people?
- Whilst reflecting on *Tiferet*-compassion in *Malchut*-nobility, establish who I have some degree of power and control over in my life, whether it is my employees, suppliers, pupils or children, and see how compassionate I am in my dealings with them. How could my leadership be more compassionate, and have I missed any opportunities to show kindness towards them?

- How does my lack of balance limit my leadership capacity/potential?
- How does my lack of compassion limit my leadership capacity/potential?
- How does my lack of compassion limit my dignity?

ADVANCED KABBALAH:

There is a fascinating Kabbalistic combination that takes place whenever somebody says a blessing (a *bracha);* it is traditional to look at the four-letter name of God but pronounce a completely different name. *Malchut*-Kingship has the same gematria (numerical equivalent) as *Adonai*[56]. The four-letter name of God represents *Tiferet*-compassion, so you look at this name (Y-H-V-H) but say the name associated with *Malchut* (which is *Adonai*). We learn that *Tiferet* represents the written Torah and *Malchut* represents the Oral Torah. Additionally, there is a masculine-feminine balance here. I understand that the *Tiferet* name is masculine in this instance and the *Malchut* name is feminine, so there is a Divine unity taking place as we say this name.

---

[56] This idea about the use of these two names of God simultaneously - reading YHVH but enunciating Adonai - is discussed extensively in Sharei Orah/The Gates of Light. In his treatise, Rabbi Joseph Gikatilla discusses this extensively, revealing many Kabbalistic secrets that can be accessed through this pairing. The combination happens on a daily basis in the home of every observant Jewish family throughout the entire word - whenever a blessing is said - but the hidden Kabbalistic dimensions are generally not known (or not discussed).

GYM SEQUENCE, DAY 45/SITTING TWIST

Lift your feet off the ground, interlace your fingers and twist to each side in rapid succession. 3 sets of 45 seconds.

.01

תפארת
Tiferet-Balance

מלכות
Malchut-Kingship

מלכות
Malchut-Kingship

.02

YOGA SEQUENCE, DAY 45/BRIDGE (SETU BANDHASANA)

To modify this position: place your block beneath your sacrum and allow it to completely take your weight. For a more dynamic stretch, lift your hips as high as possible and focus on opening out the front of your thighs.

.01

תפארת
Tiferet-Balance

מלכות
Malchut-Kingship

.02

DAY 46 / **ENDURANCE IN NOBILITY** / THE BATTLE FOR YOURSELF / נצח שבמלכות

KABBALAH SUTRA: *Netzach She b'Malchut* – Endurance in Nobility. INTENTION: To become the most powerful version of yourself through ongoing application. To increase your sphere of influence through dignified endurance. To become an enduring leader.

There are plenty of people who were rejected on their path to success. Thomas Edison was reportedly told by teachers he was "too stupid to learn anything" and it took him almost 1000 attempts to successfully invent the lightbulb. A studio executive at Fred Astaire's first screen tests wrote "Can't sing, can't act. Slightly balding. Can dance a little". J.K. Rowling was a single mother living on social security money and writing in cafes. She was rejected by 12 publishing houses, being told that she "had little chance of making money in children's books" before they finally published *Harry Potter*[57]. But these are some of the most famous rejections. We do not hear about the majority of people who get rejected because many will eventually give up, allowing someone else's opinion of them to trump their own vision.

WHEN TO GIVE UP

Continuing to strive for our mission is *Netzach*-endurance in *Malchut*-kingship. It is leading the charge with your vision and staying true to your beliefs. When we fail in our leadership, whether it is the internal leadership of giving up on our vision or the external leadership of directing other people, this quality is essential when we hit inevitable challenges.

KING DAVID AT WAR

The tales of King David in combat represent *Netzach*-endurance in *Malchut*-kingship and they reveal personality attributes of the king when he was fighting his enemies. Whether he was fighting Goliath

---

57   Blais, Jacqueline. "Harry Potter has been very good to JK Rowling. USA Today 9 July 2005. Retrieved 26 May 2009.

hand-to-hand or at war with the entire Philistine army, King David's attitude was crucial.

We have spiritual battles which affect our relationship with God. The ultimate battle being fought by King David was that of the spirit and in service of his creator. The *Tanya* explains that

> "By exercising the attribute of *Netzach, [a man seeks] to prevail triumphantly against anything that would restrain [him] from the service of God and from cleaving unto Him, and against anything that would restrain [the state of revelation in which] the entire earth is filled with the glory of God, like the wars for God fought by King David, peace to him,* which derived from his attribute of *Netzach*"[58].

As we fight against the things that restrain us and continue to bind those energies that elevate us, we are staying true to the spirit of King David and gradually fulfill our destiny and potential.

YOU ARE KING DAVID

When aiming for long-term success, an ongoing reality is that we have to fight these internal battles, whether it is overcoming our anger, doubt or other obstacles. King David ruled for a remarkable 40 years, *"reigning for seven years in Hebron and 33 years in Jerusalem"*[59]. There is however a deeper secret in this, as on an internal kabbalistic level, we could read his first seven years as corresponding to the seven *sefirot* in the body (the theme and structure of this book), and the 33 years as corresponding to the 33 vertebrae of the spine.

33 CHANNELS

The plague on Rabbi Akiva's students also ceased on the 33rd day. Is it coincidence that Jesus also reportedly died at the age of 33, in the year AD 33, or was that a reworking of this previous story? The real story, it seems, is the story of us: We have these 33 support points that form our spine - which might also be considered as shaped like a ladder - and our goal in life is to raise our consciousness up this ladder, just like

58   Sefer Tanya, Iggeret HaKodesh, Epistle 15.
59   1 Kings 2:22.

Jacob saw the angels ascending and descending a ladder. Rabbi Joseph Gikatilla explains how you can use two names of God to ascend and descend this ladder, depending upon your ability and intention:

> *"When one pronounces YHVH Adonoy (Elohim Adonoy) in this order, the influx descends through all the Sefirot, from the highest to the lowest, until the influx of blessing and essence reaches the name Adonoy. When this occurs, all the world is enhanced with a perfect blessing.*
>
> *At other times, Adonoy is pronounced first, followed by YHVH. An example of this is, "Abraham said: Adonoy YHVH, what will You give me"[60] . Another example is, "Adonoy YHVH, You have begun to show Your servant Your greatness"[61]. Still another is, "Adonoy YHVH, destroy not Your people[62].*
>
> *When the Name is pronounced Adonoy YHVH (Adonoy Elohim, it denotes the mystery of the ascent of the Sefirot and their unification with one another, until a person's concentration reaches the Source of Will....When the name is written YHVH Adonoy, it denotes the mystery of the divine influx of Binah–Understanding, which descends through the channels and reaches the name Adonoy. When this happens, all the Universe is blessed"[63].*

These meditations can be very dangerous. I speak from hard experience. If you have intuition and ability it is absolutely possible to open the Divine channels. However, if you practice without the supervision of a master teacher, you can get into trouble. Just like pouring massive amounts of water into a bowl which is not large enough or strong enough to hold the liquid, one can take in forces for which you are unprepared. Like placing thousands of concrete pieces onto a building foundation that is secure; rather than creating a strong building, the entire structure may be built on a slant or even collapse. Spiritual work is not a game and the Divine spheres are not to be played with for our amusement.

---

60 Genesis 15:2.
61 Deuteronomy 3:24.
62 Deuteronomy 9:26.
63 Gates of Light/Shaaret Orah, p42b, translated in Meditation & Kabbalah p133.

STEP INTO INFINITY

We might also see *Netzach* as eternity, the endlessness of the Universe, the unfathomable vastness of creation, and the infinity of God within. We are aiming for a continual awareness of the oneness of God, similar to the "Echad" ("One") that is intoned at the end of the *Shema* prayer. Interestingly, the numerical value for *Echad* is 13, which is the same as *Ahava* - "love"[64]. This is also representative of God. Love, Unity and God are all connected as one. The Shema can be used as an eternal mantra[65]. The Bhagavad Gita reminds us of the yogi's aim for "eternal oneness[66]" and this is the paradox we have to live with throughout our entire life: We are born into a physical plane of existence that is full of separation. It is a life where we can feel alone, separate and full of longing to re-enter this state of oneness/*Echad* through joining with a life partner.

Netzach-endurance is our connection to the Eternal. *Netzach*-endurance in *Malchut*-nobility, is a way that we might experience God within, as the continual majesty and dignity inside our body. We are blessed on a daily basis with a myriad of physical abilities, material possessions, food, shelter, love and support. As God's love for us endures and allows us to live with dignity (*Malchut*), we can be thankful and live our life with grace, thanks and strength.

TODAY'S PRACTICE

YOGA PRACTICE GUIDELINES:

Raja Yoga, or Royal Yoga is a name for the yogic school of philosophy, but also corresponds with the *sefira*-energy of *Malchut*-Kingship. As the mixture of asana and vinyasa helps our bodies become more powerful, we attain more strength with which to endure the trials of life. Yoga gives us the ability to become more sensitive to pains within our bodies and to sense paths towards healing. Our *Malchut*-sovereignty tangibly increases as we become more powerful human beings, more able to

---

64 Jewish Meditation, p127.
65 There is a helpful chapter about this in Rabbi Aryeh Kaplan's book Jewish Meditation, p122.
66 The Bhagavad Gita 6:33.

express the will of our soul, and more holistically integrated on every level.

Begin today's yoga practice by sitting quietly, noticing your breath and slowly counting the blessings that you have been given today. Your body, the clothes you are wearing, any food that you have eaten since waking up, the room you are in, the heat that is fuelling the temperature in the room, and any streams of income that are supporting your lifestyle.

My teacher Edward has said that "Yoga can teach us to do anything" because it allows us to slow down the mind and view reality on a piece-by-piece, breath-by-breath basis. Today's challenge is to notice an area of your life where you have felt powerless, unable to realise an ambition through feeling out of control. By regularly applying yourself, breath by breath and step by step, you can use the energy of Endurance in Nobility to increase your sphere of influence and achieve your goals.

GYM PRACTICE GUIDELINES:

Malchut-Kingship is the unification of your thought, speech and action so that you are the King in your own life. Focus on working your entire body and keeping your thoughts in line with your actions. During your workout, use the quality of *Netzach*-endurance to increase your self-control and inner power.

QUESTIONS FOR MEDITATION

RELATIONSHIPS:

- Where are my thoughts, speech and actions out of alignment with my relationship? Where do I say one thing and do another? Or speak in a way that does not build the relationship? How can I be more consistent in the way I speak, think or act? (*Netzach*)

YOGA/BODY/GYM:

- Where have I declared one goal for my body and not acted in alignment with this? How can I get back in line with my stated goals and really stick with my intentions over a sustained period?

BUSINESS:

- Where do I say one thing and do another in my workplace? (e.g. say I want to obtain much more business and then not do the appropriate marketing or new business lead-generation?). How can I increase my endurance factor? (Netzach)

LEADERSHIP:

- Where am I not fulfilling my leadership potential? How can I be a better leader and be more enduring?
- Where am I giving up too easily as a leader?

GYM SEQUENCE, DAY 46/DONKEY KICK

Start with your hands and knees in parallel position and use a yoga mat if necessary. As you raise each leg, do so whilst connecting your breath and keeping in alignment, being careful not to kick quickly which may adversely impact your hip or lower back. Hold each "kick" for 3 breaths. Do 5 repetitions on each leg.

.01

.02

YOGA SEQUENCE, DAY 46/BOW (DHANURASANA)

To modify you can take hold of a strap and place it around the fronts of your ankles. Whatever your position. draw your shoulder blades down and together whilst deepening your backbend.

מלכות
Malchut-Kingship

מלכות
Malchut-Kingship

נצח
Netzach-Endurance

DAY 47 / HUMILITY IN NOBILITY / GREATNESS THROUGH GRATITUDE / הוד שבמלכות

KABBALAH SUTRA: *Hod She b'Malhut* – Humility in Nobility.
INTENTION: To gain greater control over your life through humbly allowing things to be as they are. Becoming great through gratitude. Be a humble leader. Humility in all our actions. Grateful Leadership. To lead with grace, gratitude and humility.

"Abram fell on his face" — Genesis 17:3

Biblical leaders seemed to frequently fall on their face, unlike today's politicians. A trite, humble heart is essential for any enduring figurehead, but demands genuine humility. This appears counter-intuitive but the more we cultivate modesty, the more we leave room for other people and can increase our impact as a leader.

Hod-humility in *Malchut*-nobility asks us to question where we have been arrogant in our leadership positions, refusing to acknowledge fault or say we were wrong in a situation.

CULTIVATING HUMILITY

The Ramak asked;

> *"How should a person train himself in the attribute of malchut-sovereignty? First of all, his wealth should not make him proud. Rather, he should always heave like a poor person, standing before his Maker like a pauper, begging and pleading. Even one who is wealthy should accustom himself to this attitude, considering that none of his possessions belong to him and that he is forsaken and requires the constant mercies of his Creator, having nothing but the bread he eats. He should humble his heart and afflict himself, especially at the time of prayer, for this is a very effective aid. In contrast the verse states: "But your heart may then grow haughty, and you may forget…"[67], for*

---

[67] Deuteronomy 8:14.

forgetfulness is common amid pride. This is the attitude to which King David made himself well-accustomed, saying:[68] "...for I am alone and humbled"[69].

There is no expectation that leaders should automatically master the trait of humility, but it is to be cultivated. The Torah's laws are extra stringent for a King and command him to write two copies of the Torah, one to travel with him and one to stay at home[70]. We can find the equivalent in our own lives, seeking the areas where we would benefit from greater humility with those around us. The importance of this is underlined by a teaching of Rabbi Ginsburg who explains that the internal aspect of Malchut-mastery is indeed humility; *"The spiritual state identified in Chassidut as corresponding to the sefirah of Malchut is that of shiflut (humility)"[71].* It can take work to master humility.

MASTERING THE EGO

The Talmudic sages explained that true strength comes from holding back. Somewhat counter-intuitively, genuine humility is a path to greatness; *"those who are insulted but do not insult in return, who are shamed but do not shame in return, it is said[72] "His lovers are like the emerging of the sun it its strength""[73].* Once again the highest level of power is not in an explosion of energy but in a focusing of our drive. Similarly, the Rabbis teach that the person who seeks glory for its own sake will rarely achieve it, and the sages taught that the person who is honoured is the one "who honours others"[74].

HARD WORK

In addition, *Hod*-humility can help get us closer to achieving our goals when we apply the wisdom of King Solomon:

---

68 Psalms/Tehillim 25:16.
69 Tomer Devorah, p125
70 We learn this from the Babylonian Talmud, Sanhedrin 21a. The verse in Deuteronomy 17:18 states *"And it will be when he sits on the royal throne of his kingdom, he shall write for himself a copy of this Torah on a scroll before the Kohanim, the Levites".*
71 http://www.inner.org/sefirot/sefmalcu.htm.
72 Judges 5:31.
73 Babylonian Talmud, Masechet Shabbat 88b.
74 Ethics of the Fathers/Pirkei Avot 4:1.

"Lazybones, go the ant;
Study its ways and learn.
Without leaders, officers, or rulers,
It lays up its stores during the summer,
Gathers in its food at the harvest.
How long will you lie there, lazybones;
When will you wake from your sleep?
A bit more sleep, a bit more slumber,
A bit more hugging yourself in bed,
And poverty will come calling upon you,
And want, like a man with a shield"[75].

This from the man who reportedly had 700 wives and 300 concubines, who nonetheless saw the value in not staying in bed for those few extra minutes of sleep. Having the humility to look into nature and see how other creatures are behaving can spur us to master our own realm, take control of what we are doing and get up earlier to make things happen.

THE HUMBLE LEADER

The list of humble leaders - *Hod*-humility in *Malchut*-kingship is so extensive that we might surmise this character trait is essential to good leadership; *"Moses and Aaron fell on their faces"*[76], *"When Moses heard this, he fell on his face"*[77], *"And Joshua fell on his face"*[78], *"David...fell on his face"*[79], *"David and the Elders of Israel...fell on their faces"*[80], *"I [Ezekiel] fell on my face"*[81], *"King Nebuchadnezzar fell on his face"*[82], and *"I [Daniel] was afraid and fell on my face"*[83].

We might think about the leaders we admire, how they are humble and how their humility contributes to the qualities we admire in them. As

---

75 Proverbs/Mishlei 6:11.
76 Exodus 14:5.
77 Numbers 16:4.
78 Joshua 5:14.
79 1 Samuel 20:41.
80 1 Chronicles 21:16.
81 Ezekiel 3:23.
82 Daniel 2:46.
83 Daniel 8:17.

we apply humility to all of our actions, we can create a greater space for other people and a more profound opening for the Divine.

TODAY'S PRACTICE

YOGA PRACTICE GUIDELINES:

The process of yoga involves mastering the act of surrender, or humility. We become humble in the face of physical postures that challenge our body and force us to realise limitations. We notice the busy workings of our mind and are forced to recognise how far we are from the goal. The yogis teach that if we can humbly recognise our smallness, to our place as a tiny particle in the vastness of the Universe, this will assist our process of union (Echad/Yoga) with God: *"The mastery of one in Union extends from the finest atomic particle to the greatest infinity"*[84], and *"When the agitations of the mind are under control, the mind becomes like a transparent crystal and has the power of becoming whatever form is presented. Knower, act of knowing, or what is known"*[85].

GYM PRACTICE GUIDELINES:

Begin your workout with gratitude for everything within your control, and continue to make that part of your workout practice today.

SPIRITUAL PRACTICE:

Our focus is on connecting with the Infinite within through unifying our entire consciousness. By really attuning ourselves to taking a humble approach with our meditation, prayer, yoga and other spiritual practices we can achieve greater stillness within and tune into the magnitude of God.

---

[84] Yoga Sutras 1:40.
[85] Yoga Sutras 1:41, Swamij translation.

QUESTIONS FOR MEDITATION

RELATIONSHIPS:
- Where are my thoughts, speech and actions out of alignment with my relationship? Where do I say one thing and do another? Where do I speak in a way that does not build relationships? How can I be more humble and grateful for being in this relationship, and how can I express that today? (*Hod*-humility).
- Where am I an arrogant leader, e.g. Refusing to acknowledge fault or ever say I am wrong in a situation? How can I remedy this? What is it costing me? Where do I spend a lot of energy trying to look good and pretend I am better than I am? Where might I be like Moses who was a strong and confident leader but also, on occasion, "falling on [*his*] face"?

YOGA/BODY/GYM:
- Where have I declared one goal for my body and not acted in alignment with this? How can I get back in line with my stated goals, but do it with humility?

BUSINESS:
- Where do I say one thing and do another in my workplace? (e.g. say I want to obtain much more business and then not do the appropriate marketing or new business lead-generation?). Where can I benefit from my humility or creating more space for others? (*Hod*)

LEADERSHIP:
- Where am I not fulfilling my leadership potential? How can I be a better leader, and be more grateful and respectful towards others?

GYM SEQUENCE, DAY 47/RAISED LEG CRUNCH

A variation on the Sit-up, place your feet on a chair with your knees bent at 90 degrees. 3 x 12 repetitions.

.01

מַלְכוּת
Malchut-Kingship

הוֹד מַלְכוּת
Hod-Humility   *Malchut*-Kingship

.02

YOGA SEQUENCE, DAY 47/SHOULDERSTAND (SALAMBA SARVANGASANA)

The Iyengar version of the backbend involves resting on two or three folded mats which will further protect your neck and make it easier to sustain the pose. You can also modify the position by doing a shoulder stand in front of a wall, bending your knees and walking up the wall a little.

מלכות
Malchut-Kingship

הוד
Hod-Humility

מלכות
Malchut-Kingship

DAY 48 / BONDING IN NOBILITY / A LITTLE LESS THAN DIVINE / יסוד שבמלכות

KABBALAH SUTRA: *Yesod She b'Malhut* – Bonding in Nobility.
INTENTION: To increase your self-control through being grounded, and to improve relationships through becoming more influential to those around you. To achieve dignified bonding.

"Ten Sefirot of Nothingness. Their end is embedded in their beginning and their beginning in the their end" — Sefer Yetzirah 1:7

When the Kabbalists connected the sefira energies with the body they gave us a set of keys to understand God through our own physicality. The process of Biblical covenants is all about human beings making agreements to improve themselves through their promises to the Divine[86]. *Malchut*-Kingship represents the actions we take in life and *Yesod*-Bonding is the way we connect with it. *Yesod* also represents the pleasure and delight we can experience along the way.

THE END IS ROOTED IN THE BEGINNING
This Kabbalistic principle is simple to explain but easily overlooked. Before we take any action, are we fully grounded? A good builder would not lay a single brick without ensuring the blueprints are solid, and the foundation is stable. The architect ensures that the end is rooted in the beginning, but can we say the same with all of our work? *Yesod*-connection to *Malchut*-action allows us to have economy of action, so that we do not try to build on an unstable foundation or go back and re-do our mistakes.

---

[86] The key example of this is *Brit Milah*/circumcision, which is seen as a refinement of the body that is being carried out by humans, who get to 'complete' creation through this act.

452

THE RIGHTEOUS ARE THE FOUNDATION

This principle is taken to new heights in Kabbalistic thinking. When our intentions are completely dedicated to a higher cause, they can impact on the entire Universe. King Solomon wrote that *"When the storm passes the wicked man is gone, but the righteous is an everlasting foundation"*[87].

The Bahir goes into this in more depth on various levels. Firstly, it explains how the presence of a righteous person on earth actually supports the very existence of the world; *"The Blessed Holy One has a single Righteous One (Tzadik) in His world, and it is dear to Him because it supports all the world. It is the Foundation (Yesod). This is what sustains it, and makes it grow, increasing and watching it. It is beloved and dear on high, and beloved and dear below; fearsome and mighty on high, and fearsome and mighty below; rectified and accepted on high, rectified and accepted below"*[88]. This spiritual dynamic ties in with the belief that at any one point there are 36 hidden righteous people in the world, and it is on their merit that the world exists[89].

MALE & FEMALE (ADVANCED KABBALISTIC MODELLING)

There are further depths to this as in another model, *Yesod* is the male organ while *Malchut* represents the female, so the combination of male and female is what creates new existence. Additionally, *Yesod* is represented by Friday and *Malchut* is Saturday/shabbat, which plays on this further explanation by The Bahir; *"[Yesod] is the Foundation of all souls.....Is it then not written*[90], *"And on the seventh day He rested and souled"? "Souls are born through the union of Yesod-Foundation and Malchut-Kingship. Therefore, Yesod-Foundation is called the "Foundation of all souls"*[91]. The well-known Kabbalistic practice of man and wife joining on Friday night is another play on this, as the end of Friday is *Yesod*, while Shabbat is *Malchut*, so this entire pro-creative drama is

---

87   Proverbs/*Mishlei* 10:25.
88   Bahir 157, p175.
89   The *'lamed vavnikim'* - the 36 righteous - based on Talmudic statements that in every generation 36 righteous people "Greet the Shechinah" - Tractate Sanhedrin 97b; Tractate Sukkah 45b).
90   Exodus 31:17.
91   The Bahir 157, p175.

being played out on many levels, from the days of the week, through the husband and wife, to the higher spiritual realms.

BE YOUR BEST LEADER

Yesod-Bonding in *Malchut*-Nobility can give you the self-confidence to lead the way forward and overcome obstacles that prevent you from bonding with other people, goals and your best future. It is easy to isolate oneself and not deal with the personal challenges that arise with regards to bonding and connecting with others, but true *Yesod*-bonding in *Malchut*-mastery happens through relating to others around us and building these connections in a way that is considered, respectful and dignified.

"What is man that You have been mindful of him, mortal man that You have taken note of him, that You have made him little less than divine, and adorned him with glory and majesty"[92].

TODAY'S PRACTICE

YOGA PRACTICE GUIDELINES:

The yogis taught that *"when [inner wisdom] is mastered, there arises the vision that is wisdom. This vision (or the eye of intuition, or the eye of wisdom, or the inner light) can be directed to many fields of observation"*[93]. Once we have truly bonded with ourselves, achieved this sense of *yesod*-bonding with our inner vision, we can reach out into the world and the possibilities are infinite.

Yesod is also the force of grounding, the force of bonding, and the energy that is rooted in the sexual organs. *Yesod*-Bonding in *Malchut*-nobility focuses us on how everything is drawn together, and at its most root element it can be related to through the root lock. Visualising how all of our energy emanates from this *mulah* region that is just beneath the perineum and allow this to drive us.

---

92 Psalm 8:5-6.
93 Yoga Sutras 3:5-6, Ventakeshananda translation.

To experience this during TODAY'S PRACTICE, move into a place of deep stillness through focusing on the placement of your root lock/mulah bandha, bringing total focus and consciousness to your every breath and action, and hold your posture with dignity.

GYM PRACTICE GUIDELINES:

Work on strengthening the foundation of your practice, standing strong and remaining focussed. Continue to build your sense of power and mastery (*Malchut*).

LEADERSHIP PRACTICE GUIDELINES:

Become aware of how you are connecting with other people and aim to do so with dignity and respect. Notice your own capacity for leadership and strengthen your capability as a leader through these subtle and sensitive human connections.

QUESTIONS FOR MEDITATION

RELATIONSHIPS:

- Where are my thoughts, speech and actions out of alignment with my relationships? Where do I say one thing and do another? Or speak in a way that does not build relationships? What is one thing I can do today that will deepen my main personal relationships so that everyone will become more connected? (*Yesod*)

YOGA/BODY/GYM:

- Where have I declared one goal for my body and not acted in alignment with this? (e.g. promising that I will get fit to run a marathon, or learning to meditate, or learning a headstand). How can I get more deeply connected to my intentions so that I bring them into being?

BUSINESS:

- Where do I say one thing and do another in my workplace? (e.g. say I want to generate more business and then not do the appropriate marketing or new business lead-generation?). How can I get more connected to my vision and mission? (*Yesod*)

LEADERSHIP:

- Where am I not fulfilling my leadership potential? How can I be a better leader and connect more deeply with others?

ADVANCED KABBALISTIC PRACTICE

The Gates of Light (*Sharey Orah* by Rabbi Yosef Gikatalia) explores how we might directly channel the attribute of *Yesod*-Bonding into this world, and explains that *"One who wishes to perceive Eternal Life should attach himself to the attribute of El Chai (Living God), [which is associated with the Sefirah of Yesod-Foundation]"*[94]. The book then goes on to explain how we can pursue this spiritual path.

In my understanding, another aspect of attaching to "eternal life" can be done quite practically. We might begin this process by looking at all of our connections and seeing the essence of eternal life in everything. We can look at our body and consider how our DNA has been passed on through the generations, how our very face resembles that of our parents and grandparents, and how the water and atomic elements in our body have been circulating the planet for millions of years. We can experience Eternal Life within ourselves if we choose to bring it into our consciousness.

---

94 Sharey Orah 2 p18a in Meditation & Kabbalah p130. He goes on to explain: *"This means that through his prayers, one should bring El Chai into Adonoy. It was regarding this that King David had passion and desire when he said, "My soul thirsts for God, for El Chai"* (Psalms 42:3). *When the attribute (Yesod), which is called El Chai, is bound to Adonoy (Malchut), then one can draw down all his needs. He can overcome his enemies, and no one can stand up to him. We must bind the Sefirot together, attaching all levels through the attribute of Adonoy (Malchut-Kingship). We therefore say "He chooses song of praise, King (Malchut), Life (Yesod) of the world. (Original footnote: this is the end of the Yishtabach prayer). If one wishes to seek a good life, he should bind himself to the attribute of El Chai. When a person is attached to Adonoy in purity, then he is also attached to El Chai. It is thus written, "And you, who are attached to YHVH your God, you are all alive (Chai) today"* (Deuteronomy 4:4)".

GYM SEQUENCE, DAY 48/MOUNTAIN CLIMBER (MT. SINAI CLIMBER)

Begin in Push-up position and alternate bringing your knees forward, in rapid succession. 3 sets of 45 seconds.

.01

מלכות
Malchut-Kingship

יסוד
Yesod-Bonding

מלכות
Malchut-Kingship

.02

YOGA SEQUENCE, DAY 48/HEADSTAND (SALAMBA SIRSASANA)

Approach with caution and ideally only having learned this from a qualified yoga teacher. Begin by taking hold of each elbow with the opposite hand, forearms on the ground. Keep your elbows in this position, interlace your fingers and place the crown of your head on the ground. Make sure you take the weight in your forearms as you raise your legs into the air. Whilst learning the position, practice in front of a wall for safety. Women who are menstruating will typically avoid this posture. Men who are menstruating should see a doctor immediately.

.01   .02

מלכות
Malchut-Kingship

יסוד
Yesod-Bonding

מלכות
Malchut-Kingship

DAY 49 / NOBILITY IN NOBILITY / KISS THE BRIDE / מלכות שבמלכות

KABBALAH SUTRA: *Malchut She b'Malchut* – Nobility in Nobility.
INTENTION: To experience deep calm by connecting with the Godliness inside. Fulfill your leadership potential and be a king.

"I heard there was a secret chord that David played and it pleased the Lord"
Leonard Cohen

We live in bodes that feel before they think - this is *Malchut*. We live on a spherical-shaped live on a feminine-shaped planet (rather than a flat earth) - this is *Malchut*. Two-thirds of our planet is covered in water - an element that is *Malchut*. We create with our hands and feet - *Malchut* and speak from our mouths - *Malchut*. Women give birth - *Malchut* and when we proclaim that there is a single Unified God, that too is *Malchut*.

THE UN-UNIFIED SELF

When our thoughts, speech and actions are not aligned, we are out of sync with the rhythm of the earth. On a subtle level this reflects a lack of unity with God, because we are saying "all is one" but not acting as if "all is one". Every time we break our word or fall short on a commitment, we are out of alignment. There are many words for this idea of "getting back into alignment", whether it is *Shalom* (from the word '*Shalem*' meaning complete or whole) or *Yoga* (from 'unification' or 'yoking').

DIVINE SEXUAL METAPHORS

The Kabbalah must speak in the language of sexual metaphor because on a symbolic level, that is all that is left. As mentioned earlier, we speak of "conceiving" an idea and then "giving birth" to it or "manifesting" it. A farmer literally "plants seeds" before watering them. *Malchut*-kingship represents the feminine because on this planet it is only through women that we are able to give birth.

Most physical diagrams of the sefira of *Malchut*-kingship show it as existing outside of the body. Some diagrams show it as between the legs, and Rabbi Yitzkah Luria understood it as 'mate', or the point when one human comes together with another in an act of procreation. The theme of *Malchut* is central to the Sabbath and alluded to in the Kabbalistic song *Lecha Dodi* which welcomes the 'bride' of the Sabbath. This too is a joining of worlds, bringing the secular week together with a day that is sanctified and made holy through human actions. There is also a custom to read the *Song of Songs* on Friday nights, welcoming the Sabbath with a poem that discusses the relationship between a man and woman. Finally, *Malchut* is also understood as speech, because it connects one person to another.

YOGIC ONENESS

The true yogi *"has inner joy"*, according to the yogic sages. In addition *"he has inner gladness and he has found inner light...he is one with God and goes unto God...because the peace of God is with them whose minds and souls are in harmony, who are free from desire and wrath, who know their own soul"*[95]. If yoga is preparation for connecting with God, for aligning our physical energy so perfectly that we rejoin the Light, then we can certainly use it to understand *Malchut*-kingship because it is one and the same. Yoga might begin on the mat, but it is to be applied in every moment as a tool of transformation. We can view *Malchut* as the connection between two people, as the way they speak to one another or how they connect through the act of procreation. It is ideal to act nobly in approaching all of these interactions.

MALACHITE AS BREATH?

Perhaps *Malchut* is also the breath; that intangible substance that connects us with other people. It is inside the body and outside of it, occupying a continually dynamic space and fuels the speech we use to communicate with others[96].

---

95 Bhagavad Gita 5:26.
96 I do not have a source for this - it is my theory based on the other descriptions of *Malchut* comparing it to the mouth and this entire realm of existence. On the other hand, breath may however also be seen as *Yesod* because it is a substance emitting from our body that is going into the world.

PREPARING FOR SHAVUOT

The end of the 49 days of the Omer are marked with the festival of Shavuot ("Pentecost") which represents the receiving of the Torah on Mount Sinai. On it, we read the *Book of Ruth* which tells of the great-grandmother of King David. She masters her own desires and joins the Jewish people, much as King David was later able to harness the spiritual forces of Israel to create peace between the tribes, secure the city of Jerusalem and write the Book of Psalms, which are some of the most powerful spiritual books of all time.

King David was described as *"much more elevated than all the other kings who descended from him and followed him"*[97] and *Malchut*-kingship in *Malchut*-kingship allows us to tap into this energy. The *Zohar* alludes to how he is the fourth 'wheel' to the Divine chariot, accompanying the other three supports of Abraham, Isaac and Jacob[98]. This takes us back to the beginning of the book, as it says *"the end is rooted in the beginning and the beginning is rooted in the end"*[99]. We master our lovingkindness (*Chesed*), strength (*Gevurah*) and compassion (*Tiferet*), and as we master ourselves we are able to create Heaven here on Earth. Shavuot represents the 50th gate.

"Rabbi Amorai asked: Where is the Garden of Eden? He replied: It is on earth"[100].

TODAY'S PRACTICE

YOGA PRACTICE GUIDELINES:

Our yogic journey takes us from chaos and confusion, *tohu v'vohu*, to a place of stillness and stability where *"one-pointedness is steadfastness of the mind"*[101]. We become free from cravings and gain *"consciousness of mastery"*[102]and at that point we can truly become joyful of what we have.

---

97   Derech Mitzvotecha, p235.
98   The footnote to Derech Mitzvotecha p.235 explains "The three patriarchs are referred to as *The Divine Chariot* (Bereishis Rabbah 47:1). Thus the chariot would have only three supports, as it were. The fourth support is King David. See Zohar 1, p 248; Moorei Or, Maareches Alef, sec.84.
99   Sefer Yetzirah 1:7.
100 The Bahir 31, p12.
101 Yoga Sutras 3:1.
102 Yoga Sutras 1:15, Swamij translation.

GYM PRACTICE GUIDELINES:

Visualise yourself as the Warrior-King David. To borrow a battle-cry from Henry V,

> *"Imitate the action of the tiger:*
> *Stiffen the sinews, summon up the blood,*
> *Disguise fair nature with hard-favored rage…*
> *I see you stand like greyhounds in the slips,*
> *Straining upon the start. The game's afoot.*
> *Follow your spirit, and upon this charge*
> *Cry "God for Harry, England, and Saint*
> *George!"*[103].

Now, find your own equivalent and master your mastery!

QUESTIONS FOR MEDITATION

RELATIONSHIPS:

- Where are my thoughts, speech and actions out of alignment with my relationship? Where do I say one thing and do another? Or speak in a way that does not build the relationship? How can I master my speech and actions so that everything is fully aligned? (*Malchut*)
- Am I truly noble in all of my actions?
- Am I the sovereign of my behaviour? Do I take responsibility for my actions?
- Can I see the light of Godly nobility in others?

YOGA/BODY/GYM:

- Where have I declared one goal for my body and not acted in alignment with this? How can I get back in line with my goals and what can I do about it right now? What commitments can I make to myself, or public declarations to stay accountable?
- Do I treat my body with respect as if it were the property of a king?

---

[103] Henry V, 3:i.

BUSINESS:

-   Where do I say one thing and do another in my workplace? (e.g. say I want to obtain much more business and then not do the appropriate marketing or new business lead-generation?). How can I use more powerful language and what different actions might I take?(*Malchut*)

LEADERSHIP:

-   Where am I not fulfilling my leadership potential? How can I be a better leader? How can I be the best leader I can be?
-   Where are things out of balance in my business or career and how can I restore balance by mastering all the different elements (being loving, disciplined, compassionate, enduring, humble and connected)?

GYM SEQUENCE, DAY 49/MOUNTAIN

Stand in Mountain Posture, draw your legs and shoulder blades closer together and reach for your ankles with your fingertips. Be ready to climb the mountain...

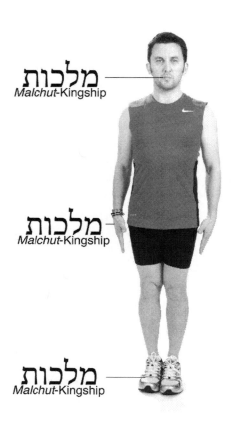

מלכות
Malchut-Kingship

מלכות
Malchut-Kingship

מלכות
Malchut-Kingship

YOGA SEQUENCE, DAY 49/SAVASANA

Lie with your heels touching and your palms close to your hips. Allow your feet to drop outwards. If your environment is cool, cover your body with a blanket. For additional uplifting extras, cover your eyes with a soft, lavender-scented bean bag.

.01

מלכות
Malchut-Kingship

מלכות
Malchut-Kingship

מלכות
Malchut-Kingship

.02

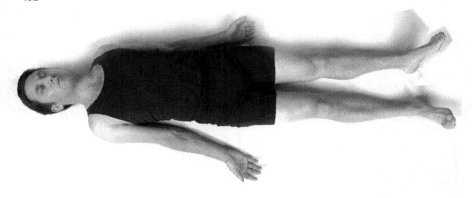

THE KABBALAH SUTRAS

BIBLIOGRAPHY

PRIMARY SOURCES

Ben HaKana, Rabbi Nehunia, *The Bahir*, translation and commentary by Rabbi Aryeh Kaplan. Maine: Weiser Books, 1989.

Bialik, Hayim Nahman and Ravnitzky, Yehoshua Hana, editors, *The Book of Legends: Sefer Ha-Haggadah. Legends from the Talmud and Midrash*, Translated by William G. Braude, New York: Shockhen Books: 1992. Originally published in Hebrew in Odessa, 1908-1911.

Cordovero, Rabbi Moshe, *The Palm Tree of Devorah/Tomer Devorah* translated by Rabbi Moshe Miller. New York: Targum/Feldheim, 1994.

Gikatilla, Joseph ben Abraham, *Gates of Light* translated and with an introduction by Avi Weinstein. London: Altamira Press, 1994.

Liadi, Rabbi Shneur Zalman, *Lessons in Tanya - The Tanya of Rabbi Schneur Zalman of Liadi. Volumes 1 to 5*. New York: Kehot Publication Society, 1998.

Kaplan, Rabbi Aryeh, *Meditation and Kabbalah*. New York: Weiser Books, 1989.

Kaplan, Rabbi Aryeh (Translation and commentary), *Sefer Yetzirah* - translation and commentary. San Francisco: Weiser Books 1997.

Luria, Rabbi Isaac, *Sha'ar HaGilgulim, The Gates of Reincarnation*, translated from the teachings of Rabbi Isaac Luria 1534-1575. Malibu: Thirty Seven Books Publishing, 2003.

Rashab, Rebbe, *LOVE LIKE FIRE AND WATER - A Guide to Jewish Meditation. Essay on the Service of the Heart by the Rebbe Rashab* (with translation and commentary by Rabbi David Sterne. New York/Jerusalem: Moznaim, 2005.

Rabbi Nosson *The Complete Artscroll Siddur* - A new translation and anthologised commentary by New York: Mesorah Publications, 1984.

Schneerson, Rabbi Menachem Mendel, *Torah, Chumash Shemot. With an interpolated English Translation and Commentary based on the works of the Lubavitcher Rebbe*. New York: Kehot, 2011.

467

Schneerson, Rabbi Menachem Mendel, *Torah, Chumash Vayikra. With an interpolated English Translation and Commentary based on the works of the Lubavitcher Rebbe.* New York: Kehot, 2011.

Solomon, David, *Tiqqunei haZohar, Qustha 1740: An English Translation.* Unpublished Manuscript version: February 2015.

Stiles, Mukunda (translation), *Yoga Sutras of Patanjali.* Boston: Weiser Books, 2002.

Scholem, Gerson, *Zohar - Basic Readings from the Kabbalah*, ew York: Schocken Books, 1949.

Ashlag, Rav Yehuda, *The Zohar: by Rav Shimon bar Yochai: from the book of Avraham: with the Sulam commentary. (*Translation Rabbi Michael Berg). New York: Kabbalah Centre International, 2003.

KABBALAH SOURCES

Aaron, Rabbi David, *Endless Light: The Ancient Path of Kabbalah.* Berkley: Berkley, 1978.

Cohen, Yedidah, *A Tapestry For The Soul - The Introduction to the Zohar* by Rabbi Yehudah Lev Ashlag. Safed: Nehora Press, 2010.

Dan, Joseph, *The Heart and the Fountain - An Anthology of Jewish Mystical Experiences.* New York: Oxford University Press, 2002.

Epstein, Perle. *Kabbalah - The Way of the Jewish Mystic.* Boston: Shambhala, 1978.

Frankiel, Dr Tamar, *The Gift of Kabbalah - Discovering the Secrets of Heaven, Renewing Your Life on Earth.* Woodstock, VT: Jewish Lights Publishing, 2003.

Goldfelder, Rabbi Gavriel, *The 50th Gate - A Spirited Walk Through the Counting of the Omer - 49 Steps to being a better human.* Boulder: Kehillath Aish Kodesh, 2011)

Ginsburgh, Rabbi Yitzchak, *Body, Mind, and Soul: Kabbalah on Human Physiology, Disease, and Healing.* Jerusalem: Gal Einai Publications, 2004.

Ginsburgh, Rabbi Yitzchak, *Living in Divine Space - Kabbalah and Meditation.* Kfar Chabad: Gal Einai, 2003.

BIBLIOGRAPHY

Jacobson, Rabbi Simon, *The Counting of the Omer: Forty-Nine Steps to Personal Refinement According to the Jewish Tradition*. Brooklyn: Vaad Hanochos Hatmimim, 1996.

Kaplan, Rabbi Aryeh, *Inner Space - Introduction to Kabbalah, Meditation and Prophecy*. Edited by Abraham Sutton. Jerusalem: Moznaim, 1990.

Kaplan, Rabbi Aryeh, *Jewish Meditation - A Practical Guide*. New York: Schocken Books, 1985.

Kramer, Chaim, *Anatomy of the Soul, Rebbe Nachman of Breslov*. Jerusalem: Breslov Research Institute, 1998.

Leet, Leonora, *The Secret Doctrine of the Kabbalah*. Vermont: Inner Traditions: 1999.

Luzzato, Rabbi Moshe Chayim, *Path of the Just/Mesillat Yesharim*, Shraga Silverstein (trans.). Jerusalem/New York: Feldheim, 1966).

Matt, Daniel C., *The Essential Kabbalah - The Heart of Jewish Mysticism*. New Jersey: Castle Books, 1997.

Rosner, Fred, *Sex Ethics in the Writings of Moses Maimonides*, New Jersey: Jason Aaronson Inc, 1994.

Scholem, Gershon, *On the Kabbalah and its Symbolism*. New York: Schocken: 1965.

Shapira, Rabbi Kalonymous Kalman, (author)*Conscious Community – A Guide to Inner Work*, Andrea Cohen-Kiener (translator). Maryland: Rowman & Littlefield, 2004.

ENERGY, HEALING, TRANSFORMATION & YOGA SOURCES

Akers, Brian Dana (trans.) *Hatha Yoga Pradipika*. Woodstock: Yogavidya. com, 2002.

Bloomfield, Dianne, *Torah Yoga*. San Francisco: Jossey-Bass, 2004.

Canfield, Jack, with Switzer, Janet, *The Success Principles - How to Get from Where You Are to Where You Want to Be*. New York: Harper Collins, 2007.

Coulter, David H., *Anatomy of Hatha Yoga – A Manual for Students, Teachers, and Practitioners*. Delhi: Motilal Banarsidass: Delhi, 2001.

Chia, Mantak, with Winn, Michael, *Taoist Secrets of Love - Cultivating Male Sexual Energy*. New York: Aurora Press, 1984.

Eliade, Merce, *Yoga: Immortality and Freedom,* (Mythos: the Princeton/ Bollingen Series in World Mythology), Willard R. Trask (Translator), David Gordon White (Introduction). Princeton University Press, 2009.

Feurstein, Georg, *The Deeper Dimensions of Yoga*. Boston: Shambala, 2003.

Iyengar, BKS, *Light on Life: the yoga journey to wholeness, inner peace, and ultimate freedom*. Emmaus, Pa.: Rodale, 2005.

Iyengar, BKS, *Light on Yoga*. New York, Schocken: 1995.

Jois, Sri K Pattahabi, *Yoga Mala*. New York: North Point Press, 2002.

Kingston, Eric Sander, *How Far to The Place of Enlightenment,* Los Angeles: Freedthinker Books, 2015.

Mezritch, R. Dov Ber, *Lekutei Yekarim & Maggid Devarav l'Yaakov*, #105, 106, Jerusalem: Kolel Mevakesh Emunah.

Michaelson, Jay, *God in your body : Kabbalah, mindfulness and embodied spiritual practice*. Woodstock, Vt.: Jewish Lights, 2007.

Myss, Caroline, *Anatomy of the Spirit: The Seven Stages of Power and Healing*. New York: Harmony Books, 1998.

Robbins, Anthony, *Awaken the Giant Within,* London: Simon & Schuster Ltd: 1992.

Satchidandanda, Sri Swami, *Yoga Sutras – Commentary on the Raja Yoga Sutras*. Yogaville, Va.: Integral Yoga Publications, 1985.

Schiffmann, Erich, *Yoga: The Spirit and Practice of Moving into Stillness*. New York: Pocket Books, 1996.

Scott, John, *Ashtanga yoga: the essential step-by-step guide to dynamic yoga*. Stroud: Gaia, 2000.

Swenson, David, *Ashtanga Yoga – The Practice Manual*. Houston, TX: Ashtanga Yoga Productions, 2000.

Tolle, Eckhart, *A New Earth*. New York: Plume, 1996.

INDEX

A

Aaron vii, 37, 186-187, 241, 280-281, 309-310, 332, 447, 468, 472

Abraham vii, 5-6, 22, 30, 35, 83, 92, 98, 146, 163, 180, 241, 350, 430, 439, 461, 467, 469, 472

Abulafia vii, 5-6, 472

altar 5, 83, 163, 472

Alter Rebbe 6, 22, 29, 106-107, 179, 197, 472, 476

angel 14, 170, 189, 357, 430, 472

anger 43, 80, 97-98, 137, 163, 196, 224, 298, 379, 421, 438, 472

anxiety 50, 164, 325, 472

Aryeh Kaplan vii, 6, 23, 43, 50-51, 83, 90-92, 131, 186, 271, 280, 357, 373, 389, 396-398, 405, 467, 472

atonement 172, 472

B

Baal Shem Tov vii, 5, 29, 131, 389, 472

Bahir 23, 51, 71, 87, 271, 381, 388, 396-397, 404-406, 410, 453, 461, 467, 472

balance xi, ix, x, 12, 20-21, 32, 35-36, 40, 43-47, 50-51, 64, 67, 71, 74-75, 80-81, 86-87, 91, 99, 101, 103, 105-107, 110, 122, 124, 133, 140, 146-154, 156-159, 162, 164-167, 170-171, 174-176, 179-183, 186, 188, 191-192, 195, 199-200, 203-205, 207-209, 221, 226, 230, 239-245, 256, 281, 285, 289, 301, 304-305, 311, 314, 336-337, 346, 361, 366, 368-369, 389, 398, 400, 428-434, 463, 472, 477

bayit 37-38, 381, 472

Ben Zoma 7, 421, 472

Bhagavad Gita 368, 431, 440, 460, 472

bitachon 472

blessing vi, vii, 5, 46, 153, 163-164, 174, 188, 296, 324, 359, 380-381, 395, 411, 430, 434, 439, 472

blockages 31, 216, 232, 239, 241, 365, 472

bonding xi, ix, x, 12, 26, 65-66, 68, 71-72, 91, 130-131, 133, 142, 150-152, 195, 199, 204, 209, 214-216, 264-265, 267, 323, 327-328, 339-342, 344, 348-351, 353, 356, 358, 361, 365, 367-368, 372, 379, 382, 387, 391, 395, 399-400, 452, 454, 472

breasts 280, 472

breath, breathing 472

C

camels 188, 472

Chanukah 2, 472

Clark, Edward 472

community vi, 30, 55, 228, 340, 389, 469, 472

confusion 6, 23, 407, 461, 472

consciousness 88, 179, 200, 217, 224, 315, 335, 342, 351, 356, 358, 390, 438, 448, 455-456, 461, 473

Cordovero vii, 5-6, 9, 29, 43, 130, 154-155, 232, 357, 467, 473, 478

Cyrano de Bergerac 35-36, 473, 478

D

death 7, 35, 71, 146, 272, 315, 343, 395, 404, 415, 473, 478

destiny 117, 189, 248, 438, 473, 478

discipline xi, ix, x, 6, 12-13, 17, 20, 35-40, 71, 73, 80, 82, 85-87, 90-91, 93-94, 97-101, 105-110, 114-118, 122, 125-126, 130-131, 133-134, 137-138, 140, 149, 151-152, 155, 162, 164, 166-167, 179, 204, 214-217, 220, 232-233, 235-236, 242, 282-283, 294-298, 356, 361-362, 366, 420, 424, 432, 473, 478

disease 45, 404, 468, 473, 478

dreams 155, 179, 373, 380, 396, 423, 473, 478

E

Ecclesiastes 107, 280, 357, 388, 420, 423, 473, 478

egoegotism 478

enemies 308, 398, 437, 456, 473, 478

enlightenment viii, 1, 4, 14, 89, 179, 233, 295, 315, 319, 335, 357, 470, 473, 478

Erich Schiffman 259, 473, 478

Ethics of the Fathers 6, 50, 80, 82, 137, 172, 195, 205, 240, 257, 271, 281, 297, 302, 309, 312, 316-318, 325, 379, 395, 408, 421, 423, 431, 446, 473, 478

eyes 7, 14, 60, 66, 85, 96, 171, 180, 190, 289, 296, 340, 344, 348, 350, 429, 465, 473, 478

F

Family Purity 7, 358, 473, 478

fire xi, x, 51, 57, 97, 138, 214, 224, 227, 356, 407, 467, 473, 478

freedom 50, 108, 140, 206, 212, 381, 407, 470, 473

G

Gikatilla vii, 5, 398, 434, 439, 467, 473

God 4-5, 7-12, 22-23, 28-30, 59, 61-62, 65-67, 71, 73-74, 82, 86, 88-89, 94, 106-107, 114, 123-125, 130, 137, 139, 141, 159, 171-172, 175, 180, 183, 187, 190-192, 196, 200, 205, 209, 212-214, 220-221, 224-225, 229, 241, 248, 258, 265, 282, 287-289, 294-295, 301, 303, 310, 316-317, 319, 324-326, 328, 332, 344-345, 349-350, 353, 358-360, 366, 368, 374, 379-381, 384, 388-389, 395, 398-399, 405-406, 411, 414-415, 422-423, 428-431, 434, 438-440, 448, 452, 456, 459-460, 462, 470, 473

Golden Calf 310, 473

Gra 18, 280, 473

INDEX

H

happiness 59, 156, 239-240, 294, 305, 326, 390, 412-413, 416, 474

Hashem 156, 172, 212, 294, 332, 388, 413, 474

healing 23-24, 28-29, 65, 105, 131, 157, 164, 170, 172, 200, 203, 213, 295, 325, 327, 343, 347, 369, 391, 395, 404, 440, 468-470, 474, 478

heart 4, 6, 43, 59, 65, 108-109, 117, 132, 149-150, 156, 162-164, 171, 173-174, 189, 207, 224, 227, 233, 265, 368-369, 445, 467-469, 474

Hillel vi, 37-38, 83, 206, 240, 280, 316-317, 325, 423, 474

humility xi, ix, x, 12, 16, 21, 26, 57-62, 71-72, 75, 91, 98, 122-127, 140, 150-152, 162, 186, 188-192, 213-216, 220, 256-261, 279, 282-290, 294-298, 301-305, 308, 310-312, 315-320, 323, 326-329, 332-336, 379, 381-384, 409, 421, 445-449, 474

I

ignorance 217, 326, 474

integrity 57, 474, 477

intuition 248, 265, 297, 406, 439, 454, 474

Isaac 35, 83, 92, 114-115, 146, 163, 180, 196, 241, 461, 467, 474

Israel 83, 114, 146-147, 164, 170, 172, 189, 200, 234, 250, 265, 272, 316, 324, 350, 365-368, 374, 422, 428, 447, 461, 474

Iyengar 383, 451, 470, 474

J

Jacob x, ix, 45-46, 98, 146-147, 153, 162-164, 170, 174, 179-180, 188-189, 200-201, 205, 240-241, 265, 341, 365, 367, 372, 374, 430, 439, 461, 474

jealousy 474

Jerusalem 7, 21, 85, 316, 318, 348, 351, 431, 438, 461, 467-470, 474

Joseph vii, 65-66, 131, 146, 200, 213, 318, 341-343, 345, 365, 367-368, 380, 388, 398, 430, 434, 439, 467-468, 474

joy 99, 164, 174, 222, 228, 359, 388, 416, 460, 474

Judah 51, 309, 474

K

Karma 6, 30-31, 44, 474

Karma Sutra 6, 474

kindness 21-22, 24, 26, 28, 40, 43, 52-54, 72-73, 98, 151, 156, 195-197, 205, 319, 382, 415, 417, 429, 433, 474

King David 22, 72, 190, 224, 265, 383, 388, 398, 422, 437-438, 446, 456, 461, 474

Kingston, Eric 470, 474

Korach 123, 474

L

Leah 180, 205, 474

liberation 99, 101, 107, 134, 140-141, 181, 274, 310, 474

473

love xi, vi, ix, x, 4, 11-13, 20-23, 26-29, 31-32, 35-36, 38-40, 43, 50, 53, 57, 59-61, 65, 67, 71, 74-75, 81-82, 86-93, 97, 105-107, 115, 130, 140, 148-156, 158-159, 174, 179, 182, 196, 198, 204, 214-216, 219-224, 226-229, 249, 265, 283-285, 287, 289-291, 295, 301, 310, 315-316, 340-343, 346, 348-350, 352-353, 372, 374, 389, 395, 405, 409, 412-417, 420, 423, 432, 440, 467, 470, 474, 477

Lovingkindness xi, ix, x, 6, 12, 16-17, 19, 24, 28, 35, 43, 47, 50, 52, 54-55, 57, 65, 71-74, 86, 90, 92, 149, 153, 155, 158, 222, 225-226, 282, 287, 348, 350, 352-353, 412, 415-416, 429, 461, 474

Lubavitcher Rebbe 5-6, 66, 249, 390, 467-468, 474

Luria vii, 5-6, 13, 196, 460, 467, 474

M

Maimonides 114, 165, 171, 173, 356, 358, 469, 474

Meditation 4-5, 10-11, 14-17, 32, 40, 47, 53-54, 61, 68, 74, 92-93, 101, 110, 118, 125, 132, 141, 150, 157-158, 166, 175, 182-183, 191, 199, 208, 224, 227-228, 236, 242, 244-245, 252-253, 260-261, 267-268, 273, 275, 290, 295, 297-298, 304, 312, 320, 324, 328, 336, 344, 353, 362, 368-369, 376, 384, 388, 392, 398-400, 415-416, 425, 432, 439-441, 448-449, 455-456, 462, 467-469, 474, 478

modesty 282, 387, 445, 474

Moses vii, 6, 114, 116-117, 186-187, 212-213, 240-241, 248-249, 257-258, 272, 280-281, 308-310, 317, 332, 358, 374, 447, 449, 469, 474

N

Nachman of Breslov 343, 469, 475

Neshama 60, 475

non-jealousy 84, 475

non-stealing 84, 475

non-violence 84, 475

O

oath 358, 379, 475

oneness 10-11, 67, 123, 259, 267, 326, 344, 440, 460, 475

P

panic 412, 475

Patanjali 31, 217, 242, 259, 303, 468, 475

peace 7, 29-30, 60, 130, 134, 173, 206, 281, 315, 327, 350, 380-381, 420-421, 438, 460-461, 470, 475

prana 351, 475

pranayama 252, 273, 424, 475

prayer 7, 53, 74, 82, 172, 216, 223, 250, 258, 273, 282, 344, 380, 398, 440, 445, 448, 456, 475

Proverbs 7, 14, 38, 80, 97-98, 137, 149, 163, 257, 265, 272, 342, 375, 405, 421, 447, 453, 475

Psalms 7, 22, 98-99, 217, 240, 282, 383, 388, 398, 422-423, 446, 456, 461, 475

psychic 323, 475

purpose 67, 106, 131, 137, 140, 204, 217, 243, 327, 343, 348, 358-359, 368, 373, 410, 475

Q

Queen Esther 317

R

Rachel vi, 180, 205, 475

Ramak 6, 9, 29-30, 94, 154, 343, 349, 357, 415, 428, 445, 475

Rambam vii, 114, 165, 475

Rashi vii, 23, 170, 188, 413, 475

Rebbe Rashab vii, 5, 222, 224, 467, 475

Rebecca vii, 92, 475

relationships ix, 13, 16, 21, 23-26, 28, 32, 36, 40, 43-45, 47, 50, 52, 54, 58-60, 65-68, 73-74, 81, 86-87, 90-93, 100-101, 105-106, 110, 115, 118, 122-123, 125, 130-133, 139, 141, 150, 158, 162, 164, 166, 175, 182, 191, 195-196, 199-200, 208, 212, 214-215, 218-219, 223-224, 227-228, 236, 239, 243-245, 252, 256-257, 260, 265, 268, 275, 281-284, 290-291, 295-296, 298, 304-305, 312, 318, 320, 325, 327-328, 336, 340, 344, 346-350, 352-353, 356, 360-362, 365-369, 372, 376, 379-381,

384, 387, 391-392, 395-397, 400, 412, 416-417, 425, 432, 441, 449, 452, 455, 462, 475

Rosh Hashanah 395, 475

S

sacrifice 218, 266, 476

Sarah 92, 272, 476

Seal xiii, xiv, 394, 476

Sefer Yetzirah 18, 43, 51, 276, 280, 357, 372-373, 398, 405-406, 411, 452, 461, 467, 476

sefirot viii, 2-3, 5, 7-9, 11-12, 14-15, 17-18, 23, 43, 57, 83, 89, 91, 123, 165, 187, 200, 207, 216-217, 223, 249, 335, 350, 372-373, 375, 388, 396, 398, 404, 406, 410-411, 438-439, 446, 452, 456, 476

self-discipline 86, 97, 282, 335, 476

Shabbat 2, 5, 7, 16, 18, 37, 139, 222, 326, 398, 406, 446, 453, 476-477

Shakespeare 46, 105, 256, 340, 420, 476

Shammai 37-38, 83, 240, 325, 476

Shimon Bar Yochai 5-6, 302, 315, 468, 476

shoulders 103, 393, 476

skin 58, 106, 197, 476

slavery 206, 476

stillness ·39, 134, 234, 273, 404, 421, 424, 448, 455, 461, 470, 476 strength ix, 12-13, 39, 79-80, 82-87, 90, 94, 97-98, 101-102, 105, 110, 114-115, 117-118, 122-126, 130, 132-133, 137, 140-142, 162, 164, 166-167, 220, 222, 232, 234, 236, 248, 271, 282, 294, 297, 305, 310, 335, 356, 361-362, 383, 387, 405, 420-423, 425, 440, 446, 461, 476-477

T

terror 180, 422, 476

teshuva 374, 476

thanksgiving 382, 476

the Alter Rebbe 22, 29, 106-107, 179, 197, 476

Tikkun 23, 31, 51, 84, 171, 223, 319, 343, 476

Tikkunei Zohar 3, 30, 43, 91, 131, 156, 170-171, 187, 207, 223, 239-240, 257, 264, 410, 476

truth 6, 150, 154-155, 162, 170, 172, 181, 187-189, 212, 225, 249, 272, 350, 375, 380, 431, 476

U

unification 4, 29, 168, 344, 352, 368, 405, 439, 441, 476

V

vinyasa 47, 73, 93, 109, 259, 297, 344, 440, 476

Vital vii, 5, 84, 106, 343, 476

W

water ix, 7, 35, 47, 50-51, 57, 59, 153, 158, 224, 227, 233, 350, 372, 396-397, 399, 405, 439, 456, 459, 467, 476

wealth 45, 138, 180, 186, 195, 205, 218, 388, 445, 476

Weinberg 21, 348, 431, 47

Y

yetzer hara 130, 343, 358

Yom Kippur 172

Z

Zohar 3, 5, 22, 30, 43, 58, 65, 71, 87-88, 91, 130-131, 156, 170-171, 187, 204, 207, 223, 239-240, 257, 264, 272, 309, 348, 359, 405, 410, 461, 468, 476

BOOK CLUB GUIDELINES

Thank you for purchasing *The Kabbalah Sutras*. Here are some thoughts on how to deepen your experience, using it as the basis of an event with your Book Club or whilst learning with a friend.

1. THEME - Pick a theme which interests you right now, such as Love, Strength, Balance, Endurance, Gratitude, Connection or Leadership. Then go to the corresponding section in the book, read one of the essays and discuss the questions.

2. LIFE QUESTIONS - What is a question that is most relevant in your life right now? Flip through the pages of the book, choose any essay and listen closely for how it may contain the guidance you are looking for. The answers may not necessarily be in the words themselves, but the thoughts they prompt while you are reading them.

3. KABBALISTIC DAY CYCLE - There is a Sefirah for every day of the week, so you might choose an essay that corresponds to the day you are reading. Based on the teachings of the Vilna Gaon, the cycle is as follows: Sunday - *Chesed*, Monday - *Gevurah*, Tuesday - *Tiferet*, Wednesday - *Netzach*, Thursday - *Hod*, Friday - *Yesod*, Saturday/Shabbat - *Malchut*. The "day" runs from sundown to sundown, so *Chesed* would be from sundown saturday night until sundown Sunday. *Gevurah* would begin at sundown Sunday, and so forth.

4. CREATIVE WRITING - You can use the Questions for Discussion as a basis for creative writing. Try answering some of the questions using "Free Writing" where your pen does not stop moving for a fixed period of time, e.g. ten minutes' continuous writing. This helps to switch off your inner censor and stay in the flow.

5. OTHER CREATIVE OUTLETS - You can also use these essays as the basis for other expressive media, such as visual arts, songwriting or plays. The key is to connect with the material in a way that feels truthful to your soul, and ideally maintains the integrity of the Kabbalistic teachings.

Good luck with your journeys!

For more resources and to join the mailing list, visit www.marcusjfreed.com.

The Kosher Sutras:
The Jewish Way in Yoga & Meditation
by Marcus J Freed
Experience Torah wisdom through the lens of yoga and meditation. The Kosher Sutras provide a new framework for learning ancient wisdom with an authentic and refreshing perspective. *"Freed's eloquently written and well-released practice manual unites the Western Jewish ritual, textual, and historical traditions with the philosophy and practice of Hatha Yoga"* - Yoga Journal.
10.6 x 8.3, 210 pages,
Paperback, ISBN 978-162407588.
Also: Kindle/E-book.
$29.99/£19.99

The Festive Sutras:
A Yogi's Guide to Shabbat & Jewish Festivals
by Marcus J Freed
How can we experience Jewish festivals & Shabbat through our body? *The Festive Sutras* contains a series of essays and practices to help get an experience of God within your body. Using the tools of torah wisdom and yoga postures, the reader is given very practical techniques to use physicality as a gateway to spirituality. T*he Festive Sutras* is three-books-in one: The Festive Sutras, concerned with the Jewish festival cycle; The Shabbat Sutras - A Yogi's guide to the Jewish Sabbath; and Ethics of the Yogis - a Jewish commentary on the classic Yoga Sutras.
6 x 9, 272 pages,
Paperback, ISBN 978-0996350686.
Also: Kindle/E-book.
$14.99/£9.99